Linguistic Advances in Central American Spanish

Brill's Studies in Language, Cognition and Culture

Series Editors

Alexandra Y. Aikhenvald (*Centre for Indigenous Health Equity Research, Central Queensland University*)
R. M. W. Dixon (*Centre for Indigenous Health Equity Research, Central Queensland University*)
N. J. Enfield (*University of Sydney*)

VOLUME 39

The titles published in this series are listed at *brill.com/bslc*

Linguistic Advances in Central American Spanish

Edited by

Brandon Baird
Osmer Balam
M. Carmen Parafita Couto

BRILL

LEIDEN | BOSTON

Library of Congress Cataloging-in-Publication Data

Names: Baird, Brandon, editor. | Balam, Osmer, editor. | Parafita Couto, M. Carmen, editor.
Title: Linguistic advances in Central American Spanish / edited by Brandon Baird, Osmer Balam, M. Carmen Parafita Couto.
Description: Leiden ; Boston : Brill, 2023. | Series: Brill's studies in language, cognition and culture, 1879-5412 ; volume 39 | Includes bibliographical references and index. | Summary: "Covering all seven countries on the isthmus, this volume presents the first collection of original linguistic studies on Central American Spanish varieties, which have long been neglected in Hispanic Linguistics. The analyses in this collection span across disciplines such as sociolinguistics, corpus linguistics, bilingualism, historical linguistics, and pragmatics. This volume bridges the gap between international and Central American scholars, as it highlights the work that has already been done by Central American scholars but is relatively unknown to scholars outside of the region. It also introduces readers to more recent work that sheds new light on Central American Spanish varieties, from both urban and rural settings as well as in bilingual communities where Spanish is in contact with indigenous languages"-- Provided by publisher.
Identifiers: LCCN 2023030739 (print) | LCCN 2023030740 (ebook) | ISBN 9789004679924 (hardback ; acid-free paper) | ISBN 9789004679931 (ebook)
Subjects: LCSH: Spanish language--Central America. | LCGFT: Essays.
Classification: LCC PC4841 .L56 2023 (print) | LCC PC4841 (ebook) | DDC 467/.9728--dc23/eng/20230802
LC record available at https://lccn.loc.gov/2023030739
LC ebook record available at https://lccn.loc.gov/2023030740

Typeface for the Latin, Greek, and Cyrillic scripts: "Brill". See and download: brill.com/brill-typeface.

ISSN 1879-5412
ISBN 978-90-04-67992-4 (hardback)
ISBN 978-90-04-67993-1 (e-book)

Copyright 2023 by Brandon Baird, Osmer Balam and M. Carmen Parafita Couto. Published by Koninklijke Brill NV, Leiden, The Netherlands.
Koninklijke Brill NV incorporates the imprints Brill, Brill Nijhoff, Brill Schöningh, Brill Fink, Brill mentis, Brill Wageningen Academic, Vandenhoeck & Ruprecht, Böhlau and V&R unipress.
Koninklijke Brill NV reserves the right to protect this publication against unauthorized use. Requests for re-use and/or translations must be addressed to Koninklijke Brill NV via brill.com or copyright.com.

This book is printed on acid-free paper and produced in a sustainable manner.

Contents

Acknowledgements VII
List of Figures, Maps, and Tables VIII
Notes on Contributors XIV

1 On the Linguistic Analysis of Central American Spanish in Monolingual and Bi/Multilingual Contexts 1
   Brandon Baird, Osmer Balam and M. Carmen Parafita Couto

2 Rhotic Variation in Northern Belize
   Beyond Tap-Trill Contrast Maintenance 17
   Trevor Bero

3 Phonological Contrast Maintenance and Language Contact
   An Examination of the Spanish Rhotic System in a Bilingual Guatemalan Speech Community 41
   Sean McKinnon

4 Variation of Absolute-Final /s/ in Tegucigalpa Spanish 72
   Julio Ventura and Brandon Baird

5 Social Evaluations of Onset /s/ Lenition in Salvadoran Spanish 94
   Franny D. Brogan, Lia Slotten and Juan Manuel Menjívar

6 An Initial ToBI Analysis of Costa Rican Spanish Intonation 121
   Eva Patricia Velásquez Upegui

7 Two Contact Induced Grammatical Changes in Spanish in Contact with Tz'utujil in Guatemala 145
   Ana Isabel García Tesoro

8 Big Data and Small Dialects
   Transitive andar *in Central American Spanish* 168
   Shannon P. Rodríguez and Chad Howe

9 Variable Number Marking in Mosquito Coast Spanish 193
   Madeline Critchfield

10   The Historical Evolution of *Usted* in Costa Rican Spanish   215
       Munia Cabal-Jiménez

11   Rates and Constraints of Present Perfect and Preterit
     in Costa Rican Spanish
     A Variationist Approach   238
       Javier Rivas and Érick Pineda

12   Address Pronouns in Panamanian Spanish
     A Historical Overview   260
       Miguel Ángel Quesada Pacheco

13   Corner-Store Service Encounters in Nicaraguan Spanish in a Rural
     Setting   284
       Jeff Michno, Evan Colby Myers and Will Przedpelski

14   Central American Spanish
     An Upward Trajectory   308
       John M. Lipski

     Index   323

Acknowledgements

We are extremely grateful to all of the reviewers who gave of their time and knowledge to make this volume possible: Alba Arias Álvarez (Universidad de Alcalá), Alberto Barahona Novoa (Universidad de Costa Rica), Mariska Bolyanatz (Occidental College), Silvina Bongiovanni (Michigan State University), Danielle Daidone (University of North Carolina Wilmington), Manuel Delicado Cantero (Australian National University), Ana María Díaz Collazos (Fort Lewis College), Jason Doroga (Ouachita Baptist University), Jenny Dumont (Gettysburg College), César Felix-Brasdefer (Indiana University), Christina Garcia (St. Louis University), Ana Isabel García Tesoro (Universidad de Antioquia), Carolina González (Florida State University), José Esteban Hernández (University of Texas Rio Grande Valley), Ji Young Kim (University of California, Los Angeles), Jennifer Lang-Rigal (James Madison University), Jorge Antonio Leoni de León (Universidad de Costa Rica), Juan Manuel Martínez López (Universidad de Granada), Terrell Morgan (Ohio State University), María Elena Placencia (Birkbeck University of London), Andrea Pešková (University of Hamburg), Miguel Ángel Quesada Pacheco (University of Bergen), Sophie Richard (Université de Tours), Adrian Rodríguez-Riccelli (University of Buffalo), Brandon Rogers (Texas Tech University), María Sánchez Paraíso (Universidad Autónoma de Madrid), Travis Sorenson (University of Central Arkansas), Nadiezdha Torres (Universidad Nacional Autónoma de México), Donny Vigil (University of St. Thomas), and Sara Zahler (University of Albany).

We dedicate this book to all the scholars from Central America that preceded us and whose work may or may not have received international visibility.

Figures, Maps, and Tables

Figures

2.1 Rhotic variants across all positions in word 29
2.2 Rates of word initial rhotic variants, overall and according to preceding phonological environment 30
2.3 Rates of word internal syllable final rhotic variants, overall and according to following phonological environment 31
2.4 Word internal syllable final rhotic variants, overall and by speaker sex 31
2.5 Word internal syllable final rhotic variants by speaker age 32
3.1 Example of the phonological distinction between the Spanish tap and trill, in the phrase *pero los perros no* 'but dogs don't' 42
3.2 Example of a canonical tap [ɾ] in the phrase *y llora* 'and s/he cries,' from participant F18 49
3.3 Example of an approximant tap [ɾ̞] in the word *pero* 'but,' from participant F18 50
3.4 Example of a perceptual tap [⁽ʳ⁾] in the word *dinero* 'money,' from participant F36 50
3.5 Example of a canonical trill [r] in the word *carro* 'car,' from participant M3 51
3.6 Example of a post-approximantized trill [rɹ] in the phrase *un arroz* 'rice,' from participant M5 51
3.7 Example of a post-approximantized tap [ɾɹ] in the phrase *carrera de [caballos]* '[horse] race,' from participant M13 52
3.8 Example of an assibilated rhotic [ř] in the word *arriba* 'above,' from participant F32 52
3.9 Duration of phonemic tap vs. trill by younger participants 59
3.10 Duration of phonemic tap vs. trill by middle-aged participants 59
3.11 Duration of phonemic tap vs. trill by older participants 60
4.1 Overall distribution of allophones of /s/ from the 278 participants 81
5.1 Screenshot of evaluation matrix (adapted from Chappell, 2016 and Walker et al., 2014) 103
5.2 Status ratings by allophone and speaker gender 107
5.3 Status ratings by allophone and listener age 107
5.4 Perceived speaker age by allophone and factor type 109
6.1 Distribution of pitch accents in broad-focus statements 127
6.2 Frequency of pitch accents according to the prenuclear position in broad-focus statements 128
6.3 Broad-focus statement. Female 36–45 years old. The woman is smoking (*La mujer está fumando*) 128

FIGURES, MAPS, AND TABLES   IX

6.4   Broad-focus statement. Female 36–45 years old. The boy is playing the piano (*El niño está tocando piano*)   130
6.5   Distribution of pitch accents in yes-no questions   131
6.6   Frequency of pitch accents according to the position in the prenuclear position in yes-no questions   132
6.7   Yes-no questions. Male 46 to 56 years old. Do you have chickens? (*¿Tenés gallinas?*)   133
6.8   Yes-no questions. Female 46 to 56 years old. Are you tired? (*¿Estás cansada?*)   134
6.9   Distribution of pitch accents in the wh-questions   136
6.10 Frequency of pitch accents according to the prenuclear position in wh-questions   136
6.11 Wh- questions. Female 36 to 45 years old. What would you like me to give you as a gift? (*¿Qué quiere que le regale?*)   137
6.12 Wh- questions. Female 46 to 55 years old. Where did you buy that washing machine? (*¿Dónde compró esa lavadora?*)   138
8.1   Frequency of *andar con* ("21st SV, CR, NI, HN" refers only to Central American varieties)   180
8.2   Transitivity by country   184
8.3   Transitivity by polarity   185
8.4   Frequency of transitive *andar* and *llevar*   187
9.1   Distribution of number marking in MCS   201
9.2   Phonic salience and number marking   204
9.3   Subject position and number marking   205
9.4   Subject type and number marking   206
9.5   Animacy and number marking   206
9.6   Age and number marking   207
9.7   Gender and number marking   207
9.8   Level of education and number marking   208
9.9   Age of acquisition and number marking   209
12.1 *Tú* vs. *Vos-VM* according to ethnic groups (Panama, 1610)   276
12.2 Pronominal inversion in Panamanian Spanish (confidence level)   278
13.1 Distribution of all customer requests by type   293
13.2 Opening act by shopkeeper and customer   296
13.3 Presence of service encounter closing according to customer gender   298

Maps

2.1   Map of Belize   24
3.1   Linguistic map of Guatemala. Reproduced image of "Languages of Guatemala" by Chabacano under Creative Commons by ShareAlike 3.0   43

4.1   Map of departments of Honduras and the capital city of Tegucigalpa. Adapted from d-maps.com   75
12.1 *Voseo* regions in Panamá (approximate situation today)   270
12.2 *Tuteo* and *ustedeo* in Panama (in present-day Panama)   277

Tables

2.1   Word position and tap/trill usage in standard Spanish (adapted from Hualde 2005:183)   20
2.2   Regression analysis of factors affecting word internal syllable final rhotics   28
3.1   Demographic characteristics of the participants   48
3.2   Distribution of phonemic tap variants   54
3.3   Multivariate analysis results for the phonemic tap (application value = canonical tap)   54
3.4   Distribution of phonemic trill variants   55
3.5   Distribution of the number of occlusions in the phonemic trill tokens   55
3.6   Multivariate analysis results for the phonemic trill (application value = canonical number of occlusions)   56
3.7   Mean tap and trill duration values by participant   57
3.8   Comparison in the distribution of phonemic tap variants in monolingual and bilingual Spanish (% of data)   61
3.9   Comparison in the distribution of phonemic trill variants in monolingual and bilingual Spanish (% of data)   62
3.10 Rhotic variant frequency distribution for participants M10 and F7   65
3.11 Change in progress in the tap vs. trill phonological contrast   66
4.1   Lipski's (1990) results (%) for realizations of /s/ in absolute-final position according to social class in Tegucigalpa Spanish (Modified from Lipski, 1990, p. 107)   76
4.2   Variation of /s/ in Tegucigalpa Spanish according to Hernández Torres (2010, p. 127). As Hernández Torres did not report the findings for all allophones, the sum of the reported data does not reach 100%   77
4.3   Rankings and classifications of occupations of the 278 participants according to 33 different individuals from Tegucigalpa   80
4.4   Distribution of allophones according to Age (*n* = 264)   83
4.5   Results of the multinomial logistic regression for Age. ">" indicates that the odds of producing the specific allophone over [s] are greater when compared to the reference category, "<" indicates that the odds of producing the specific allophone over [s] are lower when compared to the reference category, "=" indicates odds are not different, "Ref." indicates the reference category for each independent variable   83

FIGURES, MAPS, AND TABLES   XI

4.6   Distribution of allophones according to Sex (*n* = 264)   83
4.7   Results of the multinomial logistic regression for Sex. ">" indicates that the odds of producing the specific allophone over [s] are greater when compared to the reference category, "=" indicates odds are not different, "Ref." indicates the reference category for each independent variable   84
4.8   Distribution of allophones according to Social Class (*n* = 264)   84
4.9   Results of the multinomial logistic regression for Social Class. ">" indicates that the odds of producing the specific allophone over [s] are greater when compared to the reference category, "=" indicates odds are not different, "Ref." indicates the reference category for each independent variable   85
4.10 Distribution of allophones according to Education (*n* = 264)   85
4.11 Results of the multinomial logistic regression for Age. ">" indicates that the odds of producing the specific allophone over [s] are greater when compared to the reference category, "<" indicates that the odds of producing the specific allophone over [s] are lower when compared to the reference category, "=" indicates odds are not different, "Ref." indicates the reference category for each independent variable   86
4.12 Comparison of overall findings of /s/ variation in Tegucigalpa Spanish in Lipski (1987, 1990), Hernández Torres (2010, 2013), and the present study. Hernández Torres and the present study do not reach 100% because their data for the allophones [z], [s̺], and [s̞] are not reported in this table. Lipski (1987, 1990) does not report findings of [ˢ]   87
4.13 Comparison of /s/ reduction by Social Class in Lipski (1990) and the present study. [ˢ] tokens were not gathered in Lipski (1990)   89
4.14 Lower and upper bounds of 95% Confidence Intervals (CI) for the main effects of the multinomial logistic regression   91
5.1   Listener demographics   104
5.2   Factor loadings   105
5.3   Linear mixed effects model for the status factor   106
5.4   Linear mixed effects model for the positive social features factor   108
6.1   Frequencies in the nuclear configuration of broad-focus statements   129
6.2   Tone frequency in the nuclear configuration according to the age variable   130
6.3   Frequencies in the nuclear configuration of yes-no questions   133
6.4   Tone frequency in the nuclear configuration according to the sex variable   134
6.5   Tone frequency in the nuclear configuration according to the age variable   135
6.6   Frequencies in the nuclear configuration of wh-questions   138
6.7   Tone frequency in the nuclear configuration according to the sex variable   139
6.8   Tone frequency in the nuclear configuration according to the age variable   139
7.1   Direct object pronouns according to the gender of the referent   151
7.2   Direct object pronouns according to the referent number   152

7.3	Direct object pronouns with female referents according to the animate +/- trait	152
7.4	Direct object pronouns with plural referents according to the +/- animate feature	152
7.5	Percentage of employment of what neutralizes the distinction of gender and number for the direct object by groups	153
7.6	Frequency of duplication by groups	155
7.7	Percentages of employment of what neutralizes the gender and number distinction for the direct object according to the +/- animate feature of the referents	156
7.8	Frequency of omission of the direct object pronoun, in contexts of postponement with respect to the referent	157
7.9	Omissions and pronouns made according to the trait [+/- animate]	157
7.10	Frequency of omission according to groups of speakers	158
7.11	Use of *en* instead of *a* with verbs of movement	160
8.1	Comparison of three Spanish corpora by number of tokens (words) and percentage relative to overall size	182
8.2	Results of raw tokens per country	184
8.3	Preposition variation by country	186
9.1	Present indicative verb paradigm of *aiwanaia* ('to sing') in Miskitu	195
9.2	Mixed-effects logistic regression predicting 3sg. number marking with 3pl. Subjects in MCS linguistic and social factors (n = 595, AIC = 577.5)	202
10.1	Address forms used in Costa Rican Spanish in colonial times (Adopted from Quesada, 2003)	216
10.2	Types of speech acts (Based on Austin (1962) and Searle (1969))	223
10.3	Other types of speech acts (Based on Brown and Levinson (1978/1987))	223
10.4	Withdrawal and approach uses in the examples provided and types of speech acts. 16th to 18th centuries	227
10.5	FTAs to the negative face in withdrawal and approach *Vuestra Merced/Usted*. 16th to 18th centuries	228
10.6	Comparison of withdrawal and approach uses in letters from the 19th to the 20th c.	230
10.7	Comparison between the withdrawal uses of *usted*. 16th–18th century vs. 19th–20th century	231
10.8	Reanalysis of the address form system in Costa Rican Spanish	231
10.9	Comparison of the context of use of the approach *usted* from the 16th to the 20th century	233
11.1	% of PP vs. Preterit in the data	248
11.2	Rates of PP vs Preterit across the Spanish speaking world (based on oral data except for VanBuren, 1992)	248

11.3   Mixed effects linear regression predicting PP in Costa Rican Spanish   249
11.4   Factors that significantly constrain PP occurrence in Costa Rica and Mexico   255
12.1   Scale of address pronouns (Spain, 16th century)   263
12.2   Etymological *vos*   268
12.3   Panamanian *voseo*   269
12.4   Psycho-ethnolectal level of addressing (Panama, colonial times)   275
13.1   Framework for analyzing pragmatic variation during service encounters adapted from Félix-Brasdefer (2015, pp. 44–46)   287
13.2   Request types with examples in order of directness   288
13.3   Request types by customer gender during service encounters   295

Notes on Contributors

Trevor Bero
(Ph.D., 2022, Pennsylvania State University) currently works for the U.S. Department of Veterans Affairs. His graduate research focused on language variation and change with a special interest in language contact situations.

Franny D. Brogan
(Ph.D., 2018, University of California, Los Angeles) is a visiting scholar in Linguistics and Cognitive Science at Pomona College (California, USA). Her research explores sociophonetic variation in Spanish and Latinx Englishes.

Munia Cabal-Jiménez
(Ph.D., 2013, University of Illinois at Urbana-Champaign) is associate professor of Spanish and Hispanic Linguistics at Western Illinois University (Illinois, USA). Her research focuses on history of Spanish, historical sociolinguistics, and Heritage Spanish in the US.

Madeline Critchfield
(Ph.D., 2021, University of Georgia) is assistant professor of Spanish at Rockhurst University (Missouri, USA). Her research focuses on bilingual morphosyntax, Nicaraguan Spanish, and Spanish-Miskitu language contact.

Ana Isabel García Tesoro
(Ph.D., 2005, Autonomous University of Madrid, Spain) is associate professor of Linguistics at University of Antioquia (Medellín, Colombia). Her research focuses on language variation, contact-induced language change, and varieties of Spanish in contact with Mayan languages and Quechua.

Chad Howe
(Ph.D., 2006, The Ohio State University) is associate professor of Spanish and Linguistics at the University of Georgia (USA). His research focuses on language variation and change using sociolinguistic and corpus-based methods.

John M. Lipski
(Ph. D., 1974, University of Alberta) is Edwin Erle Sparks Professor of Spanish and Linguistics at the Pennsylvania State University (USA). His research focuses on language contact, utilizing experimental techniques in field settings.

Sean McKinnon

(Ph.D., 2020, Indiana University Bloomington) is assistant teaching professor of Spanish at Arizona State University (USA). His research focuses on language variation and change, with an emphasis on Spanish-Kaqchikel Maya (in Guatemala) and Spanish-English (in the United States) language contact.

Juan Manuel Menjívar

(M.S., Georgetown University), is a Spanish Linguistics Ph.D. candidate at Georgetown University, Washington, D.C. His research focuses on Spanish phonetics, Salvadoran Spanish, and Spanish as a Heritage Language in the United States.

Jeff Michno

(Ph.D., 2017, University of Texas, Austin) is assistant professor of Spanish and Linguistics at Furman University (South Carolina, USA). His research focuses on sociolinguistic and pragmatic variation, Nicaraguan Spanish, and second language acquisition.

Evan Colby Myers

(B.A., 2021, Furman University) is an editor and writer in Washington, D.C. His work focuses on technology and religion in modern American life.

Érick Pineda

(M.A., University of Colorado, Boulder) is currently pursuing a Ph.D. at the University of New Mexico (USA). His research focuses on morphosyntax, language variation, and Spanish in contact with the Purépecha language.

Will Przedpelski

(B.S., 2021, Furman University) is a consultant for a turnaround and restructuring firm in New York City, with an avid interest in modern languages. His current work centers around resolving financial and operational problems for distressed businesses.

Miguel Ángel Quesada Pacheco

(Ph.D., 1986, University of Cologne, Germany) is professor of Spanish and Latin American Studies at the University of Bergen (Norway). His research focuses on Central American Spanish, dialectology, language attitudes and Chibchan languages.

Javier Rivas
(Ph.D., 2003, Universidade de Santiago de Compostela, Spain) is associate professor of Hispanic Linguistics at University of Colorado, Boulder (USA). His research focuses on the study of processes of language variation and language change from a functionalist usage-based perspective.

Shannon P. Rodríguez
(Ph.D., 2022, University of Georgia) is a postdoctoral research associate with the Center for Latino Achievement and Success in Education (CLASE) at the University of Georgia (USA). Her research focuses on the intersections of language, ethnicity, and identity, specifically regarding Latino English in the Southeastern US.

Lia Slotten
(B.A., 2021, Scripps College) worked as a research assistant for the linguistics department of Pomona College her senior year (California, USA). Her studies included focuses on phonology, psycholinguistics, and sociolinguistics.

Eva Patricia Velásquez-Upegui
(Ph.D., 2013, El Colegio de México) is profesor of Linguistics at Universidad Autónoma de Querétaro (Mexico). Her research focuses on phonetics and phonology, more specifically, in the area of prosody and its relationship to pragmatics and discourse analysis.

Julio Ventura
(M.A, 2002, Real Academia Española, Spain) is professor of Linguistics at Universidad Nacional Autónoma de Honduras and former president of the Central American Linguistics Association (ACALing). He specializes in Honduran Spanish and indigenous languages of Honduras.

CHAPTER 1

On the Linguistic Analysis of Central American Spanish in Monolingual and Bi/Multilingual Contexts

Brandon Baird, Osmer Balam and M. Carmen Parafita Couto

1   Introduction

In 1983, John Lipski wrote that, in comparison to the rest of Latin America, the linguistic study of Central American Spanish (henceforth CAS) varieties was "still in diapers" (p. 272). More recently, similar observations have been made in dialectological work by Quesada Pacheco (2008). Comprising seven countries (i.e., Belize, Guatemala, Honduras, El Salvador, Nicaragua, Costa Rica, and Panama), the Central American isthmus is one where Spanish has long co-existed with many indigenous languages throughout the region and with English-based Creoles along its Caribbean coast. Despite the remarkable linguistic diversity that has long characterized this contact zone, Central America has historically been kept in the periphery of Hispanic linguistic research. The overarching goal of this book is to bring together the first volume of original linguistic studies from different scholars working on Spanish varieties across different linguistic subfields in every country in Central America.

Research on CAS can be traced back to the 19th century, when scholars examined CAS varieties in a fragmented manner and primarily focused on lexicography and prescriptive grammar descriptions (e.g., Batres Jáuregui, 1892; de la Rocha, 1858/2002; Gagini, 1892; Ulloa, 1870; among others). It was not until the 1950s and 1960s, however, that descriptive linguistic research on CAS began to appear (Quesada Pacheco, 2008), particularly on Costa Rican Spanish (for further discussion on earlier work on CAS, see Lipski, this volume). During this time, Lipski (this volume) observes that scant or no research had been conducted on the Spanish varieties spoken in Honduras, Guatemala, and Belize. It is noteworthy that even in more recent decades, studies on CAS varieties were limited in terms of the scope and breadth of topics examined.

A survey of antecedent scholarship shows that prior to 2010, studies largely focused on analyzing phonetic inventories or specific segments, morphological suffixes, and forms of address. Some of the important volumes of linguistic analysis between 1950 and 2010 include, but are not limited to, Alvarado de Ricord's volume on the phonetics and phonology of Panamanian Spanish (1971), Lipski's similar volume on Honduran Spanish (1987), Herranz's compilation of previously published linguistic studies on Honduran Spanish (1990) and his volume on the sociopolitical linguistic history of Honduras (Herranz 1996), Mántica's collection of essays on the morphosyntax, semantics, and pragmatics of Nicaraguan Spanish (1989), and Agüero Chaves' study of the evolution of Costa Rican Spanish (2009). These of course do not include smaller-scale studies that have scarcely appeared as journal articles or book chapters. Importantly, many scholarly works published on CAS during this time refer to Canfield's (1981) *Spanish Pronunciation in the Americas*, which includes brief, 1–2 page accounts of the Spanish of different Central American countries.

Within the last decade or so, however, research on CAS has started to gain notable traction. This emerging body of work has cast valuable light on the Spanish varieties spoken by monolingual and bi-/multilingual populations in the region. Important contributions, conducted from a dialectological approach, include Quesada Pacheco's edited volumes, which provide the results of the exact same phonetic survey (2010) and morphosyntactic survey (2013) for the Spanish variety spoken in each Central American country. Herrera Morera et al. (2016) provide a similar description of CAS, but from a pedagogical perspective. Research on second person forms of address continue to play a prominent role (for Salvadoran Spanish in the U.S.: Sorenson, 2013; Woods & Shin, 2016; for Costa Rican Spanish: Michnowicz et al., 2016; Schmidt-Rinehart & LeLoup, 2017; for Nicaraguan Spanish: Michno, 2019; for Nicaraguan Spanish in the U.S.: López Alonzo, 2016; for Honduran Spanish: Melgares, 2018). Sociolinguistic work has seen an increase in several countries, including Belize (Balam & Prada Pérez, 2017; Schneider, 2021) Guatemala (Baird, 2021a, 2023a, 2023b; McKinnon, 2020, 2023), Nicaragua (Chappell, 2020), El Salvador (Brogan & Bolyanatz, 2018), Costa Rica (Chappell, 2016), and Panama (Lamy, 2016), among others: Among these are a series of studies on language attitudes in different countries: Belize (Balam, 2013), Guatemala (Baird, 2019; García Tesoro, 2011), Nicaragua (Chappell, 2017), and those included in Chiquito and Quesada Pacheco's volume of attitudes towards Spanish in the Americas (2014). See Baird (2023c) for a more detailed review of recent sociolinguistic studies in Central America.

Crucially, other studies have examined linguistic outcomes in previously unexplored and abundant bi/multilingual communities in Central America; thus, contributing to our knowledge of the diverse contact situations that characterize this region. These studies, for instance, analyze phonetic outcomes among K'iche'/Spanish (Baird, 2015, 2017, 2018, 2020, 2021b) and Kaqchikel/Spanish bilinguals (McKinnon, 2020, 2023) in Guatemala; Spanish/English/

Kriol trilinguals in Belize (Balam, 2014); and Spanish/English Creole/Miskitu/Ulwa multilinguals in Nicaragua (Chappell, 2020; López Alonzo, 2016); as well as morphosyntactic outcomes among Spanish/English bilinguals in Belize (Balam 2015, 2016; Balam et al., 2014; Balam & Parafita Couto, 2019; Balam et al., 2021), Tz'utujil/Spanish bilinguals in Guatemala (García Tesoro, 2018), and Kaqchikel/Spanish bilinguals in Guatemala (Bierings et al., 2019).

Comparative research involving CAS varieties, which attests to the scholarly attention that is increasingly being given to these varieties, has also grown. Platz (2014), for instance, compared advice-giving strategies between speakers of Panamanian and Nicaraguan Spanish. Wagner and Roebuck (2010) compared the production of apologies in Mexican versus Panamanian Spanish, whereas Félix-Brasdefer (2010) comparatively analyzed regional variation in request strategies between native female speakers of Mexican versus Costa Rican Spanish. Sorenson (2016) examined forms of address between speakers of Salvadoran and Argentinian Spanish speakers in the U.S. Furthermore, cross-community comparisons that have investigated Spanish/English/(Creole) code-switching varieties in Central America and the U.S. have also been carried out: For an analysis of mixed nominal constructions in production data from the South Caribbean Coast Autonomous Region of Nicaragua, and Miami, Florida, see Blokzijl et al. (2017); for an analysis of intuitional data on bilingual verbs from Belize vs. the U.S., see Balam et al. (2020); for an analysis of bilingual diminutives in production data from Belize and Miami, Florida, see Vanhaverbeke et al. (2021); for an analysis of intuitional data on bilingual passives from Belize and the Southwest U.S., see Balam et al. (2022).

Although an invigorated interest in the study of CAS varieties has certainly blossomed in the last decade, including the aforementioned volumes on pedagogical and dialectal aspects (Herrera Morera et al., 2016; Quesada Pacheco, 2010, 2013), there is no volume comprising original studies that examine these varieties from linguistic perspectives. This collection fills this gap by bringing together work being conducted by a diverse group of scholars, whose research sheds light into phonological, morphosyntactic, sociopragmatic, dialectological, and historical frameworks of CAS varieties. By elucidating different linguistic phenomena in CAS varieties, we hope this volume serves as an impetus for further interest and research on this singular linguistic frontier with a rich mosaic of bi/multilingual contexts where Spanish is in intense contact not only with many indigenous languages (Guatemala, Belize, El Salvador), English as an official language (Belize), but with English-based Creoles as well (Belize, Guatemala, Honduras, Nicaragua, Costa Rica, Panama). The chapters in this volume represent diverse perspectives and approaches in the linguistic study of CAS varieties, and they offer valuable insight to other scholars and practitioners from other fields interested in the Spanish varieties spoken in Central America and the Central American diaspora.

2   Chapter Summaries

The remaining chapters in this volume are organized by linguistic subfield and represent the growing body of work on CAS. Chapters 2–6 present phonetic analyses of the Spanish spoken in Belize, Guatemala, Honduras, El Salvador, and Costa Rica whereas Chapters 7–13 comprise studies on different morpho-syntactic variables in Guatemala, Honduras, El Salvador, Nicaragua, Costa Rica, and Panama. As the linguistic study of CAS is still growing, the chapters in this volume employ a wide array of areas, such as sociolinguistics, pragmatics, historical linguistics, corpus linguistics, and dialectology. Nonetheless, all authors here have focused on the shared objective of this volume: pursuing a richer understanding of the linguistic features of CAS. The final commentary in this volume, penned by John Lipski, offers both a historical overview of seminal work on this region as well as promising avenues for further research on CAS varieties.

Chapters 2 and 3 present sociophonetic analyses of rhotics in CAS. In Chapter 2, Bero provides a variationist analysis of rhotic production in the Spanish variety spoken in Corozal, the northernmost district in Belize. Basing his analysis on interview data from 10 speakers, he investigates whether there is phonemic merger in this variety, particularly in word-initial and word-internal syllable-final positions. Bero does not find evidence of a phonemic merger. Whereas the tap is overwhelmingly produced in intervocalic tap position, the trill and the retroflex variant are used in the intervocalic trill context. In word-initial position, the retroflex rhotic is consistently used by six out of ten speakers. In the case of speakers who showed variability, rhotics preceded by consonants favored production of the canonical trill whereas those preceded by vowels favored retroflex rhotic use. In word-internal syllable-final position, when preceded by alveolar and dental consonants, the retroflex variant was produced at rates of 29% and 46%, respectively. Bero found that women in particular produced the retroflex variant. Notably, no effect was found for age, as younger speakers ages 40 and younger did not employ the retroflex variant more frequently than older speakers in word-internal syllable-final position.

Similarly, McKinnon sociophonetically analyzes the production of Spanish rhotics in a bilingual community in Guatemala in Chapter 3. In this study, bilingual speakers of Spanish and the Mayan language Kaqchikel were analyzed via sociolinguistic interviews. Like Bero's study in Chapter 2, the results demonstrate that these speakers of Central American Spanish are more consistent in producing the tap than the trill. However, the production of trills shows greater variation. Older speakers tend to use a noncanonical assibilated rhotic instead of a trill that is primarily contrasted from taps in terms of duration, particularly in minimal pairs. On the other hand, younger groups of speakers tend to demonstrate trill productions with the canonical 2+ occlusions. Based on these findings, McKinnon proposes that a change is in progress. The non-canonical realizations of the trill are becoming less common among younger generations as trill production falls more in line with general Spanish. In other words, it may be assumed that some effects of Kaqchikel on Guatemalan Spanish may be diminishing over time.

Chapters 4 and 5 analyze the production and perception of /s/ across two different Central American countries. In Chapter 4, Ventura and Baird provide the first sociophonetic study of Honduran Spanish published in English in over three decades. This chapter analyses absolute-final /s/ in Honduran Spanish, which is somewhere in the middle of the variation seen between Salvadoran and Nicaraguan varieties with high rates of lenition and deletion, and the very low rates in Guatemalan Spanish. Using a rapid anonymous survey methodology, they provide an initial analysis of the production of absolute-final /s/ among 278 Spanish speakers from Tegucigalpa, the epicenter of variation in Honduran Spanish. Ventura and Baird's analyses demonstrates an even higher rate of variation than found in broader studies of /s/ in Honduran Spanish from previous decades. Furthermore, this is the first study on /s/ in Honduran Spanish to include extra-linguistic features in the statistical analysis and these results demonstrate more variation in /s/ among speakers that are younger, male, less educated, and lower class. Although the authors readily admit that a rapid anonymous survey only offers a first step in understanding this variation, these results indicate that /s/ in Tegucigalpa Spanish is becoming more heterogeneous, much like Salvadoran and Nicaraguan Spanish.

In Chapter 5, Brogan, Slotten, and Menjívar analyze the social meaning of /s/ lenition and its interaction with gender in Salvadoran Spanish, in which /s/ is commonly produced as one of three variants in onset position: namely, the voiceless strident [s] or one of two lenited forms: the voiced variant [z], or the gesturally undershot variant [s̠]. Brogan et al. analyze data from a matched guise experiment, in which 104 Salvadoran speakers heard speech samples produced by six Salvadorans and evaluated each speaker on a set of social characteristics. With respect to gender, their results show that male guises were rated more favorably than female guises for status and positive social feature dimensions, regardless of which variant is employed. Their study also finds supporting evidence for the allophonic hierarchy of onset /s/ in terms of social status; namely, [s] is associated with the highest social status, followed by [z], and lastly by [ṣ]. Importantly, this hierarchy is attested among younger listeners only, in contrast to older listeners who give relatively similar ratings to the three variants for status. Brogan et al. contend that this is a reflection of a recent standardized process in which lenited variants are stigmatized, particularly among younger generations. Thus, only speakers perceived as "older" are able to access covert prestige when producing the lenited variant.

Velásquez-Upegui provides one of the first analyses of intonation in Costa Rican Spanish in the study presented in Chapter 6. Using the Autosegmental-Metrical Model, Velásquez-Upegui proposes a tone inventory and ToBI transcription system for broad-focus statements, yes-no questions, and wh-questions based on the analysis of six participants from San José. The results indicate that in all three types of statements indicate a rise of intonation in the pre-nuclear position and that the high tone is often realized in post-tonic syllables. Additionally, common intonational contours in nuclear syllables include H+L* L% for broad-focus statements and L+(¡) H* L% for both yes-no and wh-questions. Velásquez-Upegui also reveals significant differences in contours that are related to participant age. Specifically, speakers from "middle" and "older" generations tended to use the same contours across all three types of statements whereas younger speakers consistently produced contours that were different from the two older generations. Between-sex differences were also found, as females used the L% boundary tone in yes-no questions more than males. Taken together, the primary trends found in this study indicate similarities with other varieties of Latin American Spanish, particularly Colombian. As a whole, this chapter provides a starting point for future analyses of suprasegmental features of Costa Rican Spanish.

The first chapter that examines a morphosyntactic feature in this volume is Chapter 7, García Tesoro's analysis on two contact-induced changes in Guatemalan Spanish in contact with the Mayan language Tz'utujil. Of these changes noted among bilingual and monolingual participants, the first is the collapse of the third personal direct object pronoun system into a single option: *lo*. García Tesoro proposes that the historical instability of the third-person pronominal system in Spanish has led to this change, which has been accelerated by intense language contact, as it is predominantly seen among bilingual participants. The second is a change among prepositions, with *en* being used instead of *a* with verbs of movement. Although this change is also seen as being contact-induced and more common among bilinguals, a semantic shift is also noted here. Specifically, bilinguals demonstrate the use of both prepositions with verbs of movement, but the use of *en* is used in a very restricted way in which the speaker signals the goal, rather than the direction of the verb.

Rodríguez and Howe offer a corpus analysis of transitive *andar* across Salvadoran, Honduran, Costa Rican, and Nicaraguan Spanish in Chapter 8. Aside from the common use of *andar* in the sense of "traversing a space", Honduran, Salvadoran, Costa Rican, and Nicaraguan Spanish also demonstrate the use of *andar* as a transtive verb with the meaning of "carrying something with you". After an account of the grammaticalization of this transitive use of *andar*, the authors provide the results of their corpus analysis and demonstrate that the use of *andar* in the sense of carrying something is significantly more common in these four Central American countries than in other Spanish-speaking countries. Furthermore, in these countries, the probability of using *andar* in this sense is greater than that of using intransitive *andar* as it is canonically used in other varieties of Spanish. Nonetheless, transitive *andar* was not deemed to be competing with similar verbs like *llevar*. As the majority of corpus data on Spanish exists for Peninsular, Mexican, and Argentine varieties, a major goal of this analysis is to demonstrate how different tools in corpus linguistics can be used to analyze varieties in which there is not ample corpus representation.

In Chapter 9, Critchfield provides an analysis of third-person subject-verb agreement in the Spanish spoken on the Mosquito Coast of Nicaragua. An analysis of oral interview data of this contact variety of Spanish demonstrates a lack of number agreement in almost a quarter of the data. However, both linguistic and social factors are shown to motivate this variation as phonic salience, subject position, animacy, and the age and sex of the speaker were all significant predictors. Nonetheless, age of acquisition of Spanish was not a significant factor. In other words, Critchfield's findings demonstrate that this particular case of lack of number agreement is more likely a characteristic of Mosquito Coast Spanish in general rather than the result of incomplete acquisition of Spanish by some speakers.

In Chapter 10, Cabal-Jiménez uses historical data in order to trace the evolution of the pronoun *usted* in Costa Rican Spanish. Based on letters and manuscripts written between the 16th and 20th centuries, the author analyzes 520 tokens of *usted* and its corresponding morphology according to the types of speech acts involved in order to understand the semantic and pragmatic change of this pronoun in Costa Rica. Cabal-Jiménez's analysis focuses on face threating acts (FTAS) and she finds that from the 16th to the 18th century FTAS to the negative face include withdrawal uses of *usted* that follow the literal meaning whereas approach uses include a verb that undergoes semantic and pragmatic change. The data also demonstrates that by the 19th and 20th centuries, withdrawal uses of *usted* had expanded to include FTAS to the positive face whereas approach uses extended far beyond the speech acts of suggestions, orders, and requests seen in the 16th–18th centuries. Thus, Cabal-Jiménez concludes that pragmaticalization/grammaticalization of *usted* occurred during this time and had become encoded on this societal pronoun/deictic in Costa Rican Spanish.

Rivas and Pineda shed light on the use of the Present Perfect (PP) and the Preterit in Costa Rican Spanish in Chapter 11. Through the variationist analysis of data from 14 interviews, their study shows that in spoken Costa Rican Spanish, the Preterit is generally used as a perfective. Imperfects overwhelmingly co-occur with Preterits (94%), which reveals that in Costa Rican Spanish, foregrounded clauses are only expressed by the Preterit. The PP particularly occurs after the Present tense. Thus, the PP is used to encode anterior aspect, associated with current relevance. Importantly, constructions with durative, frequency, and proximate adverbials significantly favor PP usage. In relation to other varieties, Rivas and Pineda find that Costa Rican Spanish is similar to Mexican Spanish in that hodiernal temporal reference disfavors PP usage, and the PP is overwhelmingly used to encode the anterior aspect. In contrast to Salvadoran Spanish, however, when the PP is used as a perfective, Rivas and Pineda did not find the PP to be more subjective than the Preterit, as similar rates of subject expression were found when the PP was used to encode either the anterior or perfective aspect.

In Chapter 12, Quesada Pacheco examines historical (from the 16th to the 19th centuries) and metalinguistic texts (from the 20th and 21st centuries) in order to provide an account of the factors that led to the geographical distribution of address pronouns in Panamanian Spanish. Quesada Pacheco finds that *voseo* was used since the beginning of the colonial era. Importantly, while the reverential *vos* was attested from the first half of the 16th century to the 19th century, the use of familiar *vos* is documented from the second half of the 16th century. The innovative use of *ustedeo* to denote closeness and affection was also documented from the 16th century. Similarly, *tuteo* was used from the beginning of the early 16th century, particularly when addressing deities or speakers in a socially inferior class. Pacheco Quesada highlights that as a result of the demographic predominance of Afro-descendants in the 17th and 18th centuries, the subsequent use of *tuteo* became increasingly dominant. By the 19th century, *tuteo* had displaced *voseo* and *ustedeo*. Quesada Pachedo asserts that one of the main factors that favored the expansion of *tuteo* was the overwhelming presence of the Black and mulatto population. Thus, from the 19th century onwards, whereas *tuteo* spread to different geographical regions of Panama, *voseo* and *ustedeo* steadily declined in terms of use.

Michno, Myers, and Przedspelski analyze service encounters in a corner store in a rural community in Southwestern Nicaragua in Chapter 13. Their analysis of 81 transactions between a male service provider and his customers shows that the most frequent request type of request were ellipticals followed by commands. In relation to the sequence of speech acts and the organization of talk, interactions were found to be largely customer-initiated and transaction-oriented. Greetings and other forms of relational talk were rare, and the absence of closings was the norm in this community of practice. Notably, Michno, Myers and Przedspelski find that in overlapping service encounter interactions, the vendor uses different pragmalinguistic devices to identity with customers and minimize face-threat to them. For example, the "*espérame* mechanism" is used as a way not only to conform to sociocultural norms of politeness, but to manage turn-taking and negotiate interactions with multiple customers. Thus, even though participants in this rural corner store do not engage in relational talk, other mechanisms are employed for the purpose of negotiating overlapping interactions while also maintaining interpersonal relationships with customers.

Finally, in his concluding commentary in Chapter 14, Lipski reflects on the seminal work he conducted in Central America during the 1980s, particularly in Honduras and Panama. He outlines different sociohistorical factors that may have contributed to the diversification of Central American Spanish varieties. He suggests, for instance, that the maritime route of travel that connected Guatemala and Costa Rica during the colonial era may account for some of the similarities (e.g., sibilant [s] retention in code position) between Guatemalan and Costa Rican Spanish varieties. He also notes that the absence of a major indigenous language that spanned across the region contributed to dialect diversification, as there was no lingua franca that could be employed by the Spanish colonizers for administrative control. Lipksi also reflects on the slow trajectory of research on Central American Spanish. He highlights that linguistic descriptions by Central American authors primarily on Costa Rican Spanish were not carried out until the middle of the 20th century and thereafter. Empirical work (mainly phonetic/phonological in nature) on Central American Spanish varieties, however, were not carried out until the 1970s. Lipski observes that while advancements have been made in the linguistic study of these varieties, there are promising avenues for future work on CAS; namely, Central American communities in the U.S., and dialect contact zones within Central America and Mexico.

3   Final Remarks

In sum, this volume addresses a substantial gap within the field of Hispanic Linguistics. The collection of studies presented here has been carried out by a group of international scholars, including several from Central America, that are both well established in the study of CAS and by those that are newer to this geographical area. The expertise of all these and more scholars is needed in order to advance the linguistic study of these under analyzed and oft ignored varieties of Spanish. We express our gratitude to each and every author, and we hope that this volume will promote continued and more robust linguistic investigations of CAS both in Central America and the diaspora and lead to future collaborations in this geographical area.

As it relates to CAS in the diaspora, it is noteworthy that there is still scant linguistic research on Central American communities in the U.S., which aligns with Arias' (2003, p. 170) apt observation that "[d]espite its numerical presence, the Central American population remains invisible within the imaginary confines of what constitutes the multi-cultural landscape of the United States." Further research needs to be conducted on Central American immigrant communities both within Central America and in other contexts such as the U.S. (see Lipski, this volume).

The Central American isthmus is a diverse contact zone that linguistically epitomizes the rich indigenous, African, and European heritage of the Spanish-speaking world. As the linguistic bridge of the Americas (Moreno Fernández, 2012), Central America has a key historical linguistic link with the Southwest U.S. that also merits further research. Citing Canfield (1981), Lipski (this volume) aptly reminds us that like the traditional Spanish of New Mexico, CAS varieties are among the most archaic in Latin America. To date, however, besides comparative research on Spanish/English bilingual compound verbs and bilingual passive constructions in Belize versus New Mexico (Balam et al., 2020; Balam et al., 2022), and Martin's (1985) observations that the archaic pleonastic possessive, e.g. *una mi vaca* 'one my cow', exist in Guatemalan Spanish but not in New Mexico Spanish, there is no study that sheds light on the archaic lexical or morphosyntactic characteristics that are similar across CAS varieties and traditional New Mexican Spanish.

Furthermore, because of the presence of English-based Creoles in several Central American countries, the Isthmus also shares an important link with Creole-speaking communities in the Western Caribbean (including Colombia), which also offer fertile ground for important linguistic research on Creole/Spanish bilingual communities (Baird 2023c). As Herzfeld (2003) reports, according to data published by Smith (1995), there were at that point of time 55,000 speakers of Limonese creole in Costa Rica, 100,000 speakers of Panamanian creole, 40,000 speakers of Miskito Coast creole and 500 speakers of Rama Cay creole in Nicaragua, and 115,000 speakers of Belizean Kriol. Herzfeld reminds us that despite the numerical importance regarding number of speakers and their long presence on the Central American coast, these cultures were 'invisible' in the official histories of Central America until the sixties. In recent times, the status of Creoles has improved, although tensions regarding Creole use still exist. To this end, Leung and Loskchy's (2021) edited volume presents recent insights into how Caribbean communities deal with the evolving Creole identity and with linguistic discrimination, showing how communal resilience manifests itself via linguistic innovation and creativity. They emphasize that this sentiment is felt even more intensely in the Rimland where Creole languages are spoken among minority populations. The Rimland, a term coined by Augelli (1962), refers to the geographic enclaves in Latin America (predominantly Central America) where English/Creole-speaking West Indians settled, and their language and culture still survive.

Overall, the present volume encourages upcoming research to consider the multiplicity of monolingual and bi/multilingual communities and influencing factors that shape the distinctively heterogeneous linguistic landscape of Central America.

References

Aaron, J. E. & Hernandez, J. E. (2007). Quantitative evidence for contact-induce accommodation: Shifts in /s/ reduction patterns in Salvadoran Spanish in Houston. In K. Potowski & R. Cameron (Eds.), *Spanish in Contact: Policy, Social and Linguistic Inquiries* (pp. 327–341). John Benjamins. https://doi.org/10.1075/impact.22.23aar.

Agüero Chaves, A. (2009). *El español de Costa Rica*. Editorial Universidad Nacional de Cosa Rica.

Alvarado de Ricord, E. (1971). *El español de Panamá: estudio fonético y fonológico*. Editorial Universitario de Panamá.

Arias, A. (2003). Central American-Americans: Invisibility, Power and Representation in the US Latino World. *Latino Studies*, *1*(1), 168–187. https://doi.org/10.1057/palgrave.lst.8600007.

Augelli, J. P. (1962). The Rimland-Mainland concept of culture areas in Middle America. *Annals of the Association of American Geographers*, 52(2), 119–129.

Baird, B. (2015). Pre-nuclear peak alignment in the Spanish of Spanish-K'ichee' (Mayan) bilinguals. In E. Willis, P. Martín Butragueño, & E. Herrera Zendejas (Eds.) *Selected Proceedings of the 6th Conference on Laboratory Approaches to Romance Phonology* (pp. 163–174). Cascadilla Proceedings Project.

Baird, B. (2017). Prosodic transfer among Spanish-K'ichee' Bilinguals. In K. Bellamy, M. Child, P. González, A. Muntendam, & M. C. Parafita Couto (Eds.) *Multidisciplinary approaches to bilingualism in the Hispanic and Lusophone world* (pp. 147–172). John Benjamins. https://doi.org/10.1075/ihll.13.07bai.

Baird, B. (2018). Syntactic and Prosodic Contrastive Focus Marking in K'ichee'. *International Journal of American Linguistics*, *84*(3), 295–325. https://doi.org/10.1086/697585.

Baird, B. (2019). Ciudadano maya 100%: Uso y actitudes de la lengua entre los bilingües k'iche'-español. *Hispania*, *102*(3), 319–334. doi:10.1353/hpn.2019.0070.

Baird, B. (2020). The vowel spaces of Spanish-K'ichee' bilinguals. In R. Rao (Ed.), *Spanish Phonetics and Phonology in Contact: Studies from Africa, the Americas, and Spain* (pp. 64–81). John Benjamins. https://doi.org/10.1075/ihll.28.03bai.

Baird, B. (2021a). "Para mí, es indígena con traje típico": Apocope as an indexical marker of indigeneity in Guatemalan Spanish. In L. A. Ortiz & E. Suárez Budenbender (Eds.) *Topics in Spanish Linguistic Perceptions* (pp. 223–239). Routledge.

Baird, B. (2021b). Bilingual language dominance and contrastive focus marking: Gradient effects of K'ichee' syntax on Spanish prosody. *International Journal of Bilingualism*, *25*(3), 500–515. https://doi.org/10.1177/1367006920952855.

Baird, B. (2023a). Social perceptions of /f/ fortition in Guatemalan Spanish. *Spanish in Context*. https://doi.org/10.1075/sic.20011.bai.

Baird, B. (2023b). Clothing, Gender, and Sociophonetic Perceptions of Mayan-accented Spanish in Guatemala. *Languages 8*(3) 189. https://doi.org/10.3390/languages8030189.

Baird, B. (2023c). Sociolinguistics in Central America. In M. Ball, R. Mesthrie & C. Meluzzi (Eds.) *The Routledge Handbook of Sociolinguistics around the Word*, 2nd edition (pp. 65–73). Routledge. https://doi.org/10.4324/9781003198345-7.

Balam, O. (2013). Overt language attitudes and linguistic identities among multilingual speakers in Northern Belize. *Studies in Hispanic and Lusophone Linguistics*, *6*(2), 247–277. https://doi.org/10.1515/shll-2013-1150.

Balam, O. (2014). Notes on the history and morphosyntactic features of Spanish in Northern Belize. *Kansas Working Papers in Linguistics*, *2*, 79–94.

Balam, O. (2015). Code-switching and linguistic evolution: The case of 'hacer + v' in Orange Walk, Northern Belize. *Lengua y Migración*, *7*(1), 83–109.

Balam, O. (2016). Semantic categories and gender assignment in contact Spanish: Type of code-switching and its relevance to linguistic outcomes. *Journal of Language Contact*, *9*(3), 405–435.

Balam, O., Prada Pérez, A., & Mayans, D. (2014). A congruence approach to the study of bilingual compound verbs in Northern Belize contact Spanish. *Spanish in Context*, *11*(2), 243–265.

Balam, O., & Parafita Couto, M. C. (2019). Adjectives in Spanish/English code-switching: Avoidance of grammatical gender in bi/multilingual Speech. *Spanish in Context*, *16*(2), 194–216.

Balam, O., Parafita Couto, M. C., & Stadthagen-González, H. (2020). Bilingual Verbs in three Spanish/English code-switching communities. *International Journal of Bilingualism*, *24* (5–6): 952–967. https://doi.org/10.1177/1367006920911449.

Balam, O., Parafita Couto, M. C., & Chen, M. (2021). Being in bilingual speech: An analysis of estar 'be' constructions in Spanish/English code-switching. *Journal of Monolingual and Bilingual Speech, 3*(2), 238–264.

Balam, O., Stadthagen-González, H., Rodríguez-González, E., & Parafita Couto, M. C. (2022). On the grammaticality of passivization in bilingual compound verbs. *International Journal of Bilingualism*. https://doi.org/10.1177/13670069221097772.

Batres Jáuregui, A. (1892). *Vicios del lenguaje y provincialismos de Guatemala.* Encuadernación y tipografía nacional.

Bierings, E., Parafita Couto, M. C., & Mateo Pedro, P. (2019). Contrasting code-switching theories: insights from Kaqchikel-Spanish code-switched nominal constructions. *Proceedings of Form and Analysis in Mayan Linguistics, 5*. Retrieved from https://escholarship.org/uc/item/6m86k8oj.

Blokzijl, J., Deuchar, M., & Parafita Couto, M. C. (2017). Determiner asymmetry in mixed nominal constructions: the role of grammatical factors in data from Miami and Nicaragua. *Languages, 2*, (20). https://doi:10.3390/languages2040020.

Brogan, F. & Bolyanatz, M. (2018). A sociophonetic account of onset /s/ weakening in Salvadoran Spanish: Instrumental and segmental analyses. *Language Variation and Change, 30*, 203–230. https://doi.org/10.1017/S0954394518000066.

Canfield, D. L. (1981). *Spanish Pronunciation in the Americas.* University of Chicago Press.

Chappell, W. (2016). On the social perception of intervocalic /s/ voicing in Costa Rican Spanish. *Language Variation and Change, 28*(3), 357–378. https://doi.org/10.1017/S0954394516000107.

Chappell, W. (2017). Las ideologías lingüísticas de los miskitus hacia la lengua indígena (el miskitu) y la lengua mayoritaria (el español). *Hispanic Studies Review, 2*(2), 117–138.

Chappell, W. (2020). Social contact and linguistic convergence: The reduction of intervocalic /d/ in Bilwi, Nicaragua. In R. Rao (Ed.), *Spanish Phonetics and Phonology in Contact: Studies from Africa, the Americas, and Spain* (pp. 84–102). John Benjamins. https://doi.org/10.1075/ihll.28.04cha.

Chiquito, A. B. & Quesada Pacheco, M. A. (2014). *Actitudes lingüísticas de los hispanohablantes hacia el idioma español y sus variantes.* Bergen Language and Linguistic Studies.

de la Rocha, J. E. (1858/2002). Equivocaciones de los centroamericanos al hablar castellano. In E. Arellano (Ed.), *El español de Nicaragua y palabras y modismos de la lengua castellana, según se habla en Nicaragua [1874] de C. H. Berendt* (pp. 85–88). Instituto Nicaragüense de Cultura Hispánica, Academia Nicaragüense de la Lengua.

Félix-Brasdefer, C. (2010). Intra-lingual pragmatic variation in Mexico City and San José, Costa Rica: A focus on regional differences in female requests. *Journal of Pragmatics, 42*(11), 2992–3011. https://doi.org/10.1016/j.pragma.2010.04.015.

Gagini, C. (1892). *Diccionario de barbarismos y provincialismos de Costa Rica*. Tipografía Nacional.

García Tesoro, A. I. (2011). Lenguas mayas e identidad en Guatemala. *Perspectivas latinoamericanas, 8*, 122–134.

García Tesoro, A. I. (2018). El sistema pronominal átono de tercera persona en la variedad de contacto con el tzutujil: hacia una concordancia de objeto. *Revista Internacional de Linguistica Iberoamericana, 32*(2): 83–96.

Herranz, A. (Comp.). (1990). *El español hablado en Honduras*. Editorial Guaymaras.

Herranz, A. (1996). *Estado, sociedad y lenguaje: La política lingüística en Honduras*. Instituto Hondureño de Antropología e Historia.

Herrera Morera, G., Núñez Alvarado, V., & Quesada, J. D. (2016). *El español de Centroamérica: Visión global y materiales para su estudio*. Editorial Universidad Nacional de Costa Rica.

Hernández, J. E. & Maldonado, R. A. (2012). Reducción de /s/ final de sílaba entre transmigrantes salvadoreños en el sur de Texas. *Lengua y migración, 4*, 43–67.

Herzfeld, A. (2003). Language and Identity in a Contact Situation: The Limonese Creole Speakers in Costa Rica. *Matatu, 27–28*, 67–83.

Hoffman, M. F. (2001). Salvadoran Spanish /-s/ Aspiration and Deletion in a Bilingual Context. *University of Pennsylvania Working Papers in Linguistics, 7*(3), 10. https://repository.upenn.edu/pwpl/vol7/iss3/10.

Lamy, D. (2016). A variationist account of voice onset time (VOT) among bilingual West Indians in Panama. *Studies in Hispanic and Lusophone Linguistics, 9*(1), 113–142. https://doi.org/10.1515/shll-2016-0005.

Leung, G.a. & Loschky, M. (Eds.). (2021). *When Creole and Spanish Collide: Language and Cultural Contact in the Caribbean*. Brill.

Lipski, J. (1983). Reducción de /s/ en el español de Honduras [Reduction of /s/ in Honduran Spanish]. *Nueva Revista de Filología Hispánica, 32*, 273–288.

Lipski, J. (1986). Central American Spanish in the United States: El Salvador. *Aztlán, 17*, 91–124.

Lipski, J. (1986). Instability and reduction of /s/ in the Spanish of Honduras. *Revista Canadiense de Estudios Hispánicos, 11*, 27–47.

Lipski, J. (1987). *Fonética y fonología del español de Honduras*. Editorial Guaymuras.

Lipski, J. (1994). *Latin American Spanish*. Longman.

López Alonzo, K. (2016). Use and perception of the pronominal trio vos, tú, usted in a Nicaraguan community in Miami, Florida. In M. I. Moyna & S. Rivera-Mills (Eds.), *Forms of address in the Spanish of the Americas* (pp. 197–232). John Benjamins. https://doi.org/10.1075/ihll.10.10lop.

Mántica, C. (1989). *El habla nicaragüense y otros ensayos*. Libro Libre.

Martin, L. (1985). Una mi tacita de café: the indefinite article in Guatemalan Spanish. *Hispania, 68*, 383–387.

McKinnon, S. (2020). Un análisis sociofonético de la aspiración de las oclusivas sordas en el español guatemalteco monolingüe y bilingüe (español-kaqchikel). *Spanish in Context*, *17*(1), 1–29. https://doi.org/10.1075/sic.00051.mck.

McKinnon, S. (2023). Las vocales glotalizadas en el español guatemalteco: Un análisis sociofonético entre los hablantes bilingües (español-kaqchikel) y monolingües. *Studies in Hispanic and Lusophone Linguistics, 16*(1), 171–207. https://doi.org/10.1515/shll-2023-2007.

Melgares, J. (2018). "El vos nuestro es, ¡Ey vos chigüín!" Honduran vos as a marker of national identity. In J. E. McDonald (Ed.), *Contemporary Trends in Hispanic and Lusophone Lingustics* (pp. 191–210). John Benjamins. doi.org/10.1075/ihll.15.10mel.

Michno, J. (2019). Gender variation in address form selection in corner-store interactions in a Nicaraguan community. In J. C. Félix-Brasdefer & M. E. Placencia, *Pragmatic variation in service encounter interactions across the Spanish-speaking world* (pp. 77–98). Routledge.

Michnowicz, J., Scott, D. J., & Gorham, R. (2016). The changing system of Costa Rican pronouns of address. In M. I. Moyna & S. Rivera-Mills (Eds.), *Forms of address in the Spanish of the Americas* (pp. 243–266). John Benjamins. https://doi.org/10.1075/ihll.10.12mic.

Moreno Fernández, F. (2012). América Central: Puente lingüístico de las Américas. *Bergen Language and Linguistics Studies* 2. https://doi.org/10.15845/bells.v2i0.275.

Moser, K. (2010). Las formas de tratamiento verbales-pronominales en Guatemala, El Salvador, Panamá (y Costa Rica): hacia una nueva sistematización en la periferia centroamericana. In Hummel, M. et al. (Eds.), *Formas y fórmulas de tratamiento en el mundo hispánico* (pp. 271–291). El Colegio de México/Karl Franzens Universitat Gräz.

Platz, R. (2014). Giving Advice in Nicaragua and Panama. *Lodz Papers in Pragmatics*, *10*(1): 89–116. https://doi.org/10.1515/lpp-2014-0005.

Quesada Pacheco, M. A. (2008). El español de América Central ayer, hoy y mañana. *Boletín de Filología, XLIII*, 145–174.

Quesada Pacheco, M. A. (Ed.). (2010). *El español hablado en América Central: nivel fonético*. Vervuert.

Quesada Pacheco, M. A. (Ed.). (2013). *El español hablado en América Central: nivel morfosintáctico*. Vervuert.

Smith, N. (1995). An Annotated List of Creoles, Pidgins, and Mixed Languages. In J. Arends, P. Muysken, & N. Smith (Eds.), *Pidgins and Creoles: An Introduction* (pp. 331–374). John Benjamins.

Schmidt-Rinehart, B. C., & LeLoup, J. W. (2017). Register and forms of address in Costa Rica: Sociolinguistic realities and pedagogical implications. *Foreign Language Annals*, *50*(1), 159–176. https:// doi:10.1111/flan.12247.

Sorenson, T. (2013). Voseo to Tuteo Accommodation among Salvadorans in the United States. *Hispania*, 96, 763–781. https://doi:10.1353/hpn.2013.0120.

Sorenson, T. (2016). "¿De dónde sos?": Differences between Argentine and Salvadoran voseo to tuteo accomodation in the United States. In M. I. Moyna and S. Rivera-Mills, *Forms of address in the Spanish of the Americas* (pp. 171–196). John Benjamins.

Ulloa, F. (1872). *Elementos de gramática de la lengua castellana, escritos expresamente para la enseñanza de la juventud en Costa Rica*. Tipografía Nacional.

Vanhaverbeke, M., Enghels, R., & Balam, O. (2021, Dec. 2). *Diminutive constructions in bi/multilingual speech: A cross-community analysis of Spanish-English codeswitching in Northern Belize and Miami* [Conference Poster]. Going Romance Conference. Amsterdam, The Netherlands.

Wagner, L., & Roebuck, R. (2010). Apologizing in Cuernavaca, Mexico and Panama City, Panama: A cross-cultural comparison of positive- and negative-politeness strategies. *Spanish in Context*, 7(2): 254–278. https://doi.org/10.1075/sic.7.2.05wag.

Woods, M. R., & Shin, N. (2016). "Fijáte ... sabes que le digo yo": Salvadoran voseo and tuteo in Oregon. In M. I. Moyna & S. Rivera-Mills (Eds.), *Forms of address in the Spanish of the Americas* (pp. 305–324). John Benjamins. https://doi.org/10.1075/ihll.10.15woo.

CHAPTER 2

Rhotic Variation in Northern Belize
Beyond Tap-Trill Contrast Maintenance

Trevor Bero

1   Introduction

Across languages, the class of sounds known as rhotics (r-sounds) is marked by extensive variation. In fact, phonetic variability is noted as "a particularly salient characteristic of rhotics" and the class as a whole cannot be reliably identified by any single phonetic correlate (Chabot, 2019 p. 5). Additionally, cross-linguistic phonological analysis demonstrates the difficulty of capturing the wide variation within phonemic categories. While most languages only contain one rhotic phoneme (Ladefoged & Maddieson, 1996), many allophones are often associated with a single phoneme. For example, in languages such as Assamese, Munda, or Temne, a single rhotic phoneme manifests in approximant, trill, and flap allophones (Hall, 1997 p. 108).

Meanwhile, prescriptive Spanish has two phonemes: an alveolar tap, defined by a single contact between tongue tip and alveolar ridge, and an alveolar trill, with multiple contacts between the same articulators. Moving beyond prescriptive phonology reveals extensive dialectal differences and vast allophonic variation across all major Spanish dialect zones. This includes varieties of the U.S. Southwest (Bills, 1997; Vigil, 2008; 2018), Mexico and Central America (Bradley & Willis, 2012; Broce & Torres Cacoullos, 2002; among many others), South America (Bradley, 1999; Kim, 2019), the Caribbean (Willis & Bradley, 2008) and Spain (Bradley, 2005; Henriksen 2014; Zahler & Daidone, 2014).

Many studies of Spanish rhotics examine the maintenance of phonemic contrast between tap and trill. Some argue that the distinction, which only applies in intervocalic position in less than 30 minimal pairs, has been lost in many varieties (see Hammond, 1999). Other studies (e.g., Bradley & Willis, 2012) demonstrate factors like mean duration of rhotic segments can differentiate the two phonemes, as opposed to the prescriptive distinction based on number of lingual contacts. Finally, given the limited instances in which the two phonemes are contrastive, Hualde (2004) proposes the idea of a "quasi-phonemic" relationship.

Aside from the implications for Spanish phonology, dialectal differences offer insight into phonetic variation. This is especially true for the trill which requires more complex articulatory movements that often facilitate non-canonical variants. For example, in place of the canonical trill, assibilated rhotics are found in the Costa Rican Central Valley (Vásquez Carranza, 2006), Highland Ecuador (Bradley, 1999; 2004), the Antigua region of Guatemala (McKinnon, this volume) and other dialects in Central and South America (see Cárdenas, 1958 for geographic range of assibilated /r/). Meanwhile, other research attests a retroflex approximant realization in Yucatan Spanish (Lope Blanch, 1975) as well as backed (i.e., velar, uvular) variants in Puerto Rico (López-Morales, 1979), Cuba, Panama, and coastal Colombia and Venezuela (Canfield, 1962; Cuéllar, 1971). Additionally, pre-aspirated or pre-breathy-voice variants have been reported in Dominican Spanish (Lipski 1994; Willis & Bradley, 2008). In sum, regarding Spanish trills, it has been observed that "outside of ... conservative Spanish speech communities, the vibrant has undergone a wide range of phonetic adjustments" (Widdison, 1998 p. 51).

To build on previous studies, the present work analyzes rhotic variability in an understudied Spanish dialect spoken in Corozal Town, Belize. A retroflex rhotic is a common characteristic found in many Belizean Spanish varieties, including Corozal (Hagerty, 1979; Cardona Ramirez, 2010; Balam, 2013b). Corozal Town and the retroflex rhotic present intriguing topics of study given the history of language contact, the understudied nature of this dialect, and the broader insights on the Spanish phonological system that can be drawn from these results. While earlier studies suggested a loss of phonemic distinction between rhotics, especially in Orange Walk and Corozal districts (Hagerty, 1979), recent work shows speakers in Orange Walk maintaining a distinction in at least some speech styles (Balam, 2013b). In an effort to expand understanding of rhotic variation in Spanish, the present study assesses claims of phonemic merger with new data while also focusing on broader patterns of variation by addressing the following research questions.

1) *Is there evidence of phonemic contrast maintenance in the present data?*
2) *What social and linguistic factors constrain the use of retroflex rhotics in Corozal Spanish?*[1]
3) *What are the implications of these findings for broader issues of variation or change in the Spanish rhotic system?*

---

[1] 'Corozal Spanish' refers specifically to the Spanish in this data set, which was exclusively collected near Corozal Town. This is in contrast to the more general terms, 'Belizean Spanish' and 'Northern Belizean Spanish', used in other works (e.g., Hagerty, 1979; Balam, 2013b) which may or may not include speakers from Corozal Town.

To provide further context for the analysis, the following section presents previous findings regarding rhotic variation and non-standard variants across Spanish dialects.

2 Rhotic Variation in Spanish

2.1 *Variation across Dialects*

As mentioned above, several studies of Spanish rhotics relate non-standard variants to the prescribed tap-trill phonemic contrast. For example, in Highland Ecuador an assibilated rhotic seems to coincide with prescriptive trill environments. However, the distribution is not identical between tap and trill in prescriptive Spanish and tap and assibilated rhotic in Ecuadorian Spanish (Bradley, 1999 p. 57). In fact, rhotic use in Ecuadorian and standard Spanish only converges in syllable initial and intervocalic positions. The assibilated [ř] in Ecuadorian Spanish occupies word initial or syllable initial post-consonantal position, matching two environments of the trill in Standard Spanish. Additionally, the assibilated variant or trill contrasts with a tap intervocalically in the respective varieties (Boynton, 1981; Lipski, 1990). In the remaining contexts, the distribution of the assibilated rhotic differs from the trill. The assibilated rhotic is used word internally in coda position before a coronal consonant, but not before a bilabial or velar. Conversely, the standard Spanish trill can appear in coda position in emphatic speech no matter the following consonant. The assibilated rhotic can also appear as the second member of a complex syllable onset while the standard trill never occurs there. Thus, this study shows that non-standard rhotic variants may pattern in unique ways as opposed to simply replacing a standard rhotic phoneme.

The maintenance of the tap-trill contrast has also been explored in Veracruz Mexican Spanish through spectrographic analysis of syllable initial rhotics on semi-spontaneous speech (Bradley & Willis, 2012). This study found four different allophones of the tap, ranging from an approximant to complete elision. As for the trill, ten speakers produced a total of eight distinct variants (Bradley & Willis, 2012:56). An acoustic analysis of Dominican Spanish (Willis & Bradley, 2008) revealed the same level of allophonic variation for the tap. However, in this case, the majority of trill variants are pre-breathy voice followed by one or multiple closures. These studies also examined the duration of each rhotic finding that, for both varieties, the contrast between tap and trill is maintained by longer average duration in trill positions as opposed to more lingual contacts. In addition to demonstrating how phonological systems can adapt new methods for distinguishing phonemes, these studies also highlight a broad range of allophonic variation for both taps and trills.

Studies of the Costa Rican Central Valley dialect also describe considerable allophonic variation with assibilated rhotics (e.g., Calvo Shadid & Portilla Chaves, 1998; Vasquez-Carranza, 2006; among others). These works describe apico-alveolar fricatives, affricates, and assibilated retroflex variants, occurring across phonetic contexts. Three assibilated retroflex rhotic allophones have been reported in formal speech of female participants from the Central Valley, comprising 16% of the data (N = 707) with the remaining rhotics including alveolar taps and trills (Calvo Shadid & Portilla Chaves, 1998). Overall, non-canonical variants in this dialect are thought to emerge from language internal processes like articulatory weakening (Vasquez-Carranza, 2006 p. 303).

As opposed to focusing on tap or trill rhotics, other studies highlight rhotic variation in specific positions in a word (as part of consonant clusters see Bradley, 2006; Sessarego, 2011; in syllable/word final: Broce & Torres Cacoullos, 2002; Kim, 2019; among others). As displayed below in Table 2.1, Spanish taps and trills can be found in almost entirely complementary phonological distribution, only contrasting in intervocalic position. Despite this fact, syllable final or word final before consonant or pause remain especially intriguing as either the tap or trill can appear. While some argue that the selection of rhotics in this position is based on emphatic or stylistic choices (Quilis, 1993), others claim that the tap is the higher frequency or canonical variant (Blecua, 2001). Studies show both linguistic and social factors affecting variation in this position.

Kim (2019) examines syllable and word final rhotics in the coastal Tupe region of Peru. Overall, acoustic analysis revealed four variants, from most to least frequent, an approximant, a tap, an assibilated rhotic, and a trill. Logistic regression analysis showed following phonetic context as the most influential factor for selection of the assibilated rhotic, with a following pause, alveolar, or dental consonant greatly increasing its likelihood. Additionally, three social

TABLE 2.1   Word position and tap/trill usage in standard Spanish

Contrast tap vs. trill	V__V	Intervocalic
Trill only	#__	Word initial
	C.__	After hetero-syllabic consonant
Tap only	C__	After tautosyllabic consonant
	V._#V	Word final before a vowel
Variable	V__C	Word internal before consonant
	V_#C	Word final before consonant
	V_##	Word final before pause

ADAPTED FROM HUALDE 2005:183

factors impact variation. Speakers in the youngest or middle age groups of the study (age 20–40 or 40–60 years), those living on the coast for less than a year, and men all had higher likelihoods of using assibilated variants (Kim, 2019:151).

Syllable final rhotics have also been explored in Taos New Mexican Spanish (TNMS) (Vigil, 2008). This study is also important because TNMS is in contact with English, much like Corozal Spanish. A later study of the dialect confirmed observations that this variant is highly favored before alveolar consonants (Vigil, 2018 p. 252), similar to other studies discussed above. Additionally, women employ the retroflex at much higher rates in this position when compared to men, signaling that the variation is constrained by social factors (Vigil, 2018 p. 249).

Overall, studies of Spanish rhotics in other dialects demonstrate the wide range of phonetic variability and possible implications for reframing the prescriptive phonological contrast. No matter the exact nature of variants, it remains clear that Spanish dialects are no exception to the crosslinguistic trend of rhotic variability. While other dialects provide important insight into broader trends, the next section reviews previous studies focused on Belizean Spanish varieties.

2.2   *Rhotics in Belizean Spanish*

The earliest study of Belizean Spanish (Hagerty, 1979) was a phonological analysis including examination of rhotic variants. The analysis described seven rhotic allophones found in different regional varieties and in different positions in the word. First, there is the canonical [ɾ],[2] a single voiced alveolar flap. According to the study, this allophone occurs syllable finally or in second position of a consonant cluster. A similar variant, the assibilated alveolar rhotic [ř], appears after /t/ as in words like *otro* 'other', and in syllable final position before a pause. The third allophone is described as a voiced retroflex approximant [ɻ]. Interestingly, this variant is only used by northern district speakers and is described as identical to the initial /r/ of midwestern American English (Hagerty, 1979 p. 79). In addition to appearing in the same contexts as [ɾ], it also occurs in syllable initial position, either word initially after a pause or word medially when preceded by a consonant. The retroflex also appears variably in syllable final position. This provides preliminary evidence of the retroflex in positions canonically occupied by both the tap and trill.

Additionally, Hagerty examines the phonemic relationship between rhotic variants. Despite recognizing distinctions in some regions of Belize, Hagerty

---

2   These symbols do not always match those employed by Hagerty (1979). For the sake of clarity, IPA symbols that match descriptions provided in Hagerty (1979 p. 79–84) are used here.

(1979 p. 82) proposes the possibility of a merger in both Orange Walk and Corozal districts. He notes that speakers always prefer the retroflex in intervocalic position. In his analysis, some younger speakers failed to make the distinction between minimal pairs such as *caro* (expensive) [ka.ɾo] and *carro* (car) [ka.ɻo], instead using the retroflex articulation for both (Hagerty, 1979:81).

Finally, Hagerty further explores the retroflex variant. Though it remains unique in the broader scope of Spanish rhotics, the retroflex also occurs in Yucatan, Mexico, a close geographic neighbor with historical ties to Corozal. In Yucatan Spanish, the retroflex is most commonly found in syllable final position and only appears on occasion intervocalically (Lope Blanch, 1975). Hagerty reports that speakers of the northern districts use retroflex variants at least as often, and possibly more often, in intervocalic position as compared to syllable final (Hagerty, 1979: 84). The high variability and salience of this feature prompted further inquiry (Cardona Ramirez, 2010; Quilis, 1990; Quesada Pacheco, 2013).

Cardona Ramirez (2010) offers an account of Belizean Spanish across five northern and western districts. In initial position, five rhotic allophones are reported including alveolar tap [ɾ], non-sibilant voiced approximant alveolar [ɹ̝], trill [r], voiced approximant alveolar [ɹ], and retroflex approximant [ɻ]. In intervocalic positions with '*rr*' spellings, where a trill would be expected canonically, the retroflex approximant appears at the highest frequency (33% or 13/36).

In syllable and word final positions, the following consonant impacts variant use. In word final position, as well as before velar or bilabial consonants, a preference for the canonical tap [ɾ] arises. However, before the alveolar consonants /n/, /s/, and especially /l/, the retroflex is used at the relatively high rates of 32%, 25%, and 38%, respectively. Overall, these patterns mirror those of non-standard rhotic use in this position from other varieties (see Bradley, 1999; Kim, 2019; Vigil, 2018).

Unlike the work reported below, Cardona Ramirez's study combines speakers of different regional Belizean dialects. Importantly, it is noted that the northern districts, most of all Corozal, have the highest rate of retroflex use in syllable final position (Cardona Ramirez, 2010). Thus, although the research is largely descriptive in nature, it serves as an important baseline for further exploration of the retroflex rhotic in Corozal.

The only major quantitative work on Belizean Spanish rhotics examined tap-trill contrast maintenance (Balam, 2013b). The data included elicited production from 10 adolescent bidialectal Spanish speakers from Orange Walk, Belize. A contrast between rhotics was found to be maintained intervocalically. A retroflex approximant occurred where a trill would occur prescriptively (i.e., with 'rr' spellings). Generalization of the retroflex to canonical tap intervocalic environments remained exceedingly rare, produced in 3 tokens by a single speaker. This finding refutes the contention that the Spanish of northern Belize was "undergoing a phonemic merger" (Hagerty, 1979: 81). Further impressionistic analysis revealed that the retroflex approximant occurs most consistently where trills would be expected canonically, in word initial and intervocalic double 'rr' positions. Additionally, the retroflex occurs variably in syllable final position before homorganic (i.e., alveolar) consonants (Balam, 2013b:296). This final observation will be further investigated in the present work and considered in light of similar patterns in other Spanish dialects.

As demonstrated in Sections 2.1 and 2.2, despite a prescriptive phonology only including alveolar tap and trill variants, Spanish is no exception to the cross-linguistic pattern of remarkable rhotic variation. Examination of studies on Spanish also showed that, while understanding the phonological nature of taps and trills is important, such prior assumptions possibly obscure other patterns of variation. Studies testing social and linguistic factors that constrain variation can provide further insight into the nature of a broader range of variants. Thus, the current study provides a more holistic understanding of rhotic variation in Corozal Spanish by relating it to other dialects and discussing implications for Spanish phonology.

3   Community and Corpus

3.1   *Historical and Linguistic Development of Northern Belize*

Corozal Town serves as the capital of Belize's northernmost district, also called Corozal. The town is located only 15 miles from the border town of Chetumal, Mexico (See Map 2.1). Corozal District, like most of Belize, has been inhabited at various times by groups of British settlers, Africans, Yucatec Mayans, and Mestizos. Through most of the 18th and 19th centuries, descendants of free and enslaved Africans, often referred to collectively as "Creoles", made up the ethnic and linguistic plurality of the nation (Gabbert, 2007). However, following various waves of migration from surrounding nations, Mestizos now near an outright majority creating a demographic and linguistic shift. Importantly, the Mestizo majority and the Spanish language have always been most prevalent in the north.

Belize remains an officially English-speaking country and the English-based creole, Belize Kriol, serves as a lingua franca across districts (Ravindranath, 2009). In addition to the presence of these languages, the northern and western districts contain considerable Spanish speaking populations. In Corozal,

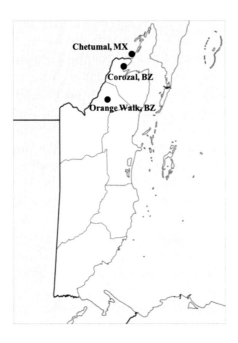

MAP 2.1
Map of Belize

the influx of Spanish speakers can be traced back to thousands of Mayans and Mestizos from Mexico fleeing the Yucatec Caste War in the mid-1800s.[3] Over the following century and a half, distinct Spanish varieties formed across northern Belize. The combination of unique linguistic, social, and historical circumstances along with a general lack of previous inquiry makes Corozal Spanish an especially intriguing case for the study of variation.

3.2   *Data Collection*

All data was collected in Corozal Town in the summer of 2019. The data analyzed here comes from 10 sociolinguistic interviews (Labov, 1984). Importantly, despite some interviewees having knowledge of English, they all used Spanish in their daily lives and were native speakers of the local dialect. Interviews took place in familiar public spaces (e.g., restaurants, small shops, a local museum) and private homes of interviewees, all within a 5-mile radius of Corozal Town. Interviews were recorded using a Zoom H1n portable recorder and lavalier lapel microphone for interviewer and participant.

---

3 Spanish varieties outside northern regions can generally be traced to later immigration, primarily of Salvadorans, Guatemalans, and Hondurans fleeing civil wars and settling in different parts of Belize during the 1980s (Shoman, 2010).

The participants come from a variety of backgrounds and professions including stay at home mothers, small business owners, and freelance handymen, among others. Participants were recruited and contacted with the help of a local community member. Their ages range from 22 to 70. The 5 male participants have the following age breakdowns: 2 from 20–40 years and 3 participants 41 and older. The 5 female participants include the following age breakdowns: 3 participants 20–40 years and 2 participants 41 and older. All participants were born and raised in Corozal District within 10 miles of Corozal Town.

4 Methodology and Analysis

The existing literature on the Spanish of Belize includes mostly descriptive accounts or explicit focus on language contact phenomena. Furthermore, studies of rhotic variation in the dialect tend to include speakers from vastly different regions or focus on maintenance of phonological contrast. Alternatively, the present study will employ the variationist method. By assuming that variation is inherent and serves a social function within speech communities (Labov, 1994), this analysis will provide a broader understanding of both the linguistic and social factors accounting for rhotic variation in Corozal Spanish.

Rhotic contexts were identified in and extracted from interview transcripts. Rhotics were then coded impressionistically. Cases of uncertainty, largely due to unclear speech, were excluded from analysis. The results presented below include a logistic regression model for Word Internal Syllable Final (WISF) position, with Speaker as a random effect. Additionally, data distributions are presented for each factor of interest in WISF and Word Initial position. The use of rhotic variants was explored based on the following factors.

4.1 *Position in Word*

The first linguistic factor is position in word, coded as WORD INITIAL, COMPLEX SYLLABLE ONSET, INTERVOCALIC (split by SINGLE or DOUBLE), WORD INTERNAL SYLLABLE INITIAL, WORD INTERNAL SYLLABLE FINAL, or WORD FINAL. In canonical Spanish, several positions are restricted to only the tap or trill as shown in Table 2.1. Additionally, as outlined above, many studies have examined rhotic variation in positions where the tap or trill usually occur or through the lens of rhotic contrast maintenance.

While the main goal of the present study is to examine variation more broadly, results will also provide insight on the question of contrast maintenance. If a merger of the type predicted by Hagerty (1979:81) has occurred in intervocalic position, there would be a preference for the retroflex in all intervocalic rhotics regardless of single or double 'r' spellings. Alternatively, evidence of contrast maintenance would be present if speakers employ different variants in these two positions.

4.2 *Phonetic Environment*

Phonetic environment is an important determinant in Spanish rhotic use for some positions in the word. For example, in word internal syllable initial position the trill is always preferred after a consonant, as in the first rhotic of the word *alrededor* (around). On the other hand, in intervocalic position the double 'r' spelling is necessary to prompt the use of the trill as in *perro* (dog). While few cases of word internal syllable initial rhotics appear in this data, a parallel context of interest is word initial rhotics. Though this position always calls for the trill in canonical Spanish, the effect of preceding context across word boundary may still play a role. It is expected that trills will be favored when preceded by words ending in consonants, while those preceded by words ending in vowels will have higher rates of non-canonical variants. To test this hypothesis, all word initial rhotics from speakers showing variation were extracted. Then, contexts were coded as either FAVORS TRILL, when preceded by a consonant, or DISFAVORS TRILL, when preceded by a vowel.

As for word internal syllable final position, all rhotics in this position were also extracted. Previous studies show widespread variation and classify this position as variable even in canonical Spanish. Following studies of other dialects (e.g., Bradley, 1999; Balam, 2013b; Kim, 2019, among many others), the following phonetic environment was coded based on place of articulation of the following consonant as: ALVEOLAR, DENTAL, LABIODENTAL, VELAR, and BILABIAL. Based on previous studies, it is expected that the non-standard rhotic variant will be favored before alveolars and dentals and disfavored before bilabials and velars.

4.3 *Age*

Early sociolinguistic studies demonstrated the importance of age as a fundamental social factor impacting variation and change (e.g., Labov, 1963). Subsequent research revealed a general pattern that younger speakers tend to use innovative variants while older speakers tend to be more conservative. Additionally, speakers in middle age tend toward more prestigious or standard forms. These generalizations have been attested in many works; however, the unique nature of social factors interacting with linguistic output necessitates further studies.

In the context of northern Belize, recent research has shown a shift in language attitudes among younger generations (Balam, 2013a; Balam & de Prada

Perez, 2017). Young native Spanish speakers in Orange Walk demonstrated an affinity for using Belizean Kriol and codeswitching (Balam, 2013a). If similar attitudes and preferences for English varieties exist in the younger generations of Corozal, higher uses of the innovative retroflex variant would be expected in younger speakers. For the present work, speakers have been split into two groups, 40 AND UNDER and 41 AND OLDER, to test for the effects of age.

4.4 Sex

The effects of speaker sex on language variation and change in monolingual communities is well documented (Eckert, 1989; Labov, 2001; among many others). While speaker sex often interacts with socio-economic status, overall, it has been found that women prefer innovative variants in some instances. Most commonly, this occurs during a change from below or when the innovative variant is not stigmatized (Labov, 1990). Belizean Spanish presents an interesting intersection of these two findings. Previous research (Balam, 2013a) and content analysis of the present data both indicate that Belizean Spanish does not carry a negative stigma. However, evidence from the interviews analyzed here, in which many speakers were asked about differences between Belizean Spanish and other familiar varieties (e.g., Mexican), indicates that the retroflex rhotic is highly salient to speakers. Thus, it is not below the level of consciousness. Previous studies of sex constrained variation led to the general prediction that women will use the retroflex at higher rates than men, though unique patterns of social life and stigmatization in Corozal will still provide a new perspective on this factor.

5 Results

Table 2.2 displays the results of a logistic regression analysis for the factors affecting word internal syllable final position, with Speaker as a random effect. The probabilities associated with levels of each factor range from 0–1, such that any probability over .5 signifies a favoring effect on retroflex use, while any below .5 signifies a disfavoring effect. The total N = 935 and excludes 3 trills, 1 rhotic with a palatal following context, and the 28 words with elided rhotics. The model selected both Following Context ($p < .001$) and Speaker Sex ($p < .01$) as significant predictors, while Speaker Age was not significant ($p = .5$).

As predicted based on previous studies of non-standard rhotics in Spanish, following DENTAL and ALVEOLAR contexts heavily favor the use of the retroflex rhotic, both with probabilities of .99. Following contexts of VELAR, BILABIAL, and LABIODENTAL all provide disfavoring contexts (factor weights < .01). Also matching the predicted outcome, the use of retroflex is heavily

TABLE 2.2 Regression analysis of factors affecting word internal syllable final rhotics

Total N: 935
Input: 0.246

	Probability	% Retroflex	Log odds	Total retroflex N	%
Following context					
Dental	.99	46%	13.7	305	33%
Alveolar	.99	32%	13.2	283	30%
Velar	.01	0%	−7.4	101	11%
Labiodental	.01	0%	−8.4	6	<1%
Bilabial	.01	0%	−11.1	240	26%
Speaker sex					
Women	0.87	44%	1.9	349	37%
Men	0.13	13%	−1.9	586	63%
Speaker age					
40 and under	[.60]	26%	0.39	435	47%
41 and over	[.40]	23%	−0.39	500	53%
Total		23%		230/935	100%

favored for women, with a probability of .87, as opposed to .13 for men. Results for Speaker Age suggest a slight favoring effect for younger speakers, though the model did not select this factor as significant.

Figure 2.1 shows the variants employed across all positions in the word for the first two hundred rhotics from each speaker. The far-left column shows the overall rate of the non-canonical retroflex variant at 11% while the tap is the majority variant at 84%. Trills and deleted rhotics make up 3% and 2% of the overall data, respectively. The next three bars show that taps make up the vast majority of rhotics in complex syllable onsets, intervocalic single, and word final positions. Taps also occupy these positions in canonical Spanish varieties. Variant choice for word internal syllable initial position is determined by the preceding consonant in canonical Spanish; however, low token counts in the present data (N = 4) preclude drawing any conclusions.

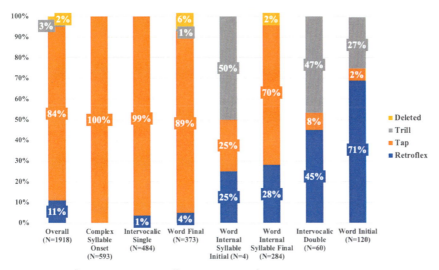

FIGURE 2.1 Rhotic variants across all positions in word
Note: Some speakers produced fewer than 200 rhotics resulting in total N < 2,000.

The final three bars show increased rates of the retroflex. The two rightmost bars represent phonological environments, word initial and intervocalic double, in which the trill appears in canonical Spanish. Focusing on these positions may lead to the conclusion that the retroflex is used variably in place of the trill, thereby not changing the phonological contrast. However, word internal syllable final position (third bar from right), also shows considerable use of the retroflex. This is a position in which the most common variant in canonical Spanish is the tap while the trill appears variably, usually for emphatic effect (Quilis, 1993). Thus, the retroflex does not seem to be serving exclusively as a variant of the trill nor simply maintaining the canonical phonological contrast. The overall results also demonstrate, through use of the tap, trill, and retroflex variants, that there is no support for a rhotic merger. In order to better understand the observed variation outside of the intervocalic double context which serves to distinguish the phonemic contrast, analysis of linguistic factors in word initial and word internal syllable final position was undertaken.

Results in Figure 2.2 are drawn from a subset, comprised of 4 speakers. The 6 excluded speakers showed no variability in their use of word initial rhotics, always using the retroflex. The right bar (Favor Trill) contains those word initial rhotics preceded by consonants (e.g., *un ruido* 'a noise') as these contexts are expected to trigger use of the trill. The middle bar (Disfavor Trill) includes those preceded by vowels (e.g., *una rama* 'a branch'). Comparing the two

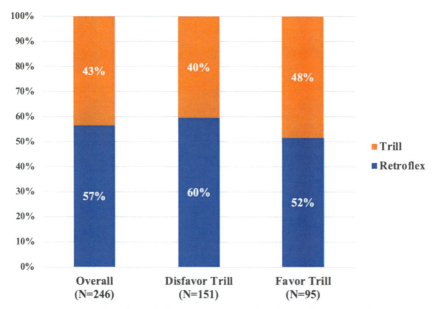

FIGURE 2.2 Rates of word initial rhotic variants, overall and according to preceding phonological environment

bars, the non-favorable trill environments promote use of the retroflex while the favorable environments promote the trill, consistent with the canonical Spanish pattern for initial position.

Moving to word internal syllable final position, several previous studies show that place of articulation of the following consonant constrains nonstandard rhotic variants. Usually, this position is occupied by a tap in canonical Spanish. However, considerable dialectal variation has been reported. All analyses of word internal syllable final position include data from all speakers (N = 967). Figure 2.3 (N = 963) excludes three instances of trills and one token with a following palatal consonant. It shows a categorical use of taps in this position before labiodental, velar, and bilabial consonants. On the other hand, when rhotics precede alveolar or dental consonants word internally, speakers employ the retroflex variant at rates of 29% and 46%, respectively.

Figure 2.4 shows the use of rhotic variants based on speaker sex, excluding three trill tokens. Speakers are split evenly with 5 men and 5 women in the data set. As shown in the middle bar, women have a marked increase in retroflex use when compared to the overall rate (42% vs. 24%). Moreover, men show more than a 10-percentage point decrease in retroflex use against the overall rate (13% vs. 24%).

Figure 2.5 shows the effect of speaker age on rhotic use, excluding three trill tokens. The speakers are split evenly, with 5 age 40 and below and 5 age 41 or

RHOTIC VARIATION IN NORTHERN BELIZE 31

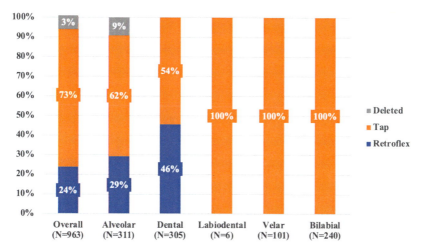

FIGURE 2.3 Rates of word internal syllable final rhotic variants, overall and according to following phonological environment

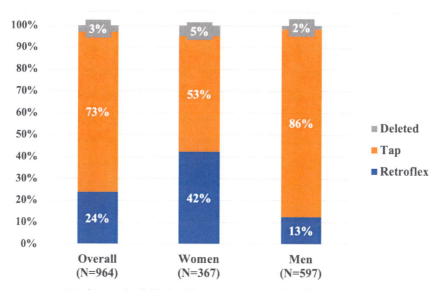

FIGURE 2.4 Word internal syllable final rhotic variants, overall and by speaker sex

above.[4] Unlike speaker sex, results suggest no effect of age on rhotic use. This is especially so for the non-standard retroflex variant, which has nearly equal usage rates when comparing the overall (24%) to the younger group (25%) and

---

4 Age was also considered as a continuous factor in analyses not shown here. No discernible pattern emerged.

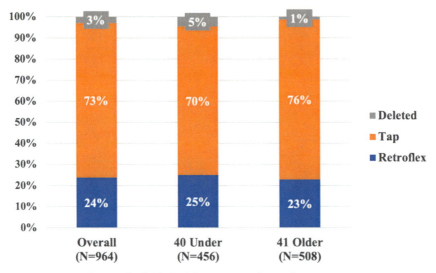

FIGURE 2.5 Word internal syllable final rhotic variants by speaker age

the older group (23%). This suggests the retroflex is an established variant in Corozal Spanish and not a locus of change across apparent time.

6   Discussion

6.1   *Maintenance of Phonemic Contrast*

In addressing the first research question, it is instructive to review findings of previous studies of phonemic contrast maintenance. Generally, results of these studies range from maintenance by various means to proposals for rhotic mergers. For example, in Central Valley Costa Rican Spanish, it is argued that an assibilated rhotic appears in all positions where a trill is used canonically (Vasquez Carranza, 2006). Alternatively, cues such as overall duration of rhotic segments have been offered as another method by which speakers maintain phonological contrast (Bradley & Willis, 2012; McKinnon, this volume). In Corozal Spanish, a merger in progress toward the use of retroflex rhotics in all intervocalic positions has been proposed (Hagerty, 1979: 81).

The results presented in Figure 2.2 show no support for a rhotic merger. Instead, it shows that Corozal Spanish maintains a distinction in intervocalic position. This is evident in the near categorical (99%) use of the tap in intervocalic position with single 'r' spellings. In fact, use of the retroflex in this position is restricted to a single lexical item, *Corozal*, by a single speaker. On the other hand, intervocalic position with 'rr' spellings vary between the retroflex and trill variants. Combining these findings with the high rates of retroflex in word initial rhotics (71%) might suggest that the retroflex is operating as an allophone of the trill. However, the use of the retroflex in word internal syllable final position shows that a focus on contrast maintenance or examining non-standard variants in comparison to the trill fails to capture the full scope of variation in Corozal Spanish.

6.2   Social Variability in Corozal Spanish Rhotics

As suggested by the second research question, social factors can provide important insight on patterns of variation while also elucidating underlying perception of retroflex usage at the community level. As seen in Table 2.2 and Figure 2.5, age shows almost no differences in distributions across groups and was not selected as significant by the logistic regression. This pattern suggests stable variation in retroflex use as opposed to a change in progress (Sankoff & Blondeau, 2007, pp. 561–562).

Speaker sex displays vastly different rates with higher retroflex usage among women. Probabilities in the logistic regression prove this to be both a strong and statistically significant predictor. Labov's (2001) principle of "the general linguistic conformity of women", predicts that women should use a stigmatized rhotic variant at a lower rate than men. As mentioned in Section 4.4, stigmatization is not a straightforward concept in Corozal Spanish. Analysis of the present data set reveals that many speakers hold Mexican Spanish in higher esteem than their native Belizean variety. However, it is also the case that men are more likely to come into contact with Mexican Spanish than women, especially older women. Thus, the higher rates of retroflex use by women could be a byproduct of generally lower levels of contact with Mexican Spanish and a resulting lack of stigmatization of the variant. In other words, some women would be operating with linguistic norms that do not stigmatize the retroflex, thereby not inhibiting their use. Overall, further analysis of social factors and possible interactions would be prudent for clarifying the incipient patterns found in this data.

6.3   Implications of Variability in Word Internal Syllable Final Position

In addition to exploring social factors, answering research question two requires examination of the linguistic factors impacting variation. The limited nature of the rhotic contrast in Spanish means that most positions in a word employ one rhotic or the other categorically. In fact, even variable positions tend to use the tap in most instances. Despite these patterns, analyses have consistently shown word internal syllable final position to be a site of high variability (see Bradley, 1999; Kim, 2019; Vigil, 2008). This holds no matter the non-standard variant in a given dialect.

Specifically, non-standard rhotic variants are favored when preceding alveolar or dental consonants, as in words like *carne* or *norte*. This is not only true in the present data set, but also finds support in studies of assibilated rhotics (Bradley, 1999; Kim, 2019), and retroflex rhotics in Taos New Mexican Spanish (Vigil, 2008). Furthermore, the following contexts of bilabial or velar consonants are also found to disfavor the use of non-standard variants in many of these other varieties. These findings highlight important facts about the retroflex rhotic in Corozal Spanish.

First, by appearing in this position and showing linguistically and socially constrained variation, the retroflex is not simply functioning as an allophone of the trill. This is further supported by the fact that the variation is constrained by similar factors in this position across Spanish dialects. Overall, the findings for word internal syllable final position demonstrate that the retroflex occurs outside of contexts canonically associated with the trill phoneme. This will be explored further in the following section.

These findings also provide preliminary insight into the origins of the retroflex rhotic. Previous studies and descriptions of Belizean Spanish often attribute the use of a retroflex rhotic to extensive contact with English and an English-based creole. While similarities certainly exist between the English rhotic and that of Corozal Spanish, the case for a contact induced change remains dubious. A contact account is especially weakened when considering the relationship between the retroflex rhotics of Corozal Spanish and other varieties. For example, a retroflex rhotic has been documented in Yucatan Spanish (Lope Blanch, 1975). Unlike in Belize, this dialect has no plausible English source for its retroflex. Also, the parallel development of a retroflex in Taos New Mexican Spanish (TNMS) presents an interesting point of comparison. Much like in Corozal, the Spanish of Taos has been in contact with English for about two centuries. Importantly, studies of that dialect described a retroflex rhotic with similar constraining factors in word internal syllable final position (Bills, 1997; Vigil, 2008). Furthermore, Vigil (2008: 231) suggests a language internal development as the source of the retroflex in TNMS, citing the use of a retroflex in the same position in Costa Rican Spanish. This argument is further supported when Vigil (2018:252) demonstrates similar conditioning factors, such as word position, phonological context, and age, for rhotic use in other varieties (see Bradley, 2006; Henriksen & Willis, 2010; Henriksen, 2014; among others).

6.4 *Reframing Spanish Rhotic Variation*

Many previous studies attempt to unify phonetic variation of rhotics within the phonological paradigm of contrast maintenance. This is especially true of studies claiming that a non-standard variant operates principally as an allophone of one phoneme or the other. While this may or may not be the case at the surface level depending on the dialect examined, the entirety of rhotic variation observed in Spanish calls into question the nature of strict and discrete phonemic separation. In fact, disagreement already exists among phonologists as to whether Spanish has one or two distinct rhotic phonemes (for arguments favoring one phoneme see e.g., Harris, 2002; for two-phoneme see Bonet & Mascaró, 1997; Quilis, 1993). This shows even the prescriptive tap-trill contrast of canonical Spanish cannot be neatly defined and provides reason to further analyze implications of findings in this study.

An alternative explanation to those presented above is that phonemic contrasts can be partially neutralized, meaning they only operate in certain contexts. For prescriptive Spanish, this is evident as phonemic opposition between tap and trill only occurs in intervocalic position, while both appear in complementary distribution in other positions. This fact led Hualde to the conclusion that the tap and trill are "clearly more closely related than other pairs of phonemes" (2004:19). This relationship is one example of what he terms "quasi-phonemic contrast", a concept that argues for gradient distinctions between some phonemes. Through this view, instead of two entirely discrete phonemes, Spanish sounds would be organized in categories. Thus, there would be a "rhotic" category that contains two other categories, "tap" and "trill", within it (Hualde, 2004: 20). Essentially, the relationship between categories "tap" and "trill" would be less well defined when compared to categorical phonemes that can be contrastive in all positions.

Interestingly, this is not the only phonemic relationship in Spanish that seems to operate in this way. Early phonological analysis of Spanish suggested a general principal that phonemic contrasts in syllable initial position are often neutralized in syllable final position (Alonso, 1945). Nasal consonants represent the main example of this phenomenon. In syllable initial position, three nasal phonemes are contrastive ([n], [ɲ], and [m], as in the words *cana* 'grey/white hair', *caña* 'cane' and *cama* 'bed'). Meanwhile, syllable final nasals undergo assimilation by matching the place of articulation of the following consonant resulting in the use of at least 6 different phonetic variants. In word final position, only [n] is used canonically, though dialectal cases of velarization also occur. This phonemic arrangement provides further evidence that the instability of rhotics in syllable final position can be linked to broader language internal phonological principles.

Results presented above introduce an extra level of complexity to the quasi-phonemic contrast approach while also lending support to it. First, the fact that the retroflex does not operate solely as an allophone of one rhotic or the other, except in intervocalic position, demonstrates the indistinct nature of the contrast in most contexts. In other words, the retroflex appears as an allophone of the trill only where the contrast is operating (intervocalic) or where the trill is used exclusively (word initial). However, as evidenced in the results for word internal syllable final position, the retroflex is also free to appear in other positions where the tap is the canonical variant.[5] Unsurprisingly, it appears at the highest rates where one could argue rhotic selection is least constrained. That is to say, in word internal syllable final position the contrast between rhotic variants is less strongly prescribed or perhaps not prescribed at all, making this a prime position for non-standard variant use. In sum, the findings presented here and in similar studies of rhotic variation suggest that a gradient phonemic contrast best captures the relationship between tap and trill in Spanish.

7   Conclusion

Results of this study refute previous claims of a rhotic merger in Corozal Spanish, instead showing the maintenance of phonemic contrast in intervocalic position. Further analysis of the non-standard retroflex rhotic indicates that it occurs in many positions in the word. In Corozal Spanish the retroflex is not an allophone of the canonical tap or trill, but rather operates independently within the rhotic system meaning it can appear in contexts canonically prescribed to either phoneme. This is in line with many previous studies of other Spanish varieties which show similar patterns of variability, revealing that some positions seem to be more susceptible to variation. Generally, such findings support the notion that the rhotic contrast in Spanish is partially neutralized or "quasi-phonemic" (Hualde, 2004) as such a relationship would allow for variable patterns across different positions in the word. Finally, despite previous claims that the retroflex rhotic resulted from contact with English, parallel developments in other dialects with no English contact (e.g., Costa Rican

---

5   A reviewer notes that the trill may appear in this position as a stylistic variant; however, the tap remains the canonically prescribed, and most common, variant.

and Yucatan Spanish) and the broad range of cross-linguistic rhotic variation suggest internal development as an equally, if not more, probable source.

References

Alonso, A. (1945). Una ley fonológica del español: variabilidad de las consonantes en la tensión y distensión de la sílaba. *Hispanic Review, 13*: 91–101.

Balam, O. (2013a). Overt language attitudes and linguistic identities among multilingual speakers in Northern Belize. *Studies in Hispanic and Lusophone Linguistics 6*(2), 247–277.

Balam, O. (2013b). Variable Neutralization of the Intervocalic Rhotic Contrast in Northern Belizean Spanish. *Borealis: An International Journal of Hispanic Linguistics 2*(2), 285–315.

Balam, O. & de Prada Perez, A. (2017). Attitudes Toward Spanish and Code-Switching in Belize: Stigmatization and Innovation in the Spanish Classroom. *Journal of Language, Identity & Education 16*(1), 17–31.

Bills, G. D. (1997). New Mexican Spanish: Demise of the earliest European variety in the United States. *American Speech 72*, 154–171.

Blecua, B. (2001). *Las vibrantes del español: manifestaciones acústicas y procesos fonéticos* [Doctoral dissertation, Universitat Autònoma de Barcelona].

Bonet, E. & Mascaró, J. (1997). On the representation of contrasting rhotics. In A. Morales-Front, A. & F. Martínez-Gil. (Eds.) *Issues in the phonology and morphology of the major Iberian languages* (pp. 103–126). Georgetown University Press.

Boynton, S. (1981). A Phonemic Analysis of Monolingual Andean (Bolivian) Spanish. In M. J. Hardman (Eds.) *The Aymara Language in Its Social and Cultural Context* [pp. 199–204]. University of Florida Presses.

Bradley, T. (1999). Assibilation in Ecuadorian Spanish. In J. Authier, B. Bullock & L. Reed (Eds.) *Formal Perspectives on Romance Linguistics. Selected Papers from the 28th Linguistics Symposium on Romance Languages* (pp. 57–71). John Benjamins.

Bradley, T. (2004). Gestural timing and rhotic variation in Spanish codas. In T. L. Face (Ed.) *Laboratory Approaches to Spanish Phonology* (pp. 195–220). Mouton de Gruyter.

Bradley, T. (2005). Systemic markedness and phonetic detail in phonology. In R. S. Gess & E. J. Rubin (Eds.) *Theoretical and experimental approaches to romance linguistics: Selected papers from the 34th Linguistic Symposium on Romance Languages* (pp. 41–62). John Benjamins.

Bradley, T. (2006). Phonetic Realizations of /sr/ Clusters in Latin American Spanish. In M. Díaz-Campos (ed.) *Selected Proceedings of the 2nd Conference on Laboratory Approaches to Spanish Phonetics and Phonology* (pp. 1–13). Cascadilla Proceedings Project.

Bradley, T. & Willis, E. (2012). Rhotic Variation and Contrast in Veracruz Mexican Spanish. *Estudios de Fonética Experimental 21*, 43–74.
Broce, M., & Torres Cacoullos, R. (2002). "Dialectología urbana" rural: la estratificación social de (r) y (l) en Coclé, Panama. *Hispania 85*(2), 382–395.
Calvo Shadid, A. & Portilla Chaves, M. (1998). Variantes retroflejas de /ɾ/ y /r/ en el habla culta de San José. *Revista Káñina 22*(1), 81–86.
Canfield, D. L. (1962). *La Pronunciación del Español en América*. Publicaciones del Instituto Caro y Cuervo.
Cardona Ramírez, M. A. (2010). La Fonética del español en Belice. In M. A. Quesada Pacheco (Ed.) *El español hablado en América Central Nivel Fonético* (pp. 20–54). Vervuert.
Chabot, A. (2019). What's wrong with being a rhotic? *Glossa 4*(1), 1–24.
Cuéllar, B. V. (1971). Observaciones sobre la 'rr' velar y la 'y' africada en Cuba. *Español Actual 20*, 18–20.
Eckert, P. (1989). *Jocks and Burnouts: Social Identity in the High School*. Teachers College Press.
Gabbert, W. (2007). In the Shadow of the Empire: The Emergence of Afro-Creole Societies in Belize and Nicaragua. *Indiana 24*, 39–66.
Hagerty, T. W. (1979). *Phonological Analysis of the Spanish of Belize*. [Doctoral dissertation, UCLA].
Hagerty, T. W. (1996). The influence of English on the Spanish language of Belize. In M. D. Phillips (Ed.), *Belize: Selected Proceedings from the Second Interdisciplinary Conference* (pp. 131–142). University Press of America.
Hall, T. A. (1997). *Phonology of coronals*. John Benjamins Publishing Company.
Hammond, R. M. (1999). On the Non-Occurrence of the Phone [r] in the Spanish Sound System. In J. Gutiérrez-Rexach & F. Martínez-Gil (Eds.) *Advances in Hispanic Linguistics* (pp. 135–151). Cascadilla Press.
Harris, J. (2002). Flaps, trills, and syllable structure in Spanish. *MIT Working Papers in Linguistics 42*, 81–108.
Henriksen, N. (2014). Sociophonetic analysis of phonemic trill variation in two sub-varieties of Peninsular Spanish. *Journal of Linguistic Geography, 2*(1), 1–21. DOI: 10.1017/jlg.2014.1.
Henriksen, N. & Willis, E. W. (2010). Acoustic characterization of phonemic trill production in Jerezano Andalusian Spanish. In M. Ortega-Llebaria (Eds.), *Selected proceedings of the 4th Conference on Laboratory Approaches to Spanish Phonology* (pp. 115–127). Cascadilla Proceedings Project.
Hualde, J. I. (2004). Quasi-phonemic contrasts in Spanish. *Proceedings of the West Coast Conference on Formal Linguistics 23*, 374–398.
Kim, K. (2019). La Variación de /r/ en Posición Posnuclear en el Español Andino del Perú. *Iberoamérica. 21*(1), 127–158.

Labov, W. (1963). The Social Motivation of a Sound Change. *Word. 19*(3), 273–309.

Labov, W. (1984). Field methods of the project on linguistic change and variation. In J. Baugh & J. Sherzer (Eds.), *Language in use: Readings in sociolinguistics* (pp. 28–53). Prentice Hall.

Labov, W. (1990). The Intersection of Sex and Social Class in the Course of Linguistic Change. *Language Variation and Change 2*(2), 205–254.

Labov, W. (1994). *Principles of Linguistic Change. Volume 1: Internal Factors*. Blackwell.

Labov, W. (2001). *Principles of Linguistic Change. Volume 2: Social Factors*. Blackwell.

Ladefoged, P., & Maddieson, I. (1996). *The Sounds of the World's Languages*. Blackwell.

Lipski, J. (1990). Spanish Taps and Trills: Phonological structure of an isolated opposition. *Folia Lingüística 24*, 153–174.

Lipski, J. (1994). *Latin American Spanish*. Longman.

Lope Blanch, J. M. (1975). Un caso de posible influencia maya en el español mexicano. *Nueva Revista de Filología Hispánica 24*, 89–100.

López-Morales, H. (1979). Velarización de la /RR/ el español de Puerto Rico: Índices de actitudes y creencias. In H. López-Morales (Ed.) *Dialectología y Sociolingüística: Temas puertorriqueños* (pp. 107–130). Hispanova de Ediciones.

Quesada Pacheco, M. A. (2013). Aspectos morfosintácticos del español hablado en Belice, In M. A. Quesada Pacheco (Ed.), *El espanol hablado en America Central: nivel morfosintáctico* (pp. 23–64). Vervuert.

Quilis, A. (1990). Notas sobre el español de Belice. *Revista Voz y Letra* I, 139–147.

Quilis, A. (1993). *Tratado de fonología y fonética españolas*. Gredos.

Ravindranath, M. (2009). *Language shift and the speech community: sociolinguistic change in a Garifuna community in Belize* [Doctoral dissertation, University of Pennsylvania].

Sankoff, G. & Blondeau, H. (2007). Language change across the lifespan: /r/ in Montreal French. *Language*, 83, 560–88.

Sessarego, S. (2011). "Phonetic analysis of /sr/ clusters in Cochabambino Spanish." In L. A. Ortiz-López (Ed.) *Selected Proceedings of the 13th Hispanic Linguistics Symposium* (pp. 251–263). Cascadilla Proceedings Project.

Shoman, A. (2010). Reflections on Ethnicity and Nation in Belize, *Documento de Trabajo 9*, 1–61.

Vásquez Carranza, L. M. (2006). On the phonetic realization and distribution of Costa Rican Rhotics. *Filología y Lingüística 32*(2) 291–309.

Vigil, D. A. (2008). *The Traditional Spanish of Taos, New Mexico: Acoustic, Phonetic, and Phonological Analysis* [Doctoral dissertation, Purdue University].

Vigil, D. A. (2018). Rhotics of Taos, New Mexico Spanish: Variation and Change. *Studies in Hispanic and Lusophone Linguistics*, *11*(1): 215–264.

Widdison, K. (1998). Phonetic motivation in Spanish trills. *Orbis: bulletin international de documentation linguistique 140*, 51–61.

Willis, E. & Bradley, T. (2008). Contrast maintenance of taps and trills in Dominican Spanish: Data and analysis. In L. Colantoni & J. Steele (Eds.) *Selected Proceedings of the 3rd Conference on Laboratory Approaches to Spanish Phonology* (pp. 87–100). Cascadilla Proceedings Project.

Zahler, S. & Daidone, D. (2014). A variationist account of trill /r/ usage in the Spanish of Málaga. *Indiana University Linguistics Club Working Papers. 14.* 17–42.

CHAPTER 3

Phonological Contrast Maintenance and Language Contact

An Examination of the Spanish Rhotic System in a Bilingual Guatemalan Speech Community

Sean McKinnon

1 Introduction

Spanish in contact with other languages is a growing area of research and scholarly interest within Hispanic linguistics (e.g., Clements, 2009), as well as contact linguistics more broadly speaking (e.g., Winford, 2020), given that there are many bilingual regions in the Spanish-speaking world. However, much of the research has focused on language contact in Spain (e.g., with Basque, Catalan, and Galician) and South America (e.g., with Quechua/Quichua). Apart from a few studies (e.g., Baird, 2017, 2020, 2021, 2023; Chappell, 2021; García Tesoro, 2005, this volume; McKinnon, 2020, 2023), there has been less of an empirical focus on language contact between Spanish and the indigenous languages of Central America.

Furthermore, while much of the recent research on Spanish in contact with other languages has focused on how the other language influences Spanish phonetics (e.g., Baird, 2020; Barnes, 2016; Chappell, 2016; Davidson, 2015; McKinnon, 2020, 2023; O'Rourke, 2010), few studies have examined if phonological contrasts are maintained in situations of language contact when the grammar of the two languages diverge (e.g., Amengual, 2016; Henriksen, 2015).

Therefore, to address these two gaps in the literature, the present study investigates the Spanish rhotic system (i.e., the tap /ɾ/ and the trill /r/) in the bilingual Spanish-Kaqchikel Maya speech community in the greater region of Antigua, Guatemala. These segments were chosen because they are phonemically contrastive, which is typologically uncommon given that only 18% of languages that have two phonemic rhotics (Ladefoged & Maddieson, 1996). Figure 3.1, taken from the present study's corpus, provides an example of how these two rhotics are contrastive (e.g., /peɾo/ *pero* 'but' vs. /pero/ *perro* 'dog').

As Figure 3.1 shows, although the segments are two different phonemes in production, they both have one measurable occlusion, which could lead to potential overlap in their perception. Due to this potential overlap, and the fact

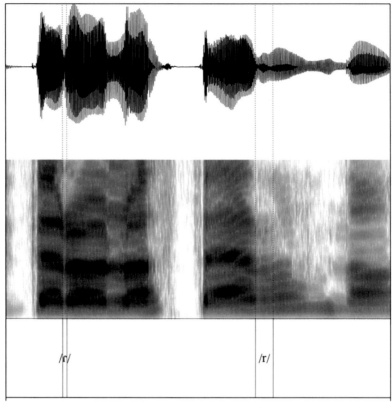

FIGURE 3.1 Example of the phonological distinction between the Spanish tap and trill, in the phrase *pero los perros no* 'but dogs don't'

that a phonemic contrast between two rhotics is not common, it is an open question whether this contrast would be maintained in situations of contact with a language (e.g., Kaqchikel Maya) that only has one rhotic phoneme.

The present study examines the extent to which and how a sample of twenty-four Spanish-Kaqchikel Maya bilingual speakers realize this phonological contrast. Overall, the data will show that these bilingual speakers maintain the contrast between the two rhotics, although the phonetic strategies they use depend on their age. Furthermore, the data will also demonstrate how the presence of rhotic minimal pairs also promotes the maintenance of the contrast.

2 Previous Literature

Guatemala is a country in Central America that is home to many minority languages, including twenty-one Mayan languages, Garífuna, and Xinca. Map 3.1 provides a linguistic map of Guatemala, showing the areas where other languages are spoken alongside Spanish.

Given the large number of languages spoken in one modern political territory previous research has documented effects of language contact in Guatemala, including Mayan language influence on Spanish (Baird, 2017, 2020; García Tesoro, 2005, this volume; McKinnon, 2020, 2023), sociolinguistic perception of Spanish-Mayan languages contact (Baird, 2021, 2023), Spanish influence on Mayan languages (Barrett, 2008; Brody, 1987, 1995), and contact between Mayan languages themselves (Barrett, 2002; Law, 2014).

MAP 3.1   Linguistic map of Guatemala. Reproduced image of "Languages of Guatemala" by Chabacano under Creative Commons by ShareAlike 3.0

The present study focuses on potential Kaqchikel Maya influence on the Spanish spoken by bilingual speakers in the greater region of Antigua, Guatemala. Kaqchikel Maya is part of the K'ichean branch within the larger Mayan language family (Law, 2014), and around 450,000 people speak it (Bennett, et al., 2016). The most recent census data by the Guatemalan government (INE, 2014) estimates that 45.1% of the Kaqchikel community are bilingual Spanish-Kaqchikel speakers, while 54.9% are monolingual speakers (38.8% in Kaqchikel, and 21.1% in Spanish); given the high level of Kaqchikel still spoken in the community, there is a strong possibility that there are effects of language contact in the Spanish spoken by this community.

2.1 *Rhotics in Spanish and Kaqchikel Maya*

Traditional accounts of the Spanish language have documented the phonological contrast between the voiced alveolar tap /ɾ/ and the voiced alveolar trill /r/ in word-medial intervocalic position (e.g., /peɾo/ *pero* 'but' vs. /pero/ *perro* 'dog'). While the canonical tap is made with one quick contact of the tongue's apex with the alveolar ridge, the canonical trill is composed of multiple contacts between the tongue and alveolar ridge, typically between two and three (Hualde, 2014). Although previous research has claimed that "in practice [the tap vs. trill contrast] is limited to less than 30 minimal pairs" (Willis & Bradley, 2008: p. 87), there are 415 documented minimal pairs in this position (Mairano & Calabrò, 2016).[1] Outside of intervocalic position the two rhotics form a complementary distribution, in which the trill appears in word-initial position and after a heterosyllabic consonant, while the tap appears in all other contexts (Hualde, 2014).

However, empirical research across the Spanish-speaking world has documented considerable variation in the production of the phonemic trill (e.g., Arias, 2019; Bero, this volume; Díaz-Campos, 2008; Henriksen, 2014; Henriksen & Willis, 2010; Lamy, 2015; Melero García, 2015; Willis, 2006, 2007; Zahler & Daidone, 2014) and tap (Bradley & Willis, 2012; Willis & Bradley, 2008) with monolingual speakers of Spanish. Although some of the variants identified are region specific, such as pre-aspirated or backed productions of /r/ in some varieties of Caribbean Spanish (Arias, 2019, Wills, 2006, 2007), other variants have been identified in many dialects. For example, the cited acoustic studies above have shown that apart from the canonical tap [ɾ] other realizations of the phoneme include an approximant tap [ɾ̞] (i.e., a rhotic sound in which the tongue apex approximates the alveolar ridge but not enough to create turbulent airflow or complete constriction) and a perceptual tap [⁽ɾ⁾] (i.e., a rhotic sound is

---

1 Furthermore, Willis and Bradley (2008) do not define what "in practice" means.

present but hard to distinguish via acoustic landmarks in the waveform and spectrogram); for the phonemic trill, in addition to the canonical trill [r] other possibilities include fricatives, approximants, and one or two+ occlusions followed by r-coloring of the following vowel (i.e., a transition period between the release of the occlusion and the following vowel that maintains a formant structure), represented as [ɾɹ] and [rɹ], respectively.

Although there is some overlap in the types of variants realized from the phonemic tap and trill (e.g., approximants, one occlusion), research has also shown that the phonological contrast can be maintained via differences in duration (Bradley & Willis, 2012; Willis & Bradley, 2008). For example, Willis and Bradley (2008) found that there was no overlap in the standard deviation values of the tap and trill in two varieties of Dominican Spanish, and in their study on Veracruz Mexican Spanish (Bradley & Willis, 2012) it was found that only one speaker (out of ten) had overlap. In addition to being an acoustic correlate that can be used in production to maintain the phonological contrast, durational differences have also been shown to be a cue in listener's perception of the phonemic tap and trill (Melero-García & Cisneros, 2020).

On the other hand, Kaqchikel, like most of the world's languages, only has one rhotic phoneme, which is the tap /ɾ/ (García Matzar, et al., 1999); two allophones exist in complementary distribution, the assibilated fricative [ɹ̝̊] in word-final position (e.g., q'or /q'oɾ/ → [q'oɹ̝̊] 'atol') and the tap [ɾ] in all other contexts. Unfortunately, there are no empirical studies on the acoustics of this rhotic phoneme in Kaqchikel. This is to say, it is possible that the phoneme may have other variants, such as what has been empirically found for Spanish (e.g., approximant and perceptual taps).

2.2   Rhotic Phonological Contrast in Bilingual Spanish

In addition to creating new phonological contrasts (e.g., French influence on the phonemicization of [v, ð, z] in English), Winford (2003) also documents how language contact can contribute to the loss of a contrast (e.g., German influence in the loss of /l/ vs. /lʲ/ in Czech). Given that Kaqchikel only has one rhotic phoneme, while Spanish has two, it is possible that Kaqchikel speakers might merge the two phonemes into one, especially since [r] is an articulatorily and aerodynamically difficult sound to produce (Solé, 2002).

However, previous research on rhotics in bilingual Spanish has shown that the tap/trill contrast is maintained, even when the other language only has one rhotic phoneme (or none). For example, Balam (2013) investigated Spanish rhotic production in a group of ten Spanish-Belizean Kriol bilingual speakers. The results for intervocalic position showed that, during an elicited production task, these bilingual speakers largely maintained the phonological contrast via the consistent use of the retroflex approximant [ɻ] for the trill and the use of approximant and perceptual taps for the phonemic tap. However, for the more controlled read-out loud task, it was found that 59% of the phonemic trill tokens were realized as a tap, leading to the conclusion that the contrast was partially lost.[2] In intervocalic position, the Shipibo-Konibo-Spanish bilingual speakers reported on in Elías-Ulloa (2020) also maintain the phonological distinction, albeit with unique variants that show influence from Shipibo-Konibo, a language which does not have rhotics. For example, in addition to the canonical variants [ɾ] and [r], these bilingual speakers also employed the voiced dental approximant [ð] for the phonemic tap and a voiced retroflex affricate [ɖʐ] and a voiced retroflex fricative [ʐ] for the phonemic trill.

Research has also examined the tap vs. trill phonological contrast with bilingual Spanish-English speakers in the United States.[3] The results from Henriksen (2015) demonstrated that the number of occlusions was an inconsistent acoustic correlate for the tap vs. trill contrast, as only some speakers from both the 1st generation (arrived in the US after the age of 13) and 2nd generation (born in the US) had a higher mean number of occlusions for the trill. However, the results did show that all speakers, except for one 2nd generation speaker (out of 16 speakers), produced phonemic trills with a longer duration value than the phonemic taps, indicating that the phonemic contrast is maintained via duration. Amengual (2016) investigated the tap vs. trill contrast with three different linguistic group (2nd generation Spanish-dominant speakers, 2nd generation English-dominant speakers, and second language Spanish speakers) and found that both the Spanish-dominant and English-dominant 2nd generation speakers used duration to distinguish between the tap and trill in production, but that only the Spanish-dominant bilinguals also used the mean number of occlusions to differentiate the two rhotic sounds.

Altogether, the findings from previous research shed light on different aspects of monolingual Spanish rhotics, namely the identification of several variants for the tap and trill (Arias, 2019; Bero, this volume; Bradley & Willis, 2012; Díaz-Campos, 2008; Henriksen, 2014; Henriksen & Willis, 2010; Lamy, 2015; Melero García, 2015; Willis, 2006, 2007; Willis & Bradley, 2008; Zahler

---

2 However, see Bero (this volume) for counter-evidence from Corozal Spanish.
3 Research has also documented the types of variants found with the phonemic tap and trill with this bilingual population. For example, Henriksen found that 1st generation speakers produced more canonical taps than the 2nd generation, while Kim and Repiso Puigdelliura (2019) found that 2nd generation speakers who use more Spanish with and are addressed more in Spanish by older speakers produce more canonical taps. With respect to the phonemic trill, Repiso Puigdelliura and Kim (2021) report on several different variants in the production of /r/.

& Daidone, 2014), the inconsistent use of the number of occlusions to maintain the rhotic phonological contrast (Bradley & Willis, 2012; Willis & Bradley, 2008), and the consistent use of duration to maintain the tap vs. trill contrast (Bradley & Willis, 2012; Melero-García & Cisneros, 2020; Willis & Bradley, 2008). Similar trends have also been found in the literature on bilingual varieties of Spanish (Amengual, 2016; Henriksen, 2015; Kim & Repiso Puigdelliura, 2019; Repiso Puigdelliura & Kim, 2021), in addition to documenting that bilinguals maintain the contrast even though their other language has only one or no rhotic phoneme (Amengual, 2016; Balam, 2013; Elías-Ulloa, 2020; Henriksen, 2015). Based on these findings, the present study is informed and guided by three research questions:

1. What is the distribution of variants for the phonemic tap and trill in bilingual Guatemalan Spanish?
2. What are the (extra-)linguistic factors that favor the canonical variants of the phonemic tap and trill in bilingual Guatemalan Spanish?
3. Is the tap vs. trill phonological contrast maintained in bilingual Guatemalan Spanish?

3 Method

The data from the present study come from a sociolinguistic corpus that was collected in the greater region of Antigua, Guatemala during the summer of 2015 with 58 speakers, 44 of whom reported being bilingual in Spanish and Kaqchikel Maya.[4] All participants completed a semi-guided sociolinguistic interview with the author that revolved around questions related to their personal life (e.g., childhood, daily routines), Guatemalan culture (e.g., popular legends, traditional dishes), and their opinions about current events. After the interview, participants also narrated the book *Frog, Where Are You?* by Mercer Mayer (1969) given that previous research has found that the book successfully elicits numerous taps and trills (e.g., Henriksen, 2015; Willis, 2006). The interview and narration task were recorded in a quiet room in the participant's house or in a private language school in Antigua, with a TASCAM DR-100mkII 2-Channel Portable Digital Recorder (sample rate of 44.1kHz) and a Shure WH20QTR Dynamic Headset Microphone. Altogether, each participant provided between 30 to 60 minutes of speech.

---

4 Unfortunately, participants were not asked additional questions about their linguistic history, proficiency, attitudes, or use. Categorizing participants according to this binary bilingual vs. monolingual distinction is acknowledged as a potential limitation of the present study.

TABLE 3.1   Demographic characteristics of the participants

Age	Women	Men	Total
18–29	4	4	8
30–39	4	4	8
50+	4	4	8
Total	12	12	24

Of the 44 bilingual speakers, 24 were selected to equally balance for biological sex (males vs. females) and age (18–29, 30–49, 50+ years old). Table 3.1 provides a summary of the demographic characteristics of the sub-set used in the present study.

3.1   Acoustic Analysis

All rhotic tokens included in the present study were manually identified in Praat (Boersma & Weenink, 2021) and extracted through a Praat script (Lennes, 2002). A maximum of 30 word-medial intervocalic tap and 30 word-medial intervocalic trill tokens were taken from each participant after the first 20 minutes of the interview in order to account for the Observer's Paradox (Labov, 1972); however, to avoid any possible effects of lexical frequency (Lamy, 2015; Zahler & Daidone, 2014), only two tokens of each lexical item were taken for each participant. Therefore, although a total number of 720 taps and 720 trills could have been extracted, only 713 taps and 276 trills were extracted for the present study given that some participants did not produce many rhotics in word-medial intervocalic position.

Another Praat script (Ryan, 2005) was utilized to demarcate each rhotic token in Praat using a text grid. While the duration was extracted through a duration script (Kawahara, 2010), each token was also classified according to the variants outlined in previous research (Bradley & Willis, 2012; Henriksen, 2015; Willis & Bradley, 2008); additionally, for the trills, the number of occlusions was also manually counted.

For the phonemic taps, three possible variants were identified by the author: canonical tap [ɾ], approximant tap [ɾ̞], and perceptual tap [⁽ɾ⁾].[5] The canonical tap is produced with a clear decrease in amplitude of the waveform and a break in the spectrogram that is consistent with a complete closure of the vocal tract. An approximant tap is one that shows a continuation of the formant structure in the spectrogram and waveform with the flanking vowels, albeit with a slight

---

5   No other variants were identified in the data.

decrease in the waveform. Perceptual taps are those that are auditorily present but do not have any distinguishing landmarks in the waveform or spectrogram to be able to delimit the segment between the flanking vowels. Figures 3.2–3.4 provide an example of each variant of the phonemic tap found in the data from the present study.

With respect to the phonemic trills, four variants were identified in the data: canonical trill [r], post-approximantized trill [rɹ], post-approximantized tap [ɾɹ], and assibilated rhotic [ř]. The canonical trill is a rhotic variant that is produced with two or more distinguishable occlusions. The two post-approximantized variants begin with either a trill or a tap and are followed by r-coloring after the rhotic, as is observed in the spectrogram and waveform by an approximant-like transition to the following vowel. The defining characteristic of the assibilated rhotic is frication throughout the segment which results in an aperiodic waveform. Figures 3.5–3.8 present examples of each of these trill variants found in the data.

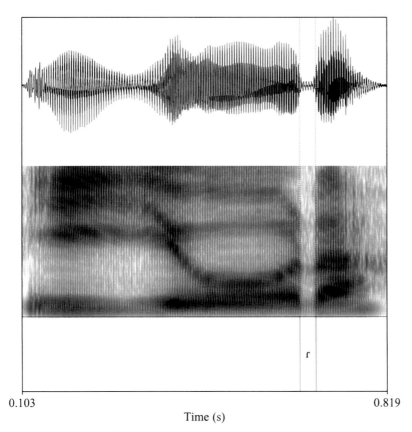

FIGURE 3.2 Example of a canonical tap [ɾ] in the phrase *y llora* 'and s/he cries,' from participant F18

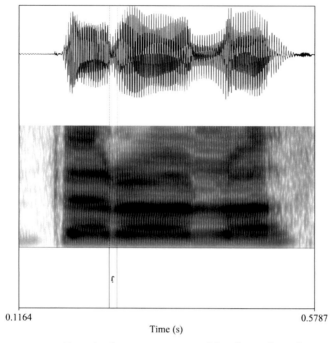

FIGURE 3.3 Example of an approximant tap [ɾ̞] in the word *pero* 'but,' from participant F18

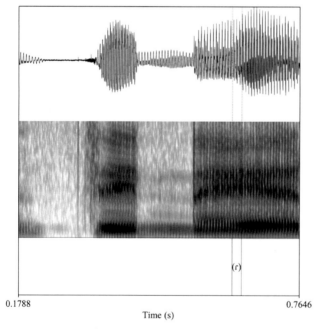

FIGURE 3.4 Example of a perceptual tap [⁽ɾ⁾] in the word *dinero* 'money,' from participant F36

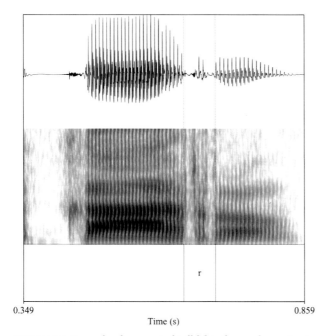

FIGURE 3.5 Example of a canonical trill [r] in the word *carro* 'car,' from participant M3

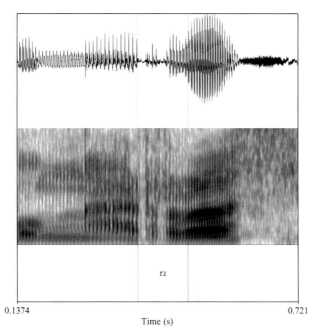

FIGURE 3.6 Example of a post-approximantized trill [rɹ] in the phrase *un arroz* 'rice,' from participant M5

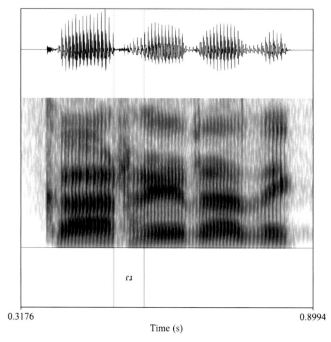

FIGURE 3.7 Example of a post-approximantized tap [ɾ̣] in the phrase *carrera de* [*caballos*] '[horse] race,' from participant M13

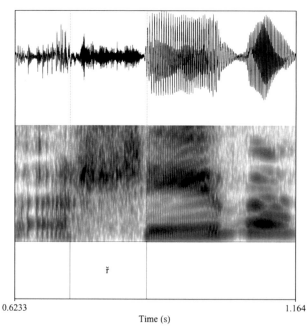

FIGURE 3.8 Example of an assibilated rhotic [ř] in the word *arriba* 'above,' from participant F32

3.2 Statistical Analysis

In addition to categorizing each token according to the rhotic variant present, its duration, and the number of occlusions (in the case of the phonemic trill), each token was also coded according to several linguistic and extra-linguistic factors. The linguistic factors were lexical stress (stressed vs. unstressed syllable) and the presence of a rhotic minimal pair, which was determined by consulting the Minimal Pair Finder website based on Mairano and Calabrò (2016).[6] Lexical stress was included as a factor given that stressed syllables typically produce more fortition, while unstressed syllables typically more lenition (Gordon, 2011); this is to say, we should expect rhotics in stressed position to favor more canonical variants (i.e., clear occlusion[s]), while rhotics in unstressed position should favor more non-canonical variants (i.e., lack of occlusions or reduced number of occlusions). While the role of phonological neighbors has been examined in previous research (Zahler & Daidone, 2014), the potential effect of the presence of rhotic minimal pairs has not yet been examined in the literature. The extra-linguistic factors were based on the demographics of the participant who produced the token in question, specifically their biological sex (female vs. male) and age group (18–29, 30–49, 50+), and they were included as factors in the present study given that previous research on Spanish rhotic variation has found age and biological sex effects (Díaz-Campos, 2008; Henriksen, 2014; Henriksen & Willis, 2010; Lamy, 2015; Melero García, 2015; Zahler & Daidone, 2014).

To identify the (extra-)linguistic factors that influence rhotic variation, two separate multivariate analyses were run in the statistical software program R (R Core Studio, 2016) and the statistical package Rbrul (Johnson, 2009) for each rhotic phoneme. In addition to the factors previously outlined, the individual lexical item and participant were included as random effects.

4 Results

4.1 Phonemic Tap

All phonemic taps were classified according to one of three possible variants (i.e., canonical tap, approximant tap, or perceptual tap) according to the criteria discussed in Section 3.1. Table 3.2 provides a summary of the frequency of each variant found in the data.

As Table 3.2 shows, the most frequent variant found in the data was the canonical tap, followed by the approximant tap and the perceptual tap. Altogether, the data show that the canonical variant of the phonemic tap was

---

6 The website address is: http://phonetictools.altervista.org/minimalpairfinder/.

TABLE 3.2 Distribution of phonemic tap variants

Variant	Raw frequency	% of data
Canonical tap [ɾ]	396	55.5%
Approximant tap [ɹ]	206	28.9%
Perceptual tap [⁽ɾ⁾]	111	15.6%
Total	713	100%

TABLE 3.3 Multivariate analysis results for the phonemic tap (application value = canonical tap)

Factor group	Factor	Centered factor weight	Percent canonical tap	n
Age group	Young (18–29)	0.66	68%	240
(p = 0.01)	Middle (30–49)	0.53	56%	240
	Older (50+)	0.32	43%	233
AIC = 874.58	DF = 8	intercept = 0.21	Overall proportion = 0.56	R^2 Fixed = 0.10 R^2 Random = 0.25 R^2 total = 0.35

the more frequent (55.5% of the data) than the non-canonical tap variants (44.5% of the data).

For the multivariate analysis the approximant and perceptual tap were combined into one category of innovative variants. Table 3.3 presents the results of the multivariate analysis, with an application value of the canonical tap.

The results in Table 3.3 indicate that only one social factor (i.e., age group) was selected as statistically significant, while no linguistic factors (i.e., presence of a minimal pair and lexical stress) were selected. Within the age group, the multivariate analysis revealed that older speakers disfavor the canonical tap variant, while middle-aged and younger speakers favored it.

4.2 *Phonemic Trill*

Each phonemic trill token was classified according to the set of criteria described in Section 3.1. The results of this classification are presented in Table 3.4.

TABLE 3.4 Distribution of phonemic trill variants

Variant	Raw frequency	% of data
Canonical trill [r]	91	33.0%
Post-approximantized trill [ɹr]	24	8.7%
Post-approximantized tap [ɹɾ]	78	28.3%
Assibilated rhotic [ř]	83	30.1%
Total	276	100%

TABLE 3.5 Distribution of the number of occlusions in the phonemic trill tokens

Variant	Raw frequency	% of data
No occlusion	83	30.1%
1 occlusion	78	28.3%
2 occlusions	71	25.7%
3 occlusions	37	13.4%
4 occlusions	5	1.8%
5 occlusions	2	0.7%
Total	276	100%

Table 3.4 shows that the canonical trill was the most frequent variant for the phonemic trill, accounting for 1/3 of the data. The next most frequent variant was the assibilated rhotic [ř], followed by the post-approximantized tap [ɹɾ] variant and the post-approximantized trill [ɹr]. Therefore, even though the canonical trill is the most frequent individual variant, the other innovative variants account for a larger portion of the data (two-thirds).

Given that the phonemic trill typically implies two or more occlusions, each phonemic trill token was also coded for the number of occlusions present. These results are presented in Table 3.5.

The results in Table 3.5 show that the most frequent number of occlusions was no occlusions, which directly corresponds to the assibilated rhotic variant. Indeed, Table 3.5 shows that the frequency of the categories decreases as the number of occlusions increase, which is not surprising given that the mean number of occlusions is 1.33 (SD = 1.15).

In order to create a binary dependent variable for the multivariate analysis, variants with 2 or more occlusions were combined (i.e., [r] and [ɹr]), and

TABLE 3.6   Multivariate analysis results for the phonemic trill (application value = canonical number of occlusions)

Factor group	Factor	Centered factor weight	Percent 2+ occlusions	n
Presence of minimal pair ($p < 0.0005$)	Yes	0.67	60%	88
	No	0.33	33%	188
Age group ($p < 0.001$)	Young (18–29)	0.72	60%	99
	Middle (30–49)	0.71	56%	77
	Older (50+)	0.13	13%	100
AIC = 296.71	DF = 8	intercept = −0.19	Overall proportion = 0.42	R^2 Fixed = 0.35 R^2 Random = 0.22 R^2 total = 0.57

variants with 1 or less occlusions (i.e., [ř] and [ɾɹ]) were combined in their own separate category. This is to say, the focus of the multivariate analysis is on which social and linguistic factors favor variants that have at least two occlusions (i.e., more canonical trill productions). The results of the multivariate analysis are presented in Table 3.6.

The results from the multivariate analysis, with the application value of 2+ occlusions, shows that two factors were selected as statistically significant: one linguistic (presence of a minimal pair) and one social (age group). With respect to the linguistic factors, phonemic trill tokens that form a minimal pair with the phonemic tap (e.g., /perito/ *perrito* 'little dog' vs. /peɾito/ *perito* 'expert') favored rhotic variants that contained two or more occlusions, while tokens that did not form a minimal pair disfavored it. Similar to the results from the phonemic tap, older speakers disfavored the more canonical variant while younger and middle-aged speakers favored the variant with 2+ occlusions.

4.3   *Maintenance of the Rhotic Phonological Contrast*

The results from the previous two sections show that there is a great deal of variation in the phonetic realization of the phonemic tap and trill. Furthermore, 28.3% of the phonemic trill tokens were classified as the post-approximantized tap [ɾɹ], which means that these tokens may have the potential to somewhat overlap with the canonical tap [ɾ] and approximant tap [ɹ] given that they share some phonetic similarities with these two phonemic tap variants.

Therefore, it is important to examine if these Spanish-Kaqchikel bilingual speakers are maintaining the phonemic rhotic contrast in Spanish. In order to explore this question, Table 3.7 presents the mean duration values of both the phonemic tap and trill for each participant, along with the standard deviation and 95% confidence interval, while Figures 3.9–3.11 present the information with boxplots.

TABLE 3.7 Mean tap and trill duration values by participant

Participant	Biological sex and age group	Mean phonemic tap duration in ms (SD) [95% CI]	Mean phonemic trill duration in ms (SD) [95% CI]	Overlap in 95% confidence interval?
F7	Female, younger	26.57 (9.19) [22.59, 30.54]	43.20 (15.73) [31.95, 54.44]	Almost
F8	Female, younger	27.00 (10.20) [22.95, 31.05]	72.00 (20.85) [59.96, 84.04]	No
F18	Female, younger	33.03 (6.00) [30.87, 35.20]	67.83 (20.46) [54.83, 80.83]	No
F27	Female, younger	34.12 (11.72) [29.28, 38.96]	105.25 (32.50) [53.53, 156.96]	No
M5	Male, younger	37.48 (8.42) [34.28, 40.69]	89.27 (19.56) [76.13, 102.41]	No
M8	Male, younger	28.25 (6.48) [25.74, 30.76]	82.95 (21.68) [73.09, 92.82]	No
M10	Male, younger	29.97 (12.11) [25.44, 34.49]	46.71 (17.93) [30.13, 63.30]	Yes
M15	Male, younger	26.44 (8.82) [23.58, 29.30]	82.00 (27.90) [68.94, 95.06]	No
F3	Female, middle-aged	21.67 (9.11) [18.06, 25.27]	85.00 (21.50) [67.02, 102.98]	No
F12	Female, middle-aged	24.87 (10.19) [21.06, 28.67]	106.00 (30.63) [77.67, 134.33]	No
F13	Female, middle-aged	39.14 (9.94) [34.73, 43.54]	71.33 (18.13) [57.40, 85.27]	No
F29	Female, middle-aged	28.36 (8.98) [24.87, 31.84]	125.00 (36.19) [80.06, 169.94]	No
M3	Male, middle-aged	23.00 (5.26) [19.96, 26.04]	89.56 (27.19) [68.65, 110.46]	No

TABLE 3.7 Mean tap and trill duration values by participant (*cont.*)

Participant	Biological sex and age group	Mean phonemic tap duration in ms (SD) [95% CI]	Mean phonemic trill duration in ms (SD) [95% CI]	Overlap in 95% confidence interval?
M4	Male, middle-aged	25.09 (7.37) [21.82, 28.36]	106.08 (13.44) [97.96, 114.20]	No
M13	Male, middle-aged	29.44 (9.04) [25.71, 33.17]	59.73 (20.16) [46.18, 73.27]	No
M17	Male, middle-aged	26.58 (6.18) [23.97, 29.20]	76.53 (17.81) [65.78, 87.30]	No
F14	Female, older	39.10 (10.89) [34.00, 44.20]	139.14 (23.59) [117.33, 160.96]	No
F32	Female, older	31.03 (12.84) [26.24, 35.83]	100.88 (33.49) [89.00, 112.76]	No
F35	Female, older	41.72 (14.51) [34.51, 48.94]	No tokens produced	N/A
F36	Female, older	30.93 (14.43) [25.22, 36.63]	198.00 (36.35) [107.71, 288.29]	No
M2	Male, older	27.65 (9.43) [23.57, 31.73]	65.24 (23.03) [53.39, 77.08]	No
M14	Male, older	30.10 (9.93) [25.58, 34.62]	95.15 (18.96) [83.70, 106.61]	No
M18	Male, older	24.27 (6.52) [21.83, 26.70]	92.50 (19.81) [79.91, 105.09]	No
M19	Male, older	27.71 (6.17) [25.10, 30.32]	92.88 (30.69) [77.11, 108.66]	No

Table 3.7 shows that one speaker (M10), and potentially another one (F7), may have overlap in the duration of the phonemic tap and trill, as defined by overlapping 95% confidence intervals; furthermore, both speakers are in the younger age group (18–29 years old). However, in order to see if there were any statistical differences at the group level, a paired-samples t-test was conducted to compare the duration between the phonemic tap and trill. Overall, there was a significant difference in duration for the phonemic tap (M = 28.86 ms, SD = 4.49) and phonemic trill (M = 90.97 ms, SD = 32.52); t(22) = −9.34, p < 0.0001.

PHONOLOGICAL CONTRAST MAINTENANCE AND LANGUAGE CONTACT 59

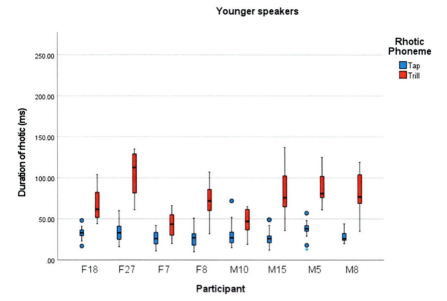

FIGURE 3.9   Duration of phonemic tap vs. trill by younger participants

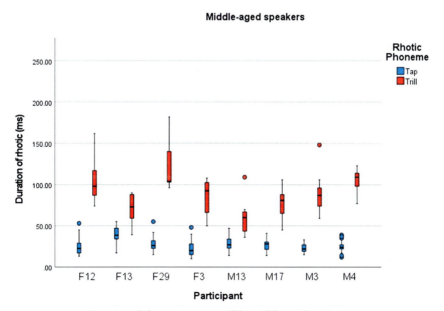

FIGURE 3.10   Duration of phonemic tap vs. trill by middle-aged participants

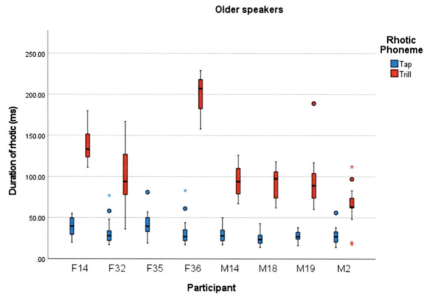

FIGURE 3.11 Duration of phonemic tap vs. trill by older participants

5   Discussion and Conclusion

The objective of the present study was to investigate not only Spanish rhotic variation in a bilingual community in Guatemala, but to also examine if these Spanish-Kaqchikel Maya speakers maintain the tap vs. trill phonological contrast. With a sample of 24 bilingual speakers, who were equally balanced for biological sex and age, 713 phonemic taps and 276 phonemic trills were extracted, categorized, and submitted for statistical analysis to uncover which (extra-)linguistic factors favor the production of the canonical variants.

With respect to the first research question, the distribution of the tap and trill variants, the findings from the present study mirror those found in previous studies on bilingual varieties of Spanish and diverge from those found in monolingual varieties of Spanish. For the phonemic tap, the most frequently produced variant was the canonical tap [ɾ] (55.5%), followed by the approximant tap [ɹ] (28.9% of the data) and the perceptual tap [⁽ɾ⁾] (15.6%). Table 3.8 compares the results of the present study with those from two monolingual varieties of Spanish and two studies on US Spanish.

As can be seen from Table 3.8, bilinguals overall have a higher rate of measurable taps (i.e., canonical + approximant taps) than what has been reported for two monolingual varieties of Spanish; however, this difference may be due

TABLE 3.8   Comparison in the distribution of phonemic tap variants in monolingual and bilingual Spanish (% of data)

Study	Dialect	Canonical tap [ɾ]	Approximant tap [ɹ]	Perceptual tap [⁽ɾ⁾]
Willis and Bradley (2008)	Dominican (Cibao and Santo Domingo)		51%	49% (includes elided tokens)
Bradley and Willis (2012)	Mexican (Veracruz)		52%	48% (includes elided tokens)
Henriksen (2015)	US Spanish (1st generation)	51.1%	33.6%	15.3%
	US Spanish (2nd generation)	25.3%	45.6%	29.1%
Amengual (2016)	US Spanish (Spanish-dominant)	84.6%	11.1%	4.2%
	US Spanish (English-dominant)	64.4%	28.8%	6.7%
Present study	Guatemalan (Bilingual Spanish-Kaqchikel)	55.5%	28.9%	15.6%

Note: Bradley and Willis (2012) and Willis and Bradley (2008) do not report the distribution of the canonical and approximant taps, but rather collapse the two into a category called "measurable taps."

the two monolingual varieties belonging to regions where consonantal weakening is more common (Lipski, 1994). It is also important to note that the cited studies employed a more controlled task to elicit the data (e.g., carrier phrases or a narrative telling of a wordless picture book), while the data from the present study come from a sociolinguistic interview and a narrative telling of the same book used in previous research.

Despite these caveats, the picture that emerges from Table 3.8 is that bilingual Spanish-Kaqchikel Maya speakers are largely producing measurable taps for the phonemic tap and have not introduced variants that have not been documented in monolingual or other bilingual varieties of Spanish. For example, Elías-Ulloa (2020) detailed how Shipibo-Konibo speakers, whose language does not have any rhotic sounds, used some variants when speaking Spanish that are found in their native inventory and closely resembled Spanish rhotics (e.g., the voiced dental approximant [ð] for the phonemic tap). The lack of

TABLE 3.9 Comparison in the distribution of phonemic trill variants in monolingual and bilingual Spanish (% of data)

Study	Dialect	0 occlusions	1 occlusion	2 occlusions	3+ occlusions
Henriksen (2014)	Peninsular (Ciudad Real and León)	11.4%	17.8%	45.2%	2.7%
Lamy (2015)	Panamanian (Panama City)	10.2%	32.7%	43.6%	13.5%
Henriksen (2015)	US Spanish (1st generation)	23.7%	36.7%	35.9%	3.7%
	US Spanish (2nd generation)	21.3%	48.8%	28.2%	1.7%
Present study	Guatemalan (Bilingual Spanish-Kaqchikel)	30.1%	28.3%	25.7%	15.9%

more innovative variants such as these in bilingual Guatemalan Spanish can be attributed to the fact that Kaqchikel Maya has the tap in its phonological and phonetic inventory.

The results from the phonemic trill also demonstrate how bilingual Guatemalan Spanish is both similar and different from other varieties of Spanish. Given that not all studies report the frequency values for individual phonetic variants, the comparison in Table 3.9 utilizes the number of occlusions present in the production of the phonemic trill.

The overall rate of phonemic trills with a canonical number of occlusions in bilingual Guatemalan Spanish is 41.6%, which is lower than the monolingual varieties of Spanish (i.e., 57.1% in Panamanian Spanish and 47.9% in Peninsular Spanish) but higher than Mexican Spanish speakers who emigrated to the US (1st generation) and the US-born 2nd generation speakers (39.6% and 29.9%, respectively). However, despite the large number of canonical occlusion productions, as a group the bilingual Guatemalan Spanish speakers had the highest percentage of phonemic trills that lacked any occlusions (i.e., the assibilated rhotic [ř]). It is important to note that the use of this variant, which closely resembles the assibilated fricative [ʝ̊] allophone of the Kaqchikel /r/, was driven exclusively by the older generation (50+ years old) speakers who accounted for 100% of its usage.

In order to better understand the results from the distributional patterns, the second research question aimed to uncover the linguistic and extra-linguistic factors that favor the production of canonical variants for the phonemic tap and trill.[7] With respect to the extra-linguistic factors, the results from the multivariate analyses show that only one factor was statistically significant in the production of the canonical tap and trill variants: age group. More specifically, the results show that both younger and middle-aged speakers favor the canonical tap and trill variants, while older speakers favor more non-canonical rhotic variants for both the phonemic tap and trill. Previous research on Spanish in contact with Yucatec Maya has frequently found that younger speakers are abandoning contact-induced variants, such as longer VOT values with voiceless stops /p, t, k/ (Michnowicz & Carpenter, 2013), fortified voiced stop /b, d, g/ productions (Michnowicz, 2011), and glottalized vowels (Michnowicz & Kagan, 2016). The proposal put forward by those studies is that the increased access to education for the younger generations is accelerating a shift away from traditional Yucatan Spanish variants towards more "standard" forms; it is also worth mentioning that the knowledge of Yucatec Maya has also been decreasing, with the younger generations showing the highest levels of language shift towards monolingualism in Spanish (Michnowicz, 2015).

A similar dynamic is at play within the ethnic Kaqchikel community in Guatemala. Although the latest census data reports that 83.9% of ethnically Kaqchikel know Kaqchikel (INE, 2014), research has also indicated that language shift from Mayan languages to Spanish is occurring in Guatemala (Garzon, et al., 1998; Hawkins, 2005). With more access to Spanish in different contexts, the younger Kaqchikel generations may be moving more towards pan-Hispanic linguistic norms as well and abandoning more traditional variants found in older generations (e.g., the assibilated rhotic [ř] for the phonemic trill). However, a move towards one set of pan-Hispanic linguistic norms does not necessarily entail a wholesale movement towards these new norms, as previous research on voiceless stop aspiration of /p, t, k/ (McKinnon, 2020) and glottalization of word-initial vowels (McKinnon, 2023) with this same sample of bilingual speakers did not find an effect for age. Therefore, future research should examine whether the more canonical rhotic variants are more positively evaluated (and/or if the more non-canonical rhotic variants

---

7 It is important to recall that, for the multivariate analysis, the post-approximantized trill [rɪ] was grouped with the canonical trill [r] to form a binary distinction between variants with non-canonical number of occlusions (i.e., 0–1) and variants with canonical number of occlusions (2+). Therefore, in this discussion, "canonical trill" refers to variants that had the canonical 2+ number of occlusions.

are more negatively evaluated), as this could help explain why there are some changes in progress (i.e., rhotics) in the Spanish spoken by Spanish-Kaqchikel bilinguals while other phonetic variation is stable across the community (i.e., VOT values for the voiceless stops, rates of vowel glottalization).[8]

To the author's knowledge, the present study was the first to consider the presence of a rhotic minimal pair in the investigation of the rhotic phonological contrast maintenance. The multivariate analysis for the phonemic trill tokens selected this factor as statistically significant, with the presence of a rhotic minimal pair favoring the production of trill variants with more canonical number of occlusions; that is, words such as /karo/ *carro* 'car' (vs. /kaɾo/ *caro* 'expensive') and /koral/ *corral* 'livestock pen' (vs. /koɾal/ *coral* 'coral') favor the production of variants with at least 2 occlusions, while words that do not have a minimal pair (e.g., /agaɾaɾ/ *agarrar* 'to grab,' /tereno/ *terreno* 'land') do not favor variants with at least 2 occlusions. A possible explanation for this result is that the use of canonical number of occlusions is another way, along with duration, to maintain the contrast specifically for words in which the distinction creates a contrast, which may be important when variants with one occlusion (e.g., the post-approximantized tap [ɾɹ]) are also produced; this it so say, if a one occlusion variant is used with the word *carro* there could be potential confusion with its minimal pair *caro*. On the other hand, if words like *agarrar* or *terreno* are produced with only one occlusion there is no potential to confuse it with another word since there are no rhotic minimal pairs for those words.

However, as an anonymous reviewer pointed out, since the post-approximantized tap [ɾɹ] is only used for the phonemic trill (and never for the phonemic tap), there should be no confusion between a one occlusion tap variant and a one occlusion trill variant. At the same time, it is important to keep in mind that Melero-García and Cisneros (2020) found, in their perceptual experiment that manipulated the duration of one-closure rhotics, that the perception of the phonemic trill significantly increased as its duration increased, despite being rated as poor exemplars of that phonemic category. With this finding in mind, it is worth examining the rhotic variant frequency distribution for the participant who had overlap in 95% confidence interval for the duration of the phonemic tap and trill (M10), as well as the participant who was close to having overlap (F7). These findings are presented in Table 3.10.

---

8 For example, Baird (2023) found that Guatemalan listeners perceive /f/ fortition (e.g., [pro̩ntera] instead of [fro̩ntera] for *frontera* 'border' as indexing speakers of Mayan languages, and they also displayed negative attitudes towards this variant (including participants who self-identified as Maya).

TABLE 3.10   Rhotic variant frequency distribution for participants M10 and F7

Rhotic phoneme	Rhotic variant	M10	F7
Tap	Perceptual tap [$^{(r)}$]	0 (0%)	7 (23.3%)
	Approximant tap [ɾ̞]	11 (36.7%)	7 (23.3%)
	Canonical tap [ɾ]	19 (63.3%)	16 (53.3%)
Total		30	30
Trill	Post-approximantized tap [ɾ̞ɾ]	6 (85.7%)	8 (80.0%)
	Canonical trill [r]	1 (14.3%)	2 (20.0%)
Total		7	10

The results from Table 3.10 show that both participants overwhelming produced the post-approximantized tap [ɾ̞ɾ] for the phonemic trill, and at least over half of the phonemic tap tokens were realized as the canonical tap [ɾ]. Said another way, the majority of the rhotics produced by participants M10 and F7 only contained one occlusion, and they were the only participants with potential overlap in the duration of the phonemic tap and trill. This finding could mean there might exist the potential for a merger between their phonemic taps and trills for these two younger speakers; future research would benefit from studies that investigate the perception of the occlusion variants for the phonemic tap and trill to better answer this open question.

The final research question was concerned with examining if the tap vs. trill contrast is maintained in this bilingual speech community, given that Kaqchikel Maya only has one rhotic phoneme. At the group level, there was a statistically significant difference between the phonemic tap and the phonemic trill, with the phonemic trill being significantly longer in duration than the phonemic tap. This finding parallels previous research on the production (Amengual, 2016; Bradley & Willis, 2012; Henriksen, 2015; Willis & Bradley, 2008) and perception (Melero-García & Cisneros, 2020) of the Spanish rhotic phonological contrast, in that duration is an acoustic correlate that can be employed to maintain the phonological distinction. As was previously mentioned, given the great deal of variation in rhotic production, which includes one occlusion variants for the phonemic trill that may overlap with the phonemic tap, having another meaningful acoustic correlate could be a useful way of maintaining the phonological contrast.

In order to obtain a more complete picture of how social factors, specifically age, interact with the phonological contrast, Table 3.11 presents a summary of

TABLE 3.11 Change in progress in the tap vs. trill phonological contrast

Age group	Majority use of canonical taps for /ɾ/?	Majority use of trill variants with canonical number of occlusions for /r/?	Use of differences in duration?
Older speakers (50+)	No (43% canonical taps)	No (13% variants with 2+ occlusions)	Yes
Middle-aged speakers (30–49)	Yes (56% canonical taps)	Yes (56% variants with 2+ occlusions)	Yes
Younger speakers (18–29)	Yes (68% canonical taps)	Yes (60% variants with 2+ occlusions)	Majority of the speakers (6 or 7 out of 8)

how each age group employs the two ways of maintaining the tap vs. trill contrast identified in the present study.

The summary in Table 3.11 shows a change in progress with respect to how the three age groups maintain the rhotic phonemic contrast. As was alluded to in the discussion about the distributional patterns of the phonemic trill, the older generation relies on duration to distinguish between the phonemic tap and trill. Specifically, this age group frequently produces the assibilated rhotic [ř], which results in a long period of frication; indeed, Table 3.7 showed that the older speakers have some of the highest mean duration values for the phonemic trill. While middle-aged speakers also use differences in segmental duration to distinguish between the two rhotics, the results from the multivariate analysis show how they also favor the use of the canonical tap variant for /ɾ/ and trill variants with 2+ occlusions for /r/. Finally, the use of canonical taps and trill variants with canonical occlusions increases even more with the youngest generation of speakers, even though 1–2 speakers may have potential overlap in the duration of their phonemic tap and trill productions. These changes across three age cohorts suggest the *manner* in which the rhotic phonological contrast is maintained may be changing within this bilingual speech community; future research should examine the social perception of these variants as a possible explanation for why this change is occurring within the community.

In summary, the present study investigated rhotic variation and the ways in which the phonemic rhotic contrast is maintained in the bilingual Spanish-Kaqchikel Maya community in Guatemala. The results from this study add to the growing body of research documenting the wide phonetic inventory contained within the phonemic tap and trill, and how segmental duration is an acoustic correlate that can be utilized to maintain the phonological contrast in spite of so much variability. Additionally, the results also provide evidence for a change in progress in how the contrast is realized across three different age groups and how the presence of rhotic minimal pairs can also promote its maintenance. However, this study, when combined with the previous literature on Spanish in contact with Mayan languages, points to the need to conduct language attitudes studies to better understand why certain phonetic variables are undergoing changes in younger speakers while other variants remain stable across generations. Regardless of what these future studies uncover, it is clear that Guatemalan Spanish, and Central American Spanish as a whole, has the potential to better inform not only our knowledge of Hispanic linguistics, but to our wider understanding of linguistic theory as well.

Acknowledgements

I would like to thank the participants for taking the time to be interviewed for this project (*matyöx chiwe, roma xetzijon wik'in pa ruwi' kik'aslem*); for their constructive feedback, I would like to thank two anonymous reviewers and the audience members at the 22nd Mid-Continental Phonetics & Phonology Conference and the 50th Meeting of the Linguistic Association of the Southwest. This research was funded by the Center for Latin American and Caribbean Studies at Indiana University through a Tinker Research Grant.

References

Amengual, M. (2016). Acoustic correlates of the Spanish tap-trill contrast: Heritage and L2 Spanish speakers. *Heritage Language Journal*, 13, 88–112.

Arias, A. (2019). Rhotic realizations of the Puerto Rican community in Western Massachusetts and Puerto Rico. In W. Valentín-Márquez & M. González-Rivera (Eds.), *Dialects from Tropical Islands: Caribbean Spanish in the United States* (pp. 7–34). Routledge.

Baird, B. (2017). Prosodic transfer among Spanish-K'ichee' Bilinguals. In K. Bellamy, M. W. Child, P. González, A. Muntendam & M. C. Parafita Couto (Eds.), *Multidisciplinary approaches to bilingualism in the Hispanic and Lusophone world* (pp. 147–172). John Benjamins.

Baird, B. (2020). The Vowel Spaces of Spanish-K'ichee' bilinguals. In R. G. Rao (Ed.), *Spanish phonetics and phonology in contact: Studies from Africa, the Americas, and Spain* (pp. 64–81). John Benjamins.

Baird, B. (2021). "Para mí, es indígena con traje típico": Apocope as an indexical marker of indigeneity in Guatemalan Spanish. In L. A. Ortiz-López & E. M. Suárez Büdenbender (Eds.), *Topics in Spanish linguistic perceptions* (pp. 223–239). Routledge.

Baird, B. (2023). Social perceptions of /f/ fortition in Guatemalan Spanish. *Spanish in Context*. https://doi.org/10.1075/sic.20011.bai.

Balam, O. (2013). Variable neutralization of the intervocalic rhotic contrast in Northern Belizean Spanish. *Borealis: An International Journal of Hispanic Linguistics, 2*, 285–315.

Barnes, S. (2016). Variable final back vowels in urban Asturian Spanish. *Spanish in Context, 13*, 1–28.

Barrett, R. (2002). The Huehuetenango Sprachbund and language standardization in Guatemala. In M. Andronis, E. Debenport, A. Pycha & K. Yoshimura (Eds.), *Proceedings of the 38th Chicago Linguistics Society: The Panels* (pp. 309–318). Chicago Linguistics Society.

Barrett, R. (2008). Linguistic differentiation and Mayan language revitalization in Guatemala. *Journal of Sociolinguistics, 12*, 275–305.

Bennett, R., Coon, J., & Henderson, R. (2016). Introduction to Mayan linguistics. *Language and Linguistics Compass, 10*, 455–468.

Boersma, P., & Weenik, D. (2021). Praat: Doing phonetics by computer (Version 6.1.50) [Software]. http://www.praat.org/.

Bradley, T. G., & Willis, E. W. (2012). Rhotic variation and contrast in Veracruz Mexican Spanish. *Estudios de fonética experimental, 21*, 43–74.

Brody, J. (1987). Particles borrowed from Spanish as discourse markers in Mayan languages. *Anthropological Linguistics, 29*, 507–521.

Brody, J. (1995). Lending the 'unborrowable': Spanish discourse markers in indigenous American languages. In C. Silva-Corvalán (Ed.), *Spanish in four continents: Studies in language contact and bilingualism* (pp. 132–147). Georgetown University Press.

Chappell, W. (2016). Bilingualism and aspiration: Coda /s/ reduction on the Atlantic coast of Nicaragua. In S. Sessarego & F. Tejedo-Herrero (Eds.), *Spanish language and sociolinguistic analysis* (pp. 261–282). John Benjamins.

Chappell, W. (2020). Social contact and linguistic convergence: The reduction of intervocalic /d/ in Bilwi, Nicaragua. In R. G. Rao (Ed.), *Spanish phonetics and phonology in contact: Studies from Africa, the Americas, and Spain* (pp. 84–102). John Benjamins.

Chappell, W. (2021). 'En esta petsa, este anio': The Spanish sound system in contact with Miskitu. In M. Díaz-Campos & S. Sessarego (Eds.), *Aspects of Latin American Spanish dialectology: In honor of Terrell A. Morgan* (pp. 181–203). John Benjamins.

Clements, J. C. (2009). *Linguistic legacy of Spanish and Portuguese*. Cambridge University Press.

Davidson, J. (2015). *Social dynamics of Catalan-Spanish contact in the evolution of Catalonian Spanish* [Doctoral dissertation, University of Illinois at Urbana-Champaign].

Díaz-Campos, M. (2008). Variable production of the trill in spontaneous speech: Sociolinguistic implications. In L. Colantoni & J. Steele (Eds.), *Selected Proceedings of the 3rd Conference on Laboratory Approaches to Spanish Phonology* (pp. 47–58). Cascadilla Proceedings Project.

Elías-Ulloa, J. (2020). Rhotics in Shipibo-Konibo Spanish: A phonetic study. In R. G. Rao (Ed.), *Spanish phonetics and phonology in contact: Studies from Africa, the Americas, and Spain* (pp. 164–206). John Benjamins.

García Matzar, P. O., Toj Cotzajay, V., & Coc Tuiz, D. (1999). *Gramática del idioma Kaqchikel*. Proyecto Lingüístico Francisco Marroquín.

García Tesoro, A. I. (2005). Español en contacto con lenguas mayas en Guatemala. In C. Ferrero, N. Lasso, & V. Lang, *Variedades lingüísticas y lenguas en contacto en el mundo de habla hispana* (pp. 25–34). Author House.

Garzon, S., Brown, R. M., & Richards, J. B., & Ajpub', W. (1998). *The life of our language: Kaqchikel Maya maintenance, shift, and revitalization*. University of Texas Press.

Gordon, M. (2011). Stress: Phonotactic and Phonetic Evidence. In M. van Oostendorp, C. J. Ewen, E. Hume, & K. Rice (Eds.), *The Blackwell companion to phonology*. Blackwell Publishing: Blackwell Reference Online. https://doi.org/10.1002/9781444335262.wbctp0039.

Hawkins, R. J. (2005). Language loss in Guatemala: A statistical analysis of the 1994 population census. *Journal of Sociolinguistics*, 9, 53–73.

Henriksen, N. (2014). Sociophonetic analysis of phonemic trill variation in two subvarieties of Peninsular Spanish. *Journal of Linguistic Geography*, 2, 4–24.

Henriksen, N. (2015). Acoustic analysis of the rhotic contrast in Chicagoland Spanish: An intergenerational study. *Linguistic Approaches to Bilingualism*, 5, 285–321.

Henriksen, N. C., & Willis, E. W. (2010). Acoustic characterization of phonemic trill production in Jerezano Andalusian Spanish. In M. Ortega-Llebaria (Ed.), *Selected Proceedings of the Fourth Conference on Laboratory Approaches to Spanish Phonology* (pp. 115–127). Cascadilla Proceedings Project.

Hualde, J. I. (2014). *Los sonidos del español*. Cambridge University Press.

Instituto Nacional de Estadística de Guatemala (2014). Publicaciones. Retrieved October 5, 2016, from https://www.ine.gob.gt/index.php/estadisticas/publicaciones.

Johnson, D. E. (2009). Getting off the GoldVarb standard: Introducing Rbrul for mixed-effects variable rule analysis. *Language and Linguistics Compass*, 3, 359–383.

Kawahara, S. (2010). Duration script. Praat Script. http://user.keio.ac.jp/~kawahara/resource.html.

Kim, J. Y., & Repiso-Puigdelliura, G. (2020). Deconstructing heritage language dominance: Effects of proficiency, use, and input on heritage speakers' production of the Spanish alveolar tap. *Phonetica*, 77, 55–80.

Labov, W. (1972). *Sociolinguistic Patterns*. University of Pennsylvania Press.

Labov, W. (2001). *Principles of linguistic change: Social factors*. Blackwell.

Ladefoged, P. & Maddieson, I. (1996). *The sounds of the world's languages.* Blackwell Publishers.

Lamy, D. S. (2015). A sociophonetic analysis of trill production in Panamanian Spanish. In R. Klassen, J. M. Liceras & E. Valenzuela (Eds.), *Hispanic Linguistics at the crossroads: Theoretical linguistics, language acquisition and language contact* (pp. 313–336). John Benjamins.

Law, D. (2014). *Language contact, inherited similarity and social difference: The story of linguistic interaction in the Maya lowlands.* John Benjamins.

Lennes, M. (2002). Save labeled intervals to wav sound files. Praat Script.

Lipski, J. M. (1994). *Latin American Spanish.* Harlow, U.K.: Longman Publishing.

Mairano, P. & Calabrò, L. (2016). Are minimal pairs too few to be used in L2 pronunciation classes? In R. Savy & I. Alfano (Eds.), *La fonetica sperimentale nell'insegnamento e nell'apprendimento delle lingue straniere. Phonetics and language learning* (pp. 255–268). Officinaventuno.

McKinnon, S. (2020). Un análisis sociofonético de la aspiración de las oclusivas sordas en el español guatemalteco monolingüe y bilingüe (español-kaqchikel). *Spanish in Context, 17,* 1–29.

McKinnon, S. (2023). Las vocales glotalizadas en el español guatemalteco: Un análisis sociofonético entre los hablantes bilingües (español-kaqchikel) y monolingües. *Studies in Hispanic and Lusophone Linguistics, 16,* 171–207.

Mercer, M. (1969). *Frog, Where Are You?* Dial Press.

Melero García, F. (2015). Análisis acústico de la vibrante múltiple en el español de Valencia (España). *Studies in Hispanic and Lusophone Linguistics, 8,* 183–206.

Melero-García, F., & Cisneros, A. (2020). No es tan simple como parece: The effect of duration on one-closure rhotics on the perception of Spanish. In D. Pascual y Cabo & I. Elola (Eds.), *Current Theoretical and Applied Perspectives on Hispanic and Lusophone Linguistics* (pp. 295–218). John Benjamins.

Michnowicz, J., & Carpenter, L. (2013). Voiceless stop aspiration in Yucatan Spanish: A sociolinguistic analysis. *Spanish in Context, 10,* 410–437.

Michnowicz, J. & Kagan, L. (2016). On glottal stops in Yucatan Spanish. In S. Sessarego & F. Tejedo-Herrero (Eds.), *Spanish language and sociolinguistic analysis* (pp. 217–240). John Benjamins.

O'Rourke, E. (2010). Dialect differences and the bilingual vowel space in Peruvian Spanish. In M. Ortega-Llebaria (Ed.), *Selected Proceedings of the 4th Conference on Laboratory Approaches to Spanish Phonology* (pp. 20–30). Cascadilla Proceedings Project.

R Core Team. (2016). R: A Language and Environment for Statistical Computing. Retrieved April 6, 2023, from http://www.rproject.org/.

Repiso-Puigdelliura, G., & Kim, J. Y. (2021). The missing link in Spanish heritage trill production. *Bilingualism: Language and Cognition, 24,* 454–466.

Ryan, K. (2005). Grid maker script. Praat Script. Retrieved April 6, 2023, from http://phonetics.linguistics.ucla.edu/facilities/acoustic/praat.html.

Solé, M. J. (2002). Aerodynamic characteristics of trills and phonological patterning. *Journal of Phonetics, 30*, 655–688.

Willis, E. W. (2006). Trill variation in Dominican Spanish: An acoustic examination and comparative analysis. In N. Sagarra & A. J. Toribio (Eds.), *Selected Proceedings of the 9th Hispanic Linguistics Symposium* (pp. 121–131). Cascadilla Proceedings Project.

Willis, E. W. (2007). An acoustic study of the 'pre-aspirated trill' in narrative Cibaeño Dominican Spanish. *Journal of the International Phonetic Association, 37*, 33–49.

Willis, E. W., & Bradley, T. G. (2008). Contrast maintenance of taps and trills in Dominican Spanish: Data and analysis. In L. Colantoni & J. Steele (Eds.), *Selected Proceedings of the 3rd Conference on Laboratory Approaches to Spanish Phonology* (pp. 87–100). Cascadilla Proceedings Project.

Winford, D. (2003). *An introduction to contact linguistics*. Blackwell Publishing Ltd.

Winford, D. (2020). The New Spanishes in the context of contact linguistics: Toward a unified approach. In L. A. Ortiz López, R. E. Guzzardo Tamargo & M. González-Rivera (Eds.), *Hispanic Contact Linguistics: Theoretical, methodological and empirical perspectives* (pp. 12–41). John Benjamins.

Zahler, S. & Daidone, D. (2014). A variationist account of trill /r/ usage in the Spanish of Málaga. *Indiana University Linguistics Club Working Papers, 14*, 17–42.

CHAPTER 4

Variation of Absolute-Final /s/ in Tegucigalpa Spanish

Julio Ventura and Brandon Baird

1   Introduction

As stated throughout this book, Central American Spanish is one of the least studied varieties of Spanish. However, even within the linguistic analysis of Central American Spanish, studies about Honduran Spanish are ever rarer. Concerning Honduran Spanish, Lipski (1990, p. 92) has stated that there is an "almost complete and enormously astonishing absence of detailed studies" and that "since the pioneering works of the lexicologist Alberto Membreño, linguistic investigations of the Honduran dialect are scarce and to the point of non-existence". Although written approximately 30 years ago, this statement remains largely true, as the studies published since continue to be rare in comparison to studies from other geographical areas of the Spanish-speaking world. Additionally, with recent exceptions such as Rodríguez & Howe (this volume), the little scholarly work on Honduran Spanish that does exist largely consists of "very general studies that describe some phenomena marked by the trends that the language follows at the Latin American level" (Hernández Torres, 2010, p. 115) and it is common for Honduran Spanish to be grouped together with Nicaraguan and Salvadoran Spanish in different analyses. However, such an aggrupation often conceals variation between the Spanish spoken in these distinct areas (Lipski, 1985).

Due to its geographical location on the isthmus, Honduran Spanish has evolved due to indigenous substrates, contact with other Central American countries, linguistic and cultural contact with pirates (Honduras was one of the most besieged countries of the 16th and 17th centuries, Lipski, 1982), African influence through imported slaves (Mariñas Otero, 1963), and other groups such as the Miskito. Thus, throughout the different dialects of Spanish spoken in Central America, Honduras has been called "a zone of linguistic transition" (Lipski, 1990, p. 94). In fact, concerning Guatemala, Honduras, Nicaragua and El Salvador, Lipski (1985) has argued that Guatemalan Spanish is the most conservative of the four and that Nicaraguan and Salvadoran Spanish are the most progressive. This of course leaves Honduran Spanish somewhere in the middle and variation in Honduran Spanish can be seen throughout the country (Hernández Torres, 2010).

Tegucigalpa is located near the geographical center of Honduras. As the capital of a small country, the majority of government agencies, the national university, television and radio stations, etc. are located there and Tegucigalpa Spanish has been said to represent the linguistic norm for the entire country. Tegucigalpa has also been the destination of migration within Honduras for many decades, if not centuries. The influx of different regional dialects into the capital has created a situation in which "the Spanish that is heard on the streets of Tegucigalpa is not necessarily a faithful representation of those that were born in the city, but rather a mosaic of the representative dialects of the entire country" (Lipski, 1990, p. 97).

The goal of the present chapter is to analyze one particular phenomenon that has shown noteworthy variation among native speakers of Honduran Spanish: the production of the voiceless alveolar fricative /s/. Although there is little experimental work on Honduran Spanish, the realization of /s/ has been discussed in a few studies in the 1980s (Amastae, 1989; Lipski, 1985, 1986, 1987, 1990[1]) and more recently (Hernández Torres, 2010, 2013; and a series of undergraduate theses: Galo Palma & Maradiaga Funes, 2016; Matute Nájera & Portillo Barahona, 2014; Méndez Ávila, 2015; Ramírez Enamorado, 2016; Ramos Molina, 2015; Rodríguez Zambrano, 2016; Rubio Montes, 2017; Suazo Martínez, 2016). In sum, these studies show that within Honduras, the area that demonstrates the most variation in the realization of /s/ is Tegucigalpa. Nonetheless, the primary focus of the majority of these studies is the phonological contexts in which different allophonic variations of /s/ tend to occur. Thus, the present study investigates different realizations of /s/ in Tegucigalpa Spanish with a primary emphasis on the effects of social factors on said variation. Specifically, this study analyzes /s/ variation in absolute-final position, i.e., at the end of an utterance before a pause, and among speakers from Tegucigalpa according to age, sex, social class, and education. The rest of this chapter is organized as follows: the next section details the existing work on /s/ in Honduran Spanish, section 3 details the present study, including the methodology, the results are reported in section 4, discussed in section 5, and concluded in section 6.

---

1 Lipski (1990) also appears in different venues: in 1983 in *Nueva Revista de Filología Hispánica* and in 1984 in *Boletín de la Academia Hondureña de la Lengua*. The 1990 version is used here, as it is the one in the authors' possession.

2 /s/ in Honduran Spanish

It has been hypothesized that in Latin American Spanish, reduction of the voiceless alveolar fricative /s/ hails from Andalusian dialects of Southern Spain and from the Canary Islands. Although difficult to pinpoint the exact moment in which these phonological processes began, these regions display /s/ lenition/aspiration (/s/ → [h]) and deletion (/s/ → ∅) at a significantly higher rate than in Central and Northern Spain and, historically, they have had more contact with the Americas than these other regions of the Iberian Peninsula (Lipski, 1990). Furthermore, Lipski (1990) argues that the phonetic and phonological behavior of /s/ is perhaps one of the most useful tools of dialectal description in the Spanish-speaking world as most dialects have generally been classified as those that maintain /s/ and those that reduce /s/ in certain phonological positions. In fact, about half of all Spanish dialects demonstrate /s/ reduction (Hualde, 2005).

Within Central American Spanish, Lipski (1985) proposes a continuum of variation from Guatemala to El Salvador and Nicaragua. Specifically, /s/ tends to be maintained in Guatemalan Spanish, but is aspirated or deleted at a much higher rate in Salvadoran and Nicaraguan Spanish. Additionally, with the exception of some areas nears coasts and international borders, the phonetics and phonology of Guatemala, El Salvador, and Nicaragua are quite homogenous within each country. In contrast, Honduran Spanish, being geographically juxtaposed between these three countries, is much more heterogeneous in terms of different realizations of /s/.

Although some descriptive studies exist (e.g. Canfield, 1990), the principal experimental and theoretical literature on /s/ in Honduran Spanish consists of a series of studies carried out in the 1980s (Amastae, 1989; Lipski, 1985, 1986, 1987, 1990), though Amastae's (1989) analysis primarily focuses on the effects of aspiration and deletion of /s/ on other consonants in word-internal position. Lipski (1985) describes the aforementioned comparison of /s/ reduction across different Central American countries. The principal phonological findings of Lipski (1986, 1987, 1990), which are based on sociolinguistic interviews and analyses of Honduran radio speech in the 1980s, indicate the following: (i) aspiration is more common than deletion; (ii) aspiration and deletion are most common in preconsonantal, word- and absolute-final position; and (iii) there are few grammatical/morphological effects on /s/ aspiration and deletion.[2]

---

2 Lipski (1987, 1990) hypothesized that since *vos* is much more common than *tú*, other phonological features would differentiate between 2nd and 3rd person singular verb inflections and the maintenance of the morphological suffix -s would not be necessary.

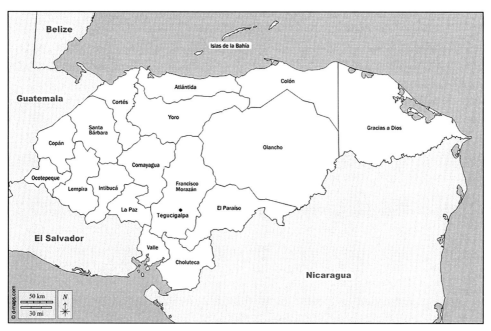

MAP 4.1   Map of departments of Honduras and the capital city of Tegucigalpa. Adapted from d-maps.com

In addition to these findings, Lipski (1986, 1987, 1990) and more recent analyses of /s/ in Honduran Spanish have shown variation throughout the country. These recent studies include the works of Hernández Torres (2010, 2013) and a series of licenciatura theses carried out by students at the Universidad Nacional Autónoma de Honduras (UNAH) between 2014 and 2017 (Galo Palma & Maradiaga Funes, 2016; Matute Nájera & Portillo Barahona, 2014; Méndez Ávila, 2015; Ramírez Enamorado, 2016; Ramos Molina, 2015; Rodríguez Zambrano, 2016; Rubio Montes, 2017; Suazo Martínez, 2016).[3] As there tends to be more phonological variation in Honduras than in the neighboring countries, the majority of these studies on /s/ in Honduran Spanish have made geographical variation a key focus. As such, refer to Map 4.1, a map of Honduras indicating the different departments and the location of Tegucigalpa, to better understand the following dialectal findings of /s/.

According to Lipski (1987, 1990), the aspiration and deletion of /s/ is most common in the northern departments of Cortés, Yoro, Atlántida, and Colón, and that in Ocotepeque, which borders both Guatemala and El Salvador, /s/

---

3   A licenciatura degree in Honduras is the equivalent of a bachelor's degree in the United States.

aspiration and deletion are less common than in Salvadoran Spanish but more common than in Guatemalan Spanish. Additionally, the southern departments of Valle, Choluteca, and El Paraíso all demonstrate heightened levels of aspiration and deletion, though not to the same degree as the aforementioned northern departments. On the other hand, Lipski states that there is less aspiration and deletion of /s/ in La Paz, Copán, Olancho, Santa Bárbara, Lempira, and Intibucá and that the variety of Honduran Spanish that demonstrates the least amount of aspiration and deletion of /s/ is that of the department of Comayagua. Lipski considers the departments of Gracias a Dios and Islas de la Bahía to be considered outliers, as Spanish is spoken as a minority language in these areas. Nonetheless, Gracias a Dios exhibits less aspiration and deletion than the other northern departments whereas Islas de la Bahía is similar to these same northern departments in terms of /s/ reduction. Finally, Lipski considers the Spanish of the department of Francisco Morazán, or more specifically, the city of Tegucigalpa, to be the epicenter of this "transitional zone" between dialects of /s/ variation (1990, p. 104) as it presents the most heterogeneous data of any department in Honduras. Lipski notes that, perhaps unsurprisingly, there is variation in the phonetic realization of /s/ according to social class, with lower social classes being much more likely to aspirate or delete. The results from Lipski (1990) for absolute-final /s/ according to social class are presented in Table 4.1.

Hernández Torres (2010, 2013) reports the findings from dialectal surveys across all 18 departments of Honduras as well. An important difference between these studies and those of Lipski is that Hernández Torres proposes that there are more possible phonetic realizations of /s/, not just the full [s], aspirated [h] and deleted ∅ varieties that form the basis of Lipski's analyses. According to Hernández Torres (2010, 2013), possible allophones of /s/ in Honduran Spanish include the voiceless alveolar fricative [s], the aspirated [h], deletion, or ∅, a voiced alveolar fricative [z], a whistled alveolar fricative [ş], a weakened voiceless alveolar fricative [ˢ], and a dental or dentalized fricative [s̪]. Lipski (1987,

TABLE 4.1   Lipski's (1990) results (%) for realizations of /s/ in absolute-final position according to social class in Tegucigalpa Spanish (Modified from Lipski, 1990, p. 107)

Social class	[s]	[h]	∅
Upper	80.0%	16.7%	3.3%
Middle	63.7%	24.6%	11.7%
Lower	53.3%	35.6%	11.1%

1990) did note the existence of this last allophone, but stated that was rather uncommon in his data.

Hernández Torres (2010, 2013) separates his dialectal findings into three groups, which are similar but not identical to those of Lipski (1987, 1990). The first group consists of departments in which /s/ is predominantly produced as [s], and includes El Paraíso, Gracias a Dios, La Paz, Intibucá, Lempira, Cortés, Islas de la Bahía, Santa Bárbara, Copán and Ocotepeque. Additionally, Hernández Torres classifies Olancho and Comayagua as part of this group, even though both present very high levels of the whistled [ṣ]. The second group is for departments that predominantly aspirate or delete /s/ and consists of the northern departments Yoro, Atlántida, and Colón, and the southern departments Choluteca and Valle. Finally, the third group is for what Hernández Torres calls "zones in transition" (2010, p. 127), in other words, areas in which the phonetic realization of /s/ is unstable, or heterogeneous, when compared to the first two groups. According to his analysis, the only department in this group is Francisco Morazán (Tegucigalpa). Hernández Torres reports the variation of /s/ in Tegucigalpa seen in Table 4.2.

The licenciatura theses carried out by students at the UNAH differ from the work of Lipski (1986, 1987, 1990) and Hernández Torres (2010, 2013) in that they do not consist of country-wide analyses, but tend to focus on a specific department. Nonetheless, these theses offer new data to the study of /s/ in Honduran Spanish as they include variables, such as age, sex, and education of the speaker, that are not readily found in the studies that have already been reported above. Matute Nájera & Portillo Barahona (2014) carried out their investigation in Olancho and found that [s] and [ṣ] were the most common allophones produced in word-final position. Additionally, they report that females produced [s] at a higher rate than males. Ramos Molina's (2015) study was done in Lempira found that although [h] and ∅ occurred more often before other consonants and in word-final position, there were no differences between females and males. The thesis from Méndez Ávila (2015) reveals that older females in El Paraíso are the most likely to pronounce the full [s], followed

TABLE 4.2 Variation of /s/ in Tegucigalpa Spanish according to Hernández Torres (2010, p. 127). As Hernández Torres did not report the findings for all allophones, the sum of the reported data does not reach 100%

[s]	[ˢ]	[h]	∅
62.50%	7.14%	19.64%	5.35%

by younger females. Males, regardless of age, demonstrate high levels of aspiration, but not deletion, in El Paraíso. In Santa Bárbara (Ramírez Enamorado, 2016), the opposite was found as females aspirated at a higher rate than males. In Comayagua (Suazo Martínez, 2016), [s] was the predominant realization of /s/. Although there were no differences between females and males, speakers that had only finished Primary school were more likely to aspirate than those that finished Secondary school or University studies. In an analysis of Valle, Colón, and Choluteca, Rodríguez Zambrano (2016) notes that in Valle and Choluteca deletion is the most common realization of /s/, followed by [h], whereas in Colón, [h] is used at the highest rate. Rubio Montes (2017) found that in Yoro, [h] is the most commonly produced allophone of /s/. Additionally, younger speakers and males were more likely to aspirate in Yoro. Finally, in a study of several municipalities in the department of Francisco Morazán, but not in Tegucigalpa, Galo Palma & Maradiaga Funes (2016) report that [s] is the most common allophone and that aspiration and deletion are more likely among younger speakers and males. It is worth noting that the additional allophones proposed by Hernández Torres (2010, 2013) were only corroborated in Francisco Morazán, Olancho, Yoro, and Comayagua.

3   The Present Study

Although sparse, the literature on Honduran Spanish indicates variation in the realization of /s/ throughout the country. In general, the departments directly to the north and south of Tegucigalpa tend to have higher rates of aspiration and deletion than other areas. Regardless, both Lipski (1986, 1987, 1990) and Hernández Torres (2010, 2013) agree that the department of Francisco Morazán, or specifically, the city of Tegucigalpa, demonstrates the highest amount of variation among speakers in Honduran Spanish. Nevertheless, aside from Lipski's analysis according to social class, these principal studies of /s/ in Honduran Spanish do not address social factors. Moreover, whereas the UNAH licenciatura theses do consider different social factors and offer insightful data, their results are largely based on comparing percentages and lack statistical analyses that would strengthen their claims. Accordingly, the research questions that this study seeks to answer are the following: (i) What is the current state of /s/ variation in Tegucigalpa Spanish in comparison to Lipski (1986, 1987, 1990) and Hernández Torres (2010, 2013)?; and (ii) How do the social factors of age, sex, social class, and education affect /s/ variation?

In order to answer these research questions, a rapid anonymous survey (Labov, 1966) was designed to elicit tokens of /s/ from a large amount of speakers across the aforementioned social variables. As with all methods, rapid anonymous surveys have advantages and disadvantages. On the one hand, they minimize the observer's paradox (Labov, 1972) as they are designed to elicit tokens in a more subtle way than other sociolinguistic methods and the likelihood of the participants producing informal speech is better than in the majority of sociolinguistic methods (Labov, 2002, p. 104). They also tend to allow for the gathering of data from a higher number of speakers than other methods. On the other hand, they usually produce fewer tokens per speaker and social judgements about each speaker are often left to the researchers' quick judgements. Additionally, this type of method lacks recorded data that can help corroborate the findings via acoustic analyses. Nonetheless, although rapid anonymous surveys are not as frequently used as other methods, recent research has shown that they are still valuable in terms of providing initial, large scale analyses of sociolinguistic variables (Ellis et al., 2006; Michnowicz, 2006).

As the primary focus of this investigation is the effects of the aforementioned social factors, the phonological context in which /s/ occurs was controlled. Specifically, all tokens of /s/ in this study come from absolute-final position, i.e., when /s/ is the very last segment in a sentence and is followed by a pause (Keating et al., 1999). Next to preconsonantal position, absolute-final position is one of the most common positions in which /s/ demonstrates variation in Honduran Spanish (Hernández Torres, 2010, 2013; Lipski, 1986, 1987, 1990). In addition, the focus on absolute-final position facilitated the creation of the question used for the rapid anonymous survey.

For the rapid anonymous survey, the first author, a native speaker of Tegucigalpa Spanish, conducted short interviews with individuals around the city. The question used in this survey was *Hola, perdone la molestia, ¿qué hora es?*, "Hello, sorry for the trouble, what time is it?". This question was asked to the participants at times in which the resulting number would end in /s/, most commonly at three (*tres*) o'clock, but also at two (*dos*), six (*seis*) and ten (*diez*) o'clock. The first author then made a note of the pronunciation of /s/ in absolute-final position. Finally, in order to mitigate some of the abovementioned disadvantages of rapid anonymous surveys, the first author informed the participants of the purpose of the study, and if they were willing, he asked about the speakers' age, sex, occupation, and education through a short conversation after the initial elicitation question. This conversation did not last longer than two minutes.

This method resulted in 278 tokens of absolute-final /s/ from 278 participants, ages 18–70 (M: 33.5, SD: 12.1), 131 males and 147 females. Of these, 110 had only completed Primary school education, 49 had completed Secondary school, and 119 had completed University studies. In the multinomial logistic regression reported in the results section, the independent variables included the following social factors: Age, following Hernández Torres' (2010, 2013) classification (18–30, 31–50, 50+), sex (female, male), education (Primary, Secondary, University), and finally, social class. The arrangement of social class was done according to a short analysis involving 33 individuals from Tegucigalpa that were not part of the rapid anonymous survey. These individuals were asked to rank the occupations of the 278 participants on a Likert scale of 1 (Lower class) to 3 (Upper class) (cf. Lang-Rigal, 2020). Following these rankings, the participants were divided up into three social classes where clear breaks in the mean responses occurred (see Table 4.3): Lower class 152 participants, Middle class 108 participants, Upper class 18 participants.

TABLE 4.3 Rankings and classifications of occupations of the 278 participants according to 33 different individuals from Tegucigalpa

Occupation	Mean (SD)	Social class
Bus fee collector	1 (0.0)	Lower
Painter	1 (0.0)	Lower
Street vendor	1 (0.0)	Lower
Vendor	1.1 (0.2)	Lower
Bus driver	1.2 (0.2)	Lower
Upholsterer	1.2 (0.5)	Lower
Security guard	1.2 (0.8)	Lower
Dress maker	1.3 (0.3)	Lower
Cobbler	1.3 (0.5)	Lower
Construction worker	1.3 (0.8)	Lower
Taxi driver	1.3 (0.9)	Lower
Student	1.8 (0.2)	Middle
Teacher	1.9 (0.6)	Middle
Host	2.1 (0.9)	Middle
Journalist	2.2 (0.4)	Middle
Office worker	2.2 (1.3)	Middle
Accountant	2.3 (1.4)	Middle
Architect	2.7 (0.3)	Upper
Business owner	2.8 (0.5)	Upper
Engineer	2.8 (0.4)	Upper
Lawyer	3 (0.0)	Upper
Medical doctor	3 (0.0)	Upper
Pharmacist	3 (0.0)	Upper

4 Results

Before presenting the analysis of the effects of the independent variables, the overall rate of use of each allophone of /s/ from the rapid anonymous survey is considered. As seen in Figure 4.1, the overall distribution of the allophones of /s/ demonstrates that the division between maintaining a full [s] and producing some other variation is almost half-and-half: 47.12% of the 278 speakers in this study produced [s] in the rapid anonymous survey whereas the remaining 52.88% produced one of the other allophonic variations. Of these other realizations, the next most common productions were deletion (∅) and aspiration, [h], at 17.63% and 16.91% respectively. Although the additional four allophones of /s/ reported by Hernández Torres (2010, 2013) were found among the participants in this study, only the weakened [ˢ] was produced somewhat regularly (13.31%), as the whistled [ṣ] (2.88%), voiced [z] (1.08%), and dental [s̪] (1.08%) allophones were scarce in this data set.

In the development of a multinomial logistic regression model that provides a good fit for the data, tokens of whistled [ṣ], voiced [z], and dental [s̪] only constituted 5% of the data (14 of 278 participants) and were deemed outliers and thus not included in the statistical analysis reported below (cf, Sarkar et al., 2011). Consequently, the remaining 264 tokens belonged to one of four categories, [s], ∅, [h] or [ˢ]. Overall, a chi-squared test reveals that the rate of these tokens in the rapid anonymous survey was significantly different, χ^2 (3, N = 264) = 20.429, p <.001. Whereas the overall rate of the tokens indicates variation in absolute-final [s] in Tegucigalpa Spanish, a consideration of the effect of social variables reveals a clearer picture of this variation. All four

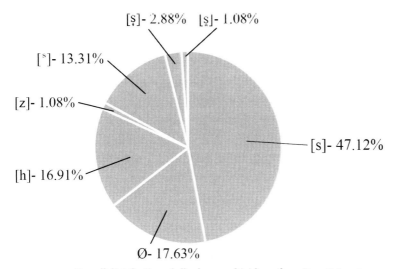

FIGURE 4.1 Overall distribution of allophones of /s/ from the 278 participants

independent variables were selected as significant predictors by the model of the multinomial logistic regression: Age ($p < .05$), Sex ($p < .001$), Social Class ($p < .01$), and Education ($p < .05$).

In addition, the multinomial regression analyzed the effects across all levels of each independent variable. As the dependent variable in this analysis has four variants, the multinomial regression compares three of these variants separately against a base level, or reference category (the fourth variant). In this analysis, [s] was chosen as the reference category for the dependent variable as it was the most frequent response in the data and ∅, [h], and [ˢ] are considered various realizations of /s/ reduction. Furthermore, each independent variable also had a reference category, which were the following: Age, 50+; Sex, Female; Social Class, Upper; Education; University. Each variant is only considered to be significantly different from the reference category if the lower and upper limits of the 95% confidence interval do not contain the value of one. If the values of both confidence intervals are greater than one, this indicates that the odds of a speaker choosing the particular variant are greater than the reference category. If the value of each confidence interval is less than one, then the odds of a speaker from that category choosing that variant are lower than the reference category (for more on multinomial logistic regressions, see Kanwit et al., 2017). In the following tables, the results of the multinomial regression are simplified to indicate odds that are greater than, equal to, or less than. The exact values for all of the following comparisons are found in the Appendix. Finally, it is important to note that although the statistical results are presented across multiple tables here, they are all the results from a single multinomial logistic regression.

The distribution of allophones according to Age is shown in Table 4.4 and the results of the multinomial regression are shown in Table 4.5. Across all three age groups, [s] was the most common response, as it occurred about half the time in each group. However, these results also indicate that speakers aged 18–30 demonstrated the most within-group allophonic variation. Of particular note, for the middle age group, 31–50, the analysis reveals that these speakers are the least likely to delete /s/ and the most likely to aspirate. Weakened [ˢ] is also much less common among the oldest group than the younger groups. In other words, the principal finding in Age is that the middle group differs the most and the younger group and older group are actually the most similar in terms of the realization of absolute-final /s/.

With respect to Sex (Tables 4.6 and 4.7), it is noted that there is more variation among the male speakers than the female. More than half of the female speakers, 61.7%, produced [s] whereas male speakers aspirated and deleted at

TABLE 4.4 Distribution of allophones according to Age (*n* = 264)

| | \multicolumn{6}{c}{Age} |
Allophone	\multicolumn{2}{c}{18–30}	\multicolumn{2}{c}{31–50}	\multicolumn{2}{c}{50+}
	N	%	N	%	N	%
∅	28	20.7%	13	12.4%	8	33.3%
[h]	18	13.3%	27	25.7%	2	8.3%
[ˢ]	21	15.6%	14	13.3%	2	8.3%
[s]	68	50.4%	51	48.6%	12	50.0%

TABLE 4.5 Results of the multinomial logistic regression for Age. ">" indicates that the odds of producing the specific allophone over [s] are greater when compared to the reference category, "<" indicates that the odds of producing the specific allophone over [s] are lower when compared to the reference category, "=" indicates odds are not different, "Ref." indicates the reference category for each independent variable

| | \multicolumn{3}{c}{Age} |
Allophone	18–30	31–50	51+
∅	=	<	Ref.
[h]	=	>	Ref.
[ˢ]	>	>	Ref.

TABLE 4.6 Distribution of allophones according to Sex (*n* = 264)

| | \multicolumn{4}{c}{Sex} |
Allophone	\multicolumn{2}{c}{Male}	\multicolumn{2}{c}{Female}
	N	%	N	%
∅	32	26.0%	16	12.1%
[h]	29	23.6%	18	12.8%
[ˢ]	18	14.6%	19	13.5%
[s]	44	35.8%	87	61.7%

TABLE 4.7 Results of the multinomial logistic regression for Sex. ">" indicates that the odds of producing the specific allophone over [s] are greater when compared to the reference category, "=" indicates odds are not different, "Ref." indicates the reference category for each independent variable

	Sex	
Allophone	Male	Female
∅	>	Ref.
[h]	>	Ref.
[ˢ]	=	Ref.

TABLE 4.8 Distribution of allophones according to Social Class ($n = 264$)

	Social Class					
Allophone	Lower		Middle		Upper	
	N	%	N	%	N	%
∅	23	16.0%	26	25.0%	0	0.0%
[h]	36	25.0%	8	7.7%	3	18.7%
[ˢ]	36	25.0%	1	1.0%	0	0.0%
[s]	49	34.0%	69	66.3%	13	81.3%

higher rates than female speakers. Thus, although there is still variation among them, the female speakers demonstrate more stability than the male speakers in this study. These findings corroborate the findings of the majority of the UNAH theses, as most noted a more stable /s/ among females.

The data for Social Class (Tables 4.8 and 4.9) indicate similar findings to those for Age and Sex. That is, one group demonstrates greater within-group variation in the production of absolute-final /s/ than the other groups: the lower class. Specifically, multinomial regressions demonstrates that speakers from the lower class are more likely to delete, aspirate, and use a weakened [ˢ] than the upper class. Additionally, deletion is the primary realization of the middle class when not producing the full [s], and the middle class is more

VARIATION OF ABSOLUTE-FINAL /S/ 85

TABLE 4.9   Results of the multinomial logistic regression for Social Class. ">" indicates that the odds of producing the specific allophone over [s] are greater when compared to the reference category, "=" indicates odds are not different, "Ref." indicates the reference category for each independent variable

	Social Class		
Allophone	Lower	Middle	Upper
∅	>	>	Ref.
[h]	>	=	Ref.
[ˢ]	>	=	Ref.

TABLE 4.10   Distribution of allophones according to Education (*n* = 264)

	Education					
Allophone	Primary		Secondary		University	
	N	%	N	%	N	%
∅	20	19.0%	6	13.0%	23	20.3%
[h]	31	29.6%	6	13.0%	10	8.9%
[ˢ]	27	25.7%	9	19.6%	1	0.9%
[s]	27	25.7%	25	54.3%	79	69.9%

likely to delete than the upper class. Finally, is it of note that almost all tokens of weakened [ˢ] in this study were produced by the lower class speakers.

In the final comparison, Tables 4.10 and 4.11 illustrate the findings for the distribution of allophones according to Education. Once again, one group shows great variation among the four allophones, as those who finished Primary school vary between all four allophones at almost equal rates. Furthermore, those that only finished primary school were more likely to aspirate and use the weakened [ˢ] than those that finished University studies. As for those that finished Secondary school, the results reveal that they were more likely to use the weakened [ˢ], but less likely to delete than those in the University education group.

TABLE 4.11   Results of the multinomial logistic regression for Age. ">" indicates that the odds of producing the specific allophone over [s] are greater when compared to the reference category, "<" indicates that the odds of producing the specific allophone over [s] are lower when compared to the reference category, "=" indicates odds are not different, "Ref." indicates the reference category for each independent variable

	Education		
Allophone	Primary	Secondary	University
∅	=	<	Ref.
[h]	>	=	Ref.
[ˢ]	>	>	Ref.

5   Discussion

This study was designed to further our knowledge on the variation of /s/ in Tegucigalpa Spanish. Although the analysis presented here does not offer data from all 18 departments as Lipski (1986, 1987, 1990) and Hernández Torres (2010, 2013) have done, and therefore cannot corroborate the nation-wide claims set forth in those studies, it can be used to compare /s/ variation within Tegucigalpa. In addition, this study provides a more in-depth analysis of /s/ variation according to social factors that were not commonly considered before. As such, the research questions posed in Section 3 are revisited and the findings of this analysis are summarized here.

The first research question was concerning the current state of /s/ variation in Tegucigalpa Spanish in comparison to the previous work. Given that Lipski's work was carried out in the 1980s and Hernández Torres' work is from the early 2010s, an aim of this study was to provide an updated account of this phonetic phenomenon. However, both Lipski (1986, 1987, 1990) and Hernández Torres (2010, 2013) primarily focus on the effects of phonological contexts on /s/ variation and little attention is paid to social factors. Thus, a seamless comparison between these studies and the present is not completely feasible. Nonetheless, in general, data from both authors demonstrate that there is more /s/ variation in Tegucigalpa than in the rest of Honduras, and the results of this study demonstrate that there is still noteworthy /s/ variation in the capital. This variation is presented in Table 4.12. For this table, the data from Lipski (1987, 1990) only includes data from the same phonological context analyzed in this study, i.e.,

TABLE 4.12 Comparison of overall findings of /s/ variation in Tegucigalpa Spanish in Lipski (1987, 1990), Hernández Torres (2010, 2013), and the present study. Hernández Torres and the present study do not reach 100% because their data for the allophones [z], [ṣ], and [ṣ] are not reported in this table. Lipski (1987, 1990) does not report findings of [ˢ]

	Allophone			
Study	[s]	[ˢ]	[h]	∅
Lipski (1987, 1990)	65.70%	N/A	25.63%	8.67%
Hernández Torres (2010, 2013)	62.50%	7.14%	19.64%	5.35%
Present study	47.12%	13.31%	16.91%	17.63%

absolute-final position whereas the data from Hernández Torres (2010, 2013) is from across all phonological contexts, as he does not present a geographical by phonological context analysis of his data.

Overall, the data in Table 4.12 reveal that although there is general variation across all of these studies, [s] appears to be even less frequent in this study than in the previous studies. Moreover, aspiration of /s/, or [h], appears to be less common now than it was during Lipski's studies in the 1980s. The present study also indicates an overall higher rate of /s/ deletion than in the two previous studies. Although some of these differences are likely due to differences in methodologies between these three studies, these overall results suggest that Tegucigalpa Spanish may be moving closer towards Nicaraguan and Salvadoran Spanish, which predominantly reduce /s/ (Brogan, 2018; Chappell, 2021; Lipski, 1985).

If Tegucigalpa Spanish is indeed headed in this direction, the question becomes how and among whom this is happening. In terms of linguistic factors, both Lipski (1986, 1987, 1990) and Hernández Torres (2010, 2013) show that /s/ reduction is most common in preconsonantal and absolute-final position, though it is true for most varieties of Spanish (Bullock, Toribio & Amengual, 2014). Therefore, with these linguistic patterns in mind, the second research question sought to address which social factors might affect /s/ variation in Tegucigalpa Spanish. As this is one of the first studies to examine this phenomenon, it analyses some of the more common social variables in sociolinguistics: age, sex, social class, and education (Labov, 1972).

The findings for Age indicated that all three age groups maintained [s] about half of the time and several studies /s/ reduction by age in different varieties of Spanish have shown similar results (Labov, 2001, p. 86). Thus, the main differences for age was not whether or not they reduced /s/, but rather *how* they reduced it. When reducing /s/, the oldest group, ages 50+, primarily deleted whereas the other two groups demonstrated variation in possible phonetic realizations of reduced /s/. Specifically, the middle group, ages 31–50, predominantly aspirated when reducing whereas the youngest group, 18–30, reveals comparable variation among all three of the common realizations of reduced /s/ in this study: deletion, aspiration, and weakening. Thus, overall findings for age do not demonstrate a change to one specific allophonic realization of absolute-final /s/, but rather suggest an overall increase in /s/ variation.

Both Lipski (1986, 1987, 1990) and Hernández Torres (2010, 2013) found higher rates of aspiration than deletion, but the opposite was found here. In fact, in the previous studies, deletion was the least common of the four principal realizations analyzed. However, deletion was the second most common realization of /s/ found in this study, the first being full [s]. As deletion was less common among the middle age group than among the younger and older groups, it may indicate a "wave-like" generational motion of variation between /s/ aspiration, which was most common among the middle age group, and /s/ deletion (Labov, 2001, p. 77). Additionally, as deletion was high among the youngest group, this indicates a possible generational change, as these speakers had not been born during Lipski's data collection and were too young to participate in Hernández Torres' studies. Finally, the results for Age also suggest that the weakened [^{s}] is a newer allophonic variation in Tegucigalpa Spanish, as it is produced more by the two younger groups and is rare among the older group. This recent increase in [^{s}] would explain why it was not found in Lipski (1986, 1987, 1990) but was later noted in Hernández Torres (2010, 2013).

The findings for Sex are rather straightforward. Female speakers are more likely to maintain a full [s] whereas male speakers are more likely to aspirate or delete. Similar findings were mentioned in several UNAH theses. Within sociolinguistics in general, these results are not necessarily surprising. Cross-linguistically, females are more likely to use prestigious forms than males, and more likely to avoid stigmatized varieties than males (Labov, 2001). To our knowledge, no study on Honduran Spanish has quantitatively analyzed sociolinguistic perceptions of /s/ reduction, although anecdotal evidence suggests that /s/ reduction can be both stigmatized and prestigious, as in other varieties of Spanish (Bullock et al., 2014; Chappell, 2021; Lipski, 1990). Thus, future perception studies would help to corroborate this claim.

The findings for Social Class reveal a great degree of variation of absolute-final /s/ among speakers from the Lower Class: The only significant difference between the Upper and Middle Classes was that the Middle Class had a significantly higher probability of deletion. Lower Class speakers were more likely to delete, aspirate, and weaken than the Upper Class and more likely to aspirate and weaken than the Upper Class. As seen in Table 4.13, the Social Class findings from this study are comparable to those from Lipski (1990). Although limited to 16 speakers, the Upper Class participants from this study are on par with the Upper Class from Lipski (1990). The findings for the Middle Class only differ in how /s/ is reduced, with aspiration being more common in Lipski (1990) and deletion being more common here. These findings may be related to the overall findings in both studies, as aspiration was more common in Lipksi and deletion is more common in this study, suggesting again that deletion is generally becoming more common in Tegucigalpa Spanish.

Although both studies indicate that the Lower Class is most likely to reduce /s/, the rates of reduction are almost 20% higher in the present study than in Lipski (1990). Again, these results indicate the likelihood that Tegucigalpa Spanish is becoming more diverse in terms of /s/ variation and more prone to reduction. Finally, the variation, or lack thereof, of the weakened [s] in the present study is worth mentioning. In fact, all but one token of weakened [ˢ] in this analysis occurred among the Lower Class group. In other words, these data demonstrate that in Tegucigalpa Spanish, this newer allophonic variation of /s/ proposed by Hernández Torres (2010, 2013) has not only begun among the Lower Class of the city, it is still largely isolated to this class.

Finally, the results of Education demonstrate comparable instability in /s/ realizations in the Primary school group to the younger, male, and lower class

TABLE 4.13 Comparison of /s/ reduction by Social Class in Lipski (1990) and the present study. [ˢ] tokens were not gathered in Lipski (1990)

	Allophone			
	[s]	[ˢ]	[h]	∅
Lipski (1990)				
Upper Class	80.0%	N/A	16.7%	3.3%
Middle Class	63.7%	N/A	24.6%	11.7%
Lower Class	53.3%	N/A	35.6%	11.1%
Present study				
Upper Class	81.3%	0.0%	18.7%	0.0%
Middle Class	66.3%	1.0%	7.7%	25.0%
Lower Class	34.0%	25.0%	25.0%	16.0%

groups discussed above. Although some comparisons thus far have indicated that for some speaker groups, the sum of their different reduced realizations is greater than their rate of realizations of a full [s], the Primary school speakers are the only group in which a specific category of allophonic reduction occurred at a greater rate than tokens of [s]. That is to say, speakers that have only completed Primary school education are more likely to aspirate than to produce a full [s]. In fact, the speakers from this group even deleted /s/ at the same rate as [s]. Concerning those with Secondary school and University education, there is again a pattern of higher rates of deletion among the more prestigious group than among the group in the middle of the social hierarchy. Thus, the lower rates of deletion among the Secondary education group than the University studies group may suggest class aspiration (Labov, 1972) among the Secondary group, as they try to mimic the speech of the University studies group but miss the mark.

Overall, the results of this study indicate a greater degree of /s/ variation in Tegucigalpa Spanish that what was noted in previous studies (Hernández Torre, 2010, 2013; Lipski, 1986, 1987, 1990). However, although the amount of variation and possible phonetic realizations of /s/ are increasing, the data here does not indicate any movement towards a single allophonic realization of absolute-final /s/. Thus, it cannot be assumed that /s/ in Tegucigalpa is headed towards any completed sound change, but rather more variation. In other words, although social factors such as younger age, male, lower class, and primary education demonstrate significant within-group variation of /s/, this social-factor specific instability likely indicates that /s/ in Tegucigalpa Spanish demonstrates overall stable variation, which, as Labov (2001, p. 75) states, "is perhaps even more common than changes which go to completion".

6   Conclusions & Limitations

The data presented in this chapter corroborate previous claims set forth by Lipski (1985, 1986, 1987, 1990) and Hernández Torres (2010, 2013) concerning the abundant variation of /s/ in Tegucigalpa Spanish. Additionally, this study has shown which social factors are significant not only in the reduction of /s/, but also how it is reduced. Overall, the findings presented here demonstrate that not only is there is overall stable /s/ variation in Tegucigalpa Spanish, but that this variation appears to be becoming more diverse. These findings lead us to predict that the variation Tegucigalpa Spanish /s/ is demonstrating will only continue to become more heterogeneous in its possible phonetic realizations and social factors will continue to play an important role in this linguistic phenomenon.

Of course, the study presented in this chapter has its limitations. Although steps were taken to mitigate some of the disadvantages of a rapid anonymous survey, this method by design only collects the one token per speaker and, in different contexts, the same speaker may produce different allophones of /s/. Thus, the data presented in this paper should be viewed as an initial analysis to a phenomenon in this scantly studied variety of Spanish. As such, further, more in-depth explorations that include recording participants in order to acoustically analyze the continuous nature of /s/ variation in Tegucigalpa Spanish according to social factors are warranted. Additionally, it has been proposed here that many of the findings can be interpreted along expected sociolinguistic hierarchies. However, as mentioned above, the overall lack of perceptual sociolinguistic studies on Honduran Spanish have left us to assume that these hierarchies also hold true in Tegucigalpa. Following perceptual studies of different realizations of /s/ in Central American Spanish, such as Brogan et al. in neighboring El Salvador (this volume), future work can better determine if /s/ reduction is indeed stigmatized in Honduran Spanish or if it has taken on another social marker.

Appendix

TABLE 4.14 Lower and upper bounds of 95% Confidence Intervals (CI) for the main effects of the multinomial logistic regression

Social variable			Allophone					
		∅		[h]		[ˢ]		
	95% CI	Lower	Upper	Lower	Upper	Lower	Upper	
Age	18–30	0.069	1.066	0.318	11.428	1.267	10.881	
	31–50	0.051	0.812	1.528	19.103	1.165	6.716	
	51+	Ref.	Ref.	Ref.	Ref.	Ref.	Ref.	
Sex	Male	1.619	7.292	1.900	9.337	1.991	5.560	
	Female	Ref.	Ref.	Ref.	Ref.	Ref.	Ref.	
Social Class	Lower	2.456	15.386	0.140	5.843	3.146	17.981	
	Middle	6.854	6.917	0.051	1.388	0.989	1.041	
	Upper	Ref.	Ref.	Ref.	Ref.	Ref.	Ref.	
Education	Primary	1.810	17.284	1.739	16.906	4.971	35.864	
	Secondary	0.354	11.428	0.222	13.543	1.261	2.343	
	University	Ref.	Ref.	Ref.	Ref.	Ref.	Ref.	

References

Amastae, J. (1989). The intersection of s-aspiration/deletion and spirantization in Honduran Spanish. *Language Variation and Change*, *1*(2), 169–183. https://doi:10.1017/S0954394500000053.

Brogan, F. (2018). *Sociophonetically-based phonology: An Optimality Theoretic account of /s/ lenition in Salvadoran Spanish* [PhD dissertation, UCLA]. UCLA eScholarship. https://escholarship.org/uc/item/4277m7v9.

Bullock, B. E., Toribio, A. J., & Amengual, M. (2014). The status of *s* in Dominican Spanish. *Lingua*, *143*, 20–35. https://doi.org/10.1016/j.lingua.2014.01.009.

Canfield, D. L. (1990). El español de Honduras. In A. Herranz (Comp.) *El español hablado en Honduras* (pp 89–90). Editorial Guaymuras.

Chappell, W. (2021). /s/ weakening in Nicaragua. In E. Núñez-Méndez (Ed.) *Sociolinguistic Approaches to Sibilant Variation in Spanish* (pp. 213–241). Routledge.

Ellis, M., Groff, C., & Mead, R. (2006). A Rapid and Anonymous Study of /r/ Vocalization in an /r/ Pronouncing City. *University of Pennsylvania Working Papers in Linguistics*, *12*(1), 57–67. https://repository.upenn.edu/pwpl/vol12/iss1/6.

Galo Palma, K., & Maradiaga Funes, M. (2016). *La realización del fonema fricativo alveolar sordo /s/ en los municipios de Ojojona, Santa Ana, Santa Lucia y Valle de Ángeles del departamento de Francisco Morazán*. [Licenciatura thesis, Universidad Nacional Autónoma de Honduras].

Hernández Torres, R. A. (2010). Fonética del español de Honduras. In. M. A. Quesada Pachecho (Ed.) *El español hablado en América Central: Nivel fonético* (pp. 115–136). Vervuert.

Hernández Torres, R. A. (2013). *Atlas lingüístico pluridimensional de Honduras. Nivel fonético*. Bergen Language and Linguistic Studies.

Hualde, J. I. (2005). *The Sounds of Spanish*. Cambridge University Press.

Kanwit, M., Terán, V., & Pisabarro Sarrió, S. (2017). Un fenómeno bien curioso: New methods for analyzing variable intensification across four dialects of Spain and Argentina. *Studies in Hispanic and Lusophone Linguistics*, *10*(2), 259–295. https://doi.org/10.1515/shll-2017-0008.

Keating, P., Wright, R., & Zhang, J. (1999). Word-level asymmetries in consonant articulation. *UCLA Working Papers in Phonetics*, *97*, 157–173.

Labov, W. (1966). *The Social Stratification of English in New York City*. Center for Applied Linguistics.

Labov, W. (1972). *Sociolinguistic Patterns*. University of Pennsylvania.

Labov, W. (2001). *Principles of Linguistic Change: Volume 2, Social Factors*. Blackwell.

Lang-Rigal, J. (2020). Prosody perception meets language attitudes: Vowel lengthening, status judgments, and stereotypes in Argentina. In T. Bugel & C. Montes Alcalá (Eds.), *New Approaches to Language Attitudes in the Hispanic and Lusophone World* (pp. 12–38). John Benjamins. https://doi.org/10.1075/ihll.25.01lan.

Lipski, J. M. (1982). Filibustero: origin and development. *Journal of Hispanic Philology*, 6, 213–238.

Lipski, J. M. (1985). /s/ in Central American Spanish. *Hispania*, 68(1), 143–149. https://doi:10.2307/341630.

Lipski, J. M. (1986). Instability and Reduction of /s/ in the Spanish of Honduras. *Revista Canadiense de Estudios Hispánicos*, 11(1), 27–47.

Lipski, J. M. (1987). *Fonética y fonología del español de Honduras*. Editorial Guaymuras.

Lipski, J. M. (1990). Reducción de la /s/ en el español de Honduras. In A. Herranz (Comp.) *El español hablado en Honduras* (pp. 91–110). Editorial Guaymuras.

Matute Nájera, D. & Portillo Barahona, M. (2014). *La /s/ fricativa ápico alveolar (silbada) en el departamento de Olancho: Estudio dialectológico pluridimensional*. [Licenciatura thesis, Universidad Nacional Autónoma de Honduras].

Mariñas Otero, L. (1963). *Honduras*. Ediciones Cultura Hispánica.

Méndez Ávila, L. (2015). *Realización del fonema /s/ en el municipio de Soledad, El Paraíso, Honduras*. [Licenciatura thesis, Universidad Nacional Autónoma de Honduras].

Michnowicz, J. (2006). Final –m in Yucatan Spanish: A Rapid and Anonymous Survey. In J. P. Montreuil (Ed.), *New Perspectives on Romance Linguistics. Vol. 2: Phonetics, phonology, and dialectology: selected papers from the 35th Linguistic Symposium on Romance Languages* (pp. 155–166). John Benjamins. https://doi.org/10.1075/cilt.276.12mic.

Ramírez Enamorado, S. (2016). *Realización del fonema /S/ en los municipios de: Ilama Gualala, Santa Bárbara, Colinas y San Luis, departamento de Santa Bárbara*. [Licenciatura thesis, Universidad Nacional Autónoma de Honduras].

Ramos Molina, J. (2015). *La realización del fonema /s/ en los municipios de San Francisco y Erandique, departamento de Lempira Honduras*. [Licenciatura thesis, Universidad Nacional Autónoma de Honduras].

Rodríguez Zambrano, D. (2016). *La realización del fonema fricativo alveolar sordo /s/ en zonas fronterizas de Honduras: Goascorán, Valle, San Marcos de Colón y El Triunfo, Choluteca*. [Licenciatura thesis, Universidad Nacional Autónoma de Honduras].

Rubio Montes, E. (2017). *Realización del fonema fricativo alveolar sordo /s/ en el municipio de Santa Rita, departamento de Yoro*. [Licenciatura thesis, Universidad Nacional Autónoma de Honduras].

Sarkar, S. K., Midi, H. & Rana, S. (2011). Detection of Outliers and Influential Observations in Binary Logistic Regression: An Empirical Study. *Journal of Applied Sciences*, 11(1), 26–35. https://scialert.net/abstract/?doi=jas.2011.26.35.

Sauzo Martínez, S. (2016). *El fonema fricativo alveolar sordo /s/ en la ciudad de Comayagua*. [Licenciatura thesis, Universidad Nacional Autónoma de Honduras].

CHAPTER 5

Social Evaluations of Onset /s/ Lenition in Salvadoran Spanish

Franny D. Brogan, Lia Slotten and Juan Manuel Menjívar

1   Introduction

Lenition of /s/ is the most studied variable in Hispanic Linguistics. A majority of work has focused on weakening in the syllable coda (see, for example, Ventura & Baird [this volume]), where both debuccalization and deletion are pervasive in approximately half of Spanish dialects (Hammond, 2001). Almost all variationist in nature, the vast body of literature on coda /s/ weakening has worked to establish the linguistic and social factors that condition its usage. In recent years, in a move to represent /s/ weakening as gradient rather than segmental, scholars have also added several instrumental studies of coda /s/ weakening to this canon, focusing on measures such as duration, center of gravity, and percent voicelessness (e.g., Erker, 2010, 2012; File-Muriel & Brown, 2011; Univaso et al., 2014).

More recent work on Spanish /s/ has also begun to examine intervocalic voicing (e.g., Bárkányi, 2013; Chappell, 2011; Davidson, 2014; García, 2015; McKinnon, 2012). Voicing, while seldom treated as weakening in this literature, is often considered a manifestation of lenition. As Kirchner (2004, p. 313) explains, "This traditional classification is [...] justified for at least two reasons: (a) the pattern of voicing is similar to that of other lenition processes in terms of its contexts and conditions; and (b) voicing does in fact conform to the constriction reduction characterisation [...] upon a closer examination of the articulatory implementation of voiced vs. voiceless consonants."

In the Spanish of El Salvador, /s/ weakening takes many forms. In addition to debuccalization and deletion, Salvadoran /s/ variably undergoes voicing as well as gestural undershoot;[1] these latter processes, in contrast to the former

---

1 Work in Spanish dialectology has sometimes referred to an allophone of Salvadoran /s/ that is perceptually similar to [θ] (e.g., Azcúnaga López, 2010; Canfield, 1981; Hualde, 2005; Lipski, 1994). Brogan (2020) argues that this allophone is a lenited variant of /s/ in which the tongue approximates the articulatory target but fails to achieve the tight and sustained constriction required to produce a strident [s]. See Brogan (2020) for a comprehensive analysis of gesturally undershot [s̞] in Salvadoran Spanish.

two, occur almost exclusively in the syllable onset. Thus, in onset position, Salvadoran /s/ is commonly produced as one of three variants:[2] [s], [z], or [s̩]. In a large-scale production study of Salvadoran /s/, Brogan (2018) shows that [z] and [s̩] are conditioned by similar linguistic constraints and are employed by similar groups of speakers (lower SES, rural, and older speakers) with one exception: [z] is overwhelmingly preferred by men while [s̩] is preferred by women. The author proposes that the two variants are "different means to the same end: both serve to reduce effort cost while preserving important perceptual distinctions in strong prosodic positions" (Brogan, 2018, p. 279). While linguistic constraints are part of the story, a more comprehensive sociolinguistic analysis is required to tease apart the attested gender asymmetries.

Moreover, recent perceptual studies of intervocalic /s/ voicing have shown that the social meaning of this variable is highly dependent on the gender of the speaker (e.g., Chappell, 2016 in Costa Rica; García, 2019 in Ecuador). The present study thus endeavors to extend the experimental paradigms employed by Chappell and García to investigate what social meaning, if any, is indexed by onset /s/ lenition (both voicing and gestural undershoot) in El Salvador, and whether and how this meaning interacts with gender.

2   Sources of Social Meaning for [z] and [s̩]

2.1   *Voicing*

In dialects of Spanish in which /s/ voicing has been broadly observed, men have often been found to employ the [z] variant more than women (e.g., García, 2015; McKinnon, 2012), including in El Salvador (Brogan, 2018). Because speakers who are (biologically) male tend to have longer and thicker vocal folds (Beck, 1999), making glottal adduction harder to control, scholars have wondered whether this asymmetry could simply be an artifact of physiology and not socially motivated variation. In an effort to explore this question, File-Muriel et al. (2015, 2021) investigate the effects that oral cavity length and vocal fold size have on the production of Barranquilla Colombian /s/. The authors find that, while both gender and the physiological variables are robust predictors of center of gravity, only the latter is a significant predictor of voicelessness, suggesting that the individual physiology of a speaker—not gender-related social meaning—may better explain observed asymmetries in voicing.

---

2   We acknowledge, of course, that the phonetic properties that differentiate these sounds are inherently gradient. That said, continuous phonetics are perceived categorically, and we thus choose to treat these variants segmentally.

Given the well-established preference of the [z] variant by men cross-dialectically, the physiological explanation is a persuasive one. That said, in a similar study of Costa Rican /s/, Chappell and Garcia (2017) show that gender and oral cavity length are better predictors of voicing than vocal fold anatomy, calling into question whether a physiological argument alone suffices to explain the observed variation. Moreover, Chappell and Garcia (2017) argue that if men have a more difficult time quelling vocal fold vibrations, they should produce more gradient voicing, yet their data show quite the opposite. Men are, in fact, more categorical than women in their production of one variant or the either (i.e., [s] or [z]), suggesting that they "may be aiming for two completely different targets: full voicelessness and full voicing" (Chappell & Garcia 2017: 30–31) in the process of constructing social meaning. Crucially, the authors conclude that, "[i]f social meaning is indexed by a phonetic variant, its production becomes socially motivated rather than indicative of a physiological response" (33). In other words, it is likely that this variant originated as a function of biomechanics, but as it became a gender marker, was seized upon as a semiotic resource to create social meaning. Because social meaning is locally constructed, one of the primary goals of the present study is to discern whether [z] is, indeed, socially meaningful for Salvadoran speakers and listeners.

2.2 *Gestural Undershoot*

While less is known about the second non-standard variant examined in the present study, [s̬], its status as a hypoarticulated variant allows us to make predictions about its potential social meaning(s). As Eckert (2008) points out in an exhaustive review of the literature on English /t/,[3] the inherent physical differences between phonetic variants may affect their social evaluation. For example, the study of /t/ and its hyper- and hypoarticulated forms reveal social meanings that align with the physical characteristics of stop production. Hyperarticulation of /t/, in which the stop is released in word-medial or word-final positions, indexes clarity as well as emphaticness due to the increased effort required to produce the hyperarticulated form. Contrastingly, hypoarticulated /t/ is more commonly associated with "loutish types", thereby "lead[ing] us to a broader view of language ideology—the association of

---

3 Eckert's analysis of /t/ release in American English is based on a number of studies, including Bucholtz's (2001) work on nerd girls, Benor's (2001) work on Yeshiva-boys, and Podesva et al.'s (2002) work on gay speech. Since the publication of Eckert (2008), the body of literature examining released /t/ has expanded to include additional work such as Podesva et al.'s (2015) study of U.S. politicians.

hyperarticulation with care and hypoarticulation with laziness" (Eckert, 2008, p.468).

Similarly, research on the (ING) variable in English suggests that—even when two variants are not clearly hyper- or hypoarticulated—the perception that one is more effortful than the other has important implications for the characteristics they index: those who produce velar [-ɪŋ] are perceived as more educated as well as more precise and intentional, while those who produce alveolar [-ɪn] may be seen as uneducated, lazy, and inarticulate (Campbell-Kibler, 2007). In her discussion of these findings, Eckert emphasizes that "[c]entral to this perception is a view of the velar form as a full form and therefore effortful and the apical form as a reduced form, hence a sign of lack of effort. One might then presume that this lack of effort can be further construed as a result of laziness, not caring, or even rebellion, and by extension, impoliteness" (Eckert, 2008, p. 466–467).

Conceiving of hyperarticulated/full and hypoarticulated/reduced variants as mapping symbolically onto personal characteristics and stances offers a compelling explanation for the stigmatization of lenited variants crosslinguistically. Within the context of the present study, it is reasonable to posit that [s] and [s̪]—and [s] and [z], for that matter—exist in a relationship akin to other full and lenited variants, with the former allophones indexing qualities similar to released /t/ and /-ɪŋ/ (educated, precise, etc.) and the latter indexing qualities such as uneducated, lazy, and inarticulate.

3 Perceptual Work on Spanish /s/

Even as perception has been a focus of English sociophonetics for some time, it remains a burgeoning field within Hispanic Linguistics; sociophoneticians working on Spanish have been primarily occupied with production studies, which tend to illuminate the "what" but not necessarily the "why." As Chappell (2019, p. 1) explains in the introduction to her edited volume on Spanish sociophonetic perception, perception studies are particularly important in that they "provide a more nuanced understanding of a variant's social meaning in context". Indeed, despite the dearth of perceptual research in Spanish sociophonetics, the work that *has* been done on Spanish /s/ has shown that listeners are well attuned to sociophonetic cues, and that their perceptions serve to bolster our understanding of well-established production patterns.

The body of sociophonetic perception research on Spanish /s/ has evolved over time from studies primarily focused on cross-dialectal processing of coda weakening (e.g., Boomershine, 2005, 2006; Figueroa, 2000; Hammond, 1978;

Schmidt, 2013) to those interested in the social meaning(s) indexed by different variants, usually [s], [h], and [∅]. In one of the first studies to investigate the social evaluation of Spanish /s/, Walker et al. (2014) examine how the social meanings of word-internal coda /s/ weakening differ based on the dialect (/s/-retaining Mexican vs. /s/-weakening Puerto Rican) of both the listener and the speaker. The authors find that, while ratings for status are similar across groups, both the listener's dialect and gender affect the social evaluation of /s/ debuccalization for ratings of heteronormativity. That is, while Puerto Ricans and Mexican men rate [s] as significantly less heteronormative than [h], Mexican women find [s] more heteronormative; the authors suggest that, as the variant [s] is associated with higher social status and gay speech,[4] it likely also indexes effortfulness, a quality that men avoid. Instead, they may favor the nonstandard variant to index qualities such as solidarity with the working class, masculinity, and heteronormativity.

In a departure from examining perceptions of /s/ debuccalization and deletion, Chappell (2016) investigates listener perceptions of intervocalic /s/ voicing in Costa Rican Spanish. The author shows that men who produce [z] intervocalically are perceived as significantly nicer, more confident, more Costa Rican, and more masculine than those who produce [s], while there is no effect, positive or negative, for female speakers. For both genders, however, the [z] variant indexes lower socioeconomic status and lower educational attainment. Faced with these differences, Chappell argues that men are able to access the covert prestige of intervocalic voicing and therefore benefit from its use despite negative socioeconomic associations; women, contrastingly do not stand to gain anything from use of the nonstandard variant and therefore choose to employ the standard [s]. Chappell's findings make a particularly good case for the importance of pairing work in production and perception: while numerous studies have shown that men voice /s/ at higher rates than women cross-dialectically, only an investigation of the social meaning of this variable can begin to explain the "whys" behind these findings.

Finally, in a study akin to Chappell's, García (2019) explores listener perceptions of intervocalic /s/ voicing in Loja, Ecuador. Distinct from Chappell, García finds that female speakers are rated significantly lower for social status when producing the non-standard [z] variant, while male speakers experience no such effect. Moreover, female speakers who use the [z] variant are rated as significantly less pleasant and significantly younger than those who

---

4   In a previous study examining the relationship between perceived sexual orientation and Spanish coda /s/, Mack (2011) shows that listeners expect gay-sounding men to produce the full sibilant [s] and experience the deletion of [s] by gay-sounding men as incongruous.

use [s], while there is again no variant effect for men. Thus, while Chappell finds that her Costa Rican male speakers benefit from use of [z] in that they are judged more favorably for a number of characteristics relating to solidarity, it appears that in Ecuador, "it is only females' use of intervocalic [z] that is socially charged, whereas males' use is not strongly associated with any of the social characteristics examined" (García, 2019, p. 125).

4 The Role of Context in Listener Assessment

Previous work in sociophonetic perception—on Spanish /s/ and otherwise— has also illuminated the role of context in listener assessment. While the sociolinguistic predictors of /s/ production are well-established, both Walker et al. (2014) and Schmidt (2013) show that listener perceptions of /s/ are often nuanced and complex. That is, regional and/or social evaluations of /s/ are not identical amongst listeners who themselves speak distinct dialects (i.e., /s/-maintaining vs. /s/-weakening) or otherwise occupy different social realms. Instead, factors such as gender and contact with speakers of other Spanish dialects affect both participants' ability to perceive variants accurately and their assignment of social meanings to variants of /s/. Fundamentally, examining the social characteristics of listeners is crucial to interpreting their social evaluations of speakers.

Just as the meaning indexed by a given variant depends on the social positioning of the listener, assignment of meaning to that variant may be further affected by the listener's assumptions about a given speaker's social identity. Campbell-Kibler (2009) demonstrates that, when general U.S. English speakers are perceived as *non*-working-class, there is no difference in intelligence ratings for different variants of (ING). However, when speakers are perceived as working-class, speaker intelligence ratings are significantly higher when they produce the velar variant [-ɪŋ] as opposed to [-ɪn]. These asymmetries show that the (ING) variable does not contribute uniformly to the construction of speakers' social identities, but rather hinges upon the perceived socioeconomic status of the speaker.

In a study that illuminates the crucial interaction of the social positioning of the listener and assumptions about speaker identity, Barnes (2019) examines the perceptions of word-final [o] (standard in Spanish and typically associated with urban speakers) and word-final [u] (standard in Asturian and typically associated with rural speakers) among bilingual speakers. When asking listeners to categorize stimuli that sit on an acoustic continuum from [o] to [u], Barnes finds that listeners who both see a photo of an urban male *and* report that they are in favor of the co-official status of Asturian and Spanish are significantly more likely to categorize acoustically ambiguous stimuli as [o]. The author posits that those in favor of co-official status have a more sophisticated understanding of the Asturian/Spanish distinction and are thus more aware of the social characteristics (e.g., rural vs. urban, respectively) associated with each.

Finally, the saliency of a given linguistic variant has been shown to affect the social indexicality of phonetic cues. Barnes (2015), for example, finds differences between the responses of Spanish and Asturian speakers to two distinct morphophonemic features in the contact language of Asturian Spanish (vowel raising of /o/ → [u] and /as/ → [es]). She posits that the source of this inequality lies in differing social salience of the variables; specifically, the appearance of an [u] where the masculine singular morpheme [-o] is expected is more surprising to listeners than the alternate feminine plural morpheme, [es]. (That is, because [-es] is found in Spanish as a plural marker and verbal morpheme, its appearance at the end of a word is not entirely unexpected.) Barnes hypothesizes that the heightened cognitive salience of [u] leads to increased social salience and facilitates a strong indexical linkage.

5 Methodology

Following Chappell (2016), the present study employs a variation of the well-established matched guise paradigm. Originally pioneered by Lambert et al. (1960), matched guise experiments ask participants to listen to a series of recordings and rate speakers, or *guises*, according to several qualities and characteristics. Crucially, each speaker contributes multiple stimuli to the experiment; these stimuli vary only with respect to the variable in question. As Kircher (2016, p. 198) explains, participants "listen to the recordings, unaware of the fact that they are hearing the same speakers more than once, in matched guises. (They are "matched" in the sense that the speaker and the semantic content of the text delivered by the speaker are the same each time—the only difference is the variety in which the speaker delivers that text.)". The forthcoming sections describe our experimental design in more detail.

5.1 *Stimuli*

Stimuli for this experiment are taken from a storybook retelling task conducted by the first author in El Salvador in 2015. Following a 45–60-minute sociolinguistic interview, speakers were asked to provide an oral narration of a wordless children's storybook, *Chalk* by Bill Thomson (Thomson 2010), chosen based on the frequent occurrence of images whose phonological representations contained /s/ in various prosodic positions and phonological environments. All speakers were native Salvadorans balanced for region, urbanicity, age, and gender. They were recorded in quiet environments using an Olympus LS-14 Linear PCM recorder digitized at 44 kHz using a 16-bit quantization with an Audiotechnica ATR 3350 lapel microphone. Six speakers (three women and three men) were chosen to contribute stimuli to the present study; all were between 18 and 41 years old at the time of recording and lived in rural areas in the western and eastern regions of the country.

Of course, the use of naturalistic speech data prompts a number of additional complications and considerations. For example, because the semantic content of the evaluated speech could potentially influence perceptions and should thus be as neutral as possible, we chose stimuli that employed colloquial language and were primarily descriptive (i.e., devoid of emotion and personal opinion). Moreover, because Salvadoran Spanish speakers frequently weaken /s/ in coda position, we tried to choose stimuli in which the only coda /s/s were those that occurred word-medially before /t/, a context in which Salvadorans of all social groups almost categorically produce overt [s] (Brogan 2018). We did this to ensure that listeners were not basing their evaluations on other socially meaningful variants. Finally, because each stimulus would be played three different times throughout the course of the experiment, we chose sentences that were unremarkable in form (e.g., speech rate, voice quality) and similar to one another in content so as to not draw attention to the repetitions.

Once stimuli had been selected, canonical tokens of [s], [z], and [ṣ] were extracted for each of the six speakers from the same narrative retelling. Three versions of each stimulus were then created: one with [s] spliced in for all occurrences of onset /s/, one with [z] spliced in for all occurrences, and one with [ṣ]. Splicing was carried out in Praat (Boersma & Weenink 2020), where the intensity of spliced segments was also manipulated to match that of the host recording. One native speaker of Salvadoran Spanish and two near-native speakers with formal training in linguistics judged the stimuli to be natural-sounding.

In addition to the experimental stimuli, four other sentences were included: two fillers and two practice items. These four items were produced by speakers whose demographics matched those of the speakers of the experimental stimuli and contained a small number of unmanipulated tokens of onset /s/ realized as [s], [z], or [ṣ]. No tokens of [h] or [∅] appeared in practice or filler items.

The next section describes the survey design in more detail.

5.2 Survey Design

All stimuli were uploaded to Qualtrics, an online survey platform that is easily accessible regardless of a user's location or device type. After providing informed consent and completing two practice items (excluded from the forthcoming analyses), listeners were told they would hear 38 different speakers in total from three different families; this was the combined number of test guises, 36, and fillers, two. This was done in order to minimize any suspicion about the similarity between guises in the survey.

Guises were presented in a pseudorandom order. First, an alternating set of male and female speakers were coupled together. This ensured that the same speaker would never appear twice in a row in any randomized iteration. Then, either four or five couples of speakers were grouped together and set to be randomly presented to each listener. Variants of /s/ ([s], [z], [s̪]) were also evenly distributed across groups of ten, with the number of each being +/-1 of the others in that group. The fillers appeared within two separate sets of ten and were placed in such a way as to fit into the male-female alternation. See Appendix for an illustration of survey flow.

Listeners were instructed to listen to each stimulus and then rate the speaker on a scale from 1–7 according to a set of social characteristics thought to be associated with Spanish /s/, adapted from Walker et al. (2014) and Chappell (2016): *de clase baja/de clase alta* 'low/high class', *menos educada/muy educada* 'less educated/very educated', *insegura de sí misma/segura de sí misma* 'not confident/confident', *antipática/simpática* 'unkind/kind', *definitivamente heterosexual/definitivamente homosexual* 'definitely heterosexual/definitely homosexual', *menos masculina/muy masculina* 'less/more masculine',[5] *menos salvadoreña/muy salvadoreña* 'less/more Salvadoran', *menos campesina/muy campesina* 'less/more rural'. Listeners were also asked to guess the age of the speaker; they were given seven options to choose from: 15–19, 20–24, 25–29, 30–34, 35–39, 40–44, and 45+. Finally, they were asked if there was anything else they noticed about the speaker. Figure 5.1 shows a sample page from the experiment.

Once listeners had heard and rated all 40 stimuli, we collected their demographic information and solicited additional comments about the study as a whole. In reviewing the responses of listeners, we noted that a few observed the repetition of audio clips. That said, this observation did not have any effect on their speaker ratings—no two matched guises were rated identically by

---

5 While previous studies have used *femenina* 'feminine' for female voices, we were interested in whether use of [z] made female voices sound more masculine, not simply less feminine. In retrospect, however, this approach was problematic; its limitations are discussed in Section 8.

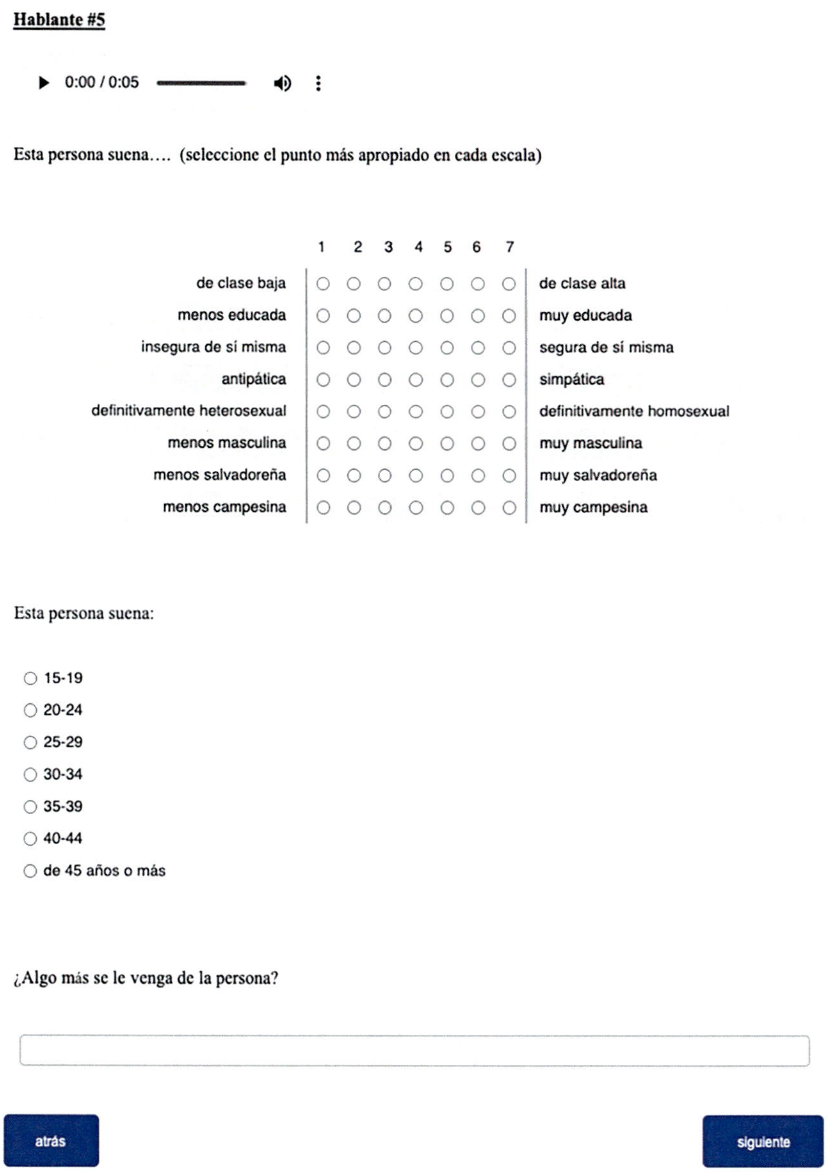

Hablante #5

▶ 0:00 / 0:05 ────── 🔊 ⋮

Esta persona suena…. (seleccione el punto más apropiado en cada escala)

	1	2	3	4	5	6	7	
de clase baja	○	○	○	○	○	○	○	de clase alta
menos educada	○	○	○	○	○	○	○	muy educada
insegura de sí misma	○	○	○	○	○	○	○	segura de sí misma
antipática	○	○	○	○	○	○	○	simpática
definitivamente heterosexual	○	○	○	○	○	○	○	definitivamente homosexual
menos masculina	○	○	○	○	○	○	○	muy masculina
menos salvadoreña	○	○	○	○	○	○	○	muy salvadoreña
menos campesina	○	○	○	○	○	○	○	muy campesina

Esta persona suena:

○ 15-19
○ 20-24
○ 25-29
○ 30-34
○ 35-39
○ 40-44
○ de 45 años o más

¿Algo más se le venga de la persona?

[   ]

[atrás]   [siguiente]

FIGURE 5.1   Screenshot of evaluation matrix (adapted from Chappell, 2016 and Walker et al., 2014)

the same listener. As Chappell (2016) notes, it would be unlikely that even a listener who noticed a speaker or clip repeating would also recall what their exact ratings were in a previous manipulation. No listeners noted that there was a change in /s/ for any such repetitions.

5.3 *Listeners*

Listeners were recruited via social media and contacts of the first and third authors in El Salvador. All but three of the listeners lived in El Salvador at the time of participation and had never lived elsewhere; three listeners were currently residing in the United States but were born in El Salvador and had lived there for more than half of their lives. Upon comparing the responses of these three listeners with those still residing in El Salvador, no clear differences were identified. Table 5.1 summarizes demographic data for our 104 listeners.

TABLE 5.1   Listener demographics

Mean age/standard deviation	23.04/7.22
Age range in years	18–68
Male, female (*n*)	55, 49
Occupation (*n*)	Student (91), engineer (2), teacher (2), food service (1), motorist (1), retired (1), supervisor (1), biologist (1), other or unspecified (4)
Region of origin	West (3), Central (94), East (1), other or unspecified (6)
Total listeners	104

5.4 *Statistical Analyses*

Following Chappell (2016), we first centered and scaled the 7-point age ratings using z-scores such that they would be comparable with the social evaluation measures. We executed this transformation in R (R Core Team 2020) using the 'scale' function. We then conducted a factor analysis which assumes that, for some collection of variables, there exists an additional set of underlying variables (or *factors*) that explain variation in the data while also capturing the interrelatedness of said variables. Using R's 'factanal' function, we identified three factors whose loadings (that is, the response variables that comprise them) aligned almost identically with Chappell's. The first (which, following Chappell, we refer to as the "status" factor) is composed of the variables of social class, level of education, and Salvadoraness. Crucially, while higher ratings of social class are positively correlated with higher ratings for education, lower ratings for Salvadoraness contribute to the status factor. In other words, speakers who were rated higher for class and education were also rated as less Salvadoran. This finding diverges from previous perceptual work on Spanish /s/ and will be discussed in more detail in Section 7.

The second factor, dubbed the "positive social features" factor, is composed of the variables of niceness and confidence. This factor loading is also identical to that of Chappell with the exception of the localness variable (Costa Ricanness contributed positively to Chappell's positive social features factor).

TABLE 5.2   Factor loadings

Status factor		Positive social features factor		Gendered factor	
High class	0.76	Very confident	0.73	Very masculine	1.00
Very educated	0.56	Very nice	0.67		
Very Salvadoran	−0.38				

Finally, again in line with Chappell, the third factor is a "gendered factor" composed of the sole attribute of masculinity. Neither age nor sexuality mapped onto any of the three factors; uniqueness scores[6] for these variables were 0.94 and 0.98, respectively. Finally, ruralness was ultimately excluded from the analysis because various listeners appeared to have accidentally inverted the scale,[7] and it was impossible to be sure of how many other listeners did the same; this limitation will be discussed in more detail in Section 8. Table 5.2 shows the loading variables and correlation coefficients for each factor.

Finally, taking the three aforementioned factors as our new dependent variables, we ran a series of linear mixed effects regressions in which both 'speaker' and 'listener' were included as random effects. All models began with the same eight fixed effects, and p values were obtained through model testing via the 'Anova' function. Variables that that did not contribute significantly to a given model were subsequently removed. Main effects tested included allophone of /s/, listener gender, speaker gender, and listener age, and interaction effects included listener gender by allophone, speaker gender by allophone, listener age by allophone, and listener gender by speaker gender by allophone. All models were constructed in R and plots were created using the ggplot2 package (Wickham 2016).

6   Results

In this section we present results for two of the three factors described in the previous section: the status factor and the positive social features factor. The only significant effect obtained for the gendered factor was speaker gender

---

[6]   A variable's uniqueness refers to "the variance that is 'unique' to the variable and not shared with other variables. It is equal to 1—communality (variance that is shared with other variables)" (Torres-Reyna n.d.: 3).

[7]   There were various instances in the data in which participants commented that a guise sounded rural yet rated that same guise low on the ruralness variable.

itself ($X \chi^2$ (1, N = 3744) = 57.6438, p < .001); in other words, listeners did not appear to separate masculinity from biological sex. This model is thus not discussed further in this section, although weaknesses in survey design that may have led to this underwhelming result are addressed in Section 8. Each model is based on 3,744 total observations and takes one of the two aforementioned factors as its dependent variable; each factor ranges in value from approximately -3 to 3. All independent variables are categorical except for age, which is analyzed continuously.

6.1 The Status Factor

The first factor identified in the factor analysis, the status factor, is composed of *class*, *education*, and *Salvadoraness*. As a reminder to the reader, Salvadoraness is negatively correlated with both class and education in this factor. The best fit model for this factor includes allophone of /s/, speaker gender, listener age, and the interaction between listener age and allophone. No significant effects obtained for listener gender, listener gender by allophone, speaker gender by allophone, or listener gender by speaker gender by allophone. The output of this model is summarized in Table 5.3.

The model presented in Table 5.3 reveals that allophone is the best predictor of status ratings. While both [z] and [ṣ] garner significantly lower ratings than [s], the effect is much larger for the latter allophone.

TABLE 5.3 Linear mixed effects model for the status factor[a]

	β (coefficient)	*t* value	*p* value
Intercept	0.43	2.26	*
Allophone			**
[s]	Ref	–	–
[z]	-0.38	-2.42	*
[ṣ]	-0.72	-4.59	***
Speaker gender			*
Female	Ref	–	–
Male	0.22	2.07	*
Listener age	-0.13	-2.02	*
Listener age x allophone			*
Listener age x [s]	Ref	–	–
Listener age x [z]	0.01	1.74	0.08
Listener age x [ṣ]	0.01	2.89	**

a *p* values for the predictors themselves were obtained via the 'Anova' function.
*p < .05; **p < .01; ***p < .001. Dashes indicate reference level of variable.

SOCIAL EVALUATIONS OF ONSET /S/ LENITION 107

With respect to speaker gender, men garner significantly higher status ratings regardless of allophone used. While the interaction between speaker gender and allophone was not significant and is thus excluded from the model, differences in ratings are nevertheless notable in that they are largest for [z] and smallest for [ṣ]. These data are visualized in Figure 5.2.

In other words, the "default" benefit in status that men get just for being men is boosted when producing [z] and (almost) neutralized when producing [ṣ].

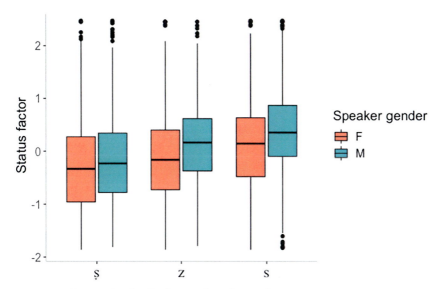

FIGURE 5.2 Status ratings by allophone and speaker gender

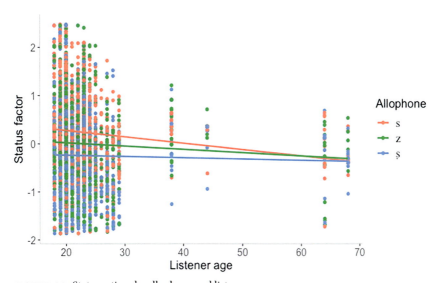

FIGURE 5.3 Status ratings by allophone and listener age

With respect to age, older listeners rate speakers lower overall, although this effect alone is relatively small. Perhaps more importantly, a significant interaction effect between listener age and allophone is obtained for [ʂ]: while older listeners rate stimuli with all three variants approximately the same for status, ratings for [s] and [z] improve among younger listeners while ratings for [ʂ] stay about the same. Figure 5.3 shows ratings for the status factor on the y-axis against listener age on the x-axis for each allophone. While the line for [ʂ] is flat, the lines for both [s] and [z] slope upward as they move from older to younger listeners. The slope of the former is steeper than that of the latter, indicating that the [s] > [z] > [ʂ] status hierarchy is most pronounced among the youngest listeners.

6.2 Positive Social Features Factor

The second factor identified in the factor analysis, the positive social features factor, is composed of *niceness* and *confidence*. The best fit model for this factor includes listener gender, speaker gender, and listener age. No significant effects obtained for allophone of /s/, listener gender by allophone, speaker gender by allophone, listener age by allophone, or listener gender by speaker gender by allophone. Crucially, neither allophone nor its interaction with any other variables is included in this model, whose output is summarized in Table 5.4.

The positive social features model reveals that, similar to status, men garner higher ratings regardless of allophone produced. Unlike status, however, male listeners also rate speakers significantly lower than female listeners regardless

TABLE 5.4 Linear mixed effects model for the positive social features factor[a]

	β (coefficient)	*t* value	*p* value
Intercept	0.21	1.05	0.30
Listener gender			*
Female	Ref	–	–
Male	−0.25	−2.20	*
Speaker gender			*
Female	Ref	–	–
Male	0.11	1.99	*
Listener age	−0.02	−2.128	*

a *p* values for the predictors themselves were obtained via the 'Anova' function.
*$p < .05$; **$p < .01$; ***$p < .001$. Dashes indicate reference level of variable.

of both allophone produced and speaker gender. Listener age is again significant: older listeners rate speakers lower overall.

6.3   Perceived Age, Status, and Positive Social Features

While perceived speaker age was excluded from the factor analysis due to its high uniqueness score, it nevertheless reveals an interesting interaction between the status and positive social features factors, as visualized in Figure 5.4.

In Figure 5.4, we see that status—while highest for [s] and lowest for [ṣ] on average—follows a similar trajectory regardless of allophone: status declines at a similar rate as the speaker's perceived age increases. This, of course, simply tells us that speakers perceived as older are also perceived as having lower status overall. What is more striking in Figure 5.4 is the trajectory of the positive social features factor. That is, while positive social features increase with age for all allophones, the increase is greatest for [ṣ], the most stigmatized of the three variants, and smallest for [s], the standard variant. In other words, speakers perceived as older get a "boost" in positive social features when they use non-standard variants (particularly [ṣ]), while speakers perceived as younger experience no such effect. These findings are discussed in more detail in the following section.

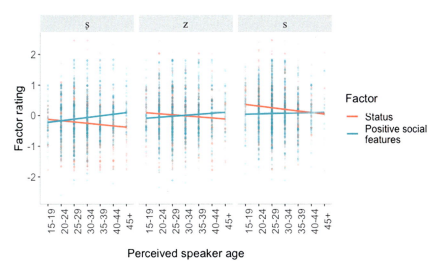

FIGURE 5.4 Perceived speaker age by allophone and factor type

7 Discussion

The preceding sections have both elucidated patterns previously observed in production data and unearthed new findings with respect to onset /s/ variation in El Salvador. In this section, we discuss four key findings from the present study and their implications.

7.1 *On the Status of [z] and [ṣ]*

Production studies have hypothesized that the Salvadoran onset /s/ variants of [s], [z], and [ṣ] exist in a hierarchy of sorts. Brogan (2018), for example, proposes that both [z] and [ṣ] serve to reduce the effort cost of the voiceless strident [s], a sound that requires particular precision in the oral cavity as well as sustained glottal abduction, in salient prosodic positions in which debuccalization and deletion are too perceptually costly. However, participant remarks in Brogan's sociolinguistic interviews suggest that [ṣ] is stigmatized while [z] remains a marker (Labov 1972),[8] and the findings of the present study corroborate these claims. That is, [ṣ] receives by far the lowest ratings for status, confirming its position at the bottom of the hierarchy, and [z] is also rated significantly lower for status than [s] (albeit higher than [ṣ]), suggesting that listeners are at least unconsciously aware of this variant and its association with non-standard speech.

While no interaction effect obtained for allophone by speaker gender, it is possible that—for biomechanical reasons discussed in Section 2.1—[z] has become associated with male speakers in the community and thereby indexes a higher social status than [ṣ] regardless of who uses it. This is reminiscent of Chappell's (2016) finding that women and men both suffer in status evaluations when using [z] (as compared to [s]), and in contrast with García (2019), who finds that women are rated significantly lower for status when employing this variant. These disparate findings remind us that "some social meanings are global and shared between dialects, while others are local" (García 2019, p. 147). The following sections explore other local meanings of /s/ in El Salvador.

---

8 Labov (1972) differentiates between *stereotypes* (features that have become the subject of overt commentary by members of the speech community) and *markers* (features whose use correlates with social groups and speech styles but are not subject to overt commentary). Crucially, speakers and listeners are thought to be unconsciously aware of markers as well as their group associations.

7.2 *Evidence for Change from above*

In a large-scale production study of Salvadoran /s/, Brogan (2018) hypothesizes that the Salvadoran dialect—once relatively isolated (Lipski, 1994)—is undergoing rapid standardization as the result of a confluence of factors including urbanization, migration, and globalization. If true, this shift would represent a change from above in which "the new element is imported from some external language or dialect. [...] Changes from above usually involve superficial and isolated features of language" (Labov, 2010, p. 185). As /s/ weakening is typically a salient and stigmatized feature in the dialects in which it persists, a move away from non-standard variants among some social groups would be a reasonable effect of dialect contact and access to education (see McKinnon [this volume] for another example of the effect of increased access to education on standardization), both of which have increased substantially in recent years (see Brogan [2018] and Brogan & Yi [2022] for a more substantive discussion of these forces).

We argue that the data obtained in the present study provide further evidence for a change in progress, particularly with respect to [ş]. That is, while older listeners rate all three variants approximately the same for status, a clear hierarchy emerges among younger listeners: [s] has the most status, followed by [z], followed by [ş]. We propose that, because the broad stigmatization of non-[s] variants in El Salvador is relatively recent, it is less potent among older speakers, and the three variants thus garner similar ratings from that cohort.

Moreover, we find that speakers perceived as older benefit from use of [ş] (and, to some extent, [z]) as compared to [s]. That is, while speakers who produce [s] are rated more or less the same along the positive social features dimension regardless of perceived age, ratings increase for "older" guises who use [z] and even more so for those who use [ş]. In other words, while all groups suffer from a loss of overt prestige (operationalized as the status factor) when using the non-standard variants, "older" speakers access covert prestige when producing [z] and [ş]; no such effect is observed for younger speakers. We argue that this asymmetry is a function of expectations: Salvadorans are aware of both the move away from stigmatized productions of /s/ (as is typical in change from above) and the rapid rate at which El Salvador as a society is changing; they therefore do not (necessarily) expect older generations to be participating in this change. When speakers perceived as younger use these non-standard variants, however, it feels unnatural and perhaps even inauthentic, preventing them from benefiting from any covert prestige indexed by these forms.

7.3 The Gender Gap

We remind the reader that one of the goals at the outset of the present study was to tease apart the relationship between onset /s/ lenition and gender. Production studies have shown a preference for [z] among male Salvadorans and a preference for [s̺] among women, and similar studies in both Costa Rica (Chappell, 2016) and Ecuador (García, 2019) have identified important gender-based asymmetries with respect to intervocalic [s] versus [z]. However, gender differences identified in the present study were, unfortunately, unrelated to /s/. Instead, we found that men garnered significantly higher ratings along both the status and positive social feature dimensions regardless of allophone produced.

These findings, while not what we expected, echo Brogan and Yi's (2022) conclusions that women in El Salvador—for reasons not within the scope of this paper—suffer from a disproportionate lack of social status and opportunity as compared to other countries in Central America (and Latin America as a whole). This "gender gap" may explain, at least in part, why women are so much more likely to employ the [s̺] variant despite its high stigma: if perceptions of both status and solidarity are fixed regardless of linguistic production, what deters women from employing the most phonetically natural variant of /s/? As a voiceless strident, [s] requires precise lingual articulation as well as sustained glottal abduction and is thus highly effortful (Kirchner, 2004). While men may mitigate this effort cost by foregoing glottal abduction—a natural remedy given the increased difficulty of controlling voicing for those with longer vocal tracts and thicker vocal folds—women may instead choose to undershoot the lingual gesture, resulting in [s̺].

While not statistically significant, it is worth noting that differences in status ratings between gender groups are the largest for [z] and smallest for [s̺], suggesting that men may benefit from producing the former and suffer from employing the latter. This finding, if corroborated with more data, could help explain the significant differences in gender-based production of these allophones.

7.4 A Local Meaning of Localness

The assumption in sociolinguistics has long been that vernacular variants are linked to local norms and values and thus carry covert prestige, and Chappell's (2016) work on the social meaning of /s/ voicing confirms as much: sounding more Costa Rican loads into her solidarity factor. In the present study, however, Salvadoraness contributed not to our positive social features factor but instead to status, as sounding "more Salvadoran" negatively correlated with both higher class and higher education ratings. We believe that this finding is curious and worth briefly addressing.

As detailed above, El Salvador is undergoing rapid social changes and is a much different place than it was just a few generations ago. For this reason, we posit that a bifurcation of society—a new El Salvador and an old—might lead listeners to perceive some of their fellow Salvadorans as "others."[9] This hypothesis is supported by the qualitative data, obtained via the optional open response sections provided for each guise. For example, while 87% of our listeners are from the central region of the country, speakers were sometimes described as sounding like they were from San Miguel, the largest region in the eastern part of the country and one of the poorest in all of El Salvador. Other unsolicited regional assessments—never in reference to where the listener him/her/themself was from—were not uncommon, and always accompanied production of the [ʂ] variant. While it is true, of course, that linguistic variants are often associated with particular geographical regions, production data show that age, urbanicity, and gender are, in fact, better predictors of [ʂ] production than region (Brogan, 2018). Particularly because our listener pool skewed young, we hypothesize that listeners heard productions of [ʂ] (and [z], to some extent) as part of an El Salvador that feels separate from their own Salvadoraness. Acutely aware of the changes that have taken place since their grandparents were their age, these listeners may associate low socioeconomic status and educational attainment with this "other" El Salvador, leading to a moderate negative correlation between ratings for Salvadoraness and those for more traditional status variables.

8 Conclusion

The primary goal of the present study was to investigate what social meaning, if any, is indexed by two variants of onset /s/ in Salvadoran Spanish: [z] and [ʂ]. Because production of these variants is highly gendered, we expected perceptions to also interact with gender in some way. Instead, we found that gender was only significant in that male guises were rated more favorably than female guises for all social characteristics, regardless of which variant they employed. That said, findings beyond gender provided both empirical confirmation of the

---

9 We remind the reader that our listeners are relatively young (mean age = 23), a fact that lends additional credence to the idea that they are responding to certain variants as something "other" Salvadorans do.

allophonic hierarchy of onset /s/ and additional evidence that a change from above is currently in progress.

A fundamental difference between production and perception studies is that, for the former, the heavy lifting occurs after data collection takes place; for the latter, the most important work takes place beforehand. As this ordering can make it difficult to identify weaknesses in a perception study until data has already been collected and analyzed, the present study has a number of limitations. First, ratings for ruralness were uniquely problematic in that a majority of the qualities listed on the right-hand side of the survey were positive, while sounding more rural (also located on the right) was perceived negatively by our listeners, as illustrated in some free responses. For this reason, it is possible that some listeners conceived of everything on the right as "better" and everything on the left as "worse," thereby inverting the scale for ruralness. It should be noted that the only other variable set up in this way was sexuality ('more homosexual' was on the right); while no listeners explicitly commented on sexuality in their free responses, ratings were so idiosyncratic that this variable was ultimately excluded from the factor analysis, suggesting that its scale, too, may have been inverted by some listeners. Future studies might consider alternating positive versus negative alignment for variables and/or instituting a comprehension check in which listeners must show that they understand the set-up of the social evaluation matrix.

A second limitation related to survey design relates to the use of the word *masculino* to mean 'masculine.' That is, while maleness and masculinity are separate (albeit related) ideas with their own lexical forms in English, Spanish *masculino* is used to mean both 'male' and 'masculine.' Moreover, it is highly likely that discussions about the differences between biological sex and gender expression/performance are much less prevalent in El Salvador, leading listeners to conflate masculinity with maleness. Future studies might consider replacing *masculino* with an alternate word such as *macho* in order to minimize this conflation.

Finally, the young skew of our listeners pool had both benefits and drawbacks. On the one hand, the demographics of our listeners are similar to those of both Chappell (2016) and García (2019), allowing us to make more direct comparisons with their findings. However, particularly given our hypotheses about change from above, it would have been valuable to garner more perspectives from older Salvadorans. While university-based recruitment is convenient, future studies on sociophonetic perception (and sociolinguistics in general) should make an effort to reach a more representative participant pool so as to avoid potential biases in their data.

Appendix

Speaker Asignment

Pseudonym	Token	Allophone	Speaker #
Maribel	1	[s]	1
Oscar	1	[s̻]	2
Marta	2	[z]	3
Oscar	2	[s]	4
Carmela	1	[s̻]	5
Rodrigo	2	[z]	6
Maribel	2	[s̻]	7
Eduardo	2	[z]	8
Carmela	2	[z]	9
Rodrigo	1	[s]	10
Maribel	1	[s̻]	11
Eduardo	1	[z]	12
Marta	2	[s]	13
Rodrigo	1	[s̻]	14
Maribel	2	[z]	15
Oscar	1	[s]	16
Carmela	1	[z]	17
Rodrigo	2	[s]	18
Marta	1	[s̻]	19
Eduardo	2	[s]	20
Maribel	2	[s]	21
Oscar	2	[z]	22
Carmela	1	[s]	23
Filler—male	–	–	24
Marta	2	[s̻]	25
Eduardo	2	[s̻]	26
Marta	1	[z]	27
Rodrigo	1	[z]	28
Carmela	2	[s̻]	29
Eduardo	1	[s]	30
Maribel	1	[z]	31
Rodrigo	2	[s̻]	32
Marta	1	[s]	33

(cont.)

Pseudonym	Token	Allophone	Speaker #
Oscar	2	[ʂ]	34
Carmela	2	[s]	35
Eduardo	1	[ʂ]	36
Filler—female	–	–	37
Oscar	1	[z]	38

Survey Flow

Introduction		
Consent		
Instructions part I		
Practice 1		
Practice 2		
Instructions part II		
Randomized block 1: Randomly present the following 5 groups	Group 1	Speaker 1
		Speaker 2
	Group 2	Speaker 3
		Speaker 4
	Group 3	Speaker 5
		Speaker 6
	Group 4	Speaker 7
		Speaker 8
	Group 5	Speaker 9
		Speaker 10
Randomized block 2: Randomly present the following 5 groups	Group 1	Speaker 11
		Speaker 12
	Group 2	Speaker 13
		Speaker 14
	Group 3	Speaker 15
		Speaker 16
	Group 4	Speaker 17
		Speaker 18
	Group 5	Speaker 19
		Speaker 20

(cont.)

Randomized block 3: Randomly present the following 5 groups	Group 1	Speaker 21
		Speaker 22
	Group 2	Speaker 23
		Speaker 24
	Group 3	Speaker 25
		Speaker 26
	Group 4	Speaker 27
		Speaker 28
	Group 5	Speaker 29
		Speaker 30
Randomized block 4: Randomly present the following 4 groups	Group 1	Speaker 31
		Speaker 32
	Group 2	Speaker 33
		Speaker 34
	Group 3	Speaker 35
		Speaker 36
	Group 4	Speaker 37
		Speaker 38

References

Azcúnaga López, R. E. (2010). Fonética del español salvadoreño. In M. A. Quesada Pacheco (Ed.), *El español hablado en América Central: Nivel fonético* (pp. 83–113). Vervuert.

Bárkányi, Z. (2013). *On the verge of phonetics and phonology: Pre-sonorant voicing in Spanish*. Phonetic and Phonology in Iberia, Universidade de Lisboa, Lisbon.

Barnes, S. (2015). Perceptual salience and social categorization of contact features in Asturian Spanish. *Studies in Hispanic and Lusophone Linguistics*, 8(2), 213–241.

Barnes, S. (2019). The role of social cues in the perception of final vowel contrasts in Asturian Spanish. In W. Chappell (Ed.), *Recent Advances in the Study of Spanish Sociophonetic Perception* (pp. 15–38). John Benjamins.

Beck, J. M. (1999). Organic variation of the vocal apparatus. In W. J. Hardcastle & J. Laver (Eds.), *The handbook of phonetic sciences* (pp. 256–289). Blackwell.

Benor, S. B. (2001). The learned /t/: Phonological variation in Orthodox Jewish English. In T. Sanchez & D. E. Johnson (Eds.), *Penn Working Papers in Linguistics: Selected Papers from NWAV 2000*.

Boersma, P., & Weenink, D. (2020). *Praat: Doing phonetics by computer.* http://www.praat.org.

Bolyanatz Brown, M. A., & Rogers, B. M. A. (2019). The social perception of intervocalic /k/ voicing in Chilean Spanish. In W. Chappell (Ed.), *Recent advances in the study of Spanish sociophonetic perception.* John Benjamins Publishing.

Boomershine, A. (2005). *Perceptual processing of variable input in Spanish: An exemplar-based approach to speech perception* [Doctoral Dissertation]. Ohio State University.

Boomershine, A. (2006). Perceiving and processing dialectal variation in Spanish: An Exemplar Theory approach. In T. L. Face & C. A. Klee (Eds.), *Selected Proceedings of the 8th Hispanic Linguistics Symposium* (pp. 58–72). Cascadilla Proceedings Project.

Brogan, F. (2018). *Sociophonetically-based phonology: An Optimality Theoretic account of /s/ weakening in Salvadoran Spanish* [Doctoral Dissertation]. University of California, Los Angeles.

Brogan, F., & Bolyanatz, M. (2018). A sociophonetic account of onset /s/ weakening in Salvadoran Spanish: Instrumental and segmental analyses. *Language Variation and Change, 30*(2), 203–230.

Brogan, F. (2020). Demystifying Salvadoran [sθ]: Evidence for /s/ lenition. In A. Morales-Front, M. J. Ferreira, R. P. Leow, & C. Sanz (Eds.), *Hispanic Linguistics. Current issues and new directions.* Benjamins.

Brogan, F., & Yi, D. (2022). Rethinking gender principles in El Salvador: Evidence from /s/ weakening. *Studies in Hispanic and Lusophone Linguistics.*

Bucholtz, M. (2001). The whiteness of nerds: Superstandard English and racial markedness. *Journal of Linguistic Anthropology, 11*, 84–100.

Campbell-Kibler, K. (2009). The nature of sociolinguistic perception. *Language Variation and Change, 21*(1), 135–156. https://doi.org/10.1017/S0954394509000052.

Campbell-Kibler, K. (2007). Accent, (ING) and the social logic of listener perceptions. *American Speech, 82*, 32–64.

Canfield, D. L. (1981). *Spanish pronunciation in the Americas.* University of Chicago Press.

Chappell, W. (2011). The intervocalic voicing of /s/ in Ecuadorian Spanish. In J. Michnowicz & R. Dodsworth (Eds.), *Selected Proceedings of the 5th Workshop on Spanish Sociolinguistics* (pp. 57–64). Cascadilla Proceedings Project.

Chappell, W. (2016). On the social perception of intervocalic /s/ voicing in Costa Rican Spanish. *Language Variation and Change, 28*(3), 357–378. https://doi.org/10.1017/S0954394516000107.

Chappell, W. (Ed.). (2019). *Recent advances in the study of Spanish sociophonetic perception.* John Benjamins Publishing.

Chappell, W., & García, C. (2017). Variable production and indexical social meaning: On the potential physiological origin of intervocalic /s/ voicing in Costa Rican Spanish. *Studies in Hispanic and Lusophone Linguistics, 10*(1), 1–37. https://doi.org/10.1515/shll-2017-0001.

Davidson, J. (2014). A comparison of fricative voicing and lateral velarization phenomena in Barcelona: A variationist approach to Spanish in contact with Catalan. In K. Lahousse & S. Marzo (Eds.), *Romance languages and linguistic theory 2012: Selected papers from 'Going Romance' Leuven 2012* (pp. 223–244). Benjamins.

Eckert, P. (2008). Variation and the indexical field. *Journal of Sociolinguistics*, 12(4), 453–476.

Erker, D. (2010). A subsegmental approach to coda /s/ weakening in Dominican Spanish. *International Journal of the Sociology of Language*, 2010(203), 9–26.

Erker, D. (2012). *An acoustically based sociolinguistic analysis of variable coda /s/ production in the Spanish of New York City* [Doctoral Dissertation]. New York University.

Figueroa, N. (2000). An acoustic and perceptual study of vowels preceding deleted post-nuclear /s/ in Puerto Rican Spanish. In H. Campos, E. Herburger, A. Morales-Front, & T. J. Walsh (Eds.), *Hispanic linguistics at the turn of the millennium: Papers from the 3rd Hispanic Linguistic Symposium* (pp. 66–79). Cascadilla Press.

File-Muriel, R., & Brown, E. (2011). The gradient nature of s-lenition in Caleño Spanish. *Language Variation and Change*, 23(2), 223–243.

File-Muriel, R., Brown, E., & Gradoville, M. (2015). *Disentangling the physiological from the socially-learned in gradient, sociophonetic processes: Evidence from s-realization in Barranquilla, Colombia* [Unpublished manuscript].

File-Muriel, R., Brown, E., & Gradoville, M. (2021). A sociophonetic approach to /s/-realization in the Colombian Spanish of Barranquilla. In E. Núñez-Méndez (Ed.), *Sociolinguistic Approaches to Sibilant Variation in Spanish* (1st ed., pp. 246–260). Routledge.

García, C. (2015). *Gradience and variability of intervocalic /s/ voicing in Highland Ecuadorian Spanish* [Doctoral Dissertation]. The Ohio State University.

García, C. (2019). Regional identity in Highland Ecuador: Social evaluation of intervocalic /s/ voicing. In W. Chappell (Ed.), *Recent Advances in the Study of Spanish Sociophonetic Perception* (pp. 125–152). John Benjamins.

Hammond, R. (1978). An experimental verification of the phonemic status of open and closed vowels in Caribbean Spanish. In H. López Morales (Ed.), *Corrientes actuales en la dialectología del caribe hispánico* (pp. 33–125). Editorial Universitaria, Universidad de Puerto Rico.

Hammond, R. (2001). *The sounds of Spanish: Analysis and application (with special reference to American English)*. Cascadilla Press.

Hualde, J. I. (2005). *The sounds of Spanish*. Cambridge University Press.

Kircher, R. (2016). The Matched-Guise Technique. In Z. Hua (Ed.), *Research Methods in Intercultural Communication: A Practical Guide* (1st ed.). John Wiley & Sons, Inc.

Kirchner, R. (2004). Consonant lenition. In B. Hayes, R. Kirchner, & D. Steriade (Eds.), *Phonetically based phonology* (pp. 313–345). Cambridge University Press.

Labov, W. (1972). *Sociolinguistic patterns*. University of Pennsylvania Press.

Labov, W. (2010). *Principles of linguistic change: Cognitive and cultural factors* (Vol. 3). Wiley-Blackwell.

Lambert, W. E., Hodgson, R. C., Gardner, C., & Fillenbaum, S. (1960). Evaluational reactions to spoken languages. *Journal of Abnormal and Social Psychology, 60*(1), 44–51.

Lipski, J. (1994). *Latin American Spanish*. Longman.

Lipski, J. M. (2012). Free at last: From Bound Morpheme to Discourse Marker in Lengua ri Palenge (Palenquero Creole Spanish). *Anthropological Linguistics, 54*(2), 101–132.

Mack, S. (2011). A Sociophonetic Analysis of /s/Variation in Puerto Rican Spanish. *Selected Proceedings of the 11th Hispanic Linguistics Symposium*, 81–93.

McKinnon, S. (2012). *Intervocalic /s/ voicing in Catalonian Spanish* [Honors thesis]. The Ohio State University.

Podesva, R. J., Roberts, S. J., & Campbell-Kibler, K. (2002). Sharing resources and indexing meanings in the production of gay styles. In K. Campbell-Kibler, R. J. Podesva, S. J. Roberts, & A. Wong (Eds.), *Language and Sexuality: Contesting Meaning in Theory and Practice* (pp. 175–190). CSLI Press.

Podesva, R. J., Reynolds, J., Callier, P., & Baptiste, J. (2015). Constraints on the social meaning of released /t/: A production and perception study of U.S. politicians. *Language Variation and Change, 27*(1), 59–87.

R Core Team. (2020). *R: A language and environment for statistical computing*. R Foundation for Statistical Computing. http://www.R-project.org/.

Schmidt, L. B. (2013). Regional variation in the perception of sociophonetic variants of Spanish /s/. In A. M. Carvalho & S. Beaudrie (Eds.), *Selected Proceedings of the 6th Workshop on Spanish Sociolinguistics* (pp. 189–202). Cascadilla Proceedings Project.

Thomson, B. (2010). *Chalk*. Marshall Cavendish.

Torres-Reyna, O. (n.d.). *Getting Started in Factor Analysis (using Stata)*.

Univaso, P., Martínez Soler, M., & Gurlekian, J. A. (2014). Variabilidad intra- e interhablante de la fricativa sibilante /s/ en el español de Argentina. *Estudios de Fonética Experimental, 23*, 95–124.

Walker, A., García, C., Cortés, Y., & Campbell-Kibler, K. (2014). Comparing social meanings across listener and speaker groups: The indexical field of Spanish /s/. *Language Variation and Change, 26*(2), 169–189.

Wickham, H. (2016). *ggplot2: Elegant graphics for data analysis*. Springer-Verlag.

CHAPTER 6

An Initial ToBI Analysis of Costa Rican Spanish Intonation

Eva Patricia Velásquez Upegui

1   Introduction

The geoprosodic study of Spanish has gained relevance in the last few years, mainly because intonation is an aspect clearly perceived by the speakers when it comes to identifying dialects and sociolects. However, it had not been considered in the criteria to delimit the dialect areas because at the Linguistic level, it has been more relevant to make the description on a segmentation basis, which is nowadays being complemented with the suprasegmental description. Therefore, for the prosodic description of Spanish it is necessary to consider not only a wide number of varieties, but also a thorough analysis of each variety, in order to recognize the common characteristics among varieties as a part of the same language, and those that mark a difference in the recognition of a particular variety.

The goal of this paper is to provide a starting inventory of the tones that form the broad-focus statements, yes-no questions, and wh-questions of Spanish spoken in Costa Rica. In other words, it is proposing a descriptive study bounded to a group of participants sharing the same sociocultural characteristics.[1] This proposal will allow not only to add up to the intonation description of this variety, but also to establish comparisons with other varieties in a way that it will contribute to the understanding of the prosody of Central American Spanish, and to the geoprosodic study of American Spanish for that matter. This is why, the purpose is to highlight the similarities between the nuclear configurations found in Costa Rican Spanish and other varieties of American Spanish compiled by Prieto & Roseano (2010). Likewise, it will also take into account the coincidences with Colombian Spanish (Velásquez-Upegui, 2013), since, as Quesada Pacheco (2014) points

---

1   It is a preliminary study on the Costa Rican Spanish intonation that seeks to prompt more complex future studies on social variables, the number of speakers, statement diversity, and spontaneity in data production.

out, speakers of San José tend to recognize similarities between their speech and that of Colombian Spanish speakers.[2]

Hereinafter, an overview of previous studies about Costa Rican intonation is outlined. Subsequently, the methodological considerations corresponding to the participants, instruments and collected data are addressed. Further on, an analysis of the statements is presented through the description of two position: the prenuclear position, and, nuclear configuration, the conclusions of the study are provided.[3]

2   Intonation of Costa Rican Spanish

There is still a scarce number of studies on the intonation of Costa Rican Spanish. One of the first contributions to this variety was made by Díaz Campos & Tevis (2002). The authors analyzed broad-focus statements from a reading test applied to two speakers, a man and a woman, from each of the following countries: Argentina, Colombia, Costa Rica, Chile, Mexico, Puerto Rico, Spain and Venezuela. Among their findings, it is mentioned that the L+H* tone is the most recurring in six varieties, one of them being the one from Costa Rica. Moreover, they explained that, in the final statements, the L% boundary tone was the most frequent in all cases.

Congosto Martín (2009) studied intonation, duration and intensity through the data of a 35 year-old speaker born in the capital city of Costa Rica, San José. For the acoustic analysis, the methodology of the International Project AMPER was followed. Nine broad-focus statements and yes-no questions with three repetitions were analyzed. Regarding intonation, a considerable resemblance between the two types of statements, which are characterized by having a falling ending, was found. Concerning the syllabic duration, the author found that

---

2 In Quesada Pacheco's (2014) work, it is not specified at what language level Costa Rican speakers ascribe this similarity. For this reason, the comparison suggested herein would be particularly interesting, in that it would allow us to determine if there are intonation similarities, provided that there are others. In this same study, the author mentions that Costa Rican speakers also find similarities with Salvadoran and Panamanian speech. However, since the literature on the intonation of these two varieties is limited or non-existent, they are not included in this review.

3 Nuclear configuration corresponds to the pitch accent of the last tonic syllable of the statement, plus the boundary tone, meaning, the final utterance of the pitch on the syllable with which the statement ends. According to Hualde (2003), a pitch accent is a pitch or sequence of pitches phonologically associated with a stressed syllable, whilst a boundary tone, is phonologically associated with the limit of a phrase. Pitch accents placed before the nuclear pitch accent are said to be in prenuclear position.

it depends on the position of the syllable in the phrase, rather than on its tonicity, with a tendency to rise if the stressed syllable is close to the end of a word or phrase. With regard to intensity, the author pointed out that it is lower in the broad-focus statements in comparison with the questions, and that, usually, the intensity tends to drop down in the last segment of the statement.

Congosto Martín (2011) described and compared the varieties from Costa Rica, Andalucía, Extremadura, and Bolivia. Regarding Costa Rican Spanish, the author presented similar results to those of her work from 2009. Furthermore, she suggested that, despite the similarities in the declension between the Costa Rican broad-focus statements and yes-no questions, in the broad-focus statements there is a staggered falling of the tone, which does not affect the presence of the last stressed syllable of the statement, while in the questions, the F0 continues rising until the last stressed syllable of the statement, where the declension begins (p.83).

López & Pešková (2020) studied the neutral and non-neutral yes-no questions from "tico" or Costa Rican Spanish. The authors recorded 6 women and 7 men of three different age groups, from different areas of Costa Rica: Cartago, San José, Desamparados, San Ramón and Turrialba, belonging to the dialect zone of the Central Valley. Eighty-nine statements were analyzed and labeled with the ToBI (*Tones and Break Indices*) system, as part of the Autosegmental-Metrical Model (Modelo Métrico Autosegmental, MA). The authors found that regardless of the questions being neutral or non-neutral, in all cases there was the presence of a rising-falling nuclear configuration transcribed as L+(¡)H* L%, although they also reported the H (+L)* L% configuration.

The previous overview allows us to acknowledge that both the broad-focus statements and the yes-no questions have been characterized by similar tones in terms of the nuclear configuration. Regarding the nuclear accent, the L+H* tone is particularly mentioned. As for the boundary tone, the L% falling endings are referred. Likewise, these findings highlight the need to know in detail the tone inventory of Costa Rican Spanish as a starting point for a wider prosodic description of this variety.

3   Methodology

3.1   *Participants*

Six participants were interviewed: three men and three women with a university-level education from three different age groups: 25 to 35 (Generation 1. G1), 36 to 45 (Generation 2. G2), and 46 to 50 (Generation 3. G3), a man and a woman of each. The statements were recorded at the participants' homes thanks to the support of the Costa Rican collaborators.[4] All the participants were born in the city of San José, which belongs to the dialect zone of the Central Valley, as per the dialect division proposed by Quesada Pacheco & Vargas (2010). According to the authors, it is possible to recognize three dialect zones in the country: 1. The Central Valley and its surrounding areas; 2. The rest of the country: the northwest area, the north pacific region and the south pacific; 3. Areas of dialect transition, like border regions, the central pacific region, the southern region, and the section adjacent to the southeast sector of the Central Valley.

Parting from the dialect division proposed by Quesada Pacheco (2013), based on the self-perception of the speakers, it is explained that most of the participants recognize the speech of San José as main point of reference. "The speech of the capital is perceived as distinctive of educated people, wealthy people, cultivated people" ("El habla capitalina se percibe como de gente educada, con dinero, gente con cultura") (p. 64). Thus, it is inferred that the speech of San José represents the renowned variety of the country (Rivas & García Pineda, this volume).

3.2 *Instruments*

For the collection of the broad-focus statements, the yes-no questions, and the wh-questions, the proposal of Prieto & Roseano (2010) was followed. In the first case, 20 photographic pictures with characters in daily life scenarios were used with the goal of making the speaker utter a descriptive broad-focus statement based on the question *What do you see in the image?* (*¿Qué ve en la imagen?*) These statements correspond to wide or informative spotlights, with no emphasis or rise in any part of the statement (Gutiérrez Bravo, 2008) and no expressive nuance. Although the same images were used with all of the participants, they did not produce identical statements. In this sense, the number of syllables forming the statements was not the same. Therefore, there was also a variation in the number of pitch accents (PA) forming each statement. Thus, to make the inventory of prenuclear pitch accents, each accent was classified according to the place of appearance in this position, which goes

---

4   While this sample size allows us to get a preview of the Costa Rican Spanish toneme inventory, in order to carry out a representative assessment of the intonational phonology, it would be worth having participants from the different Costa Rican Spanish varieties, with different education levels. However, this is a task that surpasses the goals set for this first descriptive approach that seeks to explore intonation in this Spanish language variety and its diversity in terms of the types of statements, as well as some of the social factors that identify the participants (Chappell, 2013).

from the beginning until the last stressed syllable of the statement. In general, the prenuclear position had a minimum of one PA and a maximum of three PAs. For example: a) one pitch accent: una mu*jer* cantando (a woman singing); b) two pitch accents: una mu*cha*cha es*tá* cantando (a young lady is singing), and c) three pitch accents: una mu*jer* joven*ci*ta es*tá* cantando (a young woman is singing).

Regarding the yes-no questions and the wh-questions, 20 discursive contexts were constructed so the participants could utter spontaneous statements according to the suggested scenario (Frota & Prieto, 2015; Prieto & Roseano, 2010). In all cases, the fictional speaker was a friend of the same sex of the participant, maintaining the same conditions of distance and power (Brown & Levinson, 1987). For example: You are with your friend and you are smoking, and you would like to know if the smoke is bothering him/her. Ask him/her. Expected answer: Does the smoke bother you? (*¿Te molesta el humo?*).

Each statement was recorded with one repetition, which was used just in case the first emission had an acoustic problem. In total, 60 statements were collected per participant, 20 statements for each modality.

3.3 Procedure

The study is based on the Autosegmental-Metrical Model (Gussenhoven, 2004; Hualde, 2003; Ladd, 1996; Pierrehumbert, 1980; Prieto, 2003) that allows stablishing contrasts in the intonation system from a phonological perspective. The statements were segmented and transcribed according to the *Sp-ToBI* (*Tones and Break Indices*) transcription system, based on the proposal of Hualde & Prieto (2015), who introduced the following modifications to the proposal of Prieto & Roseano (2009–2013). Particularly, the rising pitch accent with the highest peak displaced towards the posttonic syllable shifted from L+>H* to L+<H*, and the boundary tone M% and HH% were substituted with !H% and H%, respectively.

With regard to the labeling of the Costa Rican statements, phonetic considerations associated with the perception threshold of 1.5 semitones (st.) (Pamies Bertrán et al., 2002) were followed. Thus, the movements lower than 1.5 st. were transcribed as monotones (H*, L*, !H*) and the rising movements higher than 1.5 st. were transcribed as L+(¡)H*, L*+H, L+<H*, and H+L* bitones in the fallings.[5] As for the boundary tones, the L% monotones were used for

---

5 According to the Sp-ToBI labeling system (Prieto & Roseano, 2009), the L+H* pitch accent corresponds to a rising pitch movement along the stressed syllable. The rise starts at the beginning of the stressed, or tonic, syllable and finishes towards the end of that same syllable. The L*+H accent has a low pitch associated with the tonic syllable, followed by a rise

the fallings, !H% for the sustained endings, both high and low, and H% for the risings. The HL% label was also included for rising and falling complex boundary tones. The diacritic marks (¡) and (!) were also used; (¡) for risings higher than 3 st. and (!) for lower risings as compared to the previous rising. For that matter, the phonological considerations of Sp-ToBI are supplementary with phonetic approximations. These two perspectives provide a much more accurate description since the labeling approach is rooted in quantitative differences associated with pitch height.

For the segmentation of the statements, the Praat software *version 6.0.55* (Boersma & Weenink, 1992) was used. Each statement was labeled orthographically and segmented into syllables and vowels, and the F0 was calculated in each segment. Moreover, a tier was added for the caesurae, and another one for the labeling of the tones. Once each statement was analyzed, a database was created to gather the frequencies of pitch accents, nuclear accents and boundary tones. To establish the differences among the data groups, the Chi square test was used in the SPSS program (IBM, 2013).[6]

4 Tone Inventory according to the Type of Statement

In order to present the inventory of the tones found in the broad-focus statements, yes-no questions, and wh-questions, the pitch accents in prenuclear position, that is, the ones located in the segment that goes from the beginning until the pre-nuclear syllable, will be displayed first, followed by the nuclear pitch accents and boundary tones constituting the nuclear configuration, specifically, the last stressed syllable plus the final posttonic syllable of the statement.

4.1 *Broad-Focus Statements*

Due to the semi-spontaneous nature of the data, the number of pitch accents varies according to the statement uttered, which in this corpus reaches a

---

in the posttonic syllable. The L+<H* accent is uttered with a rising movement starting at the tonic syllable and ending at the posttonic syllable. Lastly, the H+L* accent is uttered with a falling movement that continues through the stressed syllable. Similarly, the (!)H* labels are included to point out that the H* and !H* pitches can occur in the same position, and the L+(¡)H* labels are included to point out that the L+H* and L+¡H*pitches can occur in the same position.

6 Although statistically significant results were obtained, they could not be extended to the whole Costa Rican population, given the characteristics and number of participants in this study.

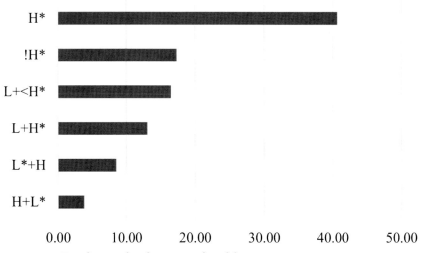

FIGURE 6.1 Distribution of pitch accents in broad-focus statements

maximum of three pitch accents. 56.66% of the statements were uttered with two pitch accents, 23.33% with one pitch accent, and 20% with three pitch accents.

Accordingly, we found 236 possible positions for the pitch accents in the set of statements, of which the H* PA accounts for 40.68%, followed by the !H* variant, which constitutes 17.37%. The rising L+<H, L+H* and L*+H PAs represent 16.53%, 13.14% and 8.47%, respectively, and finally, the falling H+L* PA only had eight occurrences, which corresponds to 3.81% of the positions (Fig. 6.1).

The H* PA corresponds to a high sustained tone, which appears mainly in statements constituted by three pitch accents, in the third place, that is, before nuclear pitch accent. Usually, the frequency of use of this PA is higher compared to the other tones reported, both in the statements that have one or two PAs and in the prenuclear position. The H* PA has the variation !H*, which also indicates a high sustained movement. However, this movement is characterized for being lower than the previous rising without being considered a falling. This pitch does not occur in the initial position. However, it is very common in the second position of statements with more than one PA (Fig. 6.2).

As for the L+<H* PA, it represents a rising movement along the stressed syllable, and it reaches the highest peak in the posttonic syllable. This PA only appears in the initial position of the statement, with a frequency of use of 32.5%, very close to the use of the H* tone (Fig. 6.3).

On the other hand, the rising L+H* and L*+H PAs showed a lower frequency of use as compared to the other tones used, and in turn, they showed a higher

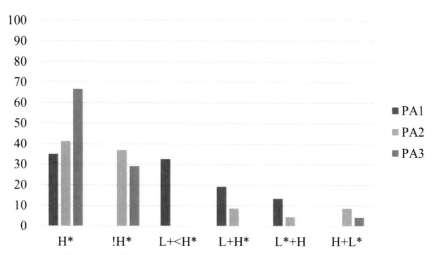

FIGURE 6.2 Frequency of pitch accents according to the prenuclear position in broad-focus statements

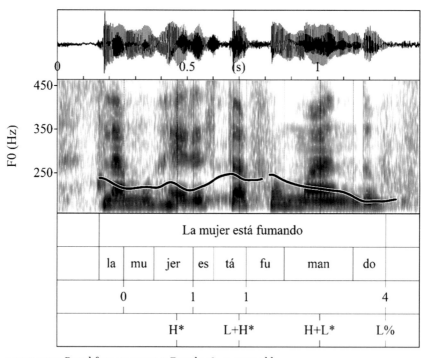

FIGURE 6.3 Broad-focus statement. Female 36–45 years old
The woman is smoking (La mujer está fumando)

tendency to appear in the initial position. The falling H+L* PA was not significantly productive in this segment of the statement. Moreover, it did not have any occurrence in the initial position.

This review of the prenuclear position in the broad-focus statements of Costa Rica reveals a preference to use high-sustained beginnings, represented as H*, with lower falling inflections in the body of the statement (!H*), which usually corresponds to a staggered falling movement (Congosto Martín 2009, 2011). The sustained beginnings can alternate with a rising along the stressed syllable, reaching its highest peak in the posttonic syllable, L+<H* (Fig. 6.4).

Regarding the nuclear configuration of the broad-focus statements, it was found that the most frequent nuclear pitch accent corresponds to the H+L* falling movement (Fig. 6.3), followed by the sustained H*, with its !H* variant. The rising L+H* nuclear pitch accent was also found, although with less occurrences (Table 6.1). This accent also has a L+!H* variant, which reveals a rising movement in the nuclear syllable that does not exceed the risings that appeared previously in the prenuclear position.

The boundary tone in all cases corresponds to the L% falling ending. Thus, the most productive nuclear configuration in the reviewed statements is H+L* L% (Fig. 6.3 and 6.4). In this sense, it is worth mentioning that this nuclear configuration was more frequent in women, with 70% of occurrences, while men preferred sustained and rising tones, with 55% of the total of accents produced by their group. The Chi square test showed that there is a statistically significant association between sex and the nuclear pitch accent produced in the $\chi^2(2) = 9.851$, p = 0.007 broad-focus statements. Therefore, even though the H+L* L% nuclear configuration is in general the most common in

TABLE 6.1 Frequencies in the nuclear configuration of broad-focus statements

Boundary tones/ Nuclear pitch accent	L% Women N	L% Women %	L% Men N	L% Men %	Total N	Total %
H+L*	42	70	27	45	69	57.5
(!)H*	16	26.67	23	38.33	39	32.5
L+(!)H*	2	3.33	10	16.67	12	10
Total	60	100	60	100	120	100

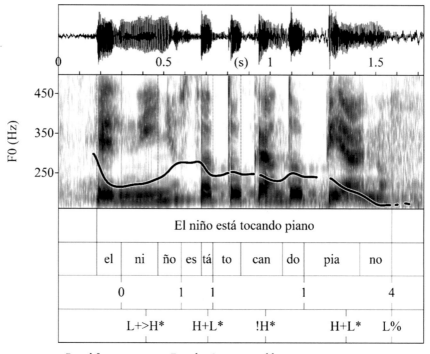

FIGURE 6.4 Broad-focus statement. Female 36–45 years old
The boy is playing the piano (*El niño está tocando piano*)

TABLE 6.2 Tone frequency in the nuclear configuration according to the age variable

Tones							
	\multicolumn{6}{c}{Nuclear pitch accent}	
	(!)H*		H+L*		L+(!)H*		Total
Age	N	%	N	%	N	%	N
G1	20	50	19	48	1	3	40
G2	9	23	26	65	5	13	40
G3	10	25	24	60	6	15	40
Total	39	33	69	58	12	10	120

the group of interviewees, its productivity seems to be determined by the sex of the participants.

The age variable revealed a statistically significant relationship with the nuclear pitch accent of the $\chi^2(4) = 10.323$, p = 0.035 broad-focus statements.

When reviewing the pairwise adjustments among the age groups, it was found that the differences lie exclusively on G1 as compared to G2 and G3. This is reflected on the greater frequency of the !H* nuclear pitch accent in G1 regarding the rest of the groups (Table 6.2).

The H+L* L% nuclear configuration is also shared with the varieties of Puerto Rico (Armstrong, 2010) and Dominican Republic (Willis, 2010), and it has also been documented in Argentina (Gabriel et al., 2010) and Chile (Ortiz et al., 2010), although less frequently. Likewise, this configuration has been reported in the Colombian variety of Bogotá (Velásquez-Upegui, 2013).

4.2   Yes-No Questions

As for broad-focus statements, the prenuclear position of the yes-no questions is characterized by having a maximum of three pitch accents. 48.33% of the statements were constituted by two PAs, and with a significantly close percentage, 47.5% of the statements were uttered with one PA. The statements with three PAs appeared in a considerably lower percentage compared with the previous data; they only appeared in 4.17% of the corpus.

The PAs that were uttered in the 188 possible positions correspond mainly to the H* tone, 42%, followed by the L+<H* tone, 28.7%, and L+H*, 17.6%. Lastly, the L*+H and H+L* tones appeared in 8% and 3.2%, respectively (Fig. 6.5).

Regarding the H* tone, it appears more frequently in the second position of the yes-no questions, besides being the only tone appearing in the prenuclear position in three pitch accent statements. The L+<H* tone appeared predominantly in the first position, and with only two occurrences in the middle of the statement. On the other hand, the rising L+H* tone appeared in the initial and

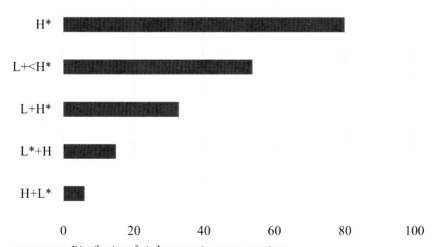

FIGURE 6.5   Distribution of pitch accents in yes-no questions

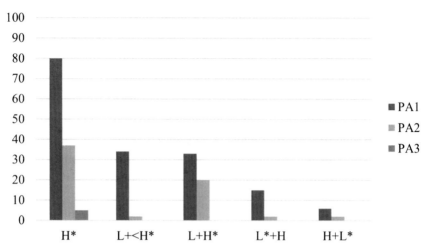

FIGURE 6.6 Frequency of pitch accents according to the position in the prenuclear position in yes-no questions

middle positions of the statements. L*+H and H+L* tones appeared in both initial and middle positions with very few occurrences (Fig. 6.6).

According to this pitch accent inventory, the prenuclear position is characterized by having a high and sustained beginning that can extend throughout the statement, and in some cases, it elapses in a rising manner (Fig. 6.6).

Regarding the nuclear configuration, the nuclear pitch accent is uttered mainly with the rising L+H* tone, which appears in 51.67% of the data, followed by the H+L* tone with 36.67% of occurrences, and finally, the H* tone that appears in 11.67% of the data. Most of these nuclear pitch accents are accompanied by the falling L% boundary tone in 86.67% of cases. Although with very low appearances, we also have the H% and !H% tones, which reveal a rising ending, as well as the HL% and LHL% compound tones. While the latter still maintain the typical falling of this variety, they show more complex tonal movements in the posttonic syllable that appear before the end of the statement. (Table 6.3).

According to the data on table 6.3, it can be inferred that the nuclear configuration in the yes-no questions corresponds to the L+(¡)H* rising with predominant L% falling endings (Fig. 6.7). This falling boundary tone is shared with the broad-focus statements of this variety (Table 6.1). The falling boundary tones in yes-no questions have also been documented in Spanish spoken in Medellín, Colombia (Muñetón Ayala & Dorta Luis, 2015; Muñoz Builes, 2020; Velásquez-Upegui, 2013), as well as in Caribbean Spanish (Venezuela, Dominican Republic and Puerto Rico), as pointed out by López & Pešková (2020), from the compilation of Prieto & Roseano (2010). The L+(¡)H* L% nuclear configuration of Costa Rican Spanish is shared specifically with the varieties of Venezuela and Medellín.

TABLE 6.3 Frequencies in the nuclear configuration of yes-no questions

Boundary tones Nuclear pitch accent	L% N	L% %	H% N	H% %	!H% N	!H% %	HL% N	HL% %	LHL% N	LHL% %	Total N	Total %
L+(¡)H*	50	41.7	7	5.83	3	2.5	2	1.67	0	0	62	51.67
H+L*	43	35.8	0	0	0	0	0	0	1	0.83	44	36.67
H*	11	9.17	0	0	3	2.5	0	0	0	0	14	11.67
Total	104	86.7	7	5.83	6	5	2	1.67	1	0.83	120	100

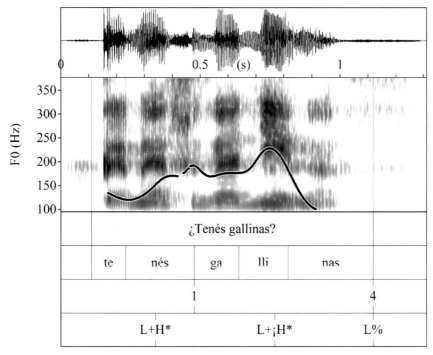

FIGURE 6.7 Yes-no questions. Male 46 to 56 years old
Do you have chickens? (*¿Tenés gallinas?*)

As in the case of the broad-focus statements, there is a statistically significant relationship between gender and the nuclear pitch accent $\chi^2(2) = 34.049$, p = 0.000, which shows a higher preference for the L+(¡)H* tone by the male groups as compared to the speakers of the opposite sex. Likewise, this same significative effect related to sex was observed in the choice of the $\chi^2(4) = 16.962$, p = 0.000 boundary tone, which revealed higher variability in the options chosen by the male group, while in the female group the L% boundary tone was more widely used. This group also presented complex boundary tones (Table 6.4).

It is worth mentioning that the complex LHL% juncture pitch only occurred in one of the cases and was uttered by a 3rd generation female speaker. Since

TABLE 6.4   Tone frequency in the nuclear configuration according to the sex variable

Tones	Nuclear pitch accent							Boundary tones								
	H*		H+L*		L+H*		Total	H%		!H%		HL%		L%		LHL%	Total
Sex	N	%	N	%	N	%	N	N	%	N	%	N	%	N	%	N	%	N
Men	12	20	7	12	41	68	60	7	11.7	6	10	0	0	47	78.3	0	0	60
Women	2	3	37	62	21	35	60	0	0	0	0	2	3	57	95	1	2	60
Total	14	12	44	37	62	52	120	7	5.8	6	5	2	2	104	86.7	1	1	120

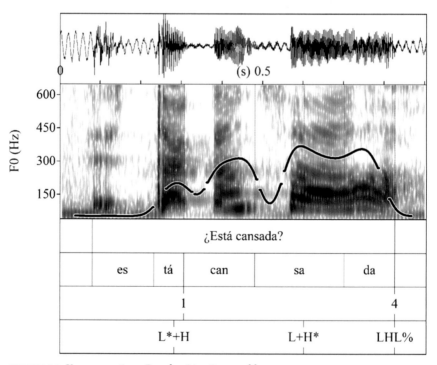

FIGURE 6.8   Yes-no questions. Female 46 to 56 years old
Are you tired? (*¿Estás cansada?*)

TABLE 6.5 Tone frequency in the nuclear configuration according to the age variable

Tones	Nuclear pitch accent								Boundary tone								
	H*		H+L*		L+H*		Total	H%		!H%		HL%		L%		LHL%	Total
Age	N	%	N	%	N	%	N	N	%	N	%	N	%	N	%	N	%	e
G1	5	13	1	3	34	85	40	0	0	1	2.5	2	5	37	92.5	0	0	40
G2	4	10	19	48	17	43	40	0	0	5	12.5	0	0	35	87.5	0	0	40
G3	5	13	24	60	11	28	40	7	17.5	0	0	0	0	32	80	1	2.5	40
Total	14	12	44	37	62	52	120	7	5.8	6	5	2	1.7	104	86.7	1	0.8	120

it was a single occurrence, it is not included as part of the Costa Rican Spanish intonation repertoire. However, it is necessary to explore, with more data and more speakers, its status within the intonation of this variety. In Figure 6.8, the post-nuclear syllable "–da" starts with a declination that comes from the nuclear syllable, followed by a rise, to end with a falling movement (Fig. 6.8).

Regarding age and nuclear pitch accent, a statistically significant relationship $\chi^2(4) = 33.872$ p = 0.000 was found. The younger speakers showed a greater frequency of the L+H* nuclear pitch accent regarding the rest of the groups. Likewise, this social variable had the same effect on the $\chi^2(8) = 27.365$, p = 0.001 boundary tone. In this case, the G3 was the only generation to show the use of rising endings. (Table 6.5).

4.3   Wh-questions

The prenuclear position in the wh-questions, like in the other statements reviewed, is formed by a minimum of one PA and a maximum of three PAs. The group of three PAs constitutes 62.5% of the data, followed by the statements with two PAs, with 23.33% of occurrences, and finally, the cases with one PA, with 14.17% of occurrences.

According to the distribution of the PAs, the 120 analyzed statements provide for 251 of the possible positions for each pitch accent. The PAs mainly used in the prenuclear position are H* (61.4%), and with a very few occurrences, the !H* variant (0.8%), followed by the L+<H* (15.94%) and L+H* (11.2%) tones, and with low appearance percentages, the L*+H (7.6%) and H+L* (3.2%) tones (Fig. 6.9).

The H* tone with a greater recurrence in the statements appears mainly in the second position, that is, after the first PA, even though it appears with high

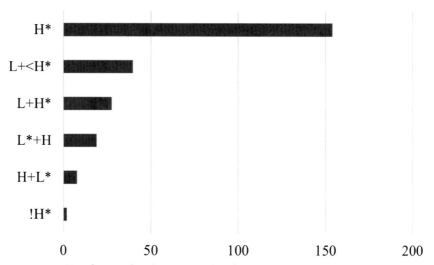

FIGURE 6.9   Distribution of pitch accents in the wh-questions

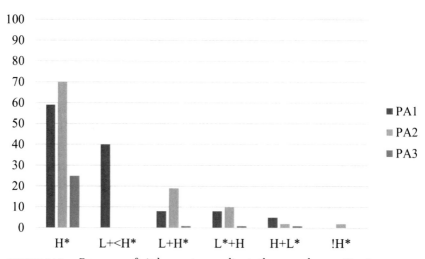

FIGURE 6.10   Frequency of pitch accents according to the prenuclear position in wh-questions

frequencies in the three positions. The L+<H* tone, like in the other reviewed statements, is preferred in the initial position. On the other hand, the L+H*, L*+H y H+L* tones appear in the three positions of the prenuclear section, with a few occurrences in each case. The !H* tone only appeared in the second PA (Fig. 6.10).

Generally, according to the PAs observed in the prenuclear position of the wh-questions, these can be characterized by a high sustained H* beginning

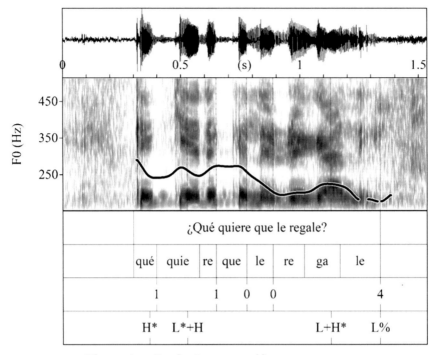

FIGURE 6.11   Wh- questions. Female 36 to 45 years old
What would you like me to give you as a gift?
(*¿Qué quiere que le regale?*)

(Fig. 6.11), which occasionally alternates with a L+<H* rising movement. For statements with two and three PAs, the F0 remains high and sustained throughout the prenuclear section.

In the nuclear configuration of the wh-questions, the more frequent nuclear pitch accents are the rising L+(¡)H* tones, followed by the sustained H* tones. H+L* and !H* tones also appear, although with less occurrences (Table 6.6).

Regarding the boundary tones, the L% type falling endings had the higher frequency. Even though !H%, HL% and H% boundary tones also appeared, their occurrences were very low (Table 6.6). According to these results, the nuclear configuration in the wh-questions is characterized by the presence of a rising movement of F0 in the stressed syllable to end with a falling L+(¡)H* L% (Fig. 6.12).

The falling endings in the wh-questions have also been documented for the varieties of Puerto Rico (Armstrong, 2010), Venezuela (Astruc et al., 2010), Argentina (Gabriel et al., 2010), and Mexico (De-la-Mota et al., 2010). As for the Colombian data, the falling have been reported in the Spanish of Medellín (Muñoz Builes, 2020; Velásquez-Upegui, 2013) and Bucaramanga (Roberto-Avilán, 2018).

TABLE 6.6   Frequencies in the nuclear configuration of wh-questions

Boundary tones/ Nuclear pitch accents	L% N	L% %	!H% N	!H% %	HL% N	HL% %	H% N	H% %	Total N	Total %
L+(¡)H*	62	51.67	4	3.33	1	0.83	3	2.5	70	58.33
H*	22	18.33	10	8.33	0	0	3	2.5	35	29.17
H+L*	10	8.33	2	1.67	0	0	0	0	12	10
!H*	3	2.50	0	0	0	0	0	0	3	2.5
Total	97	80.83	16	13.33	1	0.83	6	5	120	100

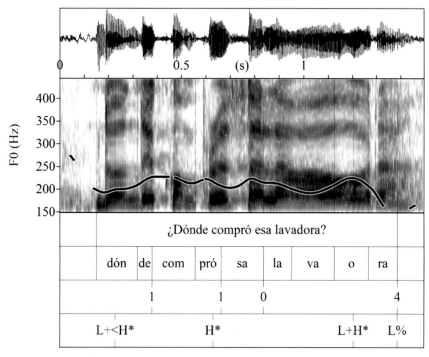

FIGURE 6.12   Wh- questions. Female 46 to 55 years old
Where did you buy that washing machine?
(*¿Dónde compró esa lavadora?*)

The sex variant does not seem to have an incidence in the production of the nuclear pitch accent, since no statistically significant effect was found χ²(3) = 6.210, p = 0.102. Nevertheless, it did have a significative effect in the χ²(3) = 13.320, p = 0.004 boundary tone. Women used the L% endings more, while men showed higher variability in boundary tones, with occurrences in each of the possibilities found (H%, !H%, HL% y L%) (Table 6.7).

TABLE 6.7 Tone frequency in the nuclear configuration according to the sex variable

Tones	Nuclear pitch accent									Boundary tones								
	H*		H+L*		L+H*		!H*		Total	H%		!H%		HL%		L%		Total
Sex	N	%	N	%	N	%	N	%	N	N	%	N	%	N	%	N	%	N
Men	18	30	2	3	38	63	2	3	60	5	8.3	12	20	2	3	41	68.3	60
Women	17	28	10	17	32	53	1	2	60	0	0.0	4	6.7	0	0	56	93.3	60
Total	35	29	12	10	70	58	3	3	120	5	4.2	16	13.3	2	2	97	80.8	120

TABLE 6.8 Tone frequency in the nuclear configuration according to the age variable

Tones	Nuclear pitch accent									Boundary tones								
	H*		H+L*		L+H*		!H*		Total	H%		!H%		HL%		L%		Total
Age	N	%	N	%	N	%	N	%	N	N	%	N	%	N	%	N	%	N
G1	18	45	0	0	22	55	0	0	40	2	5	12	30	0	0	26	65	40
G2	12	30	8	20	18	45	2	5	40	1	2.5	3	7.5	2	5	34	85	40
G3	5	13	4	10	30	75	1	3	40	2	5	1	2.5	0	0	37	93	40
Total	35	29	12	10	70	58	3	3	120	5	4.2	16	13.3	2	2	97	81	120

On the other hand, age showed a statistically significant relationship both on the $\chi^2(6) = 20.457$, $p = 0.002$ nuclear pitch accent and on the $\chi^2(6) = 19.275$, $p = 0.004$ boundary tone. In the first case, G1 did not have any H+L* and !H* PAs occurrences as compared to the rest of the groups. Just like in the nuclear pitch accent in the boundary tone G1 presented a relatively low use of the !H% sustained ending and no cases of the H% rising endings (Table 6.8).

5   Tone Inventory in Costa Rican Spanish

According to the review of broad-focus statements, yes-no questions, and wh-questions in highly educated speakers, it is possible to propose the following inventory of pitch accents and nuclear pitch accents.

H* This is a sustained high tone. It is very productive in the three types of statements. However, it is used more in the wh-questions. This pitch accent shows a phonetic variation !H*, this is a sustained high tone characterized by being lower than the previous high tone. It is used mainly in the broad-focus statements as part of the staggered falling.

L+<H* This tone has the highest rise of Fo in the posttonic syllable. It is used in the three types of statements, preferably in the initial position, and it is more frequent in broad-focus statements.

L*+H In this case, the stressed syllable coincides with a low movement followed by a rising of Fo in the posttonic syllable. It has only a few occurrences in the three types of statements.

L+H* In this tone, the Fo elapses in a rising way along the stressed syllable. Although it is used in the prenuclaer position of the three types of statements, it appears mainly in the nuclear configuration of questions, with risings from 1.5 to 3 st. It usually reaches the highest tonal peak before the nuclear syllable ends. This pitch accent shows phonetic variations like L+¡H and L+!H*. In first one, Fo rises than 3 st, and it even reaches 6 st, and in second one, Fo rises lower than the rise before.

H+L* This tone has a falling of the Fo along the stressed syllable. As in the previous case, it appears only a few times in the prenuclear position, while in the nuclear configuration of the broad-focus statements, it is used more frequently.

In relation to the boundary tones, the data delivers the following tones:

L% This tone represents a falling movement of the Fo in the last syllable of the statement. This boundary tone is typical of the three types of Costa Rican statements, and it is the only boundary tone registered in the broad-focus statements.

H% This tone corresponds to a rising ending in the last syllable of the statement. It is used in yes-no questions and wh-questions.

 !H% This tone has a sustained ending, with no rising or falling of the Fo, with regard to the statement. It is used more frequently in wh-questions.

 HL% This a complex boundary tone that maintains the rising of the Fo from the previous nuclear pitch accent and ends with a fall. It was registered in the two types of questions with very few occurrences.

6 Conclusions

The goal of this paper was to provide a first proposal of a tone inventory for Costa Rican Spanish based on the description of broad-focus statements, yes-no questions and wh-questions in speakers with a high educational level, as a foundation for the comparison of future descriptions given that, to a large extent, the reviewed data favors the exchange of information without any expressive nuance. In other words, it is their unmarked use.

In this sense, it could be stated that, in general, the three types of statements have considerable similarities in the prenuclear position, which is characterized by sustained beginnings or by having a shift of the tone toward the post-tonic syllables, from which the high tone is maintained or has slight risings. As for the nuclear configuration, the broad-focus statements are characterized by having the H+L* L% nuclear configuration, while the yes-no questions and the wh-questions show a greater use of the L+(¡) H* L% nuclear configuration.

The distribution of accents in the statements seems to favor PAs in certain positions, as in the case of the H+L* and L+(¡) H* nuclear accents, which were not widely used in the prenuclear sections of the statements in which they are the nucleus. Likewise, some PAs showed almost exclusive positions like L+<H*, which was registered mainly in the initial position of the statement, and the !H* accent in middle position, as part of the distinctive staggered falling of the broad-focus statements.

Although the configurations mentioned above are in general the most frequent in the statements, the comparison between male and female groups revealed statistically significant differences related to the sex of the participants. This is clearly reflected in the nuclear configuration of the broad-focus statements and the yes-no questions, while in the wh-questions this variation was not present in the nuclear pitch accent, but it was maintained in the boundary tone. Similarly, the age variable provides relevant information regarding nuclear configuration, mainly in relation to G1 comprising of younger speakers who consistently differed in the three types of statements analyzed, from age groups 2 and 3.

As for other variants of American Spanish, whereas the Costa Rican variety shares some characteristics with Caribbean Spanish, as pointed out by López & Pešková (2020), it also shares similarities with Colombian Spanish in regions that, according to the dialect classification of Montes Giraldo (2000), form the Central Andean Superdialect that includes the cities of Bogotá, Medellín and Bucaramanga. This seems to confirm the similarity perceived by speakers between the Colombian and the Costa Rican Spanish variety.

From the findings of this study, a series of future challenges arises, including the need to determine if the differences between the yes-no questions and the wh-questions depend exclusively on the presence of the interrogative pronoun, or if, on the contrary, prosodic factors like tonal peak alignment, duration, intensity, and others, play a role. Similarly, it is necessary to continue the study of intonation from a geolinguistic and sociolinguistic approach, so that the characteristics of Costa Rican intonation in its dialect variants and the effects that the different social variants can have on the use of certain nuclear configurations can be more precisely established. Lastly, it is necessary to carry out perceptual studies that contribute to the acknowledgement of prosodic resources that allow speakers to differentiate between the reviewed enunciative modalities.

References

Armstrong, M. E. (2010). Puerto Rican Spanish Intonation. In P. Prieto & P. Roseano (Eds.), *Transcription of Intonation of the Spanish Languagecrition* (pp. 155–190). Lincom.

Astruc, L., Mora, E., & Rew, S. (2010). Venezuelan Andean Spanish Intonation. In P. Prieto & P. Roseano (Eds.), *Transcription of Intonation of the Spanish Language* (pp. 191–226). Lincom Europa.

Boersma, P., & Weenink, D. (1992). *Praat: doing phonetics by computer*. Universidad de Amsterdam. http://www.fon.hum.uva.nl/praat/.

Brown, P., & Levinson, S. (1987). *Politeness: Some universals in language usage*. Cambridge University Press.

Chappell, W. (2013). Intonational Contours of Nicaraguan Granadino Spanish in Absolute Questions and Their Relationship with Pragmatic Meaning. In C. Howe, S. E. Blackwell, & M. Lubbers Quesada (Eds.), *Selected Proceedings of the 15th Hispanic Linguistics Symposium* (pp. 119–139). Cascadilla Proceedings Project.

Congosto Martín, Y. (2009). L'Atlas Multimédia Prosodique de l'Espace Roman (AMPER) au Costa Rica. *Géolinguistique*, 11, 119–148.

Congosto Martín, Y. (2011a). Contínuum entonativo: declarativas e interrogativas absolutas en cuantro variedades del español peninsular y americano. *Revista Internacional de Lingüística Iberoamericana*, 9(17), 75–90.

Congosto Martín, Y. (2011b). Contínuum entonativo: declarativas e interrogativas absolutas en cuatro variedades del español peninsular y americano. *Revista Internacional de Linguistica Iberoamericana*, IX(1), 75–90.

De-la-Mota, C., Martín Butragueño, P., & Prieto, P. (2010). Mexican Spanish intonation. In P. Prieto & P. Roseano (Eds.), *Transcription of Intonation of the Spanish Language* (pp. 319–350). Lincom.

Díaz Campos, M., & Tevis McGory, J. (2002). La entonación en el español de América: Un estudio acerca de ocho dialectos hispanoamericanos. *Boletín de Lingüística*, 18, 2–26.

Frota, S., & Prieto, P. (2015). Intonation in Romance: Systemic similarities and differences. In S. Frota & P. Prieto (Eds.), *Intonation in Romance* (pp. 392–418). Oxford University Press.

Gabriel, C., Feldhausen, I., Pešková, A., Colantoni, L., Lee, S.-A., Arana, V., & Labastía, L. (2010). Argentinian Spanish Intonation. In P. Prieto & P. Roseano (Eds.), *Transcription of Intonation of the Spanish Language* (pp. 285–318). Lincom Europa.

Gussenhoven, C. (2004). *The Phonology of Tone and Intonation*. Cambridge University Press.

Gutiérrez Bravo, R. (2008). La identificación de los tópicos y los focos. *Nueva Revista de Filología Hispánica*, 56, 363–401. https://nrfh.colmex.mx/index.php/nrfh/article/view/969.

Hualde, J. I. (2003). El modelo métrico y autosegmental. In P. Prieto (Ed.), *Teorías de la entonación* (pp. 155–184). Ariel.

Hualde, J. I., & Prieto, P. (2015). Intonational Variation in Spanish: European and American varieties. In S. Frota & P. Prieto (Eds.), *Intonational Variation in Romance* (pp. 350–391). Oxford University Press.

IBM. (2013). *SPSS Statistics for Windows* (22.0). IBM Corp.

Ladd, D. R. (1996). *Intonational Phonology*. Cambridge University Press.
López, J., & Pešková, A. (2020). Interrogativas absolutas en el español "tico." In C. Gabriel, A. Pešková, & M. Selig (Eds.), *Contact, variation and change. Studies in honor of Trudel Meisenburg* (pp. 593–610). Erich Schmidt.
Montes Giraldo, J. J. (2000). *Otros estudios sobre el español de Colombia*. Instituto Caro y Cuervo.
Muñetón Ayala, M. A., & Dorta Luis, J. (2015). La entonación declarativa e interrogativa en el español colombiano de Medellín: voz femenina vs. masculina. *Boletín de Filología*, 50(2), 103–122.
Muñoz Builes, D. M. (2020). *Estudio sociolingüístico de la entonación del español de Antioquia*. Pontificia Universidad Católica de Chile.
Ortiz, H., Fuentes, M., & Astruc, L. (2010). Chilean Spanish Intonation. In P. Prieto & P. Roseano (Eds.), *Transcription of Intonation of the Spanish Language* (pp. 255–284). Lincom Europa.
Pamies Bertrán, A., Fernández Planas, A. M., Martínez Celdrán, E., Ortega Escandell, A., & Amorós Céspedes, M. C. (2002). Umbrales tonales en español peninsular. *Actas Del II Congreso Nacional de Fonética Experimental*, 272–278.
Pierrehumbert, J. B. (1980). *The phonetics and phonology of English intonation*. [Massachusetts Institute of Technology]. http://www.phon.ox.ac.uk/jpierrehumbert/publications.html.
Prieto, P. (2003). *Teorías lingüísticas de la entonación*. Ariel.
Prieto, P., & Roseano, P. (2009). *Atlas interactivo de la entonación del español*. Universitat Pompeu Fabra. http://prosodia.upf.edu/atlasentonacion/.
Prieto, P., & Roseano, P. (2010). *Transcription of Intonation of the Spanish Language*. Lincom.
Quesada Pacheco, M. Á. (2013). División dialectal de Costa Rica según sus hablantes. *Dialectologia et Geolinguistica*, 21, 36–69. https://doi.org/10.1515/dialect-2013-0003.
Quesada Pacheco, M. Á. (2014). División dialectal del español de América según sus hablantes. Análisis dialectológico perceptual. *Boletín de Filología*, 2, 257–309. https://boletinfilologia.uchile.cl/index.php/BDF/article/view/35862/37524.
Quesada Pacheco, M. Á., & Vargas Vargas, L. (2010). Rasgos fonéticos del español de Costa Rica. In M. Á. Quesada Pacheco (Ed.), *El español hablado en América Central. Nivel fonético* (pp. 155–175). Lingüística Ibeoamericana.
Roberto-Avilán, Y. J. (2018). *Acercamiento a la entonación del español de Bucaramanga* [Instituto Caro y Cuervo]. http://bibliotecadigital.caroycuervo.gov.co/1307/.
Velásquez-Upegui, E. P. (2013). *Entonación del español hablado en Colombia*. El Colegio de México.
Willis, E. (2010). Dominican Spanish Intonation. In P. Prieto & P. Roseano (Eds.), *Transcription of Intonation of the Spanish Language* (pp. 123–154). Lincom Europa.

CHAPTER 7

Two Contact Induced Grammatical Changes in Spanish in Contact with Tz'utujil in Guatemala

Ana Isabel García Tesoro

1   Introduction

Guatemala presents an intense situation of linguistic contact since, in addition to Spanish, which is the official language, 22 Mayan languages, Xinka and Garifuna are spoken, officially recognized as national languages (Baird, 2019). This linguistic variety corresponds to its ethnic and cultural wealth as it is estimated that slightly more than half of the population is mestizo, 41% belonging to some Mayan ethnic group,[1] and there are Xinka and Garifuna groups that constitute a smaller percentage, less than 1% of the population.

The Mayan languages have more than six million speakers,[2] the majority languages, with more than 400.000 speakers, are Q'eqchi' (1,127,387), K'iche' (1,054,818), Mam (590,641), and Kaqchikel (411,089); the minority languages, with less than 200.000, are Q'anjob'al (166,261), Poqomchi' (133,074), Achi (124,338), Ixil (114,997), Tz'utujil (72,436), Jakalteko/Popti' (32,568), Chuj (58,592), and Akateco (55,290); those with less than 25,000 speakers are, Chalchiteko (21,550), Ch'orti' (16,663), Awakateko (10,145), Poqomam (10,787), Sakapulteko (6,528), Uspanteko (5,125), Sipakapense (4,155), Tektiteko (3,009), Mopan (2,011), and Itza' (406).

Although, in strict terms, the Mayan languages and Spanish have coexisted for more than 500 years, the situation of generalized bilingualism within indigenous communities began in the mid-twentieth century, when the Mayans began to access formal education and learn Spanish as a second language. The introduction of primary school in the departments of the indigenous population meant the first contact with Spanish for many families, in the majority of cases their children received at least two or three years of primary education, nevertheless only a minority managed to complete middle or higher studies. At the same time, the working population, especially men, were forced to learn

---

1   According to the 2018 national census, the population of Guatemala was 14.901.286 people, 6.207.503 of them were Mayan people (https://www.censopoblacion.gt/).
2   According to the 2018 national census (https://www.censopoblacion.gt/).

Spanish to carry out their jobs outside the community and to engage in commerce or other economic activities. As has happened with other indigenous communities in America, Mayan communities have maintained a high degree of Mayan-Spanish bilingualism for years since they acquired the Mayan language in the family nucleus and needed to learn Spanish to function in school, work and other areas of daily life. At present, there is no definitive data on the percentage of the monolingual population in Mayan languages although it is estimated that it does not exceed 3% or 4% (Richards, 2003).

This process of bilingualism oriented towards learning Spanish has undoubtedly been motivated by the situation of diglossia between Spanish and the Mayan languages. Despite this unfavorable social situation, the bilingual population has not abandoned its first language in favor of Spanish, which has led to a situation of intense contact between both languages in the regions where the Mayan languages have historically been spoken.

In the bilingual regions where Mayan languages are spoken, the local varieties of Spanish are not well known. However, the studies and descriptions that were carried out point to a series of traits that are interpreted as variations resulting from the intense contact with the Mayan languages. The most prominent of these are the fall of the vowels in final position, a strong consonantism, variation in the intonation, a reorganization of the third-person unstressed pronominal system, changes in the use of prepositions, or lexical loans of the different Mayan languages (Baird, 2017, 2020, 2021a, 2021b; García Tesoro, 2008; McKinnon, 2020, this volume; on the variety of contact with the Yucatec Maya in Mexico that presents similar characteristics, see Hernández & Palacios, 2015; Michnowicz & Kagan, 2016; Uth & Bravo Gutiérrez, 2020).

To contribute to a better understanding of these varieties and to provide new data, this chapter address the analysis of two contact-induced grammatical changes in the variety of Spanish in contact with the Tz'utujil language, spoken by some 50,000 speakers in the departments of Sololá and Suchitepéquez. Firstly, the reorganization of the unstressed third-person pronominal system, characterized by two changes, which are the use of *lo* as an invariable form to mark the direct object (*si es posible deja tirado la **tinaja** y lo quiebra*) and the omission of the same pronoun with determined referents ([...] *la cande-la$_i$ también $\varnothing_i$ usaron los antepasados*). The second change was the use of the preposition *en* with verbs of movement (*si yo **voy en** la escuela uno no puede hablar en Tz'utujil*).

This change is analyzed from a theoretical point of view, taking into account that it involves factors traditionally considered internal (internal evolution and grammaticalization processes of the Spanish language itself), and external (contact with Tz'utujil), which is analyzed from the proposal of Jarvis and

Pavlenko (2008) and Palacios and Pfänder (2014). This study postulates that both are involved in the outcome and in the process by which change is shaped.

First, the unstressed third-person pronominal system of Spanish, given its instability and variation since the Middle Ages, is prone to change and, in fact, is immersed in a process of change in the peninsular varieties.[3] Therefore, in a situation of intense contact such as the one analyzed, it could be seen that there is an acceleration in its grammaticalization, which translates into a reorganization of the paradigm. Likewise, the variation in the use of the prepositions *a* and *en* with verbs of movement in Spanish is well known in medieval Spanish and shows some vestiges in uses of current Spanish. It is also an element susceptible to change in the Spanish language.

Second, this study considers contact to be a trigger for linguistic change, and tries to show that Tz'utujil has characteristics that have enhanced the phenomena described. In line with authors such as Jarvis and Pavlenko (2008) and Palacios and Pfänder (2014), in situations of intense contact between bilingual speakers who have at their disposal two codes for meanings that they perceive similar, it is possible to see changes that encourage the linguistic convergence between the two languages; and it is precisely in those areas that are perceived as similar where change can occur, despite the typological distance of the languages, as has been shown in several investigations on Spanish in contact with Amerindian languages (Palacios, 2011, 2013; Palacios & Pfänder, 2014). Thus, it could be seen that the changes observed in Spanish tend to converge with the Tz'utujil language in areas prone to change.

Finally, this study would like to highlight that the evolution of the pronominal system of the unstressed third person is unusual in other variants of Spanish but presents notable parallels with other varieties of contact with Amerindian languages; thus, we consider that we are facing processes of general change in Spanish with intense contact. The reorganization of the pronominal system in the unstressed third person in varieties of Spanish in contact with Amerindian languages has been interpreted in several studies as a process of contact-induced linguistic change. Quechua, Guarani, Mayan languages, Otomi, Tepehuano, and other languages that have the absence of the grammaticalization of gender and number in common, which is considered to be behind the changes observed in Spanish (Avelino Sierra, 2017; García Tesoro & Fernández Mallat, 2015; Hernández & Palacios, 2015; Palacios, 2005, 2006,

---

3   Beyond the phenomena known as Leísmo, Laísmo, and Loísmo, there are various reorganized systems in which the features of continuity, gender, and the number of the referent are revealed as determining factors in the selection of clitics. Likewise, the case distinction tends to be omitted in the so-called referential system (see Fernández Ordóñez 2001, 2012).

2011, 2013, 2015, 2021; Sánchez Paraíso, 2019, 2021; Torres, 2018). Likewise, the reinterpretation of the values and uses of prepositions has been observed in various varieties of Spanish in contact with Amerindian languages, and such changes have also been attributed to the influence of Amerindian languages (Palacios, 2019).

2 The Corpus

The corpus event on which this research is based corresponds to a field of study carried out in San Pedro Cutzán, located in the municipality of Chicacao in the south of the department of Suchitepéquez near the coast. Chicacao is made up of an urban nucleus of 40,000 inhabitants and 11 villages, which are subdivided into cantons, including San Pedro Cutzán, which has about 11,000 inhabitants. It presents a complex linguistic situation, and there are no reliable censuses that establish the percentage of the bilingual and monolingual population. However, a visit to Chicacao reveals that an important part of the inhabitants of the urban area are indigenous and speak Tz'utujil. In the villages, on the other hand, the percentage of indigenous population is very high and clearly predominates over the non-indigenous population. Most of the indigenous people are bilingual and have learned Spanish in school or in adulthood; they generally occupy the lowest social strata and carry out different trades or work as day laborers in one of the 115 farms that surround the town.[4]

On the other hand, the rest of the population is non-indigenous and monolingual in Spanish; the majority have received basic instruction in school and tend to perform skilled jobs. Neither group has a close relationship, except in commercial or service exchanges. The official language in all contexts is Spanish, and Tz'utujil has been relegated to the family sphere among the indigenous population or to very specific contexts such as festivals or masses in the villages. In a few cases, there are attempts to bring non-indigenous people closer to the Tz'utujil culture or language, and in general, the attitudes towards Mayan languages on the part of the non-indigenous population are negative. Proof of this is that the school abstention rate for the indigenous population is very high in Chicacao since there is no bilingual education program that takes

---

4 Most of the indigenous people are workers from the nearby department of Sololá who migrated to the coastal area to work on the coffee plantations. The exploitation of the lands in the departments near the coast, such as Suchitepéquez, produced for years the migration of thousands of indigenous people, as well as the construction and foundation of "Indian villages" for their permanent settlement in the vicinities of the agricultural holdings of the landowners.

the needs of these students into account, except in some villages that have schools with bilingual education, as is the case of San Pedro Cutzán. In recent years in Guatemala, a minority sector of the indigenous population has prospered economically and has had the opportunity to study and gain access to qualified work in the capital or in a nearby city. These people tend to renounce their first language since they hardly practice it, and they do not usually pass it on to their children. Likewise, they abandon other signs of identity such as indigenous regional dress and active participation in certain customs and festivities; thus, they try to integrate into the majority non-indigenous society and maintain their social and economic status (Baird, 2019; García Tesoro, 2011). Moreover, in San Pedro Cutzán there were some people who had the following characteristics: they only spoke Spanish, they were from indigenous ethnicity, and their family spoke Tz'utujil.

This study analyzes a spoken language corpus made up of 24 semi-directed interviews carried out with bilingual and monolingual speakers. We also analyzed the duration of the recordings oscillating between 30 and 60 minutes. In order to undertake the analysis of the pronouns, sociolinguistic groups are differentiated according to the level of instruction and the degree of bilingualism of the informants,[5] which are the factors proposed as most relevant in this community in order to understand the extent of the change in the pronominal system (see García Tesoro, 2018, 2021). Likewise, they are factors that have proven to be fundamental in the study of other situations of linguistic contact (Thomason, 2001).

Considering these factors, four sociolinguistic groups that are taken into account for the analysis of the following point are distinguished.
- Group I: Monolinguals who have no contact with bilinguals. In general, it is a non-indigenous population; they have a high level of education and perform skilled jobs. They all work in the urban nucleus of Chicacao (6 interviews).
- Group II: Monolinguals who live in bilingual environments. That is, they come from families where parents or other relatives speak a Mayan language but have not transmitted it to them. They have completed primary or secondary education (6 interviews).
- Group III: Fluent or symmetrical bilinguals. They speak both languages fluently and handle them daily in different contexts. They have generally learned Spanish in school and use it in their work. They have completed primary or secondary education (6 interviews).

---

5 Following the classification of Vallverdú (2002).

- Group IV: Instrumental bilinguals. They have learned Spanish informally and hardly use it in their daily lives. Most are older people who have worked as peasants or are women. In both cases, they have not had access to basic schooling, and in most cases, they went to school for a short time and dropped out (6 interviews).

3 Analysis of Two Contact-Induced Grammatical Changes

3.1 The Reorganization of the Third-Person Unstressed Pronominal System

In the variety of Spanish in contact with the Tz'utujil, there is variation in the third-person unstressed pronominal system, and the two phenomena mentioned are detected:[6] the tendency to use *lo* as the only form for the direct object and the omission of the same.

3.1.1 The Tendency to Employ the Invariable 'Lo' in a Singular Way

The examples below demonstrate the trend towards the use of the unique form taken from the corpus:

(1)   *Entonces buscaba a su niño en la noche, toda la gente oye un lamento en la noche, se le dice que es la ciguanaba, o la llorona, por lo general a las doce de la noche sale y empieza: "miiijo, ay mi hiiijo", muchos aseguran que la*[7] *han oído, otros que* lo *han visto, y la ven como una mujer alta, elegante con una capa blanca, ¿verdad?, un vestido blanco, los que* lo *han visto, a saber si es cierto que grita.* (Monolingual Group I)
'Then she would look for her child at night. Everyone hears a cry at night. They are told that it is the ciguanaba, or the *weeping woman*. She usually comes out at midnight and begins: "miiijo [my son], oh my son!" Many say they have heard her; others who have seen *her* [lo], and see her as a tall, elegant woman with a white cloak, right? A white dress, those who have seen *her* [lo]; who knows if it is true that she screams?' (Monolingual Group I)

---

6   As we know, in standard (normative) Spanish there is the pronoun *lo* to refer to the masculine singular COD, the pronoun *los* to refer to the masculine plural COD, the pronoun *la* for the feminine singular COD, and the pronoun *las* for the feminine plural COD.
7   In some cases, the canonical form of the feminine *la* is used, both the invariable form *lo* and those of the etymological system that refer to gender and the number of the referent *los*, *la* and *las*, are used and present differences depending on the groups of speakers, as it will be seen later.

(2) *Yo le traigo la* foto *mañana, ahí* lo *tengo, ahí tiene que mirar alguno*
(Monolingual Group II)
'I'll bring you the *photo* tomorrow. I have *it* [lo] there. You have to look at someone there' (Monolingual Group II)

(3) P: [...] *lo que sí nos han obligado es que haya tradiciones, las* tradiciones lo *practican la gente ladina (no indígena) y nuestra raza más que todo ahí en la comunidad ...* (Bilingual Group III)
'Q: [...] what they have forced us is for there to be traditions, the traditions are practiced by the ladino people (not indigenous), and our race more than anything else in the community ...' (Bilingual Group III)

(4) *Si es el cocido de la hierba, hay gente que viene a buscarnos así, en los cafetales, une que va por los cafetales, en el monte así, consigue esa* hierba *y* lo *trae,* lo *trae comprada o regalada, viene a que* lo *lave bien y* lo *coce, tres veces al día un vaso ...* (Bilingual Group IV)
'If it is grass stew, there are people who come to look for us like this, in the coffee plantations, going through the coffee plantations, in the mountains like this. They get that *grass* and bring *it* [lo], they bring it [lo] bought or given away, they come to wash it [lo] well and cook *it* [lo], a glass three times a day ...' (Bilingual Group IV).

As can be seen in the examples, all kinds of *lo* [it] references are indicated. These occur according to a pattern that would preserve the distinction of case but not that of gender and number, in which the form *lo* would lose its referential characteristics and would function as a mark of case that only refers to the direct object. The trend is clear in the corpus if we look at data related to the use of the form *lo* [it] with female referents and with plurals (Tables 7.1 and 7.2), where the predominant use of *lo* [it] with all kinds of referents is evidenced with very high percentages, 56.2% for the feminine ones and 32% for the plural ones. The use of the singular feminine form *la* with plural feminine referents is much lower (only in 8.3% of the cases), which leads us to think that we are facing a tendency to simplify the system through the use of the form *lo*.

TABLE 7.1   Direct object pronouns according to the gender of the referent

	Lo(s)	*La(s)*
Masculine	536/536 (100%)	
Feminine	122/217 (56.2%)	95/217 (43.8%)

TABLE 7.2 Direct object pronouns according to the referent number

	Lo	*Los*	*La*	*Las*
Singular	517/517 (100%)		71/71 (100%)	
Plural	45/141 (32%)	96/141 (68%)	2/24 (8.3%)	22/24 (91.7%)

TABLE 7.3 Direct object pronouns with female referents according to the animate +/- trait

	Feminine *la*(s)	**feminine *lo*(s)**
Animate	36/72 (50%)	36/72 (50%)
Inanimate	59/145 (40.7%)	86/145 (59.3%)

$\chi^2 = 0.65$, df = 1, p < 0.20

TABLE 7.4 Direct object pronouns with plural referents according to the +/- animate feature

	Plural *los*	**Plural *lo***
Animate	67/84 (79.7%)	17/84 (20.3%)
Inanimate	29/57 (50.9%)	28/57 (49.1%)

Additionally, it can be seen that gender is neutralized to a greater extent than number, which is expected and does not contradict the universal principles of change since number is a more nuclear category than gender. Therefore, the latter is more susceptible to change and simplification.[8]

On the other hand, the selection of *lo* as the only form for the direct object occurs with all kinds of referents; but it is favored to a greater extent with inanimate referents, both when it points to feminine and plural, especially the latter, as can be seen in Tables 7.3 and 7.4.

It is possible to affirm then that the change is spreading fundamentally through the objects categorized as inanimate; therefore, there is an underlying hierarchy of animation that favors its extension.

---

8 From Greenberg's universals, the more nuclear character of the number with respect to gender is deduced (universals 32 and 36) (taken from the Spanish version in Moure, 2001, p. 199).

TABLE 7.5 Percentage of employment of what neutralizes the distinction of gender and number for the direct object by groups

	Group I	Group II	Group III	Group IV
Gender	4.2%	33.3%	84%	100%
Number	2.3%	23.4%	33.5%	87.9%

Below, the breakdown of the data according to the groups of speakers, which offers interesting results, is found. In order to explain the detected linguistic variation, social parameters that could condition or limit the use of pronouns have been taken into account, and the informants have been divided into four groups based on their degree of bilingualism and their level of education. These factors, as has been pointed out in numerous studies (Palacios, 2013; Thomason, 2001, among others), and have proven to be fundamental in situations of language contact. In the study, therefore, it is interesting to check whether these parameters influence the selection of clitics made by speakers belonging to different sociolinguistic groups as has been postulated. It is important to observe that both bilingual and monolingual speakers present the change, although its frequency manifests itself in different degrees, that is, the reorganized system coexists and competes with the etymological system. The percentages of employment of the unique form in the different groups can be seen in Table 7.5.

The most significant aspect of this breakdown of the results is the progression in the frequency of use in each group according to the factors considered during the study. Thus, Group I of monolinguals shows the change but in an incipient way (4.2% and 2.3%). In Group II of monolinguals who have contact with bilinguals, the changes are not so widespread, and although they manifest themselves in a considerable percentage of variation (33.3% and 23.4%), the etymological system is still predominantly maintained, as in Group I. In the bilingual groups, the change is generalized, and a reorganized system works, especially in Group IV (100% and 87.9% use of *lo* with feminine and plural referents). The results allow us to verify that the change is originated in bilingual speakers, of whom it can practically be said that the reorganized system operates, which later spreads to monolinguals. However, these latter, although showing variations, still maintain the etymological system. Therefore, in the same community, both systems coexist, the etymological predominantly among monolinguals, and the reorganized system in bilinguals.

Conversely, as a consequence of the tendency to use *lo* [it] as a unique form, in this system, its appearance is observed in contexts of duplication (as in Examples 5 and 6), that is, prepended in the same sentence as the nominal referent, which presents strong restrictions in Spanish except in some variants of Argentina and Venezuela:

(5) *Los que están en Estados Unidos, los padrinos le dicen,* lo *han adoptado sus niños, mandan ... un poco de alimento para ellos, ¿sí?* (Bilingual Group IV)
'Those who are in the United States, the godparents call him, their children have been adopted by *him* [lo], they send ... some food for them, yes?' (Bilingual Group IV)

(6) *Ahora ya no* lo *dejan el octavo (alcohol) así, en envase, sino que ya lo riegan sobre la tierra donde está enterrado el difunto, para que no sea el otro el que se lo vaya a tomar.* (Bilingual Group III)
'Now they no longer leave *it* [*lo*] the *eighth* (alcohol) like this, in a container, but now they water it on the ground where the deceased is buried so that it's not someone else who takes it.' (Bilingual Group III)

In these cases, the *lo* form, by losing the deictic character on the information of the gender and number traits of the referent, becomes an object mark that only indicates its appearance, and its presence is becoming necessary in an increasing number of contexts; therefore, it extends to those that are restricted in the Spanish standard. There is thus, a reanalysis of the function of the pronoun, which is also evidenced in the rigid syntactic order that requires duplication in all cases: pronoun-verb-direct object. This syntactic rigidity in the duplications that is manifested in the adjacency between pronoun, verb, and referent as well as in the use of *lo* as an invariable form more clearly shows characteristics of an object agreement since it only anticipates that after the verb a direct object appears. Suñer (1993) already interprets the duplication in the varieties of Argentina and Venezuela as a phenomenon of verb-object agreement that is subject to the following principle: folding with clitics is only performed with specific referents, and animation is the second necessary feature in the most cases. The author relies on the studies of several researchers who have proposed for the pronominal clitic system of Spanish, if not an objective conjugation, a concordance between the verb and the object. In the case of the variety of contact with Tz'utujil, duplication always occurs with the unique form *lo* and with all kinds of referents, although inanimate ones are more frequent, it is even possible with indeterminate referents, as can be seen in the examples below:

(7) *En cambio, en la Semana Santa sí* lo *preparamo un* pan *con* ... (Bilingual Group III)
'On the other hand, at Easter we do prepare a bread with ...' (Bilingual Group III)

(8) *Algunos sí lo usan para casarse (el güipil), pero otros solo lo usan así blusas para casarse, blusas blancas, pero ya no güipiles* ... (Bilingual Group IV)
'Some do use it to get married (the güipil, traditional embroidered blouse), but others only use *it* [lo] like this, *blouses* to marry, white blouses, but no longer güipiles ...' (Bilingual Group IV)

The frequency of duplications is not high in the corpus. It represents only 7% of the cases (52 of 753 pronouns that appear in other contexts). However, after breaking down their frequency according to the sociolinguistic groups, it is possible to visualize the progression of higher to lower from the bilingual to monolingual groups (see Table 7.5) so that the highest incidence shows in Groups III and IV, 12.6% and 16.4%, respectively, since again, they constitute the origin of the change. On the contrary, monolingual groups present a much lower percentage of duplications. Group II barely reached 2%, and Group I does not show any case of duplication since this is a minority and very marked change, identified with the speech of bilinguals. It is significant, however, that the change is manifested in Group II of monolinguals, albeit in a very low proportion.

In contrast, congruently with the tendency to use [*lo*] as a unique form, it is favored with inanimate referents since it accounts for 71.1% of cases of duplication, as can be seen in Table 7.6. This differs from what was observed in other varieties with duplication in Argentina and Venezuela in which specific and animate referents tend to duplicate and have a higher degree of topicality (Suñer, 1993) since in this case, it would be a consequence of the change induced by contact and the tendency of the system to acquire characteristics of an object match (Jaeggli, 1982).

TABLE 7.6　Frequency of duplication by groups

	Pronouns that do not duplicate	**Pronouns that duplicate**
Group I	172/172 (100%)	0/0 (0%)
Group II	256/261 (98%)	5/261 (2%)
Group III	125/143 (87.4%)	18/143 (12.6%)
Group IV	148/177 (83.6%)	29/177 (16.4%)

TABLE 7.7 Percentages of employment of what neutralizes the gender and number distinction for the direct object according to the +/- animate feature of the referents

Referent	Duplications
Animate	15/52 (28.9%)
Inanimate	37/52 (71.1%)

3.1.2 Tendency to Pronominal Omission

The second phenomenon related to the reorganization of the pronominal system is the omission of the direct object clitic with semantically or syntactically defined referents, which does not occur in other varieties of Spanish (Campos, 1986). The omission in the corpus always occurs in contexts of postponement with respect to the referent so that it is possible to recover the information. Its frequency with respect to the use of full pronouns is considerably high in the corpus, 18.5% (Table 7.8), and it is also favored with inanimate referents (Table 7.9).

As mentioned earlier, the omission is interpreted as an object-verb agreement zero morpheme that operates within the case marking system in combination or as an alternative to the invariable. In the studies carried out on languages that have object agreement, the relationship between verbal agreement and the tendency to indicate the third person with a zero mark is shown (Franco, 1991). The first and second persons, on the other hand, tend to express themselves with an explicit verbal affix. Therefore, the analyzed system would also manifest a characteristic tendency of these systems: the agreement by means of a zero morpheme of the third person object, which implies the phonetic non-realization of the pronoun in Spanish. Note that this tendency, at least to pronominal omission with inanimate referents, has already been verified in other varieties of contact, which confirms that it is a common tendency that operates in processes of change in the pronominal system of Spanish in situations of intense contact with other languages.

On the other hand, as with the tendency to use *lo* as an object mark, omission is favored with inanimate referents. The percentage of omission, although it is certainly significant, does not yet allow us to think about an extension to other contexts. To explain this trend, focus is drawn to a hierarchy of animacy in the organization of the concordance schemes since it has been proposed as an essential factor in case marking (Blake, 138 et seq.). It is important to remember that elements that are higher in the animation hierarchy are the first and second persons, followed by the third, then the personal, human,

TABLE 7.8   Frequency of omission of the direct object pronoun, in contexts of postponement with respect to the referent

Plenary pronouns	Omission
753/924 (81.5%)	171/924 (18.5%)

TABLE 7.9   Omissions and pronouns made according to the trait [+/- animate]

	Plenary pronouns	Omission
Animate	284/300 (94.7%)	16/300 (5.3%)
Inanimate	469/624 (75.2%)	155/624 (24.8%)

$\chi^2 = 51.16$, df = 1, p < 0.001

animate, and finally, the inanimate nouns. Thus, in the analyzed system, the inanimate ones referred by third-person pronouns would be interpreted as defective categories found at the lowest level of the hierarchy and, consequently, would suppose a *lo* mark without a lexical reference or a zero in order to mark their concordance. On the contrary, the speaker prefers to use *la(s)*, which is the form that still maintains referential content, to mark preferably and animate human female entities, that is, those that are in the highest position in the hierarchy.

As noted earlier, the omission of the direct object pronoun is a very widespread phenomenon that appears in monolingual and bilingual speakers, as illustrated in the examples below:

(9)   R: [...] ¿Ya conoce el hule$_i$?
P: No.
R: ¿No ∅$_i$ conoce? A ver qué, cuándo la llevamos a ver la plantación ... (Monolingual Group I)
'A: [...] Do you already know hule$_i$?
Q: No.
A: You don't know ∅$_i$? Let's see what, when do we take her to see the plantation ...' (Monolingual Group I)

(10) [...] también ha de haber también personas que practican la magia negra, pero yo digo que cada pueblo tiene su libro$_i$ y, no sé ... porque dicen que

después que ellos $\varnothing_i$ terminan de leer y ya ponen en práctica algo, ellos tienen una pelea con el diablo y lo hacen en el cementerio ... (Monolingual Group II)
'[...] there must also be people who practice black magic, but I say that each town has its own book$_i$ and, I don't know ... because they say that after they finish reading $\varnothing_i$ and already put something into practice. They have a fight with the devil and they do it in the cemetery ...' (Monolingual Group II)

(11) *[...] cuando uno solicita un trabajo ahora lo primero que le preguntan, estudio, qué curso, o sea, qué título tiene, qué ha estudiado, en fin, ese es el obstáculo para uno de ahora cuando quiere trabajar o sale a buscar un trabajo$_i$, le $\varnothing_i$ dan pero si tienes un título, una profesión.* (Bilingual Group III)
'[...] when you apply for a job now, the first thing you are asked, studies, what course, that is, what degree do you have, what have you studied. In short, that is the obstacle for you now when you want to work or look for a job$_i$, they give $\varnothing_i$ to you but if you have a degree, a profession.' (Bilingual Group III)

(12) *Hay unos (tejidos) que lo hice, ese tejido$_i$ me $\varnothing_i$ pidieron la gente para el quince, pa los patojitos ...* (Bilingual Group IV)
'There are some (fabrics) that I made, that fabric$_i$ people asked me for $\varnothing_i$ for the fifteen, for the children (patojitos) ...' (Bilingual Group IV)

In the cited examples, the clitic omission occurs in all groups of speakers; however, this phenomenon does not manifest itself with the same frequency in those same groups. Table 7.10, presented below, shows the relative frequency of omissions compared to the use of the pronoun according to the four groups considered.

A clear difference can be observed between the bilingual groups (III and IV) and the monolingual groups (I and II). Note that the frequency of omissions

TABLE 7.10 Frequency of omission according to groups of speakers

	Plenary pronouns	**Omission ($\varnothing$)**
Group I	172/184 (93.5%)	12/184 (6.5%)
Group II	261/298 (87.6%)	37/298 (12.4%)
Group III	143/192 (74.5%)	49/192 (25.5%)
Group IV	177/250 (70.8%)	73/250 (29.2%)

is very similar to that observed for the use of *lo* as a unique form, which shows that they are phenomena that are part of the same process of linguistic change and are conditioned by the same sociolinguistic factors.

3.2   Use of the Preposition en *with Verbs of Movement*

The second change analyzed is less extensive, and it is registered only among bilinguals so that it can therefore be considered a contact induced change. It is about the use of the preposition *en* with verbs of movement, as can be seen in the following examples:

(13) *[…] porque hay gente que no domina el español, entoes tiene que pagar a otra persona (un intérprete), cuando va con el doctor, cuando van con un abogado, tiene que pagar una persona, cuando van* en *el centro de salud, si solo hablan el Tz'utujil tiene que pagar a una persona, darle de comer, pagarle el día, pasaje …* (Bilingual Group III)
'[…] because there are people who do not speak Spanish, then (entoes) they have to pay another person (an interpreter), when they go to the doctor, when they go to a lawyer, a person has to pay, when they go *to* [en] the health center, if they only speak Tz'utujil, they have to pay a person, feed him, pay him for the day, fare …' (Bilingual Group III)

(14) *[…] el día venticinco, es el día del magisterio pues nacional de Guatemala, pero en la noche ya van* en *la feria, es la … cómo se llama, la investidura de la reina del deporte …* (Bilingual Group III)
'[…] on the twenty-fifth day, it is the day of the magisterium, as a national of Guatemala, but at night they already go *to* (en) the fair, it is the … what is it called, the investiture of the queen of sport …' (Bilingual Group III)

(15) *Sí, es que antes solo en lengua (Tz'utujil) nos hablaban, pero nos costó mucho porque cuando nos vamos* en *la escuela, cuando el profesor nos habla nos da miedo, nos ponemos así a chillar.* (Bilingual Group IV)
'Yes, it is that before only in language (Tz'utujil) they spoke to us, but it cost us a lot because when we go *to* (en) school, when the teacher speaks to us, we are scared, we start screaming like that.' (Bilingual Group IV)

(16) *Ahora al entrar ahí en el campo santo pues hay muchos panteones, ¿verdá?, sí, casi la mayoría se van* en *los panteones propios, no es de la municipalidad, sí, es propio, cada uno.* (Bilingual Group IV)
'Now when entering the holy field there, there are many cemeteries, right? Yes, most of them go *to* (en) their own cemeteries, it is not owned by the municipality, yes, it is their own, each one.' (Bilingual Group IV)

TABLE 7.11 Use of *en* instead of *a* with verbs of movement

Group I	0/15 (0%)
Group II	0/10 (0%)
Group III	4/19 (21%)
Group IV	12/21 (57%)

If the cases of the use of the preposition *a* in front of *en* with movement verbs in the corpus are counted, it is possible to see that it is a change that is originated in bilingual speakers since, in fact, monolingual speakers do not manifest it. Only four in Group III bilingual speakers and twelve in Group IV instrumental bilinguals have been registered as seen in the Table 7.11.

These data suggest that a change is being induced by contact with Tz'utujil, which originates in instrumental bilinguals (57%) and is spreading to the rest of bilinguals (21%) but not to monolinguals for the moment. In any case, it is a phenomenon with a very low frequency of use that could spread in the future but currently has a very limited presence.

4   Discussion

As postulated in the introduction, the two phenomena analyzed as contact-induced changes are considered. Tz'utujil has characteristics that would allow us to explain the observed changes (Dayley, 1985).

For the reorganization of the pronominal system, it was observed that Tz'utujil does not grammaticalize the agreement of gender and number in a compulsory way as in Spanish. This characteristic would explain the tendency to neutralize gender and number traits that is taking place in the marking system for the direct object. It also has a different object marking system than the unstressed pronoun system of Spanish. Tz'utujil, like the rest of the Mayan languages, is an ergative language in which there is not the same distinction between transitivity and intransitivity for the third person. This information is given by the verb and by the number of participants; therefore, they do not establish the same dative/accusative distinction for objects as Spanish. They have a system of patient object suffixes for transitive verbs, whose presence is mandatory in all cases, which are incorporated into the verb to indicate the person but do not mark the case distinction or gender and number traits. This characteristic would also support the tendency to neutralize gender and number traits in the pronominal system observed in Spanish. Finally, these suffixes appear for the first and second person, but not with the third, which would explain the tendency to omit the third person pronoun in Spanish.

Then, it would be an indirect change induced by contact (in the sense of Palacios 2011, 2013) with Tz'utujil in which there is no direct import of the contact language into Spanish, but its influence is translated into a reorganization of the unstressed pronominal system of Spanish that brings it closer to the object marking system of Tz'utujil and to an extension of the use of the preposition *en* as an alternative of the preposition *a* with movement verbs. The bilingual speaker perceives cognitive similarities (following Jarvis & Pavlenko, 2008 and Palacios & Pfänder, 2014) between the object marking system in Tz'utujil and in Spanish and assumes that it is possible to mark the object with an invariable form (lo) or a phonetic zero in Spanish.[9] Thus, from the perception of related categories, it produces changes consistent with their communication needs, and conceptual outlines are produced that lead to the readjustment of the paradigm.

On the other hand, Spanish is a language that shows variation in the pronominal system in some areas where there is no contact (in peninsular Spanish) and that also knows varieties of pronominal duplication (Venezuela, Argentina ...), although this last phenomenon is subject to many restrictions, so that it is postulated that the changes studied are introduced through structures that in the Spanish language are already immersed in grammaticalization processes and are prone to change. That is, contact would be the trigger for a process of change, which, although it may follow an unknown and unexpected evolution in other varieties of Spanish, is not chaotic and follows a specific orientation.

In fact, general processes of change of the third-person unstressed pronominal system in contact with different Amerindian languages are observed (Avelino Sierra, 2017; Avelino Sierra & Torres, 2021; García Tesoro & Fernández Mallat, 2015; Hernández & Palacios, 2015; Palacios, 2005, 2006, 2011, 2013 2015, 2021a; Torres Sánchez, 2015, 2018; Sánchez Paraíso, 2019; 2021; among others), which in all cases are typologically very different but have the absence of the category of gender and number in common. In such cases, there is always a reorganization with invariable object marks that sometimes appear with a phonetic zero, and that in the most simplified systems also lose the distinction

---

[9] In the case of omission, it must be remembered that Spanish can elide direct objects when they are undefined, unspecific (Fields). Regarding the tendency to mark the direct object with the invariable form *lo*, it is necessary to remember that the pronominalization of the indirect object in Spanish is insensitive to the gender of the referent and, increasingly, to the referent number since the tendency is to use the singular form *le* for plural referents.

of case (since the form *le* tends to be used only for direct object and indirect object, see Palacios, 2006, 2011, 2013).

Regarding the use of the preposition *en* with verbs of movement, it is also considered that it could be explained by the influence of Tz'utujil since the value of *en* as a goal with verbs of movement in Spanish is expressed in a similar way in Tz'utujil through the postpositional -pa and -chi, which can denote movement focused on the direction and the goal, as can be seen in the examples (taken from Cholotío & García Ixmatá, 1998, pp. 147, 179).

(17) *Ja nuutee' pa jaay*
'My mom went home.'

(18) *Ja nuutee' eel k'in xb'e chi ya'*
'My mom went out and went to (in) the beach'.

However, it is not interpreted as a copy or a mere loan, but as a contact-induced change in which bilinguals perceive similarities in their two languages and make them converge (Jarvis & Pavlenko, 2008; Palacios & Pfänder, 2014), they try to exploit the communication strategies of their first language in the second language. In this case, it is a variation that puts the emphasis on the goal, not so much in the direction indicated by the movement verb. Likewise, it is considered that this process occurs in Spanish as it is susceptible to this change. The variation of *a* (to) and *en* (in) with verbs of movement has been documented in the history of Spanish and in dialect varieties of Spain, and it has also been recorded in other varieties of contact with Amerindian languages such as Paraguayan Spanish (Palacios, 2019, p. 241 ss.).

Finally, from a sociolinguistic point of view, it has been observed that the reorganization of the pronominal system is manifested equally in monolingual and bilingual speakers and is part of the norm of local Spanish, although it manifests itself to a different degree. However, its extension is determined by social factors since its presence depends on the degree of bilingualism and level of education of the informants (the analysis shows a progression from less to greater frequency of changes depending on the sociolinguistic groups distinguished in this studio). Likewise, the reorganized local systems are negatively evaluated by the non-indigenous population and strongly penalized at school, where the etymological system is imposed, which also contributes to not being generalized among the entire population. In any case, the change originates and spreads from the bilingual groups, but the frequency of use decreases depending on their distance from the Mayan language. This sociolinguistic progression reinforces the hypothesis of language contact to explain the linguistic changes produced in the study area. Thus, it is appreciated that the reorganized system is the one used and is working in bilinguals, while monolinguals maintain the etymological system with some variations towards the local system. Thus, it is shown that in the same speaking community the two systems coexist; and depending on the social factors taken into account, degree of bilingualism, and level of instruction, they show a gradation within the groups of monolingual and bilingual people in a *continuum* and not as isolated and completely differentiated systems.

On the other hand, the use of the preposition *en* with verbs of movement shows a very limited frequency of use and it only occurs among bilingual speakers. Thus, it is possible to postulate that it is a change in the initial phase that has been originated in bilinguals, and it is not possible to venture whether in the future it will have acceptance and will spread; however, it is used by bilinguals in a productive way to denote another meaning and to focus the movement on the goal and not on the direction.

5 Conclusions

In order to recapitulate, it is important to point out that this work set out to show that there are two grammatical changes induced by the contact of Spanish with the Mayan Tz'utujil language. It considers that contact is the trigger for changes since Tz'utujil has a series of characteristics that the bilingual speaker tends to assimilate in the second language. Likewise, internal factors in the Spanish language itself intervene in the changes observed, that is, trends of change that are accelerated in a process of grammaticalization induced by contact. Consequently to the pronominal system, there is a reorganization of the paradigm and the generalization of certain forms, in this case, an invariant *lo* and a phonetic zero for the marking of the direct object.

In line with Palacios (2011, 2013), the goal is to emphasize that it is not a chaotic or random change, but rather a process of change that is also documented in the unstressed third-person pronominal system of Spanish in contact with Amerindian languages, which, in all cases, are typologically very different but do not have the category of gender, in which there is always a reorganization with invariable object marks that also manifest themselves with a phonetic zero, and which in the most simplified systems lose the distinction of case. Another statistically relevant linguistic factor for the reorganization of the pronominal system has also been observed in the corpus, the animation hierarchy for the referent, which is also in line with trends observed in other varieties of Spanish in contact.

In the case of the preposition *en* with verbs of movement, it is used as an alternative to the preposition *a* to denote the goal rather than the direction; and although in a very limited way, in the groups of bilingual speakers, the two options coexist.

Acknowledgements

This chapter is part of the project "Spanish project in contact with Mayan languages in Guatemala: analysis of the grammatical variation of Spanish in contact with Tzutujil", that has received funding from the Committee for the Development of Research of the University of Antioquia (minute number 2016-12806, February 15, 2018).

References

Avelino Sierra, R. (2017). *Contacto lingüístico entre el español y el otomí en San Andrés Cuexcontitlán*. Universidad Nacional Autónoma de México.

Avelino Sierra, R. & Torres Sánchez, N. (2021). Efectos del contacto en la duplicación de objeto directo en dos situaciones de contacto en México. In A. Palacios & M. Sánchez Paraíso. (Coords.) *Dinámicas lingüísticas de las situaciones de contacto* (pp. 95–116). Vervuert.

Baird, B. (2017). Prosodic transfer among Spanish-K'ichee'Bilinguals. In K. Bellamy, M. W. Child, P. González, A. Muntendam & M. C. Parafita Couto (Eds.), *Multidisciplinary approaches to bilingualism in the Hispanic and Lusophone world* (pp. 147–172). John Benjamins.

Baird, B. (2019). Ciudadano maya 100%: Uso y actitudes de la lengua entre los bilingües k'iche'-español. *Hispania, 102*(3), 319–334.

Baird, B. (2020). The Vowel Spaces of Spanish-K'ichee' bilinguals. In R. G. Rao (Ed.), *Spanish phonetics and phonology in contact: Studies from Africa, the Americas, and Spain* (pp. 64–81). John Benjamins.

Baird, B. (2021a). "Para mí, es indígena con traje típico": Apocope as an indexical marker of indigeneity in Guatemalan Spanish. In L. A. Ortiz-López & E. M. Suárez Büdenbender (Eds.), *Topics in Spanish linguistic perceptions* (pp. 223–239). Routledge.

Baird, B. (2021b). Bilingual language dominance and contrastive focus marking: Gradient effects of K'ichee' syntax on Spanish prosody. *International Journal of Bilingualism, 25*(3), 500–515.

Blake, B. (1994). *Case*. Cambridge University Press.

Campos, H. (1986). Indefinite Object Drop. *Linguistic Inquiry*, 17, 354–359.

Cholotío, A. y García Ixmatá, P. (1998). *Gramática Tz'utujiil*. Proyecto Lingüístico Francisco Marroquín.

Dayley, J. P. (1985). *Tz'utujil Grammar*. University of California Press.

Fernández Ordóñez, I. (2001). Hacia una dialectología histórica. Reflexiones sobre la historia del leísmo, laísmo y loísmo. *Boletín de la Real Academia de la Historia*, 81, 389–464.

Fernández Ordóñez, I. (2021). Dialect areas and linguistic change. Pronominal paradigms in Ibero-Romance dialects from a cross-linguistic and social typology perspective. In G. de Vogelaer & G. Seiler (Eds.), *The Dialect Laboratory. Dialects as a testing ground from theories of language change* (pp. 73–106). John Benjamins.

Franco, J. (1991). Spanish Object Clitics as Verbal Agreement Morphemes. MIT *Working Papers in Linguistics*, 14, 99–113.

García Tesoro, A. I. (2008). Guatemala. In A. Palacios (Coord.), *El español en América. Contactos lingüísticos en Hispanoamérica* (pp. 95–117). Ariel.

García Tesoro, A. I. (2011). Lenguas mayas e identidad en Guatemala. *Perspectivas latinoamericanas*, 8, 122–134.

García Tesoro, A. I. (2018). El sistema pronominal átono de tercera persona en la variedad de contacto con el tzutujil: hacia una concordancia de objeto. *Revista Internacional de Lingüística Iberoamericana*, 2(32), 83–96.

García Tesoro, A. I. (2021). Tipos de hablantes y contextos comunicativos en situaciones de contacto: el caso de Guatemala. In S. Gómez Seibane, M. Sánchez Paraíso, & A. Palacios. (Coords.), *Traspasando lo lingüístico: factores esenciales en el contacto de lenguas* (pp. 15–29). Vervuert.

García Tesoro, A. I. & Fernández Mallat, V. (2015). Cero vs. *lo* en español andino. *Círculo de Lingüística Aplicada a la Comunicación*, 61, 131–157.

Gómez Seibane, S. (2012). La omisión y duplicación de objetos en el castellano del País Vasco. *El español del País Vasco* (pp. 193–214). Universidad del País Vasco / Euskal Herriko Unibertsitatea D.L.

Hernández Méndez, E. & Palacios, A. (2015). El sistema pronominal átono en la variedad del español en contacto con el maya yucateco. *Círculo de Lingüística Aplicada a la Comunicación*, 61, 36–78.

Instituto de Estadística Nacional de Guatemala. (2014). *Publicaciones*. Retrieved April 6, 2023 from https://www.ine.gob.gt/index.php/estadisticas/publicaciones.

Jaeggli, O. (1982). *Topics in Romance Syntax*. Foris Publications.

Jarvis, S., Pavlenko, A. (2008). *Crosslinguistic Influence in Language and Cognition*. Routledge.

McKinnon, S. (2020). Un análisis sociofonético de la aspiración de las oclusivas sordas en el español guatemalteco monolingüe y bilingüe (español-kaqchikel). *Spanish in Context*, 17 (1), 1–29.

Michnowicz, J. & Kagan, L. (2016). On Glottal Stops in Yucatan Spanish: Language Contact and Dialect Standardization. In S. Sessarego & Tejedo-Herrero, F. (Eds.) *Spanish Language and Sociolinguistic Analysis* (pp. 217–240). John Benjamins.

Moure, T. (2001). *Universales del lenguaje y linguo-diversidad*. Ariel.

Palacios, A. (2005). Aspectos teóricos y metodológicos del contacto de lenguas: el sistema pronominal del español en áreas de contacto con lenguas amerindias. In N. Volker, K. Zimmermann & I. Neumann-Holzschuh (Eds.), *El español en América: Aspectos teóricos, particularidades, contactos* (pp. 63–94). Vervuert.

Palacios, A. (2006). Cambios inducidos por contacto en el español de la sierra ecuatoriana: la simplificación de los sistemas pronominales (procesos de neutralización y elisión). In *Huellas del contacto, Tópicos del Seminario* 15 (pp. 197–230). Universidad Autónoma de Puebla.

Palacios, A. (2011). Nuevas perspectivas en el estudio del cambio inducido por contacto: hacia un modelo dinámico del contacto de lenguas. *Revista de Lenguas Modernas*, *38*, 17–36.

Palacios, A. (2013). Contact-induced change and internal evolution: Spanish in contact with Amerindian Languages. In I. Léglise & C. Chamoreau (Eds.), *The Interplay of Variation and Change in Contact Settings. Morphosyntactic Studies* (pp. 165–198). John Benjamins.

Palacios, A. (Coord.) (2015). *El sistema pronominal átono de 3a persona: variedades de español en contacto con otras lenguas, Círculo de Lingüística Aplicada a la Comunicación*, 61. Número monográfico.

Palacios, A. (2019). La reorganización de las preposiciones locativas *a, en* y *por* en el español en contacto con guaraní. *Círculo de Lingüística Aplicada a la Comunicación*, 78, 233–254.

Palacios, A. (2021). Sobre el contacto y los contactos: algunas reflexiones a partir del análisis de los sistemas pronominales átonos de zonas de contacto lingüístico. In A. Palacios & M. Sánchez Paraíso (Coords.) *Dinámicas lingüísticas de las situaciones de contacto* (pp. 47–76). Mouton de Gruyter.

Palacios, A. & Pfänder, S. (2014). Similarity effects in language contact: Taking the speakers' perceptions seriously. In J. Besters-Dilger, C. Dermarkar, S. Pfänder, & A. Rabus (Eds.), *Congruence in Contact-Induced Language Change. Language Families, Typological Resemblance, and Perceived Similarity* (pp. 219–238). De Gruyter.

Richards, M. (2003). *Atlas Lingüístico de Guatemala*. SEPAZ/UVG/URL/USAID.

Sánchez Paraíso, M. (2019). La omisión del objeto directo en el español andino (Juliaca, Perú). *Cuadernos de la ALFAL*, 11 (2), 147–158.

Sánchez Paraíso, M. (2021). La duplicación del objeto directo posverbal del español andino de Juliaca (Perú). In A. Palacios & M. Sánchez Paraíso (Coords.). *Dinámicas lingüísticas de las situaciones de contacto* (pp. 117–138). Mouton De Gruyter.

Suñer, M. (1993). El papel de la concordancia en las construcciones de reduplicación de clíticos. In O. Fernández Soriano (Ed.), *Los pronombres átonos* (pp. 174–204). Taurus.

Thomason, S. (2001). *Language Contact*. Edinburgh University Press.

Torres Sánchez, N. (2015). El sistema pronominal en el español de bilingües tepehuano del sureste-español. *Círculo de Lingüística Aplicada a la Comunicación, 61*, 10–35.

Torres Sánchez, N. (2018). *Aquí hablamos tepehuano y allá español. Un estudio de la situación de bilingüismo incipiente entre español y tepehuano del sureste (o'dam) en Santa María de Ocotán y Durango*. [Doctoral dissertation, El Colegio de México].

Vallverdú, F. (2002). Introducción al Bilingüismo. In *Bilingüismo en América y Cataluña (Actas del I Foro de Bilingüismo Amer-I-Cat)* (pp. 9–15). Institut Català de Cooperació Iberoamericana.

Uth, M., & Gutiérrez Bravo, R. (2020). Language Contact and Intonation: Evidence from Contrastive Focus Marking and Loanwords in Yucatecan Spanish and Yucatec Maya. *Bulletin of Hispanic Studies, 97*(1), 31–58.

CHAPTER 8

Big Data and Small Dialects
Transitive andar *in Central American Spanish*

Shannon P. Rodríguez and Chad Howe

1   Introduction

The analysis of low-frequency phenomena presents a number of interesting challenges for linguists, not the least of which is determining a reliable source of data large enough to provide adequate opportunities for discovering the target structure(s). This challenge expands as one considers other facets of the data coverage, such as dialect diversity, which can complicate an otherwise complex topic. This paper leverages contemporary corpus resources to address an issue that sits at the convergence between low-frequency linguistic phenomena and under-represented dialects in Spanish. Specifically, we provide a corpus-based analysis of *andar* in varieties of Central American Spanish with the objective of demonstrating a lexical shift towards increasingly transitive contexts that is specific to this dialect region. This pattern, referred to by scholars as "transitive *andar*" (Rivas, 1987; Hernández, 2002; Lipksi, 1994, 2008), is illustrated in examples (1) and (2) taken from the *Corpus del Español: Web/Dialects* (CdE, Davies 2016–) and Twitter, respectively.

(1) *Había que contestarle a la guardia, todos nosotros* **andábamos** UNAS PISTOLAS VIEJAS.
'We had to answer to the guard/police, we all carried old guns.'
(Nicaragua, CdE)

(2) *Y esta es la razón por la que* **no ando** NOVIA.
'And this is the reason that I don't have a girlfriend.'
(Twitter, DÍAZ M. 2014[1])

The lexical shift in *andar* discussed in this analysis can be observed in the fact that both *andábamos* in (1) and *ando* in (2) occur with nominal complements

---

1   The data from Twitter has been revised for ease of understanding. Also, the text has been replicated in the example along with the user handle. All tweets cited in this work were extracted using San Salvador as a target for geo-tagged tokens.

producing a meaning akin to 'to carry' or 'to have'. In fact, the *Diccionario de la Real Academic Española* (DRAE) notes that *andar* can denote the meaning of "[l]levar algo consigo" 'to carry on one's person', specifically in Costa Rica, El Salvador, Honduras, and Nicaragua. In the vast majority of Spanish dialects, the verb *andar* is an intransitive verb of motion—similar to other verbs like *caminar* 'to walk', *pasear* 'to go for a walk', *moverse* 'to move oneself', and *trotar* 'to jog'—that, at least canonically, occurs with prepositional adjuncts. This use of *andar*, shown in examples (3) and (4), is the basic intransitive pattern with the meaning of 'to walk, to go'. The prepositional phrases *en grupo* and *en bicicleta* function as adjuncts, making them distinct from the complements in examples (1) and (2) with respect to their relationship with *andar*.

(3) *O sea que existen Coyotes que* **andan** *solos, Coyotes que* **andan** EN GRUPO
'Um, there are coyotes that walk alone, coyotes that travel in groups' (Colombia, CdE)

(4) *Mira a otros niños y practica, luego en unos días* **anda** EN BICICLETA.
'[She/he] watches the other kids and practices, then in a few days [she/he] is going to ride his bicycle (going riding on his bicycle).' (Mexico, CdE)

Andar can also occur with an adjectival adjunct with a concomitant meaning of 'to have been feeling' as in (5). Here, *andar* most readily collocates with adjectives like *bueno* 'good', *malo* 'bad', or *alegre* 'happy', according to the DRAE. Other uses of *andar* noted in the DRAE include its use as an interjection (6) and as an existential (7).

(5) *Que cuando uno* **anda triste** *todo le sale mal.*
'When one is sad, everything goes bad for him.'
(Honduras, CdE)

(6) *¡**Anda**! Pero sí, esta canción me encanta.*
'Wow! But yeah, I love that song.' (Spain, CdE)

(7) ***Andan** muchos locos sueltos por la calle.*
'There are a lot of crazy people loose in the street.'
(DRAE)

Finally, across a number of dialects, *andar* has grammaticalized as a progressive, parallel to *andar* + GERUND as illustrated in examples (8) and (9) (Torres Cacoullos, 2001:444), similar to the grammaticalization of the present perfect (see Rivas & García, this volume). Hernández (2002:103) notes that "the verb *andar*, as in *anda buscando algo* 'he is looking for something', functions as an auxiliary in progressive and copular constructions, as well as a lexical verb meaning 'walk, go, and go around.'" This use of *andar* is widespread among dialects of Spanish.

(8) *Ando buscando a una chica que está embarazada.*
'I'm looking for a girl that's pregnant.'
(Dominican Republic, CdE)

(9) *Desde hace unos meses **ando pensando** que puede valer la pena intentar explotar esta posibilidad.*
'It's been a few months that I've been thinking that it might be worth trying to take advantage of that possibility.'
(United States, CdE)

We maintain that the grammaticalization process proposed by Torres Cacoullos (2001) for the *andar* + GERUND construction is distinct from transitive *andar*, and, though it may be possible that these two developments occur in tandem, a broader exploration of the interplay between the two will be left for a subsequent analysis. With this in mind, our analysis will proceed in Section 2 with a more fine-grained discussion of the transitive properties of *andar* in these varieties focused specifically on determining (i) the range of complements that occur in these contexts and (ii) the meanings that arise with these complements. Section 3 provides a discussion of valency and possession in language change in the context of the observed patterns of lexical shift proposed for transitive *andar*. Section 4 discusses the methods and initial results of the corpus analysis of *andar* using data extracted from the CdE, followed by Section 5 which discusses these results both across four target Central American Spanish varieties (Costa Rica, El Salvador, Honduras, and Nicaragua) and compared to other varieties. A summary of the overall results is given in Section 6 along with conclusions and discussion of the implications for further research.

2   Transitive *andar*

As stated above, *andar* functions as an intransitive verb of movement in all varieties of Spanish, also displaying a number of other constructional behaviors (e.g., use with adjectival adjuncts and gerunds). More to the point, *andar* is unergative verb whose "single argument ... is syntactically equivalent to the subject of a transitive verb" (Sorace, 2000:879) and involves "willed, volitional, controlled acts" (van Gelderen, 2011:108). Thus, in example (3), the two tokens of *andar, andan solos* and *andan en grupo*, both have as their subjects the NP *coyotes* which expresses the agentive role.

For this analysis, we distinguish two types of transitive *andar*. The first, seen in (10) and (11), are widespread and available across dialects of Spanish, as are the examples in (3)-(9). This transitive use of *andar* is only used in the sense of 'traversing a space' and is similar to the transitive use of the English verb "to walk", as in *I walk the trail to the top of the mountain*. What is important about these examples is that the ostensibly nominal complements play same role as other complements headed by the prepositions *por* or *en*, which can be added to these NPs with little change in meaning—i.e. *anda en el camino*. In contrast with examples like (1) and (2), the NPs in examples (10) and (11) function as locative adjuncts.

(10) *Y no tiene metas, solo **anda el camino** despierto.*
'And he/she doesn't have goals, he/she just walks his/her path awake.' (Spain, CdE)

(11) *A estos ladrones, solo les recuerdo que cuando **anden la calle** con su familia y los mire alguno de los que fuimos víctimas de sus estafas.*
'To those thieves, I only remind them that when they walk the streets with their family, they will see some of us that were victims of their scams.' (Guatemala, CdE)

Regarding the target phenomenon, Hernández (2002:103) notes "*andar* has also acquired an innovative use that expresses the idea of carrying something on one's person" (see also Lipski, 1994: 260). When conveying this meaning, *andar* is used as a transitive (unergative) verb, not entirely dissimilar from verbs such as *llevar* 'to wear/carry', *cargar* 'to carry/load', *portar* 'to carry/bear', *traer* 'to bring/wear' etc., all of which can be used to convey the sense of transient possession expressed in (12) and (13). We will refer to these cases of *andar* as marking alienable possession; that is, "those with whom it is possible to in some way sever or terminate the relationship of possession (e.g., through loss, sale or theft)" (Zeshan & Perniss, 2013:7). A similar use of the verb *ta* is observed in Swedish, shown in example (14). Viberg (2010) explains that *tog* (< *ta* 'take') is "both a motion verb and a possession verb" which is under the control of the agent (*hon* 'she').

(12) *Es el maje que, aunque **ande ropa** de marca, galán se le mira, al desnudo, lo maje.*
'It's the guy that, even though he may have on (wear) name-brand clothes, one can well see with the naked eye the (his) foolishness.' (Honduras, CdE)

(13) *SUBES,[2] ayudará que la gente no **ande dinero** en su bolsa y no sea víctima de robo*
'SUBES will help so that the people don't carry money in their bags and aren't victims of theft.' (El Salvador, CdE)

(14) *Hon **tog** med sig en kopp te upp på rummet*
'She took a cup of tea up to her room.'

Beyond these cases, there is evidence, albeit tentative, that transitive *andar* can be used to indicate inalienable possession as well. In examples (2, repeated below) and (15) and (16) cited from Twitter (Central America), *andar* takes animate NPs *novia* 'girlfriend' and *un bebé* 'a baby' as a complement with a resultant meaning akin to that of *tener*. Possession in these cases is not necessarily transient and occurs beyond the temporal boundaries of the walking 'event'. Although a proper understanding of these cases of inalienable possession are important for a broader understanding of the distribution of *andar* in these transitive contexts, we will focus primarily on the uses of *andar* to mark alienable possession.

(2) *Y esta es la razón por la que **no ando** NOVIA.*
'And this is the reason that I don't have a girlfriend.'
(Twitter, DÍAZ M. 2014)

(15) *Quiero decirles que ya **ando novia** y me quiere demasiado.*
'I want to tell you all that I have a girlfriend and she loves me a lot.'
(Twitter, ALEXANDER, 2014)

(16) *Aunque uds no lo crean me veo igual que @EnitaValle en su foto, con la diferencia que no **ando un bebé** en la panza.*

---

2 SUBES is a type of credit card. We also thank one of the reviewers for a number of insightful suggestions regarding the translations of the examples.

'Even though you all don't believe me that I look the same as @EnitaValle in her photo, with the difference that I don't have a baby in my belly.' (Twitter, TURKITA, 2016)

The possibility of *andar* to mark inalienable possession notwithstanding, determining what constitutes a transitive use of *andar* is relevant for our current purposes since the meaning that arises is parallel to that expressed with certain prepositional adjuncts. To illustrate this, we present the examples in (17) and (18) all of which express the meaning of 'to carry' despite the fact that, in (17a) and (18a), the would-be nominal complement occurs as the object of the preposition *con* 'with'. We thus use the term "transitive" somewhat loosely when referring to *andar* since we are not claiming that the PPs in (17a) and (18a) and the NPs in (17b) and (18b) have the same syntactic status vis-à-vis *andar*. Moving forward we distinguish these two situations, setting aside examples like (17b) and (18b) as cases of transitive *andar* while treating those with an overt preposition[3] as adjuncts.

(17) a. *¡El que **ande con armas** en la calle sin el permiso, preso!*
'Whoever carries a gun in the streets without permission, (send him) to jail!' (El Salvador, CdE)

b. *¡cómo era posible que alguien que decía predicar un evangelio de paz simplemente **andaba un arma** de fuego para matar!*
'How was it possible that someone who said they preached the gospel of peace simply carried a fire arm to kill!' (El Salvador, CdE)

(18) a. *Yo lo creo, porque el que anda en malos negocios **anda con dinero**.*
'I believe it, because whoever deals in dirty business has money.' (Honduras, CdE)

b. *Disculpe señor, en este momento no **ando dinero**.*
'Pardon sir, in this moment I don't have any money' (Honduras, CdE)

---

3 We are not discounting the possibility of a null preposition in examples like (16b) and (17b).

In summary, the argument structure of transitive *andar* is not the canonical structure of VP + PP, such as in examples (3) and (4), where the PP contains a nominal object that, in some cases, is in fact compatible with a possession meaning. Instead, transitive *andar* has the structure of VP + NP, where the absence of the preposition triggers the meaning of alienable possession. Before turning to our corpus analysis, we provide an overview of the issues underlying *andar* as an emergent form of possession in Central American Spanish.

3 *Andar* as Lexical Change

To begin, we need to provide a clarification regarding the type of structure represented by transitive *andar*. In our analysis, *andar*, like other verbs in Spanish such as *tener* 'to have', *llevar* 'to carry/to wear', and *cargar* 'to carry', is referred to as predicative possession, which has clausal syntax (Zeshan & Perniss, 2013:3). This structure contrasts with attributive possession such as *la casa de Belén* 'Belén's house'. Among the different source domains that give rise to possessive constructions, Heine distinguishes eight domains, which he refers to as "event schemas", the most important of which, at least for the purposes of the current analysis, are the Action domain (i.e. "what one does"), the Location domain ("where one is"), the Accompaniment domain (i.e. "whom one is with), and the Existence domain (i.e. the being of things around us") (Heine, 1997, Zeshan & Perniss, 2013:5). According to Zeshan and Perniss, the Action schema "is inherently propositional in nature, containing a transitive verb of taking or seizing" which then "grammaticali[z]es to possessive constructions expressing predicative possession" (2013:6). Our analysis does not make a specific claim regarding the source domain represented by the development of transitive *andar*. Nevertheless, it is certainly feasible that the three aforementioned event schemata could be argued to constitute jointly an approach to modeling the source of the possessive meaning of *andar* in Central American Spanish. We will leave this issue for further investigation.

Moreover, the notion of possession adopted for this analysis requires further comment as well. Lehmann (1998) observes that prototypical possession occurs between a human *possessor* and an inanimate (nonhuman) *possessum*. Thus, our previous example, *la casa de Belén* 'Belén's house', would represent a case of prototypical alienable possession, though it is certainly possible that the possessor is not human (e.g., *la casa del perro* 'the dog's house') or that the *possessum* is animate/human (e.g, *la tía de Belén* 'Belén's aunt'). It is also worth noting that inalienable possession implies control over the *possessum* by the possessor in such a way that the *possessum* is "inherently and permanently possessed" (2013:7).[4] We will not provide a more detailed account of this possible distinction as it relates to transitive *andar* in Central American Spanish, especially in light of the fact that the instances of inalienable possession, inasmuch as they are attested in our data, are relatively uncommon.

One final component of the meaning of *andar*, as an intransitive verb of motion, requires particular comment as we believe it may be useful in understanding how it emerges with this innovative meaning in Central American Spanish. As mentioned above, the verb *andar* is unergative, and, as such, its subject is agentive (see also Perlmutter, 1978 and Levin & Rappaport-Hovav, 1995). We have, however, already noted an important deviation from this characterization with example (5) where *andar* occurs with an adjectival complement—*anda triste* 'is sad'. This quasi-copular use of *andar* is not unlike Spanish *estar* which gives rise to stage-level interpretations of the type that would be expected with an adjective like *triste*. Similarly, the subject in (5) is not agentive, which is another property of stative verbs like *estar* and *ser* and indeed verbs indicating possession, like *tener* 'to have'. The point here is that a non-agentive subject, we argue, is a precursor to the development of possessive meaning observed with *andar*. In example (19) we can see that non-animate subjects are in fact attested with *andar* indicating a transient state. It remains to be seen how, if any, the role of the subject may play in the development of the meaning illustrated in (20a) and, importantly, if the subject in (20a) has properties parallel to those of a more canonical verb of possession shown in (20b).

(19) *Se ve que mi teléfono **anda** mal.*
 'You see that my telephone is not working.' (Argentina, CdE)

(20) a. ***Ando** una camisa roja.*

 b. ***Llevo** una camisa roja.*
  'I am wearing a red shirt.'

---

4 The notion of inalienable possession as it applies to examples like (2), (14), and (15), while not crucial for this analysis, nonetheless deviates from that described by Zeshan and Perniss. Unlike the relationship indicated in a prototypical case of inalienable possession such as *la mano de Jules* 'Jules' hand', which is permanent, the relationship indicated by *novio* 'boyfriend' in example (2) is certainly not permanent in the same sense.

3.1 andar *in Diachrony*

For this brief summary, we will not treat the development of *andar* using the entire analytical apparatus afforded by a grammaticalization approach (Bybee, 2008, Company Company, 2008, Heine & Narrog, 2009, Howe 2018) because the shift in this case is primarily lexical—i.e. related to the selectional restrictions of the predicate. That said, it will be shown later in the analysis that structural changes are indeed observed when we take into account the range of prepositions that co-occur with *andar*. In this way, transitive *andar* constitutes a distinct process of change from that proposed by Torres Cacoullos (2001) for *andar* as a progressive auxiliary. With this in mind, we argue, following Rodríguez (2019), that the case of transitive *andar* in Central America is an example of lexical shift. *Andar* stems from the Romance variant of Latin *ambulāre* (DRAE), which was an intransitive verb (Mahoney 2002) meaning 'walk, walk about, take a walk' (Perseus Digital Library). We consider the intransitive uses of *andar*, as exemplified above in (3) and (4), as the prototypical use in Spanish, despite the fact that there are historical instances in which *andar* is ambiguously transitive, as in example (21a).

(21)   a. *pero en la corte no hay bobos:* **anda** *el dinero en la mano*
'But in the court, there aren't any fools: money is carried in the hand.' (17th century, CdE)

     b. *Tenga cuidado con los que* **andan** EN MOTO, *porque uno nunca sabe.*
'You should be careful with those who ride motocycles because you never know.'
(Honduras, CdE)

     c. *No es recomendable ni* **andar** UNA MOTO *tan baja que lo haga a uno encorvarse ni una tan alta que no nos permita apoyar al menos ambas puntas de los pies en el suelo.*
It is not recommended either to **ride/own** A MOTORCYCLE so low to the ground that it makes you stoop nor so tall that it does not allow the rider to maintain at least two points of the foot on the ground.' (Costa Rica, CdE)

     d. *Me imagino que tu otro negocio anda bien, porque veo que no sos el único que* **anda** MOTO *en Nicaragua.*
'I imagine that your other business is going well, because I see that you are not the only one who **rides/owns** A MOTORCYCLE in Nicaragua.'
(Costa Rica, CdE)

This instance of *andar* is, at least relative to broader diachronic changes in Spanish, late and thus may represent a viable candidate for a bridging context in which a novel meaning arises that contrasts with the source meaning (Evans & Wilkins, 1998; Heine, 2002). The ambiguity in (21a) is both structural and semantic. The (inanimate) subject of the verb *anda* is structurally *el dinero* 'the money' with a resultant passive reading that also requires that the subject be understood as an object—i.e. *Se lleva el dinero en la mano (por uno)* 'Money is carried in the hand (by one)'.[5] This token represents a critical step in the shift from intransitive to transitive meaning allowing for the wider generalization of transitive uses described in this analysis. In the contemporary data, ambiguities persist despite the fact that the transitive meaning is stable. Consider examples (21b-d). In (21b), the verb *andar* has an animate subject (*los que*) and occurs with a circumstantial adjunct *en moto*, which is common in Spanish for indicating modes of transportation (e.g., *viajo en tren* 'I travel by train') and, we argue, does not give rise to the ambiguity discussed in (21a). The infinitival case of *andar* in example (21c), however, does not have a lexical subject and lacks a preposition to introduce the complement *moto*, factors that we believe gives rise to an ambiguity between the transportation reading ('ride') and the possession meaning ('own'). In the absence of the preposition *en* with *moto*, a similar ambiguity can be observed in example (21d). Again, these types of ambiguities are critical to the type of shift observed with *andar* in Central American Spanish and, as will show, can be tracked through specific structural features, such as the presence vs. absence of prepositions.

3.2 *Evidence for Lexical Change*

To reiterate, we propose that transitive *andar* represents a lexical shift in Central American Spanish. In these dialects, transitive *andar* is grammatically productive and generalized to a variety of contexts. For instance, nominal complements can be pronominalized, as in (22), where transitive *andar* is used first with a nominal complement (*possessum*) *el celular* 'the cell phone', which is subsequently pronominalized with the clitic *lo* 'it' in the next clause.

(22) *me preguntó que si ella (Yamileth)* **andaba** EL CELULAR *o* LO **andaba** *yo*
'he asked me if she (Yamileth) **was carrying** THE CELLPHONE or if I **was carrying** IT' (El Salvador, CdE)

---

5 The compatability of *andar* with impersonal and passive structures in Spanish is somewhat unclear. A full explanation of the results with *se* passives (e.g., *se anda una camisa roja* 'one wears a red shirt') and *ser* passives (e.g., ?*la camisa roja fue andada por Dani* 'The red shirt was worn by Dani') is required.

By the same token, transitive *andar* can take propositional (i.e. abstract) complements, representing an additional sign of lexical shift. To illustrate this point, examples (23) and (24) demonstrate that *andar* can occur with abstract complements—in this case, temporal complements—in parallel fashion to *llevar*. Compatibility with abstract complements like *año* 'year' is, we maintain, an additional indicator of lexical shift.

(23) *Tía Julia, necesito que me des un consejo con mi ex. **Anduvimos un año** pero nada formal nos peleamos porque yo en realidad quiero algo en serio y él no.*
'Aunt Julia, I need you to give me advice about my ex. We were together a year, nothing formal, but we fought because I, in reality, want something serious, and he doesn't.' (El Salvador, CdE)

(24) ***llevo año y medio** con mi pareja*
'I've been with my partner for a year and a half'
(Spain, CdE)

One of the mechanisms involved in semantic change, as described by Bybee (2008, 2011), is chunking, referring more specifically to "sequences of units or word strings that are often produced together" (2011: 70). This mechanism, while typically evoked in discussions of structural change, can also play a role in lexical shifts where properties of a surrounding linguistic environment may be absorbed into the meaning of a lexical item. This is the proposal made by Rodríguez (2019), and the one defended here, namely that *andar* forms a strong collocation—a chunk—with *con*. The following examples illustrate what we maintain is the predecessor construction for transitive *andar* in Central American Spanish.

(25) *el que se acompaña con sabios, será sabio, y el que **anda con** RECOGIDOS Y DEVOTOS, será como ellos*
'he who accompanies wise men, will be wise, and he who walks with the cloistered and the devout, will be like them' (16th century, CdE)

(26) *y esto todo lo vi yo, y **anda con** MUCHO DINERO*
'and all of this I saw, and [he] is walking with [carrying] a lot of many' (17th century, CdE)

(27) *Hice, hermana, resistencia al justicia mayor, que **anda con** orden del rey expresa para prenderme*
'I did it, Sister, resistance to the higher justice who was walking with [carrying] AN ORDER FROM THE KING to arrest me' (CdE, 17th century)

Each of these tokens represents a relationship between the NP in capital letters whose meaning is negotiated, as it were, by the preposition *con*. In example (25), this relationship can only be understood as adjunctival, where *con recogidos y devotos* is understood as a circumstantial modifier. Examples (26) and (27), on the other hand, present two possible interpretations: one is the canonical meaning of *andar* and the other is the meaning innovative meaning of 'to carry' or 'to possess'. These instances of ambiguity are precisely the types of contexts required to give rise to a systematic association directly between the verb *andar* and the NP introduced by *con*, a relationship that, with time, would not require the intervention of the preposition. Bybee (2011: 71) notes that "increases in frequency strengthen the sequential relations within the chunk while weakening the relations of component members to cognates elsewhere." In this view, a chunk such as *ando con dinero* and *andan con armas*, do not continue to signal the canonical (i.e. intransitive) meaning of *andar*, as in 'to walk, go, go around', but rather they represent a new pragmatic meaning, namely 'to carry on one's person', that takes its cue from the semantic properties of its adjunct NP (Roberts & Roussou, 1999). This emergent shift in the structural properties of *andar*, when employed in its innovative form, gives rise to one of the additional mechanisms of semantic shift—i.e. gradual constituent structure and category change. Again, we attenuate the claim of category change since, in the grammaticalization literature, this typically involves a change in lexical class—i.e. verbs to bound morphology (Hopper, 1991). We use "category" change in this analysis to refer to change from intransitive to transitive without any implications regarding the status of *andar* as a verb.

Rodríguez (2019) proposes that, following an increase in the frequency of *andar con* around the 16th century, this collocation began patterning as a phrasal verb.[6] Figure 8.1 demonstrates the tokens per million of *andar con* taken from the Historical/Genre sub-corpus of the CdE (Davies, 2002–) to represent its frequency in all countries until from the 13th to the 20th centuries, and then from the Web/Dialects sub-corpus (Davies, 2016–) to represent the frequency of this structure in all Spanish speaking countries in the 21st century.

Hereafter, reanalysis, most likely occurred as a direct result of chunking, causing a change in constituent structure, from *andar* [*con* NP] to [*andar con*] NP which resulted in a change in the semantic and pragmatic properties of *andar* from 'walk about, walk' to 'carry on one's person'. Rodríguez maintains that a type of elided *con*, as in (20) above and (28) below, began to appear, about which Rodríguez-Puente (2012) notes that phrasal verbs often develop non-transparent meanings, akin to the notion of loss of compositionality or analyzability (Bybee, 2011). This process occurs with *andar* around the

---

6 We follow Rodríguez-Puente who describes phrasal verbs as "lexicalized combinations of a verb and a particle which function semantically and syntactically as a single unit" (2012:71).

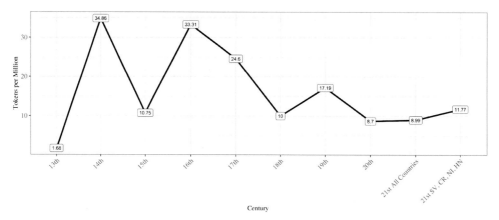

FIGURE 8.1 Frequency of *andar con* ("21st SV, CR, NI, HN" refers only to Central American varieties)

17th century and 19th century where the transitive use first appears and where the frequency of *andar con* starts to stabilize as attested in the data from the *Corpus del Español*.

(28)   *El capitán **andaba** (con) UN ARMA 9 milímetros, oficial, Beretta.*
       'The captain carried a 9-millimeter gun, oficial, Beretta.'
       (20th century, CdE)

With *andar (con)* NP reducing the necessity for *con*, the change in semantic meaning from 'walk about, walk' to 'carry on one's person' began to increase. By the 21st century, *andar con* NP was consistently reduced to *andar* NP, representing the emergent transitive structure, where the innovative, narrowed semantic meaning of 'carry on one's person' is intended. In contemporary Central American Spanish, this meaning has expanded to include alienable possession, akin to *tener* 'to have'.

To review, this diachronic sketch is intended to provide a general starting point for the corpus analysis provided in the forthcoming section, and there are two primary conclusions to draw. First, transitive *andar* is a lexical change in contemporary Spanish, albeit one with a limited dialectal distribution as will be demonstrated shortly. Second, the source structures for transitive *andar*—intransitive *andar* and the collocation *andar con*—continue to be used widely across Spanish dialects. As we will see, it is only in select dialects—namely Central American varieties—that we observe competition between *andar con* and its modern predecessor transitive *andar*.

4　Transitive *andar*: A Corpus Approach

Working with low-frequency phenomena from a functionalist perspective requires access to a large and reliable data set. Added to this is the complication of finding adequate coverage of under-represented varieties, particularly those with limited institutional prestige. Fortunately, recent additions to the collection of Spanish corpora have made it possible to expand our inquiries beyond those that are possible with smaller, limited corpora. This increased functionality greatly facilitates our ability to look for otherwise difficult to find patterns among varieties of Spanish that typically receive less attention in the scholarly literature. Our analysis makes use of the 2 billion-word *Corpus del Español* (Davies, 2016–) and attempts to address the following research questions:

1. What is the dialectal distribution of transitive *andar*?
2. Which linguistic variables are the best predictors for transitive *andar*— specifically regarding nouns that convey transient possession, where alienable possession refers to a non-permanent status?
3. How does transitive *andar* compare to other same sense verbs, like *llevar*?

In this section, we take a quantitative, corpus-based approach to the study of transitive *andar* in seeking to discover patterns of co-occurring forms within particular variable contexts (Torres Cacoullos, 2011). The results are divided into two different sections, one in which we compare the distribution of transitive *andar* across a selection of Spanish dialects and another that compares transitive *andar* to semantically similar verbs, specifically *llevar*. The results of these two analyses explain distributional facts for transitive *andar* and help to demonstrate the utility of a 'Big Data' approach to dialect variation and, from a diachronic perspective, lexical change.

Before turning to our analysis, we offer a few comments here regarding the coverage of under-studied varieties of Spanish. Among the options available for cross-dialectal analysis of lexical variation, there are only a few that provide wide coverage across all Spanish-speaking countries, including the *Proyecto para el Estudio Sociolingüístico del Español de España y América* (PRESEEA, Moreno Fernández, 1996, 2005, Moreno Fernández & Cestero, 2020) the *Corpus del Español del Siglo XXI* (CORPES XXI), the *Corpus del Español* (Davies, 2016–), and Sketch Engine's esTenTen18 (Kilgarriff *et al.*, 2014). Each of these sources provide wide coverage of different varieties of Spanish, albeit at a remarkably larger scale with the latter two (2 billion and 17.6 billion, respectively). In Table 8.1 below, we provide summary data from three different corpora,

TABLE 8.1 Comparison of three Spanish corpora by number of tokens (words) and percentage relative to overall size

	CORPES XXI	Corpus del Español	esTenTen
Spain	133.1 (34.7%)	459.3 (21.9%)	3.6 billion (17.5%)
Mexico	41.2 (10.7%)	260.6 (12.4%)	1.5 billion (7.2%)
Argentina	34.6 (9%)	182.7 (8.7%)	1.8 billion (8.8%)
Costa Rica	5.1 (1.3%)	31.7 (1.5%)	94.7 (.46%)
El Salvador	5.1 (1.3%)	39.1 (1.9%)	18.3 (.09%)
Honduras	5 (1.3%)	38.9 (1.9%)	13.4 (.07%)
Nicaragua	5 (1.3%)	34.6 (1.9%)	40.3 (.19%)

CORPES XXI, *Corpus del Español*, and esTenTen, comparing three high-resource dialects—Spain, Mexico, and Argentina—and four target varieties in Central America—Costa Rica, El Salvador, Honduras, and Nicaragua. As expected, the target varieties comprise only a small portion of the overall tokens in the three corpora: 5.2% for CORPES XXI, 7.2% for the *Corpus del Español*, and > 1% for esTenTen. Despite being the largest of these corpora by far, the esTenTen dataset provides relatively minimal access to these varieties. Taken together, the overall number of tokens and the percentage of coverage available through the *Corpus del Español* makes this an ideal tool for analyzing lexical variation.

4.1   Methodology

To quantify the dialectal variation between transitive and intransitive *andar*, we extracted tokens from the *Corpus del Español* Web/Dialects sub-corpus (Davies, 2016–). Specifically, we isolated collocates of [andar] + (*dinero* 'money', *plata* 'silver/money', *efectivo* 'cash', *dinero en efectivo* 'cash', *en efectivo* 'cash', *moneda(s)* 'money/coins', *arma(s)* 'weapon(s)/gun(s)', *pistola(s)* 'gun(s)', *ropa* 'clothes', *zapato(s)* 'shoes', *pantalón(es)* 'pants', *camisa(s)* 'shirt', *short(s)* 'shorts', *tenis* 'sneakers', *chanclas* 'sandals') in different subcorpora: Central America (Honduras, El Salvador, Costa Rica, Panama, Nicaragua, and Guatemala), Spain, Argentina, Chile, Mexico, and the US. These particular nouns were chosen for their compatibility with alienable possession nature and are based on common nouns found with other same-sense transitive verbs (Hernández, 2002). We began with 1104 tokens, and, after removing duplicates, cases of *andar* + GERUND, *andar* + adjective, and *andar* + *sin* 'without' (a negative preposition that makes the verb transitively ambiguous), we were left with 455 useable data points.

These tokens were then coded for the following variables: Country, Collocating Noun, Transitivity (transitive 'no preposition' or non-transitive 'preposition intervening between verb and noun'), Verb Form (tense), Habituality (habitual or not), Preposition (if present, which preposition was used), Determiner (if present before noun, which determiner was used), Adjective (if present, which adjective modified the noun), and Polarity (negative or positive). Transitivity represents the response variable and was, for the purposes of this analysis, coded determined based on the presence or absence of the preposition of an intervening preposition between *andar* and one of the following target nouns. In this way, *ando dinero* was coded as transitive while *ando con dinero* was not. The data was then subjected to a generalized linear mixed-effects model (GLMM) in RStudio using the lme4 package (Bates *et al.*, 2015). The GLMM is a model statistically robust enough to handle non-normal, categorical data and also has predictive power, in that log-likelihoods can be extracted from them for different variable coefficients. This allowed us to treat Transitivity as the response variable for the fixed effects, and Noun as the random effect, testing which of the other variables were best suited as the fixed effect operators.

4.2 Results for Analysis of Dialectal Variation

An overview of the data, as seen in Table 8.2, reveals that there is a high degree of variation observed with the transitive and non-transitive use of *andar* in Costa Rica, El Salvador, Honduras, and Nicaragua, but not in samples from Guatemala and Panama. There is also little to no variation in the other countries represented in this sample.

The best fit model included Transitivity as the response variable, Noun as the random variable, and Country and Polarity as predictor variables. These variables, along with the rest of the variables in the data, proved to be statistically insignificant (p = .9998 in most cases). Figure 8.2 demonstrates the significance of Transitivity by Country where the results of a Chi-squared test shows no significant difference between the non-transitive and transitive forms in Nicaragua, Honduras, El Salvador, and Costa Rica (Nicaragua: χ-squared = 0.5814, df = 1, p = 0.4458; Honduras: χ-squared = 0.18367, df = 1, p = 0.6682; El Salvador: χ-squared = 2.5, df = 1, p = 0.1138; Costa Rica: χ-squared = 0.14754, df = 1, p = 0.7009). This corroborates the competing variation between transitive *andar* and non-transitive *andar*. Figure 8.3 shows the results of Transitivity by Polarity, where the affirmative tokens favor the transitive form.

Taking a closer look at the four countries where transitive *andar* competes with its canonical (i.e. intransitive) counterpart, we calculated the log-odds that a speaker from each of these countries would use transitive *andar*, based on the best predictor variables given by the GLMM, namely Country

TABLE 8.2 Results of raw tokens per country

Country	Non-transitive	Transitive
Argentina	35 (100%)	0 (0%)
Chile	70 (96%)	3 (4%)
Costa Rica	32 (52%)	29 (48%)
El Salvador	15 (37 %)	25 (63%)
Spain	31 (94%)	2 (6%)
Guatemala	15 (79%)	4 (21%)
Honduras	23 (47%)	26 (53%)
Mexico	48 (88%)	6 (12%)
Nicaragua	19 (44%)	24 (66%)
Panama	10 (100%)	0 (0%)
United States	36 (95%)	2 (5%)
TOTAL	**334 (73%)**	**121 (27%)**

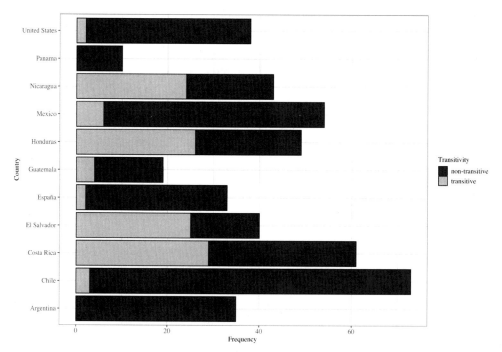

FIGURE 8.2 Transitivity by country

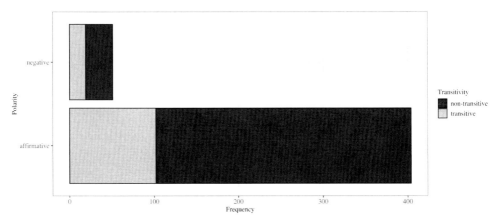

FIGURE 8.3 Transitivity by polarity

(El Salvador, Nicaragua, Costa Rica, and Honduras) and Polarity (affirmative). The results were as follows, where the percentage represents the probability transitive *andar* would be used. Observe that the probability is greater than 50% in each of these subsamples of the data that *andar* will be used with a transitive sense, as operationalized by the lack of an intervening preposition. Also important in examples (29)–(32) is the meaning of alienable possession that is expressed.

(29) **El Salvador** = 71%
*Tenía su faldita y blúmer abajo, a la altura de las rodillas. Él **andaba un short** y el zipper lo tenía abajo.*
'She had her little dress and bloomers underneath, to the length of her knees. He was wearing shorts and he had the zipper down.'

(30) **Nicaragua** = 63%
*... caminar con garbo de bailarín como **si anduviesen la ropa** más holgada del mundo.*
'to walk with the grace of a ballet dancer as if they wore the most loose-fitting clothes in the world.'

(31) **Costa Rica** = 57%
*... correr el riesgo de chocar así con un infeliz de estos. ¿Y si **anda un arma**? ¿Y si no le importa y sigue su marcha?*
'... to run the risk of running into one of those wretched people. And if he has a gun? And if he doesn't care and continues his march?'

(32)   **Honduras = 57%**
*Es conveniente **andar siempre dinero en efectivo**, especialmente billetes de baja denominación, ya sea en lempiras ...*
'It's convenient to always carry cash, especially bills of smaller amounts, even in Lempiras.'

Regarding preposition variation, we considered whether the tokens from these countries displayed variation among preposition usage, which may be used as an indicator of lexical change (Schøsler, 2007). Indeed, the data seem to show that there is variation in preposition usage, including the choice to not include a preposition, namely to use transitive *andar*. Table 8.3 shows the cases of intransitive *andar* that appeared with a preposition in each country along with the number of cases of transitive *andar* (i.e. no preposition). Here, there is a high degree of variation among the inner four Central American countries, as seen in the competition between the lack of a preposition and the use of *con* 'with'. In the countries where transitive *andar* is not widely attested, there is still variation, but variation does not always indicate language change the way language change requires variation. Here, there is notable overlap between the use of *con* and that of other prepositions, but little to no competition occurring with the transitive use, suggesting a lack of lexical shift in these particular subsets of the data. In Costa Rica, El Salvador, Honduras, and Nicaragua, where *andar* has experienced increased grammaticalization (Rodríguez, 2019), it seems that preposition variation has also been restricted, meaning that if a

TABLE 8.3   Preposition variation by country

Country	No preposition (transitive)	*con*	Other (*de, en*)	Total
Argentina	0 (0%)	31 (89%)	4 (11 %)	35
Chile	3 (4%)	68 (93%)	2 (3%)	73
Costa Rica	29 (45%)	22 (36%)	10 (19%)	61
El Salvador	25 (63%)	13 (33%)	2 (4%)	40
Spain	2 (6%)	19 (55%)	12 (39%)	33
Guatemala	4 (21%)	14 (74%)	1 (5%)	19
Honduras	26 (53%)	15 (31%)	8 (16%)	49
Mexico	6 (19%)	31 (54%)	17 (28%)	54
Nicaragua	24 (56%)	15 (35%)	4 (9%)	43
Panama	0 (0%)	7 (70%)	3 (30%)	10
United States	2 (5%)	29 (76%)	7 (19%)	38

speaker were to use transitive *andar* with a preposition, it would almost always be *con*. In other words, the preposition *con* is not required to produce a transitive meaning.

4.3   Competing Verbs
Lastly, we took a subset of the data described above (52 tokens), namely the tokens of *andar* + *dinero/arma(s)* in the four inner Central American countries, as they have the highest frequency in our dataset. We then extracted similar tokens (211) from the Web/Dialects sub-corpus of the CdE (Davies, 2016–) with the verb *llevar* to understand whether *andar* overlaps with other verbs used to indicate alienable possession. This data set was comprised of 263 tokens.

4.4   Results of Competing Verbs
The results of this comparison can be seen in Figure 8.4 where the light gray reflects the frequency of *llevar*, which is high, and the black reflects the frequency of *andar* in each country, which is low. In Figure 8.1, the high *p*-values indicated a small difference in the distribution of transitive *andar* and non-transitive *andar*, suggesting competition between these two variants. However, here in Figure 8.4, transitive *andar* does not seem to contrast with

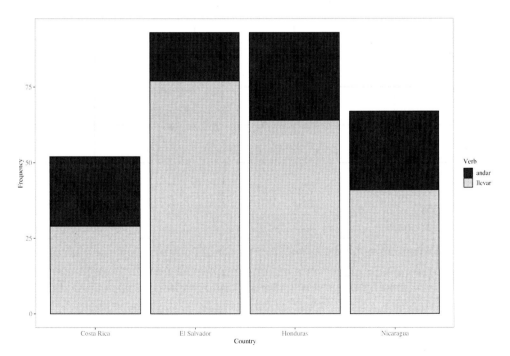

FIGURE 8.4   Frequency of transitive *andar* and *llevar*

llevar, at least insofar as overall frequency is concerned. We maintain that this is due largely to the fact that *llevar* is simply more frequent. Chi-squared tests revealed that the differences in frequencies of the two verbs were statistically significant, meaning that the frequencies are so statistically different that it is unlikely that they are competing for the same meanings. Further analysis could reveal that this is due to the choice in nouns, being that *arma(s)* may be more frequent with a verb like *cargar* and *dinero* with a verb like *traer*, both of which are semantically primed for nouns that are compatible with a meaning of alienable possession (e.g., 'gun' and 'money'). However, what is relevant here is that there is a type of layering of meaning occurring in these dialects, which is characteristic of forms undergoing lexical change.

To summarize, we maintain that transitive *andar* competes with nontransitive *andar* in Costa Rica, El Salvador, Honduras, and Nicaragua. Here, Polarity, specifically an affirmative reading, proved to be a significant predictor for the use of transitive *andar*. There is, however, no overt competition in our data between transitive *andar* and *llevar* in these four Central American countries where the transitive use of *andar* is most widely attested.

5   Conclusions and Discussion

Based on the results of the quantitative corpus analysis, we conclude that *andar* is indeed used with the transitive sense described by Lipski (1994) and Hernández (2002) particularly in varieties of Central American Spanish, namely Costa Rica, El Salvador, Honduras, and Nicaragua. Moreover, its transitive use has become a common way in some varieties to communicate the idea of 'to wear or carry on one's person' or even 'to have' with [+ transient possession] nouns. The results of a GLMM point to Country and Polarity as the best predictors for the transitivity of *andar* with the nouns selected for the corpus search.

In comparing the results of the mixed-effects model with those of the hypothesized competition between *andar* and *llevar*, we further conclude that transitive *andar* is not in direct competition with *llevar* specifically, though a layering of meaning is observed both in our data and diachronically (Hopper & Traugott, 2003). However, it clearly overlaps with the intransitive canonical form followed by the preposition *con*. Speakers and writers from these varieties of Spanish use this structure with a possessive meaning, marking for the most part alienable possession. And while the data are limited at this point, transitive *andar* appears to be available to mark inalienable possession, occurring with nouns like *bebé* 'baby' or *novio/a* 'boyfriend/girlfriend'. The data analysis thus far has not produced tokens of transitive *andar* (i.e. without *con*) with complements that are explicitly intransient—a hallmark of prototypical inalienable possession—or perceived as permanent, such as *esposo/a* 'spouse' or *hermano/a* 'brother/sister'. However, abstract nouns such as *año* as complements occur with transitive *andar*, much in the same way that they do with *llevar* 'to wear/carry' or even *tener* 'to have'. The exact role of these complements in the development of *andar* is left for future study.

These results are provided in the context of a proposed case of lexical shift that involves both the gradual diversification of the collocation profile of *andar* and the subsequent entrenchment and expansion of the meaning that arises with the structure *andar con* (Rodríguez, 2019). Here, there is a loss of compositionality and analyzability leading to lexical change wherein *andar con* no longer signifies "to walk with" but "to carry on one's person." It is also in this stage where *andar con* appears to take on the properties of a transitive phrasal verb. An additional step involves the gradual, though not necessarily complete, loss of the preposition *con* with expanded use of *andar* as a type of alienable possession similar to *tener* 'to have'. Beyond this, we have observed initial evidence that *andar* in Central American Spanish can be used with animate complements to produce a meaning akin to inalienable possession. The extent to which transitive *andar* is employed with a broader range of possessive uses is one of a number of interesting questions left open in this study.

The thread running throughout this analysis is the use of large-scale corpora to uncover patterns in low-resource dialects. This approach relies heavily on access to reliable data that can be understood to reflect, at least in general terms, the language used in particular varieties of the language. Use of the *Corpus del Español* (Davies, 2016–) and other large corpora, such as esTenTen18 (Kilgarriff *et al.*, 2014), for tracking lexical change allows for reproducible results that reflect broad patterns of linguistic change, provided (a) that the research questions need not be tied specifically to the demographics of the speakers/users and (b) that the scale of the data samples and subsamples be understood as a countermeasure to issues of representation. Indeed, the claims presented in this analysis would most certainly be even more robust if an exhaustive extraction of *andar* were conducted across each of the large corpora mentioned here (i.e. the *Corpus del Español*, CORPES, esTenTen18), though we will leave this task for future research. Finally, it perhaps goes without saying that a more detailed understanding of lexical change in varieties of Central American Spanish requires an understanding of the socio-historical contexts in which users produce and shape language, and even contact with indigenous languages (Critchfield, this volume, García Tesoro, this volume), factors that are difficult to operationalize in a corpus of 2.1 billion words. But the Big Data approach does help to introduce questions that, in the absence of suitable resources for under-represented varieties, frequently go unanswered or completely unexamined.

References

Bates, D., Mächler, M., Bolker, B. & Walker, S. (2015). Fitting Linear Mixed-Effects Models Using lme4. *Journal of Statistical Software*, 67(1), 1–48.

Bybee, J. L. (2008). Mechanisms of Change in Grammaticalization: The Role of Frequency. In B. D. Joseph & R. D. Janda (Eds.), *The Handbook of Historical Linguistics* (pp. 602–623). Blackwell Publishing Ltd.

Bybee, J. L. (2011). Usage-Based Theory and Grammaticalization. In B. Heine & H. Narrog (Eds.), *The Oxford Handbook of Grammaticalization* (pp. 69–78). Oxford University Press.

Company Company, C. (2008). Gramaticalización, debilitamiento semántico y reanálisis. El posesivo como artículo en la evolución sintáctica del español. In J. Kabatek (Ed.), *Sintaxis histórica del español y cambio lingüístico: nuevas perspectivas desde las Tradiciones Discursivas.*, vol. 31 (pp. 17–51). Iberoamericana.

Davies, M. (2002–) *Corpus del Español: 100 million words, 1200s–1900s*. Retrieved April 6, 2023 from http://www.corpusdelespanol.org/hist-gen/. (Historical / Genres).

Davies, M. (2016–) *Corpus del Español: Two billion words, 21 countries*. Retrieved April 6, 2023 from http://www.corpusdelespanol.org/web-dial/. (Web / Dialects).

Evans, N. & Wilkins, D. (1998). *The knowing ear: An Australian test of universal claims about the semantic structure of sensory verbs and their extension into the domain of cognition.* (Arbeitspapier 32, NF.) Cologne: Institut für Sprachwissenschaft.

Heine, B. (1997). Grammaticalization theory and its relevance to African linguistics. In R. Herbert (Ed.), *African linguistics at the crossroads: Papers from Kwaluseni* (pp. 1–15). Köppe.

Heine, B. (2002). On the role of context in grammaticalization. In I. Wischer & G. Diewald (Eds.), *New Reflections on Grammaticalization* (pp. 81–101). John Benjamins.

Heine, B. & Narrog, H. (2009). Grammaticalization and Linguistic Analysis. In B. Heine & H. Narrog (Eds.), *The Oxford Handbook of Linguistic Analysis* (pp. 401–423). Oxford University Press.

Hernández, J. E. (2002). Accommodation in a dialect contact situation. *Revista de Filología y Lingüística de la Universidad de Costa Rica*, 28(2). 93–110.

Hopper, P. (1991). On some Principles of Grammaticalization. In E. C. Traugott & B. Heine (Eds.), *Approaches to Grammaticalization* (Typological Studies in Language), vol. 19. (pp. 17–35). John Benjamins.

Hopper, P. & Traugott, E. C. (2003). *Grammaticalization, 2nd Ed.* Cambridge University Press.

Howe, C. (2018). Grammaticalization. In K. Geeslin (Ed.), *The Cambridge Handbook of Spanish Linguistics* (pp. 604–624). Cambridge University Press.

Kilgarriff, A., V. Baisa, J. Bušta, M. Jakubíček, V. Kovář, J., Michelfeit, P. Rychlý y V. Suchomel. (2014). The Sketch Engine: Ten Years on. *Lexicography 1*, 7–36.

Lehmann, C. (1998). *Possession in Yucatec Maya: Structures—Functions—Typology.* Munich: Lincom Europa.

Levin, B. & Rappaport-Hovav, M. (1995). *Unaccusativity. At the Syntax-Lexical Semantics Interface.* MIT Press.

Lipski, J. M. (1994). *Latin American Spanish.* Longman.

Lipski, J. M. (2008). *Varieties of Spanish in the United States.* Georgetown University Press.

Mahoney, K. D. (2002). ambulare. *Latdict.* http://www.latin-dictionary.net/search/latin/ambulare.

Moreno Fernández, F. (1996). Metodología para el "Metodología del 'Proyecto para el estudio sociolingüístico del Español de España y de América' (PRESEEA)," *Lingüística 8*, 257–287.

Moreno Fernández, F. (2005). Corpus para el estudio del español en su variación geográfica y social. El corpus PRESEEA. *Oralia 8*, 123–139.

Moreno Fernández, F. y Cestero, A. M. (2020). El Corpus PRESEEA. Desarrollos analíticos. *Verba. Anuario Galego de Filoloxía, 80*, 119–138.

Perlmutter, D. (1978). Impersonal passives and the unaccusative hypothesis. In J. J. Jaeger, A. C. Woodbury, F. Ackerman, C. Chiarello, O. D. Gensler, J. Kingston, E. E. Sweetser, H. Thompson, and K. W. Whitler (Eds.), *Proceedings of the 4th annual meeting of the Berkeley Linguistics Society* (pp. 157–189). Berkeley: Berkeley Linguistics Society.

Perseus Digital Library. Ed. Gregory R. Crane. Tufts University. http://www.perseus.tufts.edu.

RAE. (2017). andar. *Diccionario de la lengua española.* http://dle.rae.es/?id=2ZGgAPa|2ZIziL7.

Rivas, P. G. (1987). *La Lengua Salvadorena.* Second Edition. Ministerio De Cultura y Comunicaciones.

Roberts, I. & A. Roussou. (1999). A formal approach to "grammaticalization." *Linguistics, 37*(6). 1011–1041.

Rodríguez, S. P. (2019). Transitive *andar*: an emerging verb of possession. University of Georgia Manuscript.

Rodríguez-Puente, P. (2012). The Development of Non-Compositional Meanings in Phrasal Verbs: A Corpus-Based Study. *English Studies: A Journal of English Language and Literature, 93*(1), 71–90.

Schøsler, L. (2007). The status of valency patterns. In T. Herbst & K. Götz-Votteler (Eds.), *Valency: Theoretical, Descriptive and Cognitive Issues* (pp. 51–66). Walter de Gruyter.

Sorace, A. (2000). Gradients in Auxiliary Selection with Intransitive Verbs. *Language*, 76(4), 859–890.

Torres Cacoullos, R. (2011). Variation and Grammaticalization. In M. Díaz-Campos (Ed.), *The Handbook of Hispanic Sociolinguistics* (pp. 148–167). Wiley-Blackwell.

Torres Cacoullos, R. (2001). From lexical to grammatical to social meaning. *Language in Society*, 30, 443–478.

van Gelderen, E. (2011). Valency changes in the history of English. *Journal of Historical Linguistics*, 1(1), 106–143.

Viberg, Å. (2010). Basic verbs of possession: A contrastive and typological study. *Cognitextes, 4*. https://doi.org/10.4000/cognitextes.308.

Zeshan, U. & Perniss, P. (2013). Possessive and existential constructions: Introduction and overview. In A. Y. Aikhenvald & R. M. W. Dixon (Eds.). *Possession and Ownership: A Cross-linguistic Typology* (pp. 1–31). Oxford University Press.

CHAPTER 9

Variable Number Marking in Mosquito Coast Spanish

Madeline Critchfield

1 Introduction

Variable number marking on verb morphology has only been observed in a few varieties of Spanish, including Dominican Spanish, Afro-Bolivian Spanish, Spanish in the U.S., and Mosquito Coast Spanish. This linguistic phenomenon is characterized by the use of non-standard number marking on verb forms, which can be phonological or morphological in nature, resulting in the non-agreement of subject and verb. In this study, agreement refers to the occurrence of a subject and its corresponding verb form, matching in person and number, via explicit agreement morphology.

This chapter discusses what linguistic and social factors predict variable number marking in Mosquito Coast Spanish (MCS), specifically on verbs of 3pl. referents. 3pl. agreement morphology on verbs in Spanish incorporates an alveolar nasal consonant suffix (/n/), that distinguishes it from 3sg. (*comen* 'they eat' vs. *come* 'he/she/it eats'). In the case of verbs in the preterite, additional morphological content distinguishes 3pl. from 3sg. (*dijeron* 'they said' vs. *dijo* 'he/she/it said'). In the context of 3pl. referents, the plural-marked form of the verb, is the expected or standard form (1a), while the singular-marked form of the verb, is the non-standard form (1b) because it results in a lack of number agreement between subject and verb.

(1) a. *en   cuanto   al   estilo   de   vida,   ellos   viv-ían*
       in   regard   to   style   of   life   they   live-PST.3PL
       diferente
       differently
       'in regard to lifestyle, they lived differently'

   b. *nuestros   ancestros   antes   viv-ía   de   la   naturaleza*
      our   ancestors   before   live-PST.3SG   from   the   nature
      'our ancestors used to live from nature'

MCS is a contact variety spoken along the northern Caribbean coast of Nicaragua by first-language speakers of Miskitu. The data for this study was collected from speakers in the city of Puerto Cabezas, the capital of the Región Autónoma de la Costa Caribe Norte (RACCN), which is the northern-most department along the Atlantic coast. In the RACCN, Miskitu and Spanish are the primary languages spoken, with 70.4% of people residing in the municipality of Puerto Cabezas identifying as Miskitu (Wilson Withe et al., 2012, p. 12). This study investigates a feature of this speech community's variety of Spanish, variable number marking, as it relates to acquisition and language contact. The current study aims to add to the body of research about Spanish varieties spoken in Nicaragua (including but not limited to Lipski, 1984, 1985; Chappell, 2014, 2015a, 2015b; Critchfield & Lívio, *forthcoming*; Michno et al., *this volume*), as they have been understudied in the linguistics literature.

MCS arose in the middle of the 20th century with the implementation of Spanish-only education via the Río Coco Pilot Project for Basic Education, a UNESCO-sponsored initiative whose goal was to Hispanicize the Miskitu people (García, 1996, p. 99; Meringer, 2014, pp. 205–207). Following the Sandinista revolution in the 1970s, a national literacy campaign was established which also promoted the use of the Spanish language as part of a collective Nicaraguan identity (García, 1996, p. 104; Escobar, 2013, p. 732). As a result of this social and political pressure, a shift toward Spanish being the dominant language in all regions of Nicaragua took place and led to the Miskitu community, both adults and children, acquiring Spanish as a second language (García, 1997; Escobar, 2013; Wilson Withe et al., 2012). This acquisition process has played an important role in the development of MCS, as the speech community underwent a rapid language shift. In addition, the community was geographically isolated from the target language in question due to a central mountain range dividing the country and preventing consistent contact with Nicaraguan Spanish speakers (Floyd, 1967, pp. 1–16). This study suggests that these circumstances resulted in the divergent acquisition (also referred to in the literature as incomplete acquisition[1]) of number marking in MCS, now a fixed feature in this contact variety.

Miskitu and Spanish differ in how they mark plurality of discourse referents. Spanish directly marks number in the verb morphology, with number also being marked in the noun phrase, if explicitly expressed. In Miskitu, plurality is marked by the presence of the pluralizer *nani* following the nominative

---

1   The term 'incomplete acquisition' has been somewhat controversial when describing bilingual speakers of Spanish, due to its possible pejorative interpretation. In this study, the term 'divergent acquisition' will be used instead to describe the acquisition of a feature that does not pattern with monolingual varieties, except when referring to work done by authors who use the term 'incomplete'.

TABLE 9.1   Present indicative verb paradigm of *aiwanaia* ('to sing') in Miskitu

	Singular subject pronouns	Plural subject pronouns	Present indicative
First-person	*yang*	*yang nani*	*aiwani-sna* sing-PRS.1 'I/we sing'
Second-person	*man*	*man nani*	*aiwani-sma* sing-PRS.2 'you/you all sing'
Third-person	*witin*	*witin nani*	*aiwani-sa* sing-PRS.3 'he/she/they sing'

ADAPTED FROM SALAMANCA, 1988, P. 115, 250

pronoun but not in the morphology of the verb (Table 9.1). Based on these differences, research on MCS offers important insight into the impact language contact can have on the acquisition of morphosyntactic features in Spanish.

2   Variable Number Marking in Spanish and Portuguese

While variation in number marking on the noun phrase, via final /s/ deletion, has been studied extensively for Spanish (Lipski & Recuero, 1996; Lipski, 2011; Penny, 2000; Guy, 2014, p. 446; Chappell, 2014, 2015a,b among others), variation in number marking on verb morphology is not widely attested. In Caribbean Spanish, this phenomenon appears to be phonological, with Dominican Spanish (2) exhibiting variation in number marking on 3pl. forms, via final /n/ deletion (Lipski & Recuero, 1996, p. 364). Caribbean Spanish appears to be moving toward a less richly inflected verb system due to this weakening (3).

(2)   *tú   cant-a*
      you   you sing-PRS.3SG
      'you sing'
      ALBA, 2004, p. 125

(3)   *com-e*
      eat-PRS.3SG
      'you eat'; 'he/she/it eats'; 'they eat'
      FOOTE & BOCK, 2012, p. 432

Unlike Dominican Spanish, the variable number marking found in MCS is morphological in nature and not a case of final /n/ deletion. Examples of verbs in the preterite demonstrate the clear use of 3sg. verb morphology and not final consonant deletion (4). Previous research shows the use of 3sg. verb forms with 3pl. referents occurs at a rate of 20.3% in MCS, with VS word order, the presence of intervening material between subjects and verbs, and high phonic salience verbs all favoring lack of agreement (Critchfield & Lívio, *forthcoming*).

(4) entonces   los   pajarito-s   dij-o   que   hab-ía   un
    then   the.PL   bird-PL   say-PST.3SG   that   there was   a
    techo
    roof
    'then the birds said that there was a roof'

Two additional varieties of Spanish exhibit a reduction in number, and also in person. Speakers of Afro-Bolivian Spanish use 3sg. morphology as an invariant verb form for all persons and numbers (5) (Lipski, 2008a,b), while bilingual speakers of English and Spanish in the United States display variation in their use of 3sg. verb forms with first-person, second-person, and 3pl. referents (6) (Lipski, 2008c:59, 2020). Both of these cases appear to be morphological in nature.

(5) yo   no   conoc-ió   hacienda
    I   no   know-PST.1SG   ranch
    'I never knew the haciendas'
    SESSAREGO, 2011, p. 128

(6) vien-e   mis   tíos
    come-PRS.3SG   my   aunt and uncle
    'my aunt and uncle come'
    LIPSKI, 2008c, p. 59

While the phenomenon of variable number marking exists in other varieties of Spanish, the characteristics and behavior of this feature differ from what has been observed in MCS (variable and morphological in nature, only occurring in the context of 3pl.), making these varieties unsuitable for comparison: the variation in number marking in Caribbean Spanish is phonological and not morphological, Afro-Bolivian Spanish does not show variation but instead utilizes one invariant verb form, and U.S. Spanish includes both person and number non-agreement.

Variable number marking on verb morphology in Brazilian Portuguese (BP) has been discussed extensively in the linguistics literature (Guy, 1981, 2005; Scherre, 1998; Naro & Scherre, 2000; Scherre & Naro, 2001, 2010, 2014; Lucchesi, Baxter, & Ribeiro, 2009; Brandão & Vieira, 2012; Mendes & Oushiro, 2015). As in MCS, this variation in BP has been observed in contexts of 3pl. (*eles fazem/faz* 'they do') (Mendes & Oushiro, 2015, p. 362). While several linguistic predictors have been identified in the research on 3pl. subject-verb agreement in BP, phonic salience, preceding markers, and animacy of the subject are the three most prominent factors that have been shown to favor singular-marked forms (Mendes & Oushiro, 2015, p. 362). Since this topic has been studied from a variationist framework for BP, the corresponding body of literature informs the methodological perspective of the current study.

In the context of 3pl., higher rates of non-agreement are found with high phonic salience verbs and lower rates with low phonic salience verbs, particularly present and imperfect indicative forms in which 3sg. and 3pl. are distinguished by only the nasalization of the final vowel (*ganha/ganham* 'he/she wins/they win') (Naro & Scherre, 2000:243). Research on BP also shows [+animate, +human] referents, as well as preceding markers (plural morphemes in the noun phrase or plural referents in previous sentences) result in higher rates of agreement (*os meninos foram/foi* 'the boys went' vs. *os menino-∅ foram/foi* 'the boys went') (Scherre & Naro, 1992; Monguilhott, 2009; Brandão & Vieira, 2012; Rubio & Gonçalves, 2012; Mendes & Oushiro, 2015; Oushiro, 2015). Finally, word order and the presence of intervening linguistic material between the subject and verb impact number marking. When the subject directly precedes the verb, agreement is strongly favored (*eles fazem/faz* 'they do'), while distantly preceding subjects (*ós ainda não casamos/casou* 'we haven't yet gotten married') and postponed subjects (*chegaram/chegou dois caras* 'two guys arrived') disfavor agreement (Mendes & Oushiro, 2015, p. 363).

The social predictors of variation in BP for 3pl. subject-verb agreement are level of education and speaker gender. Higher rates of singular-marked forms are observed in speakers with less formal education (Brandão & Vieira, 2012; Naro & Schere, 2013; Mendes & Oushiro, 2015; Oushiro, 2015). In regard to speaker gender, men produce more singular-marked forms than women; however, in rural communities specifically, women produce higher rates of non-agreement because men are exposed to different speakers via employment opportunities outside their respective communities (Guy, 1981; Rodrigues, 1987; Labov, 2001; Rubio & Gonçalves, 2012; Mendes & Oushiro, 2015).

Due to the lack of variationist literature on variable subject-verb number marking in Spanish, this study will draw heavily from the research of this phenomenon in BP to guide its methodology, specifically the analysis of linguistic and social factors that predict non-standard, singular-marked forms.

3 Methods

The current study involved a sociolinguistic interview and 20 MCS speakers. All participants who were interviewed resided in Puerto Cabezas, Nicaragua and self-identified as being Miskitu-dominant or balanced bilingual speakers of Miskitu and Spanish. Anyone who learned Miskitu after Spanish, or as a second language, was not included in the study. An official bilingual profile was not administered but participants were asked several questions related to their linguistic background as part of the sociolinguistic interview.

In the beginning of the interview, participants were asked what languages they spoke. All 20 participants stated that they spoke only Miskitu and Spanish, and that they learned Miskitu at home with their families from birth. Their acquisition of Spanish varied, with 15 of the 20 speakers having learned Spanish at home from a family member or after starting primary school (before age six). The other 5 speakers learned Spanish upon entering secondary school and had little contact with the language at home. Miskitu would be considered the first language for all participants and Spanish would be either an additional first language for those with a more balanced level of bilingualism, or a second language.

Another language-related question that was asked of the speakers during the interview involved situations in which they tend to use Miskitu and Spanish. All participants said they use Miskitu at home with friends and family; Spanish, however, is used depending on who they are with. Some use Spanish as a way to accommodate non-Miskitu speakers: "el español también, bueno, lo usamos siempre porque siempre tenemos amigos españoles" 'Spanish also, well, we always use it because we always have Spanish friends', and others use Spanish only when it is necessary for communication: "yo casi hablo más el miskito y una persona me habla en español, hablo en español" 'I speak mostly Miskitu and if a person speaks to me in Spanish, I speak in Spanish'. Several participants stated that they base their language use on who they are talking with. If the person with whom they are talking does not speak Miskitu, they will use Spanish but if the person does speak Miskitu, that is the preference. Spanish was described as being a language used at school and in other public spheres, while Miskitu could be used both at home or in public if the interlocutor also spoke Miskitu.

The interviews were conducted in June and July of 2017 in Puerto Cabezas. Interviews were transcribed and coded for variable number marking. All cases of explicit 3pl. subjects and their corresponding verbs were extracted from the transcriptions (this included possible cases of non-specific, generic, or indefinite reference). Verbs directly followed by a word beginning with a nasal were excluded from the data set. 595 total tokens were analyzed.

3.1 Description of Factors

The factors analyzed in the current study were based on predictors found to be significant in Brazilian Portuguese, which also is characterized by variable number marking on verb morphology (Mendes and Oushiro, 2015; Oushiro, 2015): phonic salience of the verb (high or low salience), subject position relative to the verb (immediately preceding, distantly preceding, or postponed), subject type (pronoun or noun phrase), animacy of the subject ([+human] or [-human]), speaker age (18–29 or 30+), speaker gender (female or male), speaker level of education (secondary or university), and speaker age of Spanish acquisition (child or adolescent).

3.1.1 Linguistic Factors

Phonic salience referred to the difference between the verb morphology that marks singular or plural number. Low phonic salience were cases in which the only distinction between plural and singular forms of the verb was a final nasal consonant (*trabajan* vs. *trabaja* in 7a and 7b). High phonic salience were cases in which there was a larger perceptible distinction between singular and plural forms of the verb (*dijeron* vs. *dijo* in 8a and 8b).

(7) a. *los   hombre-s   trabaj-an*
       the.PL   man- PL   work-PRS.3PL
       'the men work'

   b. *ellos   trabaj-a   de   la   agricultura*
       they   work-PRS.3SG   of   the agriculture
       'they work in agriculture'

(8) a. *ellos   le   dij-eron   que   no   les   llevara*
       they   him   tell-PST.3PL   that   no   them   take-PST.SBJV.3SG
       'they told him not to take them'

   b. *entonces   los   pajarito-s   dij-o   que   hab-ía   un
       then   the.PL   bird-PL   say-PST.3SG   that   there was   a
       techo*
       roof
       'then the birds said that there was a roof'

Subject position involved two parts: the order of the subject in relation to the verb and the presence or absence of linguistic material between the subject and verb. The three designations were immediately preceding (9), distantly preceding (10), and postponed (11).

(9) ellos   viv-en   allí
    they   live-PRS.3PL   there
    'they live there'

(10) ellos   nunca   aguant-aba   de   nada
     they   never   tolerate-PST.3SG   of   nothing
     'they never tolerated anything'

(11) vien-en   mi-s   prima-s
     then   the.PL   bird-PL
     'my cousins come'

Subject type was coded as being either a pronoun (personal, indefinite, relative, and demonstrative) (12) or noun phrase (both simple and compound) (13). Only explicit forms were analyzed in order to avoid any ambiguity in identifying the referent while coding the data.

(12) ellos   mand-aban   en   el   parlamento
     they   send-PST.3PL   in   the   parliament
     'they were in charge in the parliament'

(13) mi-s   ancestro-s   and-aba   en   el   mar
     my.PL   ancestor-PL   go-PST.3SG   in   the   sea
     'my ancestors went around in the sea'

Subjects were coded as being either [+human] (14) or [-human] (15). Both [+animate] and [-animate] subjects that were nonhuman were grouped under [-human].

(14) la-s   mujer-es   miskita-s   nac-ieron   para   tener
     the-PL   woman-PL   Miskitu-PL   born-COND.3SG   for   have.INF
     hijos
     children
     'the Miskitu women were born to have children'

(15) la-s   bebida-s   típica-s   ser-ía   chicha
     the-PL   drink-PL   typical-PL   be-COND.3SG   chicha
     'the typical drinks would be chicha'

3.1.2 Social Factors

Participants were placed into one of two age categories: 18–29 and 30+. The groups were divided around the age of 30, which corresponds with the counterrevolution that occurred in Nicaragua in the late 1980s. Speakers born after this event would have been required to speak Spanish in school due to the Spanish literacy campaign that was established by the Sandinistas.

Participants self-identified their gender and were then assigned to one of two groups: male or female. Level of education was also divided into two categories: secondary and university. Speakers were grouped based on the highest level they had attended but did not have to have completed that course of study in its entirety. Finally, age of acquisition was divided into two categories: child and adolescent. If the speaker reported having learned Spanish before the age of 6 (upon entering primary school), they received the designation of 'child' and if they reported learning Spanish at or after the age of 12 (upon entering secondary school), they received the designation of 'adolescent'. All participants fell into these two age groups.

4 Data Analysis

The general frequency results (Figure 9.1) show lack of agreement occurred in 23.87% of the data set, with 142 occurrences out of 595. All 20 speakers

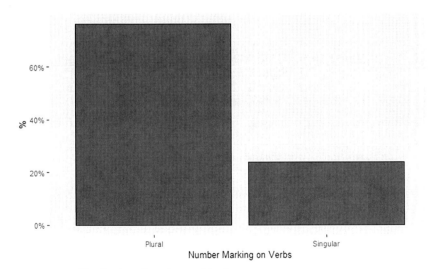

FIGURE 9.1 Distribution of number marking in MCS

TABLE 9.2   Mixed-effects logistic regression predicting 3sg. number marking with 3pl. Subjects in MCS: linguistic and social factors (n = 595, AIC = 577.5)

	Estimated/Simple log odds	SE	$Pr(>|z|)$	n	% 3sg.
Number marking	−4.5/.011	.71	3.00e-10 ***	453	76.13%
(vs. plural)				142	23.87%
singular					
Phonic salience	1.67/5.29	0.43	9.31e-05 ***	103	6.8%
(vs. high)				492	27.4%
low					
Subject position	.75/2.13	.25	.00240 **	317	16.1%
(vs. immediately preceding)	.68/1.97	.32	.03266 *	189	30.7%
distantly preceding				89	37.1%
postponed					
Subject type	.18/1.2	.24	.43998	277	19.1%
(vs. pronoun)				318	28%
noun phrase					
Animacy	.77/2.16	.32	.01654 *	518	22.4%
(vs. [+human])				77	33.8%
[−human]					
Age	.96/2.6	.39	.01395 *	332	16.9%
(vs. 18–29)				263	32.7%
30+					
Gender	.98/2.67	.36	.00608 **	369	17.1%
(vs. female)				226	35%
male					
Level of education	.67/1.95	.35	.05653	343	22.2%
(vs. university)				252	26.2%
secondary					
Age of acquisition	.04/1.04	.44	.93001	435	20.5%
(vs. child)				160	33.1%
adolescent					

displayed variability in number marking. The overall distribution of number marking aligned with what was previously attested by Critchfield & Lívio (*forthcoming*), who observed lack of agreement in 20.3% of the cases they analyzed in MCS.

The current analysis included a categorical dependent variable: plural number marking or singular number marking, and eight different independent variables: phonic salience, subject position, subject type, animacy of the subject, speaker gender, age, level of education, and age of acquisition.

The model selection began by running an initial logistic regression model in R using lrm(). The output indicated an overall significance (small p-value of the Model Likelihood Ratio Test < 0.0001) and goodness-of-fit of the model with all eight independent variables (concordance index C of 0.757). The model was reviewed for any signs of data sparseness or multicollinearity by examining the standard errors for each object in the model, all of which were small and indicated no evidence of multicollinearity. A generalized linear regression was used to run three different stepwise tests: forward, backward, and bidirectional. The results of these tests showed that all predictors, other than subject type and age of acquisition, significantly improved the model (evaluated using the AIC). An ANOVA was run to compare the AIC of a model with all eight independent variables and a model without subject type and age of acquisition. The results showed no significant difference in the AIC between the two models, so all variables were kept. Finally, possible interactions between the independent variables were reviewed but none were found to be statistically significant.

The final model was a mixed-effects logistic regression with speaker as a random effect and phonic salience, subject position, subject type, animacy of the subject, speaker gender, age, level of education, and age of acquisition as fixed-effects. Phonic salience, subject position, animacy, age and gender were all significant predictors[2] (Table 9.2).

4.1 Linguistic Factors

Phonic salience was the factor with the strongest predictive power (p = 9.31e-05 ***). Low phonic salience tenses/moods such as present indicative (16) and imperfect indicative (17) were the strongest predictors of singular number marking in the data set, 5.29 times more likely to result in non-agreement.

(16) los   miskito-s   también   tien-e   derecho   a   su
     the.PL   Miskitu-PL   also   have-PRS.3SG   right   to   their
     tierra   natal
     land   native
     'the Miskitus also have a right to their home land'

---

2   *p < 0.05, **p < 0.01, ***p <0.001.

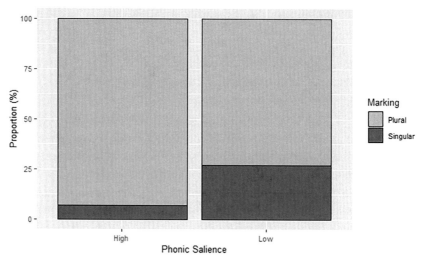

FIGURE 9.2 Phonic salience and number marking

(17) antes   los   líder-es   no   permit-ía   eso
     before   the.PL   leader-PL   no   permit-PST.3SG   that
     'before the leaders didn't permit that'

Singular number marking occurred 27.4% of the time when the verb had low phonic salience and only 6.8% of the time when the verb had high phonic salience (Figure 9.2).

High phonic salience verb forms therefore did not frequently motivate the production of non-agreement, with only seven cases being observed in the data (18 and 19). These results align with what has been found in MCS and BP.

(18) eso-s   buzo-s   como   vin-o   aquí,   hac-en
     that-PL   diver-PL   like   come-PST.3SG   here   make-PRS.3PL
     huelgas
     strikes
     'those divers, like they came here, they make strikes'

(19) ellos   fu-e   guerrilleros
     they   be-PST.3SG   warriors
     'they were warriors'

The results for subject position indicated that both distantly preceding and postponed subjects were statistically significant in predicting singular number

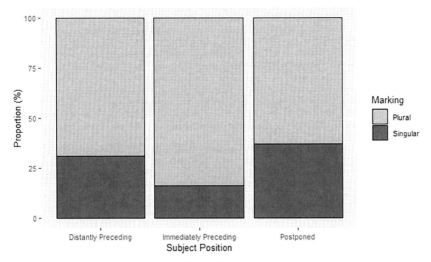

FIGURE 9.3 Subject position and number marking

marking (p = .00240** and .03266* respectively). The likelihood of getting singular number marking was 2.13 times greater when the subject was distantly preceding and 1.97 times greater when it was postponed. When the subject was immediately preceding the verb, singular number marking occurred 16.1% of the time, versus 30.7% when distantly preceding and 37.1% when postponed (Figure 9.3). These results also align with MCS and BP (Critchfield & Lívio, *forthcoming*; Mendes & Oushiro, 2015, p. 363).

Subject type was the only linguistic factor that was not a significant predictor of variable number marking; however, the model did show a slight favoring effect, with 3sg. tokens occurring 28% of the time with noun phrases and 19.1% with pronouns (noun phrases 1.2 times more likely to result in non-agreement) (Figure 9.4). According to Zanini, Chiara, et al. (2020), number is easier to assign to more salient referents, who are generally represented by more minimal subject forms (Gundel, Hedberg and Zacharski, 1993). The increased agreement rate with pronouns reflects this tendency.

The results for animacy showed that [-human] subjects were 2.16 times more likely to predict singular number marking compared to [+human] subjects (p = .0165*) (20 and 21). Non-agreement occurred 33.8% of the time with [-human] subjects and 22.4% of the time with [+human] subject (Figure 9.5). These findings reflect what has been found for BP (Mendes and Oushiro, 2015, p. 363). The more animate a referent is, the more salient it is in the mind of the speaker. This saliency results in a greater ease of assigning number to any given referent (Zanini, Chiara, et al., 2020).

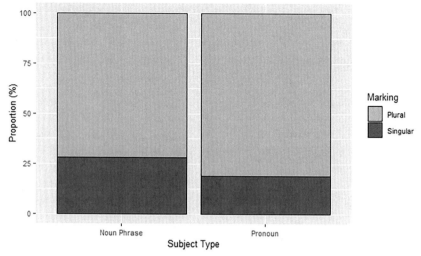

FIGURE 9.4 Subject type and number marking

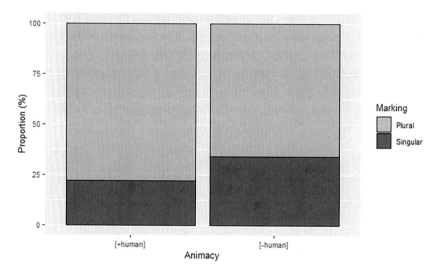

FIGURE 9.5 Animacy and number marking

(20) *antes   ven-ía   uno-s   proyecto-s*
      before   come-PST.3SG   some-PL   project-PL
      'some projects used to come here'

(21) *eso-s   canal-es   no   es   bueno   para   nosotros*
      that-PL   canal-PL   no   be-PST.3SG   good   for   us
      'those canals are not good for us'

4.2 Social Factors

The logistic regression showed age and gender to be the only social factors that were statistically significant in predicting variable number marking (p = .01395* and p = .00608** respectively). Speakers over the age of 30 were 2.6 times more likely than speakers 18–29 to produce non-agreement (a rate of 32.7% vs. 16.9%, shown in Figure 9.6), and male speakers were 2.67 times more likely than female speakers (a rate of 35% vs. 17.1%, shown in Figure 9.7).

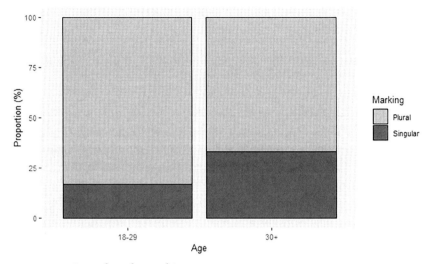

FIGURE 9.6 Age and number marking

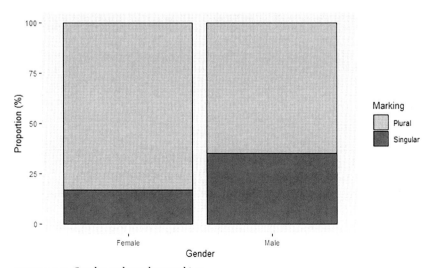

FIGURE 9.7 Gender and number marking

A variety of conclusions could be drawn based on the current findings for age. Trends in the sociolinguistics literature show younger speakers use more non-standard variants, unless stigmatized (Silva-Corvalán, 2001, p. 102; Chappell, 2015a, p. 225). The results in this study could suggest that variable number marking is a stigmatized feature in the community; however, without independent evidence of negative evaluation, this cannot be confirmed. It is also unclear if these results indicate that this phenomenon in MCS is decreasing in the community over time, with younger speakers producing less non-agreement, or if speakers are changing their speech habits as they age.

In regard to gender, female speakers generally have a tendency to use variants that are more standard, which is reflected in the results for this study. This pattern has been explained by Silva-Corvalán (2001, p. 98), as reflecting the expectation women have to behave in a polite and courteous manner, including using speech that is considered standard.

Level of education did not meet the < .05 threshold for statistical significance in predicting singular number marking (p = .05653); however, speakers with a secondary level of education were 1.95 times more likely to produce non-agreement when compared to speakers with a university level of education (Figure 9.8).

Age of acquisition was also not a statistically significant predictor (p = .93001); however, speakers who acquired Spanish after the age of 12 produced non-agreement at a higher rate (33.1% vs. 20.5% by speakers who acquired Spanish before the age of 6, shown in Figure 9.9). Based on the lack

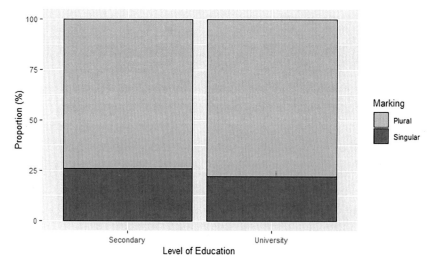

FIGURE 9.8 Level of education and number marking

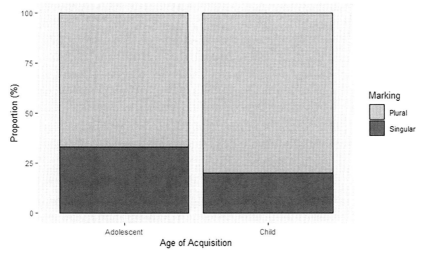

FIGURE 9.9 Age of acquisition and number marking

of significance age of acquisition plays in the analysis, the variable number marking found in the MCS speech community does not appear to be the result of the current population's acquisition process, otherwise the group of participants who acquired Spanish after the age of 12 would have produced more non-agreement at a significant rate.

5 Discussion and Conclusions

Both linguistic and social factors motivate the use of 3sg. verb morphology with 3pl. subjects in MCS, including phonic salience, subject position, animacy, age, and gender, all of which were significant predictors in the statistical model. The probability of getting non-agreement in the data set was 4.38 times higher when the phonic salience of the verb was low, the subject distantly preceded the verb, was a noun phrase, was [-human], the speaker was over the age of 30, a male, had a secondary level of education, and acquired Spanish as an adolescent. These findings correlate with the trends discussed for MCS in previous studies and with Brazilian Portuguese.

Interestingly, one of the factors that failed to demonstrate statistical significance is one of the most telling in the analysis. The lack of statistical significance shown regarding age of acquisition provides important information about the evolution of variable number marking in MCS. Based on the current findings, the age the participants acquired Spanish had no significant impact on the production of non-agreement. Based on this finding, as well as the presence of variable number marking across all social categories, it could be concluded that this phenomenon is a characteristic of MCS, likely originating from the group language shift that occurred when Spanish was established in the education system on the Caribbean coast in the middle of the twentieth century. During this shift, geographic isolation from Spanish-speaking populations in Nicaragua could have led to the divergent representation of certain features in MCS. According to Montrul (2006, 2008), incompleteness (or divergence) in language acquisition is a result of insufficient target language input. When the shift to Spanish began, there was no direct ground access to the Pacific coast capital, Managua, and telegraph was the only means of communication (*The Miskitos in Nicaragua, 1981–1984*, 1984). This isolation would have meant limited contact with Nicaragua Spanish-speaking populations, outside of the educational sphere. The lack of input these first speakers of MCS experienced would have greatly impacted the acquisition of Spanish in a target-like manner. Unlike the first speakers of MCS, the current target language in this speech community is not necessarily Nicaraguan Spanish, as most speakers now acquire Spanish from other speakers of MCS: family, friends, or teachers. It would, therefore, be expected that speakers would acquire features of MCS.

Evidence of influence from Miskitu is also present in the effect of number. When learners have not acquired a second language in its entirety, they rely on L1 influence as a strategy, particularly when the L1 and the L2 differ (Winford, 2003). Number marking on verbs in Miskitu contrasts with Spanish as it is not morphologically marked in the verb. The use of 3sg. verb forms with both 3sg. and 3pl. referents can be attributed to the lack of number distinction in the Miskitu verb paradigm, as learners tend to reduce or eliminate target language inflectional morphemes, such as those used to mark number, when a typological difference exists in the L1 and L2 (Winford, 2003, p. 213).

While the findings do not suggest that current speakers of MCS possess a divergent use of number marking (based on MCS being the target language and not Nicaraguan Spanish), they do suggest that speakers rely on cognitive processes, such as salience, to compensate for the difference in number marking in Spanish vs. Miskitu. The effect of salience on the distribution of the linguistic factors is a clear example of speakers employing a normal cognitive process in the context of a divergent patterning of features in the Spanish number marking system. The more salient the referent, both semantically or structurally, the more likely the speaker was to produce agreement. Structurally speaking, more minimal forms such as pronouns, are used when the referent is more salient in the mind of the speaker (Levinson, 2000; Lubbers Quesada, 2015, p. 265). Semantically speaking, human referents are more salient (Zanini, Chiara, et al.,

2020). Along with high phonic salience verbs, pronouns and [+human] subjects favored agreement in the data analysis. While variable subject-verb number agreement indicates the presence of divergent acquisition (a result of initial language shift), higher rates of agreement in more salient contexts reflect normal cognitive patterns.

The findings for the social predictors suggest that the less a speaker is exposed to language norms, the more likely they are to diverge from patterns found in Nicaraguan Spanish. In the data set, the non-standard variant (singular number marking) was produced at higher rates by older speakers, males, speakers with lower levels of education, and those who acquired Spanish at a later age.

Age was a statistically significant motivator in the analysis, with speakers aged 18–29 less likely to produce non-agreement. The general trend for younger speakers to use more non-standard language, except when the feature in question is stigmatized, may indicate that variable number marking in MCS has some level of stigmatization attached to it (Silva-Corvalán, 2001, p. 102). This could be a result of younger speakers being more exposed to standard language norms via education and media. As time passes and contact between Nicaraguan Spanish and MCS increases, less non-agreement may be observed.

The results for gender also suggest that variable number marking is a stigmatized feature as men were more likely to produce non-agreement. Women tend to use more standard language, which has been attributed to their awareness of the social consequences of speech choices. Since women have historically had fewer opportunities for advancement, the use of standard language has been a strategy to communicate socioeconomic status (Silva-Corvalán, 2001, p. 98).

Level of education was not a statistically significant factor in the analysis; however, speakers with a secondary level of education produced more non-agreement. General trends in sociolinguistics show speakers with less formal education deviate more from standard language norms (Brandão & Vieira, 2012; Naro & Schere, 2013; Chappell, 2015; Oushiro, 2015). Level of bilingualism has been connected to the use of non-standard language and while level of education is distinct from level of bilingualism, speakers with more formal education would also have had more exposure to prescriptive language norms in the classroom.

Based on the findings for linguistic and social constraints, number marking in MCS appears to be strongly connected to bilingualism and language contact, a result of the divergent acquisition of Spanish. Previous research on both Spanish and Portuguese supports this claim as there are no attested cases of variable number marking in varieties of these languages that have no history of significant contact with other languages. While similar phenomena have been observed in varieties of Spanish with no recent language contact (i.e. Dominican Spanish), final /n/ deletion is distinct from the variable number marking presented here.

MCS is a contact variety that experienced rapid language shift, and as a result, divergent acquisition of a linguistic feature that differs in its distribution in the contact language/L1, Miskitu. Based on the findings from this study, as well as the history of MCS, it appears that variable number marking is now a fixed feature in the grammar, decreasing in speakers who are exposed more to Nicaraguan Spanish and standard language norms.

References

Alba, O. (2004). *Cómo hablamos los dominicanos: Un enfoque sociolingüístico*. Grupo León Jimenes.

Brandão, S. F., & Vieira, S. R. (2012). Concordância nominal e verbal: Contribuições para o debate sobre o estatuto da variação em três variedades urbanas do português. *Alfa: Revista de Linguística (São José do Rio Preto), 56*(3), 1035–1064.

Chappell, W. (2014). Reanalysis and hypercorrection among extreme/s/reducers. *University of Pennsylvania Working Papers in Linguistics, 20*(2), 5.

Chappell, W. (2015a). Formality strategies in Managua, Nicaragua: A local vs. global approach. *Spanish in Context, 12*(2), 221–254.

Chappell, W. (2015b). Linguistic factors conditioning glottal constriction in Nicaraguan Spanish. *Italian Journal of Linguistics, 27*(2), 1–42.

Critchfield, M. & Lívio, C. (Forthcoming). Variable concord in two American Romance varieties: Using Brazilian Portuguese to inform Mosquito Coast Spanish. *Proceedings from the 49th Linguistics Symposium on Romance Languages*.

Escobar, A. M. (2013). Bilingualism in Latin America. In T. K. Bhatia & W. C. Ritchie (Eds.), *The handbook of bilingualism and multilingualism* (pp. 725–744). Wiley-Blackwell.

Floyd, T. S. (1967). *The Anglo-Spanish struggle for Mosquitia*. University of New Mexico Press.

Foote, R., & Bock, K. (2012). The role of morphology in subject–verb number agreement: A comparison of Mexican and Dominican Spanish. *Language and cognitive processes, 27*(3), 429–461.

García, C. (1996). *The making of the Miskitu people of Nicaragua: The social construction of ethnic identity*. Uppsala University.

Gundel, J. K., Hedberg, N., & Zacharski, R. (1993). Cognitive status and the form of referring expressions in discourse. *Language*, 274–307.

Guy, G. R. (1981). Linguistic variation in Brazilian Portuguese: Aspects of the phonology, syntax, and language history. University of Pennsylvania. (Doctoral dissertation).

Guy, G. (2005). A questão da crioulização no português do Brasil. In A. M. Stahl Zilles (Ed.), *Estudos de variação lingüística no Brasil e no Cone Sul* (pp. 15–38). Editora da Universidade Federal do Rio Grande do Sul.

Guy, G. (2014). Variation and change in Latin American Spanish and Portuguese. In P. Amaral & A. M. Caravalho (Eds.), *Portuguese-Spanish interfaces: Diachrony, synchrony, and contact* (pp. 443–464). John Benjamins.

Labov, W. (2001). *Principles of sociolinguistic change: Social factors*. Malden: Blackwell.

Lipski, J. (1984). /s/ in the Spanish of Nicaragua. *Orbis*, 33(1–2), 171–181.

Lipski, J. (1985). /s/ in Central American Spanish. *Hispania*, 68(1), 143–149.

Lipski, J. (2008a). *Afro-Bolivian Spanish*. Iberoamericana Editorial.

Lipski, J. (2008b). Afro-Bolivian Spanish and Helvécia Portuguese: Semi-creole parallels. *PAPIA-Revista Brasileira de Estudos do Contato Linguístico*, 16(1), 96–116.

Lipski, J. M. (2008c). *Varieties of Spanish in the United States*. Georgetown University Press.

Lipski, J. M. (2011). Socio-phonological variation in Latin American Spanish. In M. Díaz Campos (Ed.), *The handbook of Hispanic sociolinguistics* (pp. 72–97). Wiley-Blackwell.

Lipski, J. M. (2020). Creoloid phenomena in the Spanish of transitional bilinguals. In *Spanish in the United States* (pp. 155–182). De Gruyter Mouton.

Lipski, J. M., & Recuero, S. I. (1996). *El español de América*. Madrid: Cátedra.

Lucchesi, D., Baxter, A. N., & Ribeiro, I. (2009). *O português afro-brasileiro*. Edufba.

Mendes, R. B., & Oushiro, L. (2015). Variable number agreement in Brazilian Portuguese: An overview. *Language and Linguistics Compass*, 9(9), 358–368.

Meringer, E. R. (2014). Accommodating mestizaje on Nicaragua's Rio Coco: Miskitu activism before the Sandinista revolution. *AlterNative: An International Journal of Indigenous Peoples*, 10(3), 203–215.

The Miskitos in Nicaragua, 1981–1984. (1984). Americas Watch Committee.

Monguilhott, I. D. O. (2009). Estudo sincrônico e diacrônico da concordância verbal de terceira pessoa do plural no PB e no PE. UFSC (Doctoral dissertation).

Montrul, S. (2006). Incomplete acquisition as a feature of bilingual and L2 grammars. In *Inquiries in linguistic development: In honor of Lydia White* (pp. 335–359). John Benjamins Amsterdam.

Montrul, S. (2008). *Incomplete acquisition in bilingualism: Re-examining the age factor*. John Benjamins Publishing.

Naro, A. J., & Scherre, M. M. P. (2000). Variable concord in Portuguese: The situation in Brazil and Portugal. *Creole language library*, 21, 235–256.

Naro, A. J., & Scherre, M. M. P. (2013). Remodeling the age variable: Number concord in Brazilian Portuguese. *Language Variation and Change*, 25(1), 1.

Oushiro, L. (2015). Identidade na pluralidade: Avaliação, produção e percepçãolinguística na cidade de são paulo. Universidade de São Paulo (Doctoral dissertation).

Penny, R. (2004). *Variation and change in Spanish*. Cambridge University Press.

Rodrigues, A. C. S. (1987). A concordância verbal no português popular em São Paulo. FFLCH-USP (Doctoral dissertation).

Rubio, C. F., & Gonçalves, S. C. L. (2012). A fala do interior paulista no cenário da sociolinguística brasileira: Panorama da concordância verbal e da alternância pronominal. *Alfa: Revista de Linguística (São José do Rio Preto)*, 56(3), 1003–1034.

Salamanca, D. (1988). Elementos de gramática del miskito. Massachusetts Institute of Technology (Doctoral dissertation).

Scherre, M. M. P., & Naro, A. J. (1992). The serial effect on internal and external variables. *Language Variation and Change*, 4(1), 1–13.

Scherre, M. M. P. (1998). Variação da concordância nominal no português do Brasil: Influência das variáveis posição, classe gramatical e marcas precedentes. *Sybille Grosse and Klaus Zimmermann (ds.), "Substandard" e mudança no português do Brasil*, 153–188.

Scherre, M. M. P., & Naro, A. J. (2001). Sobre as origens estruturais do português brasileiro: Crioulização ou mudança natural?. *Papia*, 41–50.

Scherre, M. M. P., & Naro, A. J. (2010). Perceptual vs. grammatical constraints and social factors in subject-verb agreement in Brazilian Portuguese. *University of Pennsylvania Working Papers in Linguistics*, 16(2), 20.

Scherre, M. M. P., & Naro, A. J. (2014). Sociolinguistic correlates of negative evaluation: Variable concord in Rio de Janeiro. *Language Variation and Change*, 26(3), 331.

Sessarego, S. (2011). On the status of Afro-Bolivian Spanish features: Decreolization or vernacular universals. In *Proceedings of the Fifth Workshop on Spanish Sociolinguistics* (pp. 125–141). Cascadilla Someville, MA.

Silva-Corvalán, C. (2001). *Sociolingüística y pragmática del español*. Georgetown University Press.

Wilson Withe, C., Oporta, P., Muller Oporta, J., Chow Smith, W., Bency, S., Taylor, A., ... & Simmons Santiago, Y. (2012). *Sari laka apu kan piuara: Antes de los días tristes: Cuaderno cultural miskitu*. UNESCO, San Jose (Costa Rica). Programa Conjunto de Revitalizacion Cultural y Desarrollo Productivo creativo en la Costa Caribe de Nicaragua, Managua (Nicaragua).

Winford, D. (2003). *An introduction to contact linguistics*. Wiley-Blackwell.

Zanini, C., Rugani, R., Giomo, D., Peressotti, F., & Franzon, F. (2020). Effects of animacy on the processing of morphological Number: a cognitive inheritance?. *Word Structure*, 13(1), 22–44.

CHAPTER 10

The Historical Evolution of *Usted* in Costa Rican Spanish

Munia Cabal-Jiménez

1   Introduction

This study deals with the evolution of *usted* in Costa Rican Spanish. In general, Spanish has been traditionally classified as a T/V system (Brown and Gilman, 1972; Brown and Levinson; 1978, 1987; Braun, 1988), in which the V uses have been performed through the pronoun *usted* and the T uses through the pronoun *tú* in countries that are *tuteantes* or by *vos* in countries that are *voseantes*. This study shows how the T/V system in Costa Rican Spanish during colonial times until the beginning of 20th c. started to display a structure that differs from the above-mentioned system.

2   History of Costa Rican Address Forms during Colonial Times[1]

The studies of Costa Rican Colonial Spanish have been carried out mostly by Costa Rican linguist Miguel Ángel Quesada Pacheco, whose studies have contributed significantly to the knowledge of Costa Rican colonial Spanish and, consequently, to the description on the use of address forms during that time in Costa Rica.

The present address form system in Costa Rican Spanish displays a very complex system, where *vos*, *tú* and *usted* compete in the non-deferential parameter. Moreover, the three pronouns, or at least two forms, can be used by the speaker with the same interlocutor in the same conversation (Quesada, 2003). Based on an analysis and comparison of Costa Rican colonial and postcolonial manuscripts, documents, private letters, newsletters and testimonies,

---

1   Due to space constraints and to avoid the anodyne repetition of the well-known and canonical evolution of the pronoun *usted* from 16th c. in Spanish, I will not address the extensive literature available on the topic that the student and scholar have already at their disposal. I will refer to the specific case of Costa Rica and close areas where *usted*, during colonial times, experienced particular changes in its use.

Quesada proposes (based on Brown and Gilman, 1972) that since colonial times in Costa Rica, the 2nd pronominal person (2ps) and verbal address form system employs various pronouns to express deferential and non-deferential distinctions.

Throughout the history of this pronoun, during the 16th and 17th centuries, *vos, vuestras mercedes, vuesa merced* and *vuesencia* appeared in texts and manuscripts and were used in hierarchical (deferential) relationships. Of particular interest is that Quesada registers the first time, in the 18th c., the use of *usted* to express solidarity. He has termed the use of *usted* with this solidarity meaning as *ustedeo* (see also Quesada Pacheco, this volume). It is also in this century when the first written evidence of *voseo americano* can be found. Towards the late 18th c., based on excerpts of manuscripts, he finds evidence of the variation between *tú* and *vos* (voseo americano) in contexts of solidarity. (Quesada, 2003). Quesada adds: "Esta alternancia cobrará valor más tarde, porque es la responsable de la actual alternancia entre *usted* y *vos*" (p. 2329). He also reports that by then *tú* already competed with *vos* in non-hierarchical (non-deferential) relationships. Quesada puts forward a visual and historical description (for each century) of the 2nd person pronoun system in Costa Rican Spanish (adapted in Table 10.1).

This multiplicity of pronouns during these centuries leads Quesada to propose an *overload* on the system (Quesada, 2003). By *overload*, Quesada refers to the abundant presence of various address forms to express the 2ps category.

TABLE 10.1 Address forms used in Costa Rican Spanish in colonial times

Century	Power	Solidarity
16th–17th	Vos	Tú
	Vuestra Merced	
18th	Usted	Vos (voseo americano)
	Su Merced	Tú
		Usted (ustedeo)
19th	Usted	Vos (voseo americano)
		Tú
		Usted (ustedeo)
20th	Usted	Vos
		Tú (incipient)
		Usted (ustedeo)

ADOPTED FROM QUESADA, 2003

He does not provide, however, an analysis to explain the changes the pronoun *usted* underwent from the deferential meaning (power) to the non-deferential meaning (solidarity). His description of the distribution of the address form system in Costa Rica is presented through the Brown & Gilman dyad of power and solidarity, isolated from any social factors that could have played a role in Costa Rican colonial society.[2]

A reanalysis of Quesada's chart suggests a different situation. From the 16th to 18th centuries in Costa Rican Spanish, the pronoun *vos* experienced a shift from use in hierarchical relationships to nonhierarchical relationships (indicating solidarity).[3] Similarly, during the 18th century, the use of pronoun *usted* is extended to being used both in hierarchical relationships and in non-hierarchical relationships. Rosenblat has explained the shift of *vos* (from a power to a solidarity pronoun) with the '*hidalguización*' hypothesis (Rosenblat, 1969).

What type of changes did the pronoun *usted* undergo that made it acquire the non-deferential meaning (ustedeo)? Quesada does not present a possible explanation about what could have caused this evolution. His description refers to the fact that the Costa Rican address forms (until the 20th c.) have displayed a sort of "pronominal entropy" that is, that pronouns oscillate, as a pendulum, between the deferential and non-deferential axis: "... ora recargándose en el plano de la solidaridad, ora en el plano del distanciamiento, sin que parezca llegar a un fin". (Quesada, 2003). *Ustedeo* development is relevant for the history of Spanish language in Costa Rica, since, as Quesada also points out: "El ustedeo irrumpe en la población con mayor fuerza, de manera que en la actualidad se observa un empleo general en todo el país, tanto en la ciudad como en el campo" (Quesada, 2003, p.2334).

Evidence of *ustedeo* during colonial and present times in other Spanish speaking countries in Latin America has been documented. Given the constraints in space we cannot offer a detailed exam of all the relevant literature. Several studies show the use of *Vuestra Merced* and *usted* in the New World, some of these studies analyze the use of this pronoun in family letters, or manuscripts that reflect certain level of orality and provide an account of the use of the pronoun *usted* in covariation with the pronoun *tú* (Bentivoglio, 2002).

---

[2] Power and solidarity are two dimensions of social life expressed through the address form pronouns. Historically, both pronouns, T and V (Brown and Gilman, 1972) were not used reciprocally. Later, these pronouns expressed a distinct use: T was used to express that a specific participant in a given interaction belonged to the same social status, and, that they were close/familiar to each other. On the other hand, V indicated that the participants in the interaction belonged to the same social group but were not close/familiar to each other.

[3] Terms which seem to better describe the situation.

Bentivoglio documents the use of *usted* in contexts of solidarity, between spouses, but in very specific instances, in letters where the general address form is *tú*. In the Andean region of Venezuela, Mérida, the inhabitants of this region use *usted* with a T value.[4] It is used between spouses, friends, and siblings. Obediente Sosa, Carrera de la Red y Álvarez provide a sociohistorical explanation about the use of *vuestra merced* and *usted* in the region of Mérida (Obediente Sosa, 2010; Carrera de la Red et al., 2004): Similar uses of *usted* with a T value have also been found in colonial times for the region of Cartagena, Colombia and the Caribbean region (Gutiérrez Maté, 2009).[5]

The purpose of this article is to offer a linguistic explanation of what mechanisms were at play that were conducive to the evolution of the pronoun *usted* in Costa Rican Spanish throughout this period.

3   Theoretical Framework

The concept of face, as presented by Brown and Levinson (1978/1987), constitutes a very important notion that will be extensively applied in the analysis of the semantic/pragmatic change of the pronoun *usted*. According to them, at the very core in any human interaction exists the concept of face, independent of any message that is conveyed or received. In those interactions, many types of actions or contents can be communicated, varying from requests to offers or complaints. Speaker (S) and Hearer (H) are competent individuals in such interaction, and each has "face", i.e., "the public self-image that every member wants to claim for himself" (p. 61). Face consists of two related aspects: negative and positive face. Negative face is the establishment of personal independence, territories, personal preserves, right to non-distraction—i.e., freedom of actions and freedom from imposition. Positive face is the positive consistent self-image (crucially including the desire that this self-image be appreciated and approved of), claimed by interactants (p. 61). The concept of face, positive and negative, is the basis of all types of social relationships.

One important aspect of Brown and Levinson's approach is that participants in any given exchange know what they are expected to do and follow specific conventions when pursuing goals. These authors posit that despite

---

4   And, inversely, tú is used with a V value, to express politeness and distance (Obediente, 2010).
5   Obediente points out, quoting Iraset Páez: "… el ustedeo es una de las peculiaridades más resaltantes de la región andina […]" And adds "Esta situación, patente ya en el siglo XVIII, es la que ha perdurado en dicha comunidad en los tiempos modernos" (Páez, Iraset, citado en Obediente Sosa, 2010, p. 93).

the different cultural outcomes of such conventions, it is a common process to all-natural languages and their speakers. In other words, an interactant possesses certain rational capacities to use specific strategies. An important aspect of face is that it is an emotional investment; it can be lost, maintained, or enhanced and should always be attended to in the interaction. Everyone's face depends on the other participant's face; therefore, there is cooperation on maintaining each other's face. Whereas the ways to carry out this task can have unique cultural expressions, Brown and Levinson assume that the existence of a public image or face and the social need that everyone has to orient him or herself in social interactions, are of universal character.

The double-sided nature of the concept of face also implies that in every single exchange both S and H must pay attention to what they are doing in terms of threatening the good standing of either of those two components of face. Those acts that can decrease the positive or the negative face of both S and H are known as "face threatening acts" (FTAs). In the interactions between S and H, the acts performed by the individuals may threaten the face intrinsically, that is, the very nature of the speech act can portray a threat to the other's face (verbally or no-verbally). FTAs can be classified according to two types: a) FTAs that threaten negative face vs. FTAs that threaten positive face, b) Threats to H's face versus threats to S's face.[6]

When the speaker acts in such a way that he impedes the hearer's freedom of action and/or does not avoid impeding hearers' freedom of action, an FTA to the negative face has been performed. For example: preventing the hearer from executing an action, or, making clear to the hearer that he must perform a specific task, the freedom of action of the H is somehow limited. Examples of these types of acts can be requests, suggestions, advice, reminders, threats, or warnings, among other actions. A second type of act through which the S threatens the H's negative face is when the S exerts pressure on H to accept or reject offers and/or promises. A third type of act in which the freedom of action of the H is threatened, is through the expression of an act in which the S communicates a desire towards H or H's goods. Examples include compliments or expression of strong or negative emotions towards H, expression of envy, admiration (the S may like something H has) or anger (attempting to harm H or H's goods).

Acts that threaten positive face are those that threaten the self-image of the H; basically, those acts that threaten H's desire that his image will be accepted and approved. Such FTAs can be performed expressing some negative evaluation of some aspect of H's positive face: disapproval, criticism, accusations,

---

6 For strategies on how FTAs are performed, see Brown and Levinson (1978, 1987: 69).

insults in which obviously the self-image of the H is not being approved, or, also, through the expression of contradictions, disagreements, or challenges. That is, through the establishment or expression that the H may be wrong, the self-image of H is also somehow "disapproved". Also, FTAs to the positive face can also be made through the mention of taboo topics or acts of irreverence through which S expresses that he does not consider the H's values. In this same set of actions that may threaten the H's positive face are those actions that may cause some distress to the H through the expression of bad news about H or good news about S (through boasting).

Together with the notion of face, the concepts of withdrawal and approach provide an alternative frame to analyze and understand the address form system in Costa Rican colonial Spanish. Withdrawal and approach provide a more generalized context that explains that individuals tend to come closer (approach) or to put more distance (withdraw) when they interact with other individuals.

Also relevant for the current analysis is the notion of intentionality related to the interaction. Expanding the concept of face, Terkourafi (2007) revisits this concept and traces its historical structure. Examining the concept based on cognitive and human emotion literature, she proposes a more universal notion of face, based on traits that are common to human nature. This principle is proposed to exist independently from cultural and societal specificities. She elaborates upon this concept establishing a.) the notion of Face 1 (which refers to face in a specific cultural context), and b.) to Face 2 as a universal concept, existing outside of any societal or cultural context. Face 2 is, in turn, based on two main components: one is the biological grounding, which supposes the dimension of approach/withdrawal on the part of the individuals, and intentionality, which refers to acts performed by individuals that are based on decision making. It is related to mental states and what they (and the individuals) are about. Intentionality is what makes the concept of face uniquely human. This approach/withdrawal trait is not only common to all human emotions but also phylogenetically primary, universal, and preconscious:

> It seems to me that such a dimension provides a natural basis for a universalizing notion of face, from which the latter can inherit two important features: its dualism between positive (approach) and negative (withdrawal) aspects, and its universality. (Terkourafi, 2007, p. 323)

Intentionality refers to actions that reflect the mental property of doing something. Acts such as beliefs, intentions, love, and judgments all are displays of intentionality. Those acts are intended for someone else, that is, for the *Other* and as Terkourafi points out: "Face is similarly intentional inasmuch as it presupposes an Other. Awareness of the Other, in turn, presupposes a notion of Self." (Terkourafi, 2007, p. 323).

The presence of another to whom the self relates to and speaks to, justifies the decision of the speaker to approach the other or to withdraw from the other. If, through intentionality, judgment is expressed, that will cause the individual to withdraw for her or his interlocutor. If through intentionality love is displayed, then the individual will opt for coming closer and express his or her intentions in a more intimate way. This, in turn, will make the individual to approach his or her interlocutor. The existence of the other also implies the existence of the self. A notion of face that presupposes the existence of a "other" means that both participants work together on directing their actions intentionally. That is equivalent to say that the notion of face in its universalizing concept is based mainly on intentionality, it is because of the intentionality that face concerns arise and are fulfilled.

These terms are used in the current study to analyze the pronouns and to offer a perspective that it is more comprehensive of the communicative dynamic and provides a better account about how and why the pronoun *usted* evolved in its meaning.

4   Methodology

The purpose of this study is to track the historical evolution of the 2ps *usted*. The materials that make possible a study with that historical perspective are written records.

The study will use official letters (Fernández; Fernández, 1882), excerpts from manuscripts, and family letters (Quesada, 1987) in the more recent periods. The letters include personal and public (official) writings where the two individuals involved were friends, relatives, or acquaintances. The study uses primarily a descriptive analysis and interprets them under the consideration of the theories of semantic change and politeness theory. The manuscripts or documents written from the 16th century on, were found in archives, anthologies, specialized publications, and history journals.[7] Parts of trials or manuscripts in which the testimony of the witnesses reproduce dialogs or interchange of information in which personal address interaction is present, are included. Although there are many materials from the 16th c. on in Costa

---

[7] For a list of documents from Costa Rican Archives and the abbreviations employed to refer to them and the documents (see Appendices A and B).

Rican archives, finding letters from the previous period and shortly after independence proved to be a difficult task. While there is an abundance of official letters, those of personal character are even more challenging to track down.[8] All these sources proceed from specialized publications, such as, Costa Rican archives, el *Archivo General de Indias* located in Sevilla, Spain (consulted electronically), and letters facilitated by family members and/or researchers. The list of letters and excerpts used in this study are forty-nine in total.[9] The letters provided by Eugenio García were collected from the private correspondence of Joaquín García Monge, it includes correspondence with and between the Costa Rican literary authors Joaquín García, Monge, Manuel Antonio González (Magón) and María Isabel Carvajal also known as Carmen Lyra, a prominent female Costa Rican writer. The letters collected and published by Alberto Montero Segura refer to the debate of nationalism in Costa Rican literature that took place between 1894 and 1902, between outstanding Costa Rican writers. The authors sustained this debate through published correspondence in newspapers.

5   Analysis

How did the pronoun *usted* in Costa Rican Spanish acquire the use as a T (or approach) pronoun? In this section, it is proposed: a.) to distinguish between the uses of the nominal address *Vuestra Merced*, and the uses of *usted* as pronoun; and b.) to provide an explanation of the semantic change experienced by the *usted* that allows for its use as a withdrawal pronoun and as an approach pronoun. This semantic change will be explained by a.) a process of grammaticalization and by b.) a process of pragmaticalization (for pragmatical variation in Central American Spanish, see Michno et al., this volume).

5.1   *Variables for the Analysis*
The analysis of the evolution of 2ps *usted* and the nominal form *Vuestra Merced* is based on two variables: a.) the subject form (the nominal address form *Vuestra Merced* or the pronominal form *usted*) and b.) the verbal form, specifically the type of speech acts (hence, SA) (Austin, 1962; Searle, 1969).

---

8   There are many factors that explain the scarcity of these letters. From factors related to conservation of materials in a semi-tropical climate environment before proper archive maintenance was possible to lack of tradition in conserving documents of private character.
9   For a complete list of sources, see bibliography.

Most of the verbs analyzed fit the classification proposed. There are other SAs that are more pragmatic in nature because they acquire their meaning in the consideration of the H, or in SA that are more related to the consideration of the speaker's self. For their classification, the examples given by Brown and Levinson (1978, 1987) are also considered.

TABLE 10.2 Types of speech acts

Types of speech acts	Examples (content communicated)
Verdictives	To belittle, to boast, to disapprove, to accuse
Exercitives	To suggest, to order, to request, to exert pressure (S > H), to advice, to excuse, to remind, to constrain
Commissives	To promise
Behavitives	Expression of sentiments from S to H, to compliment, to admiration, negative emotions, thanks, to offer an excuse/to apologize, to make an offer, to express an emotion, to accept a compliment/gift
Expositives	To confess, to make a statement
Declaratives (Searle)	To warn

BASED ON AUSTIN (1962) AND SEARLE (1969)

TABLE 10.3 Other types of speech acts

Speech act centered on the speaker	Centered on the consideration of both, hearer and speaker	Centered on the hearer	Other
To express self-humiliation (e.g., admission of wrongdoing)	To express/communicate no common values between S/W and H/R	To express indifference to the positive face needs H/R	To communicate/express a speech act with increased possibility that and FTA will occur (sensitive topic)
		To express/communicate same values of the H	

BASED ON BROWN AND LEVINSON (1978/1987)

The nominal address form *Vuestra Merced*, which appeared in Spanish around 15th century evolved into *usted* through a process of grammaticalization that finished around 17th c. According to Traugott and Dasher (2005), grammaticalization is the process through which lexemes evolve to acquire grammatical functions (Traugott; Dasher, 2005). The brief description below offers a timeline in the grammaticalization process of *usted* (the *focus* of this study though, will be the *pragmatic strengthening* of the pronoun).[10] Grammaticalization is constituted by the following factors:

1. A specific construction
   Vuestra Merced, is constructed with the possessive "Vuestra" and the noun "Merced". Morphologically, this compound is reanalyzed and becomes one word.[11]
2. Bleaching
   The possessive meaning of *Vuestra* disappears; bleaching of the meaning is considered part of the morphological reanalysis.
3. Phonological attrition
   This is the more evident factor in the evolution of *usted* throughout the 500 years of change. Plá Cárceles (1923) refers in detail to the intermediate phases of the phonological attrition of this form.

According to Quesada, the first documentation in Costa Rica of the form *usted* can be established during the first quarter of 18th c. (Quesada Pacheco, 2009).

The present analysis is based on the notion of face (Brown and Levinson 1978/1987). Additionally, the notions of withdrawal (instead of deferential) vs approach (instead of non-deferential) proposed by Terkourafi (2005) are also applied. In previous linguistic literature where both uses of *usted* have been documented (Quesada, 2010), little attention has been given to elucidate how that distinction came to be.[12]

5.1.1   Withdrawal Uses of *Usted* 16th to 18th Centuries (Manuscripts)
The examples offered in this section display uses of *usted* (withdrawal) in manuscripts.

---

10   For all the intermediate steps of the phonetical/phonological changes, see Plá Cárceles, (1923).
11   See Plá Cárceles (1923).
12   Some authors have discussed the pragmatic aspects on the use of the pronouns (Quesada, 2011, Obediente, 2010).

(1) *"Como usted me enlaze el buey de que me dio noticia le daré una petaca de tabaco"* Cubujuquí, 1749. Archivo Nacional. Complementario Colonial, fo.2.
'usted me enlaze, performative'

(2) *Tengo nota qe* Vd. determina *hacer dejacn (sic, dejación) de tres ramos de capellanía qe son a su cargo ... (como* Vd.sabe) *Espero su respuesta (en caso qe concienta)* (AN:PG 158; fo .11) Cartago, 1782; PG 158; fo. 11]
'Usted determina (you determine), sabe (you know), consienta (you agree). W/S puts pressure on R/H to perform "X" act'.

In sample (1) the speech act is performative and the meaning of the verb *to lasso* is literal. As a performative speech act, in this context, there is no semantic exploitation of the verb.

In sample (2) a man writes to his brother about an administrative procedure. The SAs portrayed in this sample are actions were the W/S puts pressure on R/H to perform a series of acts such as *onsenter, saber, onsenter*, things the brother asks the priest to get done. As in the previous example, the meaning conveyed by the speech act equals the meaning of the verb.

5.1.2   Approach Uses of *Usted*. 16th to 18th Centuries
The next examples correspond to uses of *usted* as an approach pronoun:

(3) *"... aquí ando en solicitud de* usted, *que es más para su bien que para el mío, me han dicho que* usted *está curando a Mathías Quezada por un mal eficio y vengo a que christianamente* me diga, *en Dios y por Dios, si es mi muchacha quien lo tiene así" Cartago, 1775.* Archivo Nacional, Complementario Colonial 22347, fo. 21.
'*me diga*, making a request, expositive'

Exchange between a woman who is trying to discourage a man of his advances as suitor:

(4) *"... que* mire *que se lo lleva el Diablo ..." Cartago, 1724* Archivo de la Curia Metropolitana: *c.*11. 1.4. fo. 434.
'*mire*, order, command'

In excerpt (3) "me diga" has the illocutive force of 'confirm' instead of 'saying' or 'telling'. The meaning of "diga" (*decir*, a expositive type of verb) undergoes a semantic interpretation as "to confirm". The parent of the girl is making the request to have the rumor verified. It is more than just "telling" the information (which W/S already knows). There is, consequently, a pragmatic exploitation of the meaning of the verb.

In example (4) the SA employed is given as a command, but also is a warning "mirar" 'to look at'. In this context, it implies "to realize". The man should "realize" that, by his advances, he risks some consequences (to be taken away by the devil). The verb *mirar* with the meaning of "realize" is used by the woman to discourage her suitor, but it is also a matter of a warning, therefore, there is a semantic exploitation of the verb.

How are the uses of *usted* as withdrawal or as an approach form differentiated in this first period? Withdrawal *usted* will be performed trough a speech act that has a literal meaning; approach *usted* will be performed with a verb that undergoes semantic and pragmatic exploitation.

5.1.3 Withdrawal Use of *Vuestra Merced*. 16th to 18th Centuries (Administrative Letters)

Two examples of the use of *Vuestra Merced* (V.Md) from this period are offered:

(5) "... *me vino el testimonio de aver rrescevido (sic) el pliego que* V. Md. *me ynvió (sic) para el rreal acuerdo de Panamá* ..." [Carta del Adelantado y Gobernador Gonzalo Vásquez de Coronado a su Teniente de Gobernador. Cartago, 1601.]
"Vuestra Merced me ynvió', sent to me, assertive"

(6) "... *en las mulas que traygo me a ydo mal, que se me han quedado doze o trece; y el macho bueno de la casta de Medina que* V.Md. *me quería comprar, rodó con la carga por una cuesta cresta abajo* ..." Carta del Adelantado y Gobernador Gonzalo Vásquez de Coronado a su Teniente de Gobernador, Cartago. 1601.
'me quería comprar, you wanted to buy from me, H states the intention of S'

In a similar fashion, in examples (5) and (6) the nominal address forms in administrative letters employ verbs that express SAs that are assertive or that express an intention, in contexts where the main meaning of the verb corresponds with the action expressed by it. Table 10.4 summarizes the subject and the verb forms (speech acts).

In the examples provided in Table 10.4, the SAS (making requests, giving orders/warning, putting pressure on the H/R), constitute FTAS to the negative face of the H: rights to non-distraction, freedom of action, freedom from

TABLE 10.4 Withdrawal and approach uses in the examples provided and types of speech acts. 16th to 18th centuries

Example		Excerpts of manuscripts		Letters
		Withdrawal [Literal use].	Approach [Semantic exploitation]	Withdrawal {Literal use}.
(1)	Usted me enlaze	Performative		
(2)	Determine, saber, concienta	Put pressure on the H/R to perform X act		
(3)	Me diga		Making a request, expositive	
(4)	Mire		Order/Warning	
(5)	Me ynvió			Making a statement, expositive
(6)	Me quería comprar			Stating an intention

imposition are all threatened by these SAs. Table 10.5 shows in a succinct manner the percentages of the different types of speech acts present in letters and excerpts analyzed from 16th to 18th c.

Two elements are of importance: both the nominal address form and the pronoun *usted* cover, within this period, the same withdrawal functions; *usted*, on the other hand, also functions as an approach pronoun, while simultaneously using SAs that are literal in some cases and/or semantically exploited in others. Therefore, there is some overlapping, with the speech acts that express suggestion, orders, and request. The letters that only employed *Vuestra Merced*, cover not only the SAs through which the W performs suggestions, orders, and request, but also other SAs such as putting pressure on the H, to give advice, express intention or to give a reminder.

All these functions, that coincide in the pronoun *usted*, both as withdrawal and as approach constitute FTAs to the negative face. With the nominal form there is not an approach meaning, but there is an overlapping with the pronoun *usted* regarding withdrawal uses. This can be interpreted as a fact that the pronoun *usted* was undergoing a process where the SAs related to *usted* and *Vuestra Merced* were already established for the withdrawal uses. The approach uses were not yet stabilized but were undergoing pragmatic exploitation.

TABLE 10.5 FTAs to the negative face in withdrawal and approach *Vuestra Merced/Usted*. 16th to 18th centuries

FTA to the negative face	Withdrawal excerpts of manuscripts (*usted*)	Withdrawal letters (*Vuestra Merced*)	Approach excerpts of manuscripts (*usted*)
	Frequency	Frequency	Frequency
Suggestion	12.50%	18.18%	33.33%
Order	12.50%	27.27%	33.33%
Request	25%	31.81%	33.33%
S putting pressure on H to perform X act	50%		
Advice		9.09%	
Excuse/Intention		9.09%	
Reminder		4.54%	

5.2 *Pragmaticalization of the Pronoun* Usted

In this second period, we see that FTAs to the negative face of the addressee are still performed, but a new element appears: SAs that reflect FTAs to the positive face of the H

5.2.1 Withdrawal Use of *Usted* (FTA to the Positive Face of the R/H)

The following examples (7) and (8) belong to a debate among Costa Rican writers around the end of 19th century and the beginning of 20th century:

(7) "*Señor Zapatero,* usted hace *admirablemente las zapatillas de señora, pero le aconsejo que* se dedique *a las botas Federicas o a las alpargatas.*"
    'usted hace 'you do', que se dedique 'you devote (yourself)'; expositive and verdictive, respectively'
    Carta de RICARDO FERNÁNDEZ GUARDIA a Pío Víquez. June 24, 1894.

Example (7) starts with a statement with an expositive type of SA: The W belittles the addressee advising him to produce a lower class of footwear, which is a metaphor to imply that the addressee, as a writer, should occupy himself with national topics, instead of trying to write about more worldwide themes. The positive face of the addressee is threatened as it disregards the desire of the H of being approved on his literary practices:

(8) *"Manifesté solamente un deseo y* usted lo ha tomado como una exigencia ..."
'usted lo ha tomado como una exigencia, [expression of not sharing the same value or perspective, behavitive'] Letter from Carlos Gagini to Ricardo Fernández Guardia. June, 29th. 1894.

Example (8) clearly states that both W and H disagree on how the interaction took place, that being a behavitive type of act. Even more, the W is disapproving the addressee's perspective (FTA to positive face) and in a way, implying that H's perspective is misguided.

5.2.2   Approach Use of *Usted*. 19th and 20th Centuries

Examples (9) and (10) come from a letter written from the father of a young woman to the father of a young man.

(9) *"Creo que* usted debe estar sabido *que su hijo Merino llevaba relaciones amorosas con la hija mía, y al mismo tiempo con el objeto de casarse, pues llo* [*sic*] *le puse un plazo de seis meses ..."*
'one parent gives a warning to the other parent, declarative'
Letter from ANTONIO ARMILIO ARCE to Amadeo Léon. March 6th. 1935.

The letter starts with a very complex declarative speech act. The construction of the verbal tense *usted debe estar sabido* states that the parent of the boy should know about the relationship between the young couple (the modal verb *debe* reinforces that). At the same time, the father of the girl, through that statement, does not give a lot of room (or freedom of choice) to the father of the boy to not know about the situation. This limitation on the freedom of action of the H is an FTA to the negative face of the addressee

(10) *"Así es que* haga lo que le paresca [*sic*], si ud. se disgusta, *pues ando por donde* quiera, *pues son pantalones lo que cargo ..."*
'haga lo que le paresca, 'do whatever you want', behavitive; si usted se disgusta 'if you get upset', behavitive; ando por donde quiera 'I am here (where you can find me)' warning/threat'
Letter from ANTONIO ARMILIO ARCE to Amadeo Léon. March 6th. 1935.

The statements *haga lo que parezca* 'do whatever you want' and *si usted se disgusta* 'if you get upset' are expressions of emotion that constitute behavitive SAs. The last statement, on the other hand, constitutes an expression of warning "ando por donde quiera pues son pantalones lo que cargo", despite that the S is telling to do what he wants (haga lo que le paresca) and giving him the freedom to do what he wants. This statement, paired up with the other phrases (si ud se disgusta) followed by "ando por donde quiera, warning is actually conveying the idea that the H cannot act freely, which in turn, constitutes and FTA to the negative face of the addressee.

Table 10.6 reflects all the cases of *usted* found in the letters from 19th and 20th century. The cases of *usted* as an approach pronoun are represented by verbs that portray FTAs to the negative face of H; the withdrawal *usted* is marked by verbs that constitute FTAs to the positive face of the H. This is the most fundamental difference between the two periods under analysis: the presence on the later period of SAs that constitute FTAs to the positive face of the addressee, a factor that was absent in the previous period.

Table 10.7 contains a comparison between the withdrawal uses in both periods under examination.

Table 10.7 shows how the *contexts are contrasting in what they communicate and are mutually exclusive*. The withdrawal *usted* seems to have "moved out" to new contexts: from contexts in which the withdrawal *usted* was an FTA to the negative face to contexts in which the use constitutes an FTA to the positive

TABLE 10.6 Comparison of withdrawal and approach uses in letters from the 19th to the 20th c.

Example	Letters from the 19th to the 20th centuries	
	Withdrawal FTA to the positive (+) face	Approach FTA to the negative (−) face
Usted hace admirablemente zapatillas de señora … le aconsejo que se dedique	Expositive (verdicitive) belittling	
Y ud. lo ha tomado como una exigencia	Not sharing the perspective of the H (behavitive)	
Echa usted en cara un desatino que creo no haber dicho	Disagreement, accusation (verdictive)	
Usted debe estar sabido		Implicit warning (you better know about this) expositive/behavitive
Haga lo que le parezca, si ud. se disgusta, ando por donde quiera		Expresión of emotion (anger) warning (behavitive)

TABLE 10.7   Comparison between the withdrawal uses of *usted*. 16th–18th century vs. 19th–20th century

Withdrawal uses

Withdrawal FTA to the negative face 16th–18th c.	Withdrawal FTA to positive face 19th–20th c.
Performative	
Put pressure on the hearer to perform X act	
Making a statement, expositive	
Giving an excuse	
	Expositive (verdictive), belittling
	Not sharing the perspective of the H (behavitive)
	Disagreement, accusation (verdictive)

face of the addressee. More importantly, *usted* moves *from one context to another, from one period to the next, without leaving the previous context "empty"*.

It is important at this point to recall the table from the beginning in which the "movement" of *usted* was already schematized based on a reinterpretation of the data offered by Quesada (2005). The chart is reproduced here again with the intention to show the migration of the pronoun from the withdrawal (deferential) column to the approach (non-deferential) column:

TABLE 10.8   Reanalysis of the address form system in Costa Rican Spanish

Century	Withdrawal (instead of power)	Approach (instead of solidarity)
16th–17th	Vos	Tú
	Vuestra Merced	
18th	Usted	Vos (voseo americano)
	Su Merced	Tú
		Usted (ustedeo)
19th	Usted	Vos (voseo americano)
		Tú
		Usted (ustedeo)
20th	Usted	Vos
		Tú (incipient)
		Usted (ustedeo)

An important issue to resolve is how the codification of the new specialized use (the FTA to the positive face) is produced.

5.2.3 Steps in the Pragmaticalization of the Pronoun *Usted*

By the pragmaticalization of the pronoun *usted*, it is meant the process through which the pronoun changes in its use (to withdraw from or approach to someone) according to the context and types of SAs used during the exchange. Terkourafi (2005) when explaining the use of the V term in Cypriot Greek, based on Dasher and Traugott, points out that, if the speech act is centered in the speaker, there is a process of subjectification, which can be defined as the type of meaning expressed from the speaker's perspective.

> While grammaticalization is a complex multilevel diachronic process leading towards grammar, subjectification is a particular type of semantic change, leading to meanings "based in the speaker's subjective belief state/attitude toward the proposition" (Traugott, 1989, p. 35).

The *subjectification* process is seen by Diewald (2011) as a component of the *grammaticalization* process and it is also considered by this author as a particular type of semantic change. Moreover, Diewald also sees a connection between subjectification and pragmatics, given the fact that subjectification is based on meaning from the perspective of the speaker, who is the central element in "any pragmatic aspect of language" (Diewald, 2011: 9). Diewald also introduces the term *pragmaticalization* to refer to certain type of changes that do not fall within the *subjectification* area or within *grammaticalization* territory. The author denominates thus *pragmaticalization* as the border line between the two, because at the end point of the change there is not a new grammar element in the traditional sense (as it would happen with "normal" grammaticalization with the creation of a new pronoun to express the new meaning of *usted*) but there is a change. Following Diewald, in the grammaticalization processes the structural scope is reduced (one *usted*) but also the semantic scope is expanded (withdrawal and approach).

The evolution of *usted* also fulfills other criteria for grammaticalization (Diewald, 2011):[13]

1. Obligatoriedness: the form *usted* or its verbal form is present or required in the language to express the(se) meaning(s). ✓
2. Paradigmatic opposition: the two linguistic features must be in paradigmatic opposition. The withdrawal *usted* is expressed through SAs in

---

13 See Diewald, 2011: pp. 366–367).

specific contexts that are different from the approach *usted*. The two meanings are distributed showing paradigmatic opposition. ✓

3. Relational meaning: Grammatical categories have a common core of meaning or *function*. The common function in this case is to address each other and keep/deal with face. The pragmatic elasticity provided by the pronoun allows the speaker to use the *usted* functionally, to satisfy his/her pragmatic needs. That option, such pragmatic elasticity, becomes part of the rules of the grammar of the language. ✓

5.3 Usted: *Form vs. Function*

So far it has been seen how the use of *usted* is used within the same community to mark different stances of the S towards the addressee. Table 10.9 shows the contexts in which the approach *usted* took place from the 16th to the 18th century (few contexts) to the increased series of contexts in which the approach *usted* took place from the 19th to the 20th centuries.

The considerable expansion of contexts in the second period goes hand in hand with the increase in the use; moreover, all the contexts are consistent

TABLE 10.9   Comparison of the context of use of the approach *usted* from the 16th to the 20th century

Context of use of approach *usted* 16th–18th c.	Context of use of approach *usted* 19th–beginning of 20th c.
	Compliment
Suggestion	Expression of admiration
Order	Reminding
Request	Warning
	Constraining
	Expression of negative emotions
	Promise
	Expression of same values of the H
	Suggestion/Advice
	Expressing thanks (damage to S)
	Offer
	Request
	Offering an excuse (damage to S)
	Expression of S's sentiments of the H
	Formulaic expression
	Putting pressure on the H to perform X act

with the fact that they constitute an FTA to the negative face of the addressee. Thus, the withdrawal *usted* "migrated" from contexts of FTAs to the negative face to the contexts of FTAs to the positive face. The approach use, on the other hand, stayed in the same "setting": FTA to the negative face and expanded the contexts in which it could take place. It is also possible to see how the two uses have become specialized over the years. *Pragmaticalization* is proposed, then, as the mechanism through which the specialization of the *usted* took place: The speakers' statements go through a process of subjectification in which S conceives the use of *usted* regarding the interaction with the addressee. The addressee receives the pronoun *usted*, he/she decodes it, that is, the addressee performs/completes the invited inference that could be either the withdrawal function or the approach use. At the last stage of the process, the specialization of *usted* as an approach pronoun is incorporated into the system, the functions become pragmaticalized/grammaticalized and encoded on the social deictic/pronoun *usted*.

6 Conclusions

This first period revealed interesting tendencies regarding the evolution of the address form system. The first period saw a clear path in the process of grammaticalization from *Vuestra Merced* to *usted*. From an internal perspective of the language, it was determined that the use of the pronoun as withdrawal was linked with the literal meaning of the verbs. It was also determined that the pronoun, with verbs that are not used literally but rather have a pragmatic exploitation, was used with the *usted* as an approach pronoun. The second process, pragmaticalization, was found to bring a further specialized use of the pronoun. Instead of deferential vs. non-deferential, the terms withdrawal and approach are proposed. Those pragmatic choices became incorporated as functions in the language.

This development of the pronoun *usted* did not happen in a vacuum. The evolution and expansion of the use of this pronoun was motivated by a series of social changes occurring over 400 years, and accounts for them.[14] Even though a focused linguistic view on the possible evolution of *usted* has been presented, language change is never dissociated from the lives and experiences of past and present communities of practice.

---

14   For a review of how sociohistorical factors exerted an impact on the evolution of *usted*, see Cabal-Jiménez (2013).

Appendix

Documents from Costa Rican Archives
Archivo Nacional. Complementario Colonial 2008. Year 1749. Cubujuquí, Heredia.
Archivo Nacional. Protocolos de Guatemala 158. Year 1782. Cartago.
Archivo Nacional, Complementario Colonial 2247. Year 1775. Cartago.
Archivo de la Curia Metropolitana: *c*.11. 1.4. Year 1724. Cartago.

List of Abbreviations
AN: Archivo Nacional de Costa Rica.
CC: Complementario Colonial.
PG: Protocolos de Guatemala.
ACM: Archivo de la Curia Metropolitana.

References

Austin, J. L. (1962). *How to do things with words*. Harvard University Press.
Bentivoglio, P. (2002). Spanish forms of address in the sixteenth century. In: I. Taatvitsainen & J. Andreas (Eds), *Diachronic perspectives on Address Terms Systems* (pp. 177–191). John Benjamins. DOI: https://doi.org/10.1075/pbns.107.09ben.
Braun, F. (1988). *Terms of address. Problems of patterns and usage in various languages and cultures*. Berlin, New York, Amsterdam: Mouton de Gruyter.
Brown, R., & Gilman, A. (1972). The pronouns of power and solidarity. In: J. Fishman (Ed). *Readings in the sociology of language* (pp 252–275). Mouton.
Brown, P. & Levinson, S. (1978, 1987). *Politeness. Some universals in language use*. Studies in Interactional Sociolinguistics 4. Cambridge University Press.
Diewald, G. (2011). Pragmaticalization defined as grammaticalization of discourse functions. *Linguistics* 49(2). 365–390.
Cabal-Jiménez, M. (2013). From deference to face: the evolution of *usted* in Costa Rican Spanish. [Doctoral dissertation, University of Illinois at Urbana-Champaign].
Carrera de la Red, M. & Álvarez, A. (2004). Tratamientos y cortesía en la elaboración de fuentes documentales de la etapa fundacional de la provincia de Mérida (Venezuela). In D. Bravo & A. Briz (Eds.) *Pragmática sociocultural: estudios sobre el discurso de cortesía en español* (pp. 227–244). Boletín de Lingüística.
Gutiérrez Maté, M. (2012). El pronombre usted en el español de Cartagena de Indias el Siglo XVII y su "divergencia" de Vuestra Merced. In E. Montero & C. Manzano (Eds.) *Actas del VIII Congreso Internacional de Historia de la Lengua Española*, Vol. 2. (pp. 1889–1904). Santiago de Compostela.

Obediente, E. (2010). Visión diacrónica y dialectal de las formas de tratamiento en los Andes venezolanos. In C. Borgonovo, M. Español-Echeverría, & P. Prévost. *Selected Proceedings of the 12th Hispanics Linguistics Symposium* (pp. 87–96). Cascadilla Proceedings Project.

Pla Cárceles, Josefina. (1923). La evolución del tratamiento 'vuestra merced'. *Revista de Filología Española, 10*. 245–80.

Quesada Pacheco, M. A. (1991/1993). *Nuevo Diccionario de Costarriqueñismos*. Editorial Tecnológica de Costa Rica. Cartago, Costa Rica.

Quesada Pacheco, M. A. (2003). Formas de tratamiento en Costa Rica: visión histórica. In J. Girón Alconchel & J. Bustos Tovar (Coords.) *Actas del VI Congreso Internacional de la Lengua Española* (pp. 2323–2335). Madrid.

Quesada Pacheco, M. A. (2005, Sept). *Formas de tratamiento en Costa Rica: Visión histórica* [Conference presentation] Forms of address forms in the Spanish Speaking World. Graz, Austria.

Quesada Pacheco, M. A. (2009). *Historia de la lengua española en Costa Rica*. Editorial de la Universidad de Costa Rica. San José.

Quesada Pacheco, M. A. (2010). *El español de América*. Editorial Instituto Tecnológico de Costa Rica. Tercera edición. Cartago, Costa Rica.

Quesada Pacheco, M. A. (2011). Ideas y actitudes lingüísticas en Costa Rica durante el siglo XIX. *Cuadernos de Ilustración y Romanticismo. Revista Digital del Grupo de Estudios del Siglo XVIII 17*. 1–18. Universidad de Cádiz.

Rosenblat, A. (1964). Base del español de América: nivel social y cultural de los conquistadores y pobladores. *Boletín de Filología Española* (pp. 171–230). Universidad de Chile.

Searle, J. (1976). A classification of illocutionary acts. *Language in Society 5*. 1–23.

Terkourafi, M. (2005). Identity and semantic change: Aspects of T/V usage in Cyprus. *Journal of Historical Pragmatics 5*(2). 283–306.

Terkourafi, M. (2007). Toward a universal notion of face for a universal notion of co-operation. In I. Keckskes & L. Horn. (Eds.). *Explorations in Pragmatics: Linguistic, Cognitive and Intercultural Aspects*. (pp. 313–344). Mouton de Gruyter.

Terkourafi, M. (2009). Finding face between Gemeinschaft and Gesellschaft: Greek perceptions of the in-group. In M. Haugh & F. Bargiela-Chiappini (Eds.) *Face, Communication and Social Interaction* (pp. 269–288). Equinox.

Traugott, E. & Dasher, R. (2005). *Regularity in semantic change*. Cambridge University Press.

Bibliography of Sources and Materials

Carta de Don Diego Vásquez de Montiel Coronado dirigida a su tía Doña Ma. Termiño Vásquez de Coronado, adelantada de Costa Rica. 10/10/1717. Transcribed by Munia

Cabal-Jiménez. In: PARES (Portal de Archivos Españoles). Archivo Histórico Nacional de España. Reference code: ES 28079.AHN/5.1.141/DIVERSOS-COLECCIONES, 37, N.2.

Carta de Don Diego Vásquez de Montiel Coronado, adelantado de Costa Rica a fray Pedro Brinigas, procurador general de la Orden de Ntra. Sra. De la Merced Calzada, agradeciéndole la remisión de las cláusulas del testamento de su tía doña María Termiño Vásquez de Coronado, y comunicándole el envío de poder a d. Manuel de Mojica para que ponga al corriente el Mayorazgo que su tía tenía en Sevilla. Copia de 22 de diciembre, remitida por la vía de Panamá. 16/12/1722. Transcribed by Munia Cabal-Jiménez. In: PARES (Portal de Archivos Españoles). Archivo Histórico Nacional de España. Reference code: ES 28078. AHN/5.1.141/DIVERSOS-COLECCIONES, 37, N.5.

Carta de Antonio Emilio Arce to Amadeo León. 1934. Transcribed by Dr. Elizet Payne. Faculty at the School of History, University of Costa Rica. Reference code: Archivo Nacional de Costa Rica. Alcaldía de Santo Domingo de Heredia. No. 8. Fo. 49 to 49v. Matter: Kidnapping.

Fernández, León; Fernández Guardia, Ricardo. (1882). *Colección de documentos para la historia de Costa Rica*. Volumes. 1–3, San José de Costa Rica, Imprenta nacional, 1881–83. Volumes. 4–5, Paris, Impr. P. Dupont, 1886. Volumes 6–10, Barcelona, Impr. Viuda de L. Tasso, 1907.

Letters from and between Carmen Lyra, Joaquín García Monge and Manuel González Zeledón were facilitated by Mr. Eugenio García, grandson of the Costa Rican author Joaquín García Monge. These letters belong to the private correspondence of Joaquín García Monge, inherited by Mr. Eugenio García. Retrieved from the blogspot "Cosas de Jota" (www.cosasdejota.blogspot.com).

Quesada Pacheco, Miguel. (1987). *Fuentes documentales para el estudio del español colonial de Costa Rica*. Editorial Alma Mater.

Segura Montero, Alberto. (Ed). (1995). *La polémica (1894–1902): El Nacionalismo en Literatura*. Editorial de la Universidad Estatal a distancia. San José, Costa Rica.

CHAPTER 11

Rates and Constraints of Present Perfect and Preterit in Costa Rican Spanish

A Variationist Approach

Javier Rivas and Érick Pineda

1   Present Perfect and Preterit in Spanish

This paper is concerned with the expression of the aspectual meanings of *anterior* and *perfective* in past time situations. Anterior aspect refers to a situation that takes place before the moment of speech but it has relevance in the present (Fleischman, 1983, p. 187, Bybee et al., 1994, p. 54). In contrast, the term *perfective* is used to describe situations that are perceived as bounded at some point prior to the moment of speech. Unlike perfectives, then, anteriors are not used to express past situations that happen sequentially in narratives. Comrie (1976) and Dahl (1985) identify four prototypical meanings associated with anterior: (1) resultative, (2) experiential/existential, (3) continuative or persistent situation, and (4) recent past/hot news. These meanings are conveyed by means of the Present Perfect[1] (PP) [*haber* (Present) + Past Participle] in Spanish, as is shown in the following examples from Costa Rica:[2]

(1)   *Lo más bonito es que, una vez que* ha pasado *el control de calidad …* (CR-10, *Inf.*)
      'The most beautiful thing is that, once it has passed quality control …'

(2)   *Yo nunca* he estudiado *eso* (CR-8, *Inf.*)
      'I (have) never studied that'

---

1   Following the trend started by Comrie (1976), we will use a lower case initial letter to refer to cross-linguistically recurrent semantic categories such as *anterior* or *perfective* and an upper case initial letter to refer to language-specific categories such as *Present Perfect* or *Preterit*.

2   All the examples included in this chapter are taken from the San José, Costa Rica data included in *Macrocorpus de la norma lingüística culta de las principales ciudades de España y América* (Samper Padilla et al., 1997). See § 2 for a description of this corpus. CR means 'Costa Rica', *9* is the interview number, *Inf.* means 'informant' and *Enc.* means 'interviewer'.

(3) *Así* he estado *durante todos esos veinte años* (CR-9, *Inf.*)
'I have been like this for the last twenty years'

(4) Enc.—*Yo tengo mucho de no ver a Flora.*
Inf.—Ha tenido *el segundo hijo* (CR-1)
Enc. 'I have not seen Flora in a long time'
Inf. 'She has had her second child'

Constructions with a stative verb such as Spanish *haber* 'have' and a Past Participle are used to express anterior aspect in Basque, Danish, Greek, and Tigre, among other languages (Bybee et al., 1994, p. 64). These constructions may in turn undergo a process of grammaticalization in which they lose current relevance and designate perfective or past actions. This grammaticalization process is attested in Spanish in different degrees, depending on the dialect. The following examples illustrate perfective uses of the PP in Costa Rican Spanish:

(5) *El Colegio Superior de Señoritas en este año* ha cumplido *los cien de su fundación* (CR-13, *Inf.*)
'This year, the *Colegio Superior de Señoritas* celebrated [has celebrated] its 100th year since its foundation.'

(6) *usted y yo* hemos leído *el ... el ... el artículo* (CR-12, *Inf.*)
'You and I read [have read] the ..., the ..., the article'

(7) p*ero ahora en mil novecientos ochenta y siete, que ya todos estamos grandes, mis padres* han tenido *que dejar su casa* (CR-7, *Inf.*)
'But now in 1987, since we are all adults, my parents have had to leave their house'

The grammaticalization path anterior-perfective/past is also found in French and German, as well as in other languages belonging to different families such as Atchin, Ewe, and Mandarin Chinese (Bybee 2015, p. 143). For Romance languages, Harris (1982) and Squartini & Bertinetto (2000) identify four stages in the process of grammaticalization of the PP towards perfective values (see also Alarcos Llorach, 1947). Stage I corresponds to the source construction, formed with [*habere* ('to have') + Past Participle], which has a resultative meaning. As such, this construction is limited to describing states that are the result of a previous action, its reference is the time of speech, and it cannot be used to express an anterior situation, regardless of how close it is to the present time.[3] In stage II, the construction is used to express situations that occur prior to the moment of speech. More specifically, the PP describes durative or iterative actions that start in the past and extend up to speech time (inclusive function). The PP displays semantic restrictions, since it does not usually occur with non-durative actions or with telic verbs, unless they express an iterative action (e.g., *ha llegado tarde muchas veces recientemente* 'he has arrived late a lot of times recently' but not **ha llegado tarde esta mañana* ('*he has arrived late this morning'). In stage III, the PP loses the semantic restrictions found in the previous stage, and it extends to all past situations that are relevant in the present. As is noted by Squartini & Bertinetto (2000), the PP in this stage expresses "some kind of psychological feeling of the speaker for what is currently relevant" (p. 414). Finally, in stage IV, the PP has been completely grammaticalized as a perfective, replacing the simple Preterit in this function (consider, e.g., the French *Passé Composé*). As a result, the PP is compatible with past time adverbials such as *yesterday* or *the other day*, and used in sequenced narratives.

Unlike Harris (1982), Squartini & Bertinetto (2000, pp. 419–420) point out that stage II should be interpreted as an independent development (a kind of hybrid aspect between imperfective and perfective), and not as the intermediate stage between the resultative and the perfective. In this same line, other linguists also support the theory of different grammaticalization paths for the PP within the pan-Hispanic world (Rodríguez Louro & Howe, 2010, Jara Yupanqui, 2011, Escobar & Crespo, 2020) due to the wide variation found cross-dialectally, which suggests that the grammaticalization path is not uniform and that it does not occur in a linear fashion.

In the comparative analysis conducted by Schwenter & Torres Cacoullos (2008) between corpus samples representing the Spanish of Madrid and the Spanish of Mexico, the authors report substantially lower frequency rates of the PP in the Mexican variety (15%) than in Spain (54%). Their variationist analysis indicates that in Mexico the PP is used to express anterior aspect, whereas perfective meanings are expressed by the Preterit. In contrast, the authors find that the Madrid data shows that the PP is at a more advanced stage of grammaticalization, because it replaces the Preterit especially in hodiernal temporal contexts, i.e., perfective actions that happened on the same day.

The PP also grammaticalizes as a perfective in Argentinian River Plate Spanish. Rodríguez Louro (2016) argues that in this variety the PP is specializing to express indefinite past situations that do not extend up to the present time. This is in opposition to the Preterit, which encodes concrete past actions.

---

3 In present day Spanish resultative constructions may be expressed by [*tener* 'have' + Past Participle]: *tengo la cama hecha* 'I made my bed, lit.: I have my bed made'.

This opposition between the PP and the Preterit is reflected in the low rate of use of the PP compared to the Preterit (10% vs. 90%). Unlike Peninsular Spanish, the PP does not occur with hodiernal references in the Argentinian variety.

In Andean varieties of Spanish, the PP seems to follow a different grammaticalization path towards the expression of subjective values such as evidentiality, i.e., the speaker's evaluation of the nature of the source on which their message is based. In this respect, the PP is used in Peruvian Spanish to express situations that the speaker has personally experienced in the past (Jara Yupanqui, 2011, 2017, Escobar, 2012, Escobar & Crespo, 2020), whereas in Ecuadorian Spanish the use of the PP has been associated with the expression of hearsay or reported information (Dumont, 2013, Pfänder & Palacios, 2013). These evidential uses of the PP are sometimes attributed to the influence of native American languages such as Quechua (but see Howe, 2013, pp. 115–117). The emergence of these evidential meanings is related to the relevance of the PP in the present since, as noted by Rodríguez Louro & Jara Yupanqui (2011), "el hablante desea enfatizar su propia perspectiva y ofrecer la situación pasada como relevante en el momento del habla [the speaker wants to emphasize their own perspective and offer the past situation as relevant at the time of speech]" (p. 71).

In comparison to other varieties of Spanish, the use of the PP and Preterit in Central American Spanish has received much less attention in the literature. Previous work has mainly focused on the Spanish of El Salvador (Hernández, 2008, 2013). Hernández (2008, p. 135) reports that 29% of PP use in his spoken corpus corresponds to contexts expressing perfective situations. In this respect, Salvadoran Spanish seems to differ from other American varieties of Spanish, such as Mexico, in which the PP mainly occurs in anterior contexts. In a later study, Hernández (2013) finds that the PP is used in narratives in El Salvador to convey perfective aspect when the speaker wants to express their affective closeness to the situation. This hypothesis is supported by the high rates of PP in combination with grammatical forms that contribute to the expression of subjectivity: first-person subjects, expressed subjects, reported and quoted speech, and psychological verbs conveying pains and feelings. On this account, Salvadoran Spanish resembles Andean varieties in that the PP is associated with subjective values.

Although there are very few studies on PP and Preterit use in Costa Rican Spanish, the available evidence suggests that this variety is moving towards the grammaticalization of the PP as a perfective, albeit at a slower pace. VanBuren (1992) makes a comparison of PP and Preterit use in Costa Rican and Peninsular Spanish using three different datasets: written press, dramatic texts, and an elicited questionnaire (aimed at measuring the speakers' acceptability of the

PP and Preterit in discrete sentences). In her analysis, the author distinguishes between iterative and durative actions, and semelfactive ones, i.e., those actions that happened only once regardless of their duration (1992, p. 144). The PP occurs in 22% of the examples in her data, and of these, 20% are semelfactive with a perfective meaning. However, only 1 example of the PP expressing a semelfactive action is evaluated as acceptable in the questionnaire (VanBuren 1992, p. 147). These results could be attributed to the association of the PP in American varieties of Spanish with a formal or prestigious construction (Squartini & Bertinetto, 2000, p. 413, Butt & Benjamin, 2004, p. 230).

Taking into account findings from previous work (summarized above), the purpose of this paper is to contribute to the ongoing discussion regarding the grammaticalization paths of the PP across varieties of Spanish by studying the PP and Preterit distribution in spoken Costa Rican Spanish. Following Schwenter & Torres Cacoullos (2008, p. 12), we define the envelope of variation functionally, as "the evolutionary perfect-to-perfective path". In the same way as these authors, we restrict our analysis to PP and Preterit forms (Schwenter & Torres Cacoullos 2008, p. 13). Using variationist methodology (Labov, 1994, Tagliamonte, 2012), we will identify the probabilistic grammar of the PP in oral Costa Rican Spanish in order to determine the degree of grammaticalization of this construction in the anterior-perfective cline. Additionally, we will also analyze the impact of subjectivity on the expression of the PP, in line with previous studies on Central American Spanish (Hernández, 2013). In the following section, we describe our data and methodology.

2   Data and Methodology

We analyze the PP and Preterit usage patterns on the data obtained from fourteen conversations between one interviewer and one informant recorded in San José, Costa Rica, as part of the *Macrocorpus de la norma lingüística culta de las principales ciudades de España y América* (Samper Padilla et al., 1997). These conversations illustrate what Labov (1994, p. 157) describes as *careful speech*. We examine approximately 66,000 words found in 7 hours of conversation. The interviews are evenly distributed according to gender (7 women, 7 men) and age—4 informants from generation I (28 to 34 years old), 6 informants from generation II (37 to 50) and 4 informants from generation III (60 and over). All informants have a university degree. Each interview is 30 minutes long.[4] From this corpus, we extract all PP and Preterit examples for a total number of 1222 tokens, after the following cases were excluded from the

---

4 For more information about this corpus, see Samper Padilla (1995).

analysis: truncated examples, such as *he mantenido* in (8), examples in the progressive form (e.g., *estuve trabajando* 'I was working' or *se ha estado celebrando* 'It's being celebrated'), examples in direct speech, like *actué* in (9), and examples in which the verbal form is ambiguous between first-person plural Preterit or Present form (e.g., *nos casamos* 'we got married/we get married'):

(8) He mantenido ... *Mire, en el colegio nocturno hace veinte años trabajo.* (CR-9, *Enc.*)
 'I have kept .... Look, I have been teaching night school for twenty years'

(9) *Y entonces le digo: "Es que yo creo que yo, inconscientemente,* actué *como debía de actuar el ser humano"* (CR-10, *Inf.*)
 'And then I told him: "I think that, unconsciously, I acted as a human being should act"'

In order to determine the probabilistic grammar of the PP in this dataset, we code each token for a number of linguistic factors. To allow for comparison with previous variationist studies on PP grammaticalization across different dialects of Spanish (e.g., Schwenter & Torres Cacoullos, 2008, Holmes & Balukas, 2011, Rodríguez Louro, 2016), we use the factors that were selected as significant in previous quantitative analyses of other Spanish varieties: Aktionsart, object number, temporal reference, temporal adverbial, clause type, and previous clause tense. We also include in our analysis two additional linguistic factors: subject grammatical person and subject expression, in order to determine whether the PP expresses subjectivity. Let us consider each of these factors in turn.

Aktionsart: We distinguish between states, activities, achievements and accomplishments (Vendler 1957, Dowty 1979). Unlike states, activities, achievements and accomplishments are dynamic. Telicity (i.e., the existence of an endpoint) distinguishes states and activities (atelic) from achievements and accomplishments (telic). Finally, whereas states, activities and accomplishments are durative, achievements are punctual. In what follows, we present some examples of each Aktionsart verb class taken from the corpus:

a) states (non-dynamic, atelic, durative): *creer* 'think', *estar en peligro de muerte* 'be in danger of death' and *existir* 'exist'.
b) activities (dynamic, atelic, durative): *hacer investigación* 'do research', *leer* 'read', *trabajar* 'work'.
c) accomplishments (dynamic, telic, durative): *hacer un trabajo* 'write a paper', *leer el artículo* 'read the paper', *madurar* 'mature'
d) achievements (dynamic, telic, punctual): *descubrir* 'discover', *ganar* 'win', *morir* 'die'.

Following previous studies (Schwenter & Torres Cacoullos, 2008, Copple, 2011, Howe & Rodríguez Louro, 2013, Rodríguez Louro, 2016), we determine the Aktionsart of each token by identifying the verb infinitive and its complements.[5] As is noted by Bybee et al. (1994, p. 74), as resultatives grammaticalize into anteriors and those in turn grammaticalize into perfectives, their compatibility with different classes of verbs gradually increases as well. This tendency has been shown empirically for Spanish in both diachronic (Copple, 2011, p. 177) and cross-dialectal synchronic (Schwenter & Torres Cacoullos, 2008, p. 23) studies. Therefore, we include Aktionsart in our statistical analysis in order to determine whether it significantly constrains the occurrence of the PP in Costa Rican Spanish. We distinguish between durative and punctual situations (cf. Schwenter & Torres Cacoullos, 2008, p. 15). If Aktionsart significantly constrains PP use in these data, we will interpret this result as evidence that the PP is behaving as an anterior.

Object number: Schwenter & Torres Cacoullos (2008, p. 16) and Rodríguez Louro (2016, p. 635) find that constructions with a plural object favor the PP in their data, because these constructions are highly compatible with the meanings of experiential and of persistent situation, and these meanings are generally associated with the PP (Comrie, 1976, p. 56–61, Dahl, 1985, p. 132). We distinguish between plural objects vs. other (singular object, none). A significant effect of plural objects on PP use will suggest that the PP maintains its meaning as an anterior.

Temporal reference: this linguistic factor is divided into three main categories: specific, indeterminate and irrelevant. Examples with a specific temporal reference refer to situations that happened at a point prior to the speech time. Within this category, three additional distinctions are made, according to the temporal distance from the speech time: hodiernal (today), hesternal (yesterday) and prehesternal (before yesterday), as is shown in (10), (11) and (12) respectively:

(10)   ... *hoy en la mañana estaba en la Caja del Seguro y* dieron *permisito para salir* (CR-1, *Inf.*)
'... Today in the morning I was at Social Security Fund and they [i.e., the young ladies attending Colegio de Señoritas] were given permission to leave'

---

5   We include verbal complements in the analysis because the presence and type of complement conditions the type of *Aktionsart*. Compare *escribir* 'to write' (activity) with *escribir una carta* 'to write a letter' (accomplishment) or *caminar hacia la entrada* 'to walk towards the front door' (activity) and *caminar hasta la entrada* 'to walk until the front door' (accomplishment).

(11) *Ayer ... ayer ... ayer* fui ... fui *a ... a ... al aeropuerto internacional El Coco* (CR-7, *Inf.*)
'Yesterday ... yesterday ... yesterday ... I went ... I went to international airport El Coco'

(12) *el ... el Código Civil* ha cumplido *en ... el año pasado ... recién pasado, su centenario* (CR-13, *Inf.*)
'The Civil Code was [has been] 100 years old last year'

Temporal reference is classified as indeterminate when the situation happened at a point prior to the speech time, but the context does not provide enough evidence to determine the temporal distance of the event. In contrast, there are situations that cannot be anchored to a specific point in time, because they happened multiple times or never happened. These situations are analyzed as having irrelevant temporal reference. Examples (13) and (14) respectively illustrate indeterminate and irrelevant temporal reference:

(13) *la profesora Angélica Gamboa, actualmente una persona que ... que pasa ya de los noventa años, me* ha dicho: *"Es que don Omar—dice—era una maravilla, era algo realmente excepcional".* (CR-13, *Inf.*)
'Professor Angélica Gamboa, a person who at present is older than 90, told [has told] me: "Don Omar—she says—was wonderful; he was really exceptional"'

(14) *nunca* aprendí *a hablar inglés* (CR-6, *Inf.*)
'I never learned how to speak English'

If the PP in Costa Rica is used as an anterior, it will be highly disfavored in constructions with a specific time reference.

Temporal adverbial: We distinguish the following types of adverbials: connective (*entonces* 'so', *luego* 'then', *después* 'afterwards'), durational (*desde* 'since' + point in time, *desde hace* 'for' + period of time, *de ahí en adelante* 'from then onwards'), frequency (*siempre* 'always', *nunca* 'never', *alguna vez* 'ever'), proximative (*ahora* 'now', *este año* 'this year', *actualmente* 'at present'), specific (*ayer* 'yesterday', *el año pasado* 'last year', *cuando*-clauses), and *ya* 'already'. In cases in which more than one temporal adverbial co-occurs in the same clause, we choose the temporal adverb with the widest structural scope (connectives before *ya*, *ya* before specific, specific before frequency).[6] For example, in (15)

---

6 A careful analysis of the data shows that, when more than one temporal adverbial occurs in the clause, the adverbial with the highest scope conditions the choice of the tense. For

we find a connective adverbial (*posteriormente*), *ya*, and a specific adverbial (*en el segundo semestre*). Since *posteriormente* is the adverbial with the widest structural scope, we classify (15) as having a connective temporal adverbial:

(15) Posteriormente el segundo ... en el segundo semestre *de ese segundo año* ya *no estudié más Medicina* (CR-2, *Inf*.)
'Then on the second semester of the second year I no longer studied Medicine'

Proximate, frequency and durational adverbials are highly compatible with the prototypical meanings associated with the PP (recent past, experiential/ existential and inclusive or persistent situation). We predict that these types of adverbs will favor the PP in the data if the PP is being used as an anterior in Costa Rican Spanish. In contrast, *ya* as well as connective and specific adverbials should disfavor the PP.

Clause type: The experiential meaning often associated with the PP as an anterior frequently occurs in language in non-assertive contexts, that is to say, negative and interrogative clauses (Dahl & Hedin, 2000, p. 378). As is noted by Schwenter & Torres Cacoullos (2008) *yes-no* questions "are less anchored temporally than WH (who, what, when, where, why) questions" (p. 10), and therefore should be more congruent with the experiential meaning. Additionally, since anteriors often encode background information that is relevant to a current situation (Howe, 2013, p. 71), they will tend to occur in relative clause constructions. Consequently, if the PP behaves as an anterior in Costa Rican Spanish, we predict that it will be favored in relative clause constructions, *yes-no* questions and negative clauses. For the quantitative analysis, we distinguish two categories within this factor group: 1) relative clauses and *yes-no* questions and 2) other. Negative clauses were included in the category of 'other' because their association with the PP is determined by its frequent occurrence (66%, N = 92/140) in constructions expressing irrelevant temporal reference (cf. Schwenter & Torres Cacoullos, 2008, p. 19).

---

example, in *nunca fui a un solo baile en toda mi carrera universitaria* (CR-2, *Inf*.) 'I never went to a single dance while I was in college' the speaker uses the preterit *fui* 'I went' with the frequency adverb *nunca* 'never' because this action is anchored in a specific time period prior to the moment of speech *en toda mi carrera universitaria* 'while I was in college'. In contrast, in *porque Liberación Nacional, siendo oposición, nunca ha perdido* (CR-12, *Inf*.) 'because Liberación Nacional, being in the opposition, has never lost', the PP *ha perdido* 'has lost' occurs with the same frequency adverb *nunca* when the time period extends up to the moment of speech.

Previous clause tense: we include this factor in our analysis in order to determine if priming has any impact on the occurrence of the PP in our data. To test this, we code for the tense of the first finite verb that occurs in the preceding discourse context of the target token. Previous studies show that priming effects contribute to the grammaticalization processes of TAM markers. For example, in his diachronic study of Spanish auxiliaries *haber*, *deber*, and *tener* as markers of deontic modality, Blas Arroyo (2018, p. 202) reports that, regardless of frequency, the presence of a deontic periphrastic construction in the immediately preceding context significantly increases the probability of its replication in the subsequent context. Likewise, Holmes & Balukas (2011, p. 87) show that the presence of a PP in the previous three clauses statistically conditions the occurrence of the PP in Peninsular Spanish constructions with prehodiernal temporal reference. If the occurrence of the PP is conditioned by priming effects, the presence of a PP in the preceding context will significantly increase the likelihood for the PP to occur in the target construction. For the statistical analysis, we distinguish the PP vs. other.[7]

Subject grammatical person: we include this factor in order to determine if subjectivity plays a role in PP expression. Following previous studies (Aaron & Torres Cacoullos, 2005, Torres Cacoullos & Schwenter, 2008, Rivas, 2011, Hernández, 2013) we operationalize this factor by coding for the grammatical person of the subject. Traugott & Dasher (2002) indicate that first- and second-person singular subjects (*I* and *you*) "are crucially grounded in the point of view of the speaker, and so they exhibit subjectivity" (p. 22).[8] If the PP is associated with subjective values, it will be favored by the occurrence of first- and second-person singular subjects.

Subject expression: Hernández (2013, p. 274) finds that PP usage strongly correlates with expressed subjects in his data of spoken Salvadoran Spanish. He argues that the high percentage of expressed subjects may be interpreted as an example of pragmatic strengthening (Traugott, 1988), more specifically, "they are used to increase the speaker's stake in what is being said" (Hernández, 2013, p. 273). In order to determine if subject expression conditions the occurrence of PP in Costa Rican Spanish, we distinguish between expressed and null subjects in our statistical analysis.

In the following section, we summarize the results of our quantitative analyses.

---

[7] Since all the interviews start with a question of the interviewer and we only analyze the informants' speech, all 1222 tokens are coded for previous clause tense.
[8] See also Cabal-Jiménez (this volume).

3   Results and Analysis

The frequency of occurrence of the PP in these data of spoken Costa Rican Spanish is 20%, as illustrated in Table 11.1. Table 11.2 shows that the percentage of the PP is similar to the rates found in written data of Costa Rican Spanish as well as in other varieties of Central American Spanish (e.g., El Salvador) and South America (e.g., Ecuador). The percentage of PP use in spoken Costa Rican Spanish is higher than in other Latin American varieties such as Mexico (15%), Peru (15%), and Argentina (10%), but lower than the one found in Spain (54%).

TABLE 11.1   % of PP vs. Preterit in the data

	N	%
Preterit	981	80
PP	241	20
Total	1222	100

TABLE 11.2   Rates of PP vs Preterit across the Spanish speaking world (based on oral data except for VanBuren, 1992)

	Preterit	**PP**
Spain (Schwenter & Torres Cacoullos, 2008)	46%	54%
El Salvador (Hernández, 2004)	78%	22%
Costa Rica (VanBuren, 1992)	78%	22%
Ecuador (Dumont, 2013)	78%	22%
Peru (Jara Yupanqui, 2013)	85%	15%
Mexico (Schwenter & Torres-Cacoullos, 2008)	85%	15%
Argentina (Rodríguez Louro, 2016)	90%	10%

Do these dialectal differences in PP rates of expression reflect divergent probabilistic grammars?[9]

In order to determine which of the linguistic factors outlined in the previous section significantly constrain the occurrence of the PP in Costa Rican Spanish, we submit our data to a generalized linear mixed model using R (R: A Language and Environment for Statistical Computing. R Foundation for Statistical Computing, Vienna, Austria). We include the speaker (N = 14) as a random effect. We run multiple models testing for significant interactions between the linguistic factors presented in section 2 and find none. Table 11.3 summarizes the results of the best model, determined by the lowest AIC:

TABLE 11.3   Mixed effects linear regression predicting PP in Costa Rican Spanish[a]

Random effects	Variance	Std. Dev.				
Speaker (Intercept)	1.19	1.09				

Fixed effect	N	% PP	Estimate	Std. Error	Pr (>|z|)	Significance
(Intercept)	1222	20	−4.59	0.51	< 0.001	***
Aktionsart: achievement	390	12	−0.47	0.25	0.06	.
Aktionsart: other	832	23	–	–	–	–
Temporal adverbial: connective, specific, *ya*	265	4	−0.99	0.41	0.016	*
Temporal adverbial: durative, frequency, proximate	130	47	0.9	0.3	0.003	**
Temporal adverbial: no adverb	827	21	–	–	–	–
Clause type: relative and yes/no questions	164	25	0.35	0.29	0.2416	n.s.
Clause type: other	1058	19	–	–	–	–
Object number: plural	97	32	0.73	0.36	0.044	*
Object number: singular, no object	1125	17	–	–	–	–

a For an explanation of the terms *estimate, standard error* and *Pr* (>|z|), see Tagliamonte (2012, p. 148–149).

[9] As previous research shows, different rates do not always entail different probabilistic grammars. For example, even though the rates of subject pronoun expression in Spanish range from 20% to 40%, depending on the dialect, previous research shows that the linguistic factors that constrain this syntactic variable remain consistently the same cross-dialectally (Carvalho et al. 2015).

TABLE 11.3   Mixed effects linear regression predicting PP in Costa Rican Spanish (cont.)

Fixed effect	N	% PP	Estimate	Std. Error	Pr (>|z|)	Significance
Previous clause tense: PP	100	73	2.2	0.35	< 0.001	***
Previous clause tense: other	1122	15	–	–	–	–
Temporal reference: indeterminate	386	8	1.59	0.42	< 0.001	***
Temporal reference: irrelevant	361	55	4.18	0.39	< 0.001	***
Temporal reference: specific (hodiernal, hesternal, prehesternal)	475	2	–	–	–	–
Subject: expressed	604	23	0.47	0.22	0.034	*
Subject: null	618	17	–	–	–	–
Subject grammatical person: first- and second-singular	428	19	0.28	0.25	0.265	n.s.
Subject grammatical person: other	794	20	–	–	–	–

Positive coefficients are associated with the occurrence of PP
Number of observations: 1222, Random effects N: Speaker = 14, AIC = 653.9
Signif. codes: 0 '***' 0.001 '**' 0.01 '*' 0.05 '.' 0.1 'ns' 1

The results of the statistical analysis show that the presence of the PP in spoken Costa Rican Spanish is conditioned by the following factors: previous clause tense, temporal reference, temporal adverbial, object number, subject expression and *Aktionsart*. Clause type and subject grammatical person do not significantly condition PP usage in these data. As is shown in Table 3, the presence of a PP in the previous clause significantly favors the occurrence of the PP in the target clause. This result indicates that priming boosts PP usage. The occurrence of the PP in the immediately preceding context acts as a prime in the following context, which leads the speaker to use the PP again. Priming effects increase the token frequency of the PP. This fact may contribute to advancing its grammaticalization process since, as is noted by Bybee (2010, p. 107), high token frequency is typical of grammaticalizing constructions.

The rates of use of PP and Preterit are significantly different depending on the tense of the previous clause. For example, when the previous clause tense is an Imperfect, the PP only occurs in 6% (N = 12/206) of the examples.[10] In other words, Imperfects combine with Preterits in 94% of the data. Since the

---

10   The percentage of the PP with a previous preterit is also very low (4%, N = 20/499).

PP hardly ever occurs after an Imperfect, this result suggests that the PP is not generally used as a perfective. In contrast, in Peninsular Spanish 27% of the PPs are preceded by an Imperfect (Schwenter & Torres Cacoullos, 2008, p. 25). This shows that, in addition to the Preterit, the PP in Peninsular Spanish can be used to express foregrounded situations, that is to say, temporally ordered past situations that convey the most relevant information of the discourse (Hopper & Thompson 1980, p. 281). In Costa Rican Spanish, however, foregrounded clauses are only encoded by the Preterit, as is shown in (16):

(16) *Sí, era un … un … una situación muy fea porque él **estaba perdiendo** demasiada sangre. Por cierto,* se salvó (CR-6, *Inf.*)
'Yes, it was a very ugly situation because he was losing too much blood. By the way, he recovered'

In the Costa Rican data, we find a correlation between PP use and a previous Present. The PP occurs after the Present tense in 33% of the examples, and this percentage is significantly higher than with the Imperfect (p = 0.000, χ^2 = 36.29716). In fact, 78% (N = 189/241) of the PPs that we find in the data occur with a preceding Present or PP. This result may be interpreted as evidence that in Costa Rica the PP retains its value of an anterior, because of its meaning of current relevance. Consider (17):

(17) *Sí … al … a los nueve meses pedí que me trajeran a San José y desde entonces **vivo** en San José. En varios lugares de San José, pero aquí ha transcurrido toda mi vida casi* (CR-6, *Inf.*)
'Yes, after nine months I asked them to bring me to San José and I have lived in San José since then. In several places in San José, but I have spent almost all of my life here'

In addition to previous clause tense, the occurrence of the PP in the data is also significantly conditioned by temporal reference. As can be seen in Table 11.3, both irrelevant and indeterminate temporal references strongly favor the use of the PP in spoken Costa Rican Spanish. Prototypically, the PP with an anterior meaning is tied to irrelevant temporal references with experiential and continuative uses. Since the situation cannot be anchored to any specific time point, it cannot be elicited by querying 'when?' (Schwenter & Torres Cacoullos, 2008, Copple, 2011). In the data, the vast majority (82%, N = 198/241) of PP constructions have irrelevant temporal reference. The other 18% (N = 43/241) are constructions whose temporal context, in opposition to the irrelevant temporal reference, can be identified either within a specific or indeterminate temporal reference.

There are 475 examples in the dataset with a specific time reference and only 11 are expressed by means of the PP. 5 of these examples occur in combination with hodiernal ('today') temporal reference and 6 with prehesternal ('before yesterday') time reference. Yet, 4 out of the 5 examples we classify as hodiernal belong to what Copple (2011, p. 172) describes as *very recent temporal reference*, i.e., those that occur "right before" the moment of speech. For example, in (18) *me he referido* 'I referred [have referred]' mentions something that was uttered by the informant in the immediately preceding context (*el elemento central de lo que se puede llamar respeto* 'the key element of what we can call respect'):

(18) Inf. *Es esa aceptación de las cosas positivas, esa aceptación también de las cosas negativas de los semejantes, de uno mismo, que quizás constituye el elemento central de lo que se puede llamar respeto.*
[10 lines later]
Enc. *¿Cómo se manifiesta el respeto en un matrimonio?*
Inf. *El respeto en un matrimonio no se aleja mucho de este contexto general al que me he referido.* (CR-5)
'Inf. It is to accept positive things and to accept negative things in oneself and others that is probably the key element of what we call respect.
[*10 lines later*]
Enc. How is respect shown in a marriage?
Inf.—Respect in a marriage is not different from this general meaning I referred [have referred] to'

Copple (2011), who bases her analysis on data extracted from dramatic texts, describes as having very recent temporal reference those events that "occurred within 25 lines of the reporting of their occurrence onstage (most generally, just before or within the same short scene")" (p. 172). In this same line, we classify as very recent temporal reference those situations that happened in the last 30 minutes, which is the time that each interview lasts, as has been mentioned above. As is noted by Copple (2011, p. 177), very recent temporal reference should be distinguished from hodiernal. In fact, in her diachronic data, she shows that very recent temporal reference favors the use of the PP in Peninsular Spanish since the 15th century, whereas hodiernal time reference disfavors the PP until the 19th century.

As for indeterminate temporal reference, which significantly favors the use of PP constructions, this result is probably of more interest since Schwenter & Torres Cacoullos (2008, p.31) identify this reference as the locus of grammaticalization toward perfective. In our data, the PP constructions with indeterminate time reference occur either with no temporal adverbials or with the proximative adverbial *ahora* 'now', as in (19):

(19) *Esa parte de estudios sociales, que muchas veces se veía antes este ... más extensa ... ahora la* han hecho *más local.* (CR-14, *Inf.*)
'That section of social studies, which it was usually seen before as ... longer ... now they have made it more local'

The results for temporal reference reveal that the PP in Costa Rican Spanish maintains its prototypical uses of durative and experiential, as is reflected in its correlation with irrelevant temporal reference. Additionally, the PP in spoken Costa Rican Spanish retains other uses such as very recent past, which cannot be considered as evidence for extension of the PP into perfective contexts. Since the occurrence of PP in prehodiernal contexts is very low (1%, N = 6/466), the only evidence we find in favor of an anterior-perfective grammaticalization in the data is the occurrence of the PP in indeterminate temporal contexts.

The results of the statistical analysis regarding temporal adverbial also suggest that the PP is being used as an anterior. Constructions with durative, frequency and proximative adverbials significantly favor the use of the PP in the data. As has already been mentioned, these adverbials are congruent with the prototypical meanings of an anterior: inclusive, experiential, and recent past. In contrast, specific adverbs and *ya* disfavor the use of the PP. Since these adverbs are used to express perfective aspect, this result indicates that Costa Rican Spanish prefers the Preterit to express perfective meanings.[11]

Another factor that is selected as significant in the quantitative analysis is object number. Constructions in which the object occurs in the plural significantly favor the use of the PP in Costa Rica. Plural objects are generally associated with iterative situations, that is to say, situations that happen more than once. For this reason, plural objects are compatible with the inclusive and experiential meanings typically associated with anteriors.

The PP is also significantly constrained by subject expression in these data. Expressed subjects favor the occurrence of the PP. As already mentioned, Hernández (2013) argues that the PP increases the subjectivity of the

---

11   Only 32% of the examples we extract from the corpus have a temporal adverbial. Similar percentages are reported in previous studies: approximately 25% in both Peninsular and Mexican Spanish (Schwenter & Torres Cacoullos, 2008, p. 16) and 27% in Argentinian Spanish (Rodríguez Louro, 2016, p. 634). The percentage of constructions with temporal adverbials is very similar for the PP (30%, N = 72) and Preterit (33%, N = 323).

construction in perfective contexts, because he finds statistically significant higher rates of expressed subjects with the PP than with the Preterit in his data. Do the results of our statistical analysis reflect these same tendencies in our corpus? Like Hernández (2013), we find that the percentage of expressed subjects is higher with the PP (53%, N = 23/43) than with the Preterit (46%, N = 380/818) in contexts of specific and indeterminate temporal reference. However, this difference does not reach statistical significance.

Finally, the occurrence of the PP in Costa Rican Spanish is also conditioned by Aktionsart verb class. Although marginally, punctual situations (i.e., achievements) significantly disfavor the occurrence of the PP. We can interpret this result as evidence that the PP expresses anterior meanings (inclusive, experiential), which are incompatible with punctual situations, especially if they are semelfactive, and not iterative. VanBuren (1992) reports a similar result for written Costa Rican Spanish and elicited questionnaires. Whereas Costa Rican speakers generally choose Preterit for situations that occur only once, speakers from Spain more frequently prefer the PP in the same context (VanBuren, 1992, p. 155). As is noted by Schwenter (1994) and Schwenter & Torres Cacoullos (2008), the PP in some varieties of Peninsular Spanish has been grammaticalized as a perfective in hodiernal contexts. Consequently, in this variety, the PP does not exhibit Aktionsart restrictions (Schwenter & Torres Cacoullos, 2008, p. 23). Similarly, Rodríguez Louro (2016) shows that Aktionsart verb classes do not significantly constrain PP use in Argentinian Spanish, where the PP has been grammaticalized to express past indefinite situations.

4   Overview

The purpose of this study is to account for the grammaticalization of the PP in a previously under-described variety, Costa Rican Spanish. Our analysis of naturally occurring data taken from 14 oral interviews reveals that the PP occurs in 20% (N = 241/1222) of the examples. This percentage is significantly higher (p = 0.0002, χ^2 = 13.76154) than the one reported by Schwenter & Torres Cacoullos (2008, pp. 20) for Mexico (N = 331/2234). Does this difference in rates of expression correlate with a difference in linguistic constraints?

As shown in Table 11.4, the linguistic constraints that statistically condition the occurrence of the PP are essentially the same in both varieties. Our statistical analysis reveals that, as is the case with Mexican Spanish, Costa Rican Spanish uses the PP as an anterior. Even though, as shown in examples (5) to (7) above, the PP may indicate perfective aspect in Costa Rica, the only tendency we find in the data that may lead to the grammaticalization of perfective uses is that the PP is significantly favored in clauses with indeterminate time reference. This context is the locus of grammaticalization of the PP as a perfective,

TABLE 11.4 Factors that significantly constrain PP occurrence in Costa Rica and Mexico

	Costa Rica	Mexico	Spain
Irrelevant temporal reference	+	+	+
Indeterminate temporal reference	+	+	+
Specific temporal reference: today	–	–	+
Specific temporal reference: yesterday and before	–	–	–
Previous clause tense: PP	+	n.a.	n.a.
Temporal adverbial: proximate, frequency, durative	+	+	+
Temporal adverbial: other	–	–	–
Object number: plural	+	+	+
Object number: singular and no object	–	–	–
Clause type: yes/no questions, relative	n.s.	+	n.s.
Subject expression: expressed	+	n.a.	n.a
Aktionsart: durative	+	+	n.s.
Aktionsart: punctual	–	–	n.s.

+ means 'favors PP', – means 'disfavors PP', n.s. means 'not significant', n.a. means 'not applicable (not included in the analysis)'

as Schwenter & Torres Cacoullos (2008) indicate: "indeterminate contexts are more open to the generalization of the PP than determinate (specific, definite) temporal reference, due to their lack of temporal anchoring" (p. 31). The PP would tend to appropriate perfective contexts that are temporally indeterminate (i.e., less specified).[12]

Another result that shows that the PP is being grammaticalized as a perfective in Peninsular Spanish is that the PP is favored by hodiernal temporal reference in this variety, as Table 4 illustrates. In contrast, in both Mexican and Costa Rican Spanish hodiernal temporal reference disfavors the PP. In fact, in Costa Rican Spanish we find that vast majority of the examples in which the PP occurs in contexts of hodiernal temporal reference actually correspond to what Copple (2011) describes as very recent temporal reference. These uses have been associated with the PP since the 15th century and therefore could be considered as evidence of retention (or persistence) of earlier meanings.

Additional evidence of retention/persistence is provided by the effect of subject expression on the occurrence of the PP. As is noted by Copple (2011,

---

12 In this way, these authors suggest that it is temporal reference (indeterminate) that determines the spread of the PP into the perfective domain and not temporal distance (hodiernal, hesternal, prehesternal), as has been previously assumed.

p. 176), expressed subjects strengthen the highlighting effect that resultative PPs set on the agent/experiencer responsible for the current situation. Although subject expression significantly constrains the occurrence of the PP through the history of Spanish (Copple, 2011, p. 177), its effect gradually decreases as the PP evolves from its original resultative meaning. Therefore, we interpret the correlation between expressed subjects and the PP we find in our data as evidence of retention of the meaning of the original resultative construction.

The results of our quantitative analyses also suggest that the PP in Costa Rican Spanish is not used in the same way as in other Central American varieties such as El Salvador. For the latter, Hernández (2013) reports higher rates of the PP expressing perfective aspect (29%) than in Costa Rica (18%). In addition, this author shows that, when used as a perfective, the PP is more subjective than the Preterit. He bases this analysis on the significantly higher percentage of the PP than the Preterit in combination with forms that contribute to increasing the subjectivity of the construction: expressed subjects and first-person singular subjects. In Costa Rican Spanish, however, we do not find evidence in favor of this analysis. As shown in the previous section, although expressed subjects significantly favor the use of the PP in our dataset, we find similar rates of subject expression in both anterior and perfective uses of the PP. Similarly, the factor of subject grammatical person was not selected as significant in our statistical analysis. In fact, when expressing perfective aspect, first-person subjects are less frequent with the PP (30%, 13/43) than with the Preterit (37%, 300/818). Therefore, our results do not substantiate Hernández's (2013) account of Salvadoran Spanish.

This work contributes to our understanding of an under-studied variety of Spanish, namely, Costa Rican Spanish, by providing a variationist analysis of PP and Preterit use. In addition to testing linguistic factors found to significantly constrain the occurrence of the PP in other Spanish dialects, we use priming data as a metric for 'current relevance'. This chapter also contributes to the body of research that debunks the traditional approach that regards Latin American Spanish as a unique variety (Hernández, 2013, Howe, 2013, Fløgstad, 2016, Rodríguez Louro, 2016, Jara Yupanqui, 2013, Escobar & Crespo, 2020, among others). Additionally, in line with Rodríguez and Howe (this volume), our findings also reveal that not all varieties of Central American Spanish behave in the same way. Our statistical analysis shows that the probabilistic grammar of the PP in Costa Rican Spanish is more similar to Mexican Spanish than to Salvadoran Spanish. Like in Mexico, the PP in Costa Rica behaves as an anterior, with little evidence of grammaticalization towards the perfective domain.

References

Aaron, J., & Torres Cacoullos, R. (2005). Quantitative measures of subjectification: A variationist study of Spanish *salir(se)*. *Cognitive Linguistics, 16*(4), 607–633. https://doi.org/10.1515/cogl.2005.16.4.607.

Alarcos Llorach, E. (1947). Perfecto simple y perfecto compuesto en español. *Revista de Filología Española, 31*, 108–139.

Blas Arroyo, J. L. (2018). Comparative variationism for the study of language change: five centuries of competition amongst Spanish deontic periphrases. *Journal of Historical Sociolinguistics, 4*(2), 177–219. https://doi.org/10.1515/jhsl-2017-0030.

Butt, B., & Benjamin, C. (2004). *A new reference grammar of modern Spanish*. Routledge.

Bybee, J., Perkins, R., & Pagliuca, W. (1994). *The evolution of grammar: tense, aspect, and modality in the languages of the world*. University of Chicago Press.

Bybee, J. (2010). *Language, usage and cognition*. Cambridge University Press.

Bybee, J. (2015). *Language change*. Cambridge University Press.

Carvalho, A. M., Orozco, R., & Shin, N. (2015). Introduction. In A. M. Carvalho, R. Orozco, & N. Shin (Eds.), *Subject pronoun expression in Spanish. A cross-dialectal perspective* (pp. xiii–xxvi). Georgetown Univ. Press.

Comrie, B. (1976). *Aspect. An introduction to the study of verbal aspect and related problems*. Cambridge Textbooks in Linguistics.

Copple, M. (2011). Tracking the constraints on a grammaticalizing perfect(ive). *Language Variation and Change, 23*(2), 163–191. http://dx.doi.org/10.1017/S0954394511000044.

Dahl, Ö. (1985). *Tense and aspect systems*. Basil Blackwell.

Dahl, Ö., & Hedin, E. (2000). Current relevance and event reference. In Ö. Dahl (Ed.), *Tense and Aspect in the Languages of Europe* (pp. 385–402). De Gruyter Mouton. https://doi.org/10.1515/9783110197099.3.385.

Dowty, D. (1979). *Word meaning and Montague grammar*. Reidel.

Dumont, J. (2013). Another look at the present perfect in an Andean variety of Spanish: Grammaticalization and evidentiality in Quiteño Spanish. In J. Cabrelli Amaro, G. Lord, A. de Prada Pérez, & J. E. Aaron (Eds.), *Selected Proceedings of the 16th Hispanic Linguistics Symposium* (pp. 279–291). Cascadilla Proceedings Project.

Escobar, A. M. (2012). Revisiting the 'present perfect': Semantic analysis of Andean colonial documents. *Lingua, 122*(5), 470–480. https://doi.org/10.1016/j.lingua.2011.10.005.

Escobar, A. M., & Crespo Del Rio, C. (2020). La gramaticalización de la subjetividad en el español andino. In L. Andrade Ciudad & S. Sessarego (Eds.), *Los castellanos del Perú: historia, variación y contacto lingüístico* (pp. 156–205). Routledge. https://doi.org/10.4324/9781003083412-7.

Fleischman, S. (1983). From pragmatics to grammar: Diachronic reflections on pasts and futures in Romance. *Lingua*, *60*(1–2), 183–214. https://doi.org/10.1016/0024-3841(83)90074-8.

Fløgstad, G. (2016). *Preterit expansion and perfect demise in Porteño Spanish and beyond: A critical perspective on cognitive grammaticalization theory*. Brill. http://library.oapen.org/handle/20.500.12657/38097.

Harris, M. (1982). The 'past simple' and 'present perfect' in Romance. In M. Harris & N. Vincent (Eds.), *Studies in the Romance verb* (pp. 42–70). Croom Helm.

Hernández, J. E. (2004, December). *Present perfect variation and grammaticization in Salvadoran Spanish*. [Doctoral thesis, University of New Mexico]. ProQuest Dissertations Publishing.

Hernández, J. E. (2008). Present Perfect semantics and usage in Salvadoran Spanish. *Revista internacional de lingüística iberoamericana*, *6*(2(12)), 115–137.

Hernández, J. E. (2013). Focus on speaker subjective involvement in Present Perfect grammaticalization: Evidence from two Spanish varieties. *Borealis: An International Journal of Hispanic Linguistics*, *2*(2), 261–284. http://dx.doi.org/10.7557/1.2.2.2525.

Holmes, B. C., & Balukas, C. (2011). Yesterday, All my Troubles Have Seemed (PP) So Far Away: Variation in Pre-hodiernal Perfective Expression in Peninsular Spanish. In J. Michnowicz, & R. Dodsworth (Eds.), *Selected Proceedings of the 5th Workshop on Spanish Sociolinguistics* (pp. 79–89). Cascadilla Proceedings Project.

Hopper, P. & Thompson, S. (1980). Transitivity in grammar and discourse. *Language*, *56*(2), 251–299.

Howe, C. (2013). *The Spanish perfects. Pathways of emergent meaning*. Palgrave Macmillan.

Howe, C., & Rodríguez Louro, C. (2013). Peripheral Envelopes: Spanish Perfects in the Variable Context. In A. M. Carvalho & S. Beaudrie (Eds.), *Selected Proceedings of the 6th Workshop on Spanish Sociolinguistics* (pp. 41–52). Cascadilla Press.

Jara Yupanqui, M. (2011). Funciones Discursivas y Gramaticalización del Pretérito Perfecto Compuesto en el Español de Lima. *Spanish in Context*, *8*(1), 95–118. https://doi.org/10.1075/sic.8.1.05jar.

Jara Yupanqui, M. (2013). *El perfecto en el español de Lima: Variación y cambio en situación de contacto lingüístico*. Pontificia Universidad Católica del Perú Press.

Jara Yupanqui, M. (2017). The Present Perfect in Peruvian Spanish: An Analysis of Personal Experience Narratives among Migrant Generations in Lima. In M. Fryd & P. Giancarli (Eds.), *Aorists and Perfects. Synchronic and Diachronic Perspectives* (pp. 42–77). Brill/Rodopi.

Labov, W. (1994). *Principles of Linguistic Change, Volume 1: Internal Factors*. Wiley-Blackwell.

Pfänder, S., & Palacios, A. (2013). Evidencialidad y validación en los pretéritos del español andino ecuatoriano. *Círculo de Lingüística Aplicada a la Comunicación*, *54*, 65–98. http://dx.doi.org/10.5209/rev_CLAC.2013.v54.42373.

R: The R Project for Statistical Computing (n.d.). About R. https://www.r-project.org/.

Rivas, J. (2011). "*Como no me trago el humo ...:*" A corpus-based approach to aspectual *se*. *Studies in Hispanic and Lusophone Linguistics, 4*(2), 379–416. https://doi.org/10.1515/shll-2011-1106.

Rodríguez Louro, C., & Howe, C. (2010). Perfect potential: Semantic change in narrative contexts across Spanish. *Revista internacional de lingüística iberoamericana, 8*(2(16)), 157–174.

Rodríguez Louro, C., & Jara Yupanqui, I. M. (2011). Otra mirada a los procesos de gramaticalización del perfecto en español: Perú y Argentina. *Studies in Hispanic and Lusophone Linguistics*, 4(1), 55–80. https://doi.org/10.1515/shll-2011-1091.

Rodríguez Louro, C. (2016). Indefinite past reference and the Present Perfect in Argentinian Spanish. *Studies in Language, 40*(3), 622–647. https://doi.org/10.1075/sl.40.3.05lou.

Samper Padilla, J. (1995). Criterios metodológicos del 'Macro-corpus' de la Norma lingüística culta de las principales ciudades del mundo hispánico. *Lingüística, 7*, 263–293.

Samper Padilla, J. A., Hernández Cabrera, C. E., & Troya Déniz, M. (1997). *Macrocorpus de la norma lingüística culta de las principales ciudades del mundo hispánico*. Universidad de Las Palmas de Gran Canaria.

Schwenter, S. (1994).The grammaticalization of an anterior in progress: evidence from a Peninsular Spanish dialect. *Studies in Language, 18*(1), 71–111. https://doi.org/10.1075/sl.18.1.05sch.

Schwenter, S., & Torres Cacoullos, R. (2008). Defaults and indeterminacy in temporal grammaticalization: the 'perfect' road to perfective. *Language Variation and Change, 20*(1), 1–39. https://doi.org/10.1017/S0954394508000057.

Squartini, M., & Bertinetto, P. M. (2000). The simple and compound past in Romance languages. In Ö. Dahl (Ed.), *Tense and Aspect in the Languages of Europe* (pp. 403–439). Mouton de Gruyter.

Tagliamonte, S. A. (2012). *Variationist sociolinguistics. Change, observation, interpretation*. Wiley-Blackwell.

Torres Cacoullos, R., & Schwenter, S. (2008). Constructions and pragmatics: Variable middle marking in Spanish *subir(se)* 'go up' and *bajar(se)* 'go down'. *Journal of Pragmatics*, 40(8), 1455–1477. https://doi.org/10.1016/j.pragma.2008.01.005.

Traugott, E. C. (1988). Pragmatic Strengthening and Grammaticalization. In *Proceedings of the Fourteenth Annual Meeting of the Berkeley Linguistics Society* (pp. 406–416). https://doi.org/10.3765/bls.v14i0.1784.

Traugott, E. C., & Dasher, R. B. (2002). *Regularity in semantic change*. Cambridge University Press.

VanBuren, P. E. (1992, March). *The Spanish Perfect: A Synchronic Study of the Functional Load of the Simple and Compound Perfect in Costa Rican and Peninsular Spanish among Educated Speakers*. [Doctoral thesis, Union Institute and University]. ProQuest Dissertations Publishing.

Vendler, Z. (1957). Verbs and times. *The Philosophical Review, LXVI*, 143–160.

CHAPTER 12

Address Pronouns in Panamanian Spanish

A Historical Overview

Miguel Ángel Quesada Pacheco

1   Delimitation of Scope

This chapter analyzes the use of the address pronouns *vos*, *tú*, and *usted* in Panamanian Spanish and elaborates on the scope of symmetrical relationships of confidence/formality (following the terminology of Fontanella, [1999]) in order to elucidate and explain, from a diachronic perspective, its current geographical distribution. Previous studies on the use and extension of address pronouns in current Panamanian Spanish (Quesada, 2017; Stanziola and Quilis, 1983; Tinoco & Quesada, 2013; Teixeira & Leal, 2017) show a clear geographic distribution: a) the massive presence of *tú* in the middle of the country and major cities; b) the extension of *ustedeo* (i.e., the use of *usted* in confidence situations in border areas) and c) the use of *vos* in its diphthongized variant (*vos cantáis, vos coméis*, etc.) in the central-western part of the country. In order to provide a diachronic explanation to the aforementioned distribution, the main goal of the present study is to analyze the historical evolution of address pronouns in this variety of Central American Spanish, in order to elucidate the causes of its current geographical distribution, as well as the linguistic and social factors that have influenced their uses throughout the last 500 years. To achieve this goal, this analysis is based on the conceptual framework of language internal diffusion (Croft, 2000; François, 2014), which takes into account the process of change within a given language due to individual, social, and geographical changes.

2   Theoretical and Methodological Approach

Unlike theoretical models applied to diachronic geolinguistics—*Stammbaumtheorie*, *Wellentheorie*, Areal Norms theory, among others—which are circumscribed to areas of large domains; that is, areas of contact among languages genetically related or not (Hernández, 1999, p. 41; Aikhenvald and

Dixon, 2001, pp. 11–19; Nocentini, 2004, pp. 102–103), there is a model applied to areas of small domains, a language or variant of a language, known as *Internal Linguistic Diffusion* (François, 2014)[1] which studies and tracks the way in which a certain innovative linguistic feature gains strength in a given speaking community, displacing the previous linguistic feature.

Following Nocentini (2004, p. 101), who states that "Given two competing linguistic phenomena A and B, in an area of segregation of propagation, it is possible to identify which of the two is innovative and which is conservative on the basis of their distribution" (my translation), the *Internal Linguistic Diffusion* model combines, within the traditional concept of dialect; i. e, "regional differences within a language" (Petyt, 1980, p. 27), dialectological and diachronic with sociolinguistic aspects, and consists of three basic phases: a) gestation, b) propagation, and c) consolidation.

Gestation refers to the emergence of a linguistic change, or innovation, which occurs at a given moment in the history of a language and usually manifests itself in one or more idiolects: "Indeed, linguistic innovations first emerge in the speech of certain individuals, in the form of novel ways of speaking—whether phonetic, lexical, phraseological, etc." (François, 2014, p. 168). According to Croft (2000, p. 174), "The propagation of a new linguistic variant is essentially the adoption of a new linguistic convention by the community." If the innovation is accepted by other individuals in the speech community, it is adopted by that community. Furthermore, it is important to highlight that change as a phenomenon concerns a set of idiolects, and the phenomenon of innovation goes hand in hand with the propagation process (Croft, 2000, p. 185); if not, it would have no reason to be. Finally, when innovation is adopted as part of the daily discourse of the speech community, the innovation takes hold, settles down and becomes part of the linguistic heritage of that community:

> After a period of competition with the previous norm, the innovation may become statistically dominant, and settle in the speech habits of a whole social group. If it does, then it becomes a property of an entire 'communalect' (i.e. sociolect, dialect or language). From that point onwards, the linguistic feature will be transmitted to descendant generations of learners, just as much as the rest of the inherited system. (François, 2014, p. 168)

---

1 The discussion about internal linguistic diffusion is not new, but goes way before François (cf. Wolfram & Schilling-Estes 2003).

Following this model, language innovations can take several generations to become established, but sometimes it does not take root at all: "This process [of propagation] takes time, and in fact may never go to completion, that is, complete replacement of the old convention by the new one. Moreover, many innovations are not selected, or do not survive very long." (Croft, 2000, p. 174). The change does not necessarily encompass the entire spectrum of a language but may well refer to a set of dialects of that language. For this reason, this model cannot be represented in the form of a tree, since the model of the genealogical tree necessarily includes a language *per se*, not a fragment of that language (François, 2014, p. 166).

Methodologically, the present study adopts a historical sociolinguistic approach, which has been previously applied in Hispanic linguistics (e.g., Bertolotti, 2015; Bravo 1990, 2002–2004; Castillo, 1982; Fernández Martín, 2012; Fontanella, 1970, 1999, among others). This method uses archive data, literary works, journalistic publications, and other historical sources as a research database and goes through each of the address pronouns in question. A chronological trajectory is then displayed in an effort to identify and explain linguistic (structural) and extra-linguistic (geographic, social, cultural) factors that contributed to changes in pronoun distribution and usage (Hummel, 2010; Moreno, 2010).

In accordance to this, the following sources were employed to gather material for a linguistic *corpus*:

a)   Unpublished historical manuscripts from Archivo General de Indias (henceforth AGI), Archivo General de Simancas (AGS) and *Corpus Diacrónico y Diatópico del Español de América* (CORDIAM), all available online;

b)   Published historical works (Fernández Alcaide, 2009; Mena, 2013; Otte, 1998; Pacheco, 1864) as well as literary works from the 17th, 18th and 19th centuries (Miró, 1985, 1999);

c)   Metalinguistic texts, particularly from the 20th and 21st centuries (Quesada, 2017; Quesada & Tinoco, 2014; Robe, 1950; Stanziola & Quilis, 1983; Tinoco, 2010) were used in order to complete a historical overview of address pronouns in Panamanian Spanish.

In the present study, the dialect level is circumscribed to the current Panamanian territory and is subdivided into: the West (Chiriquí and Veraguas provinces), the Central-West (Herrera, Los Santos and Coclé), the Middle (Colón, West Panama and Central Panama), and the East (Darien).[2] Note that in this chapter I refer to Panama as the territory that in colonial times was called Royal Audience and Chancery of Panama in Tierra Firme, excluding the

---

2   Source: https://www.inec.gob.pa/archivos/P6221DIV-DISTRITOS2013.pdf.

part that belonged to present-day Colombia, and is today part of the Republic of Panama (cf. Robe 1953; see also Miró 1985; Mena 2000, 2001, 2013).

3 Address Pronouns in Spain in the 16th Century: An Overview

According to Bravo (1990, pp. 177–180), the address pronouns in Spain at the time of the conquest of the New World showed a complex system consisting of some courtesy formulas and two pronouns. The most common courtesy formulas were *Vuestra Señoría* ~ *Excelencia* ~ *Majestad* ~ *Merced* and were used in asymmetric address, usually in situations of complete distance, in formal discourse, particularly among people of lower positions towards people of higher positions in the social scale, with *vuestra majestad* used only to address royalty. *Vuestra Merced* was reserved for formal and informal situations, and it was particularly used among people of the same social / familiar scale (symmetrical types of address), and from people of lower social status to people of higher status (asymmetrical types of address).

The pronouns were *vos* and *tú*. *Vos* had two uses: as F (formality) and as C (confidence). F-*Vos* was used in formal, asymmetric situations when addressing people of lower social status (the king, a governor, etc. to their subalterns), while C-*Vos* was employed in informal situations, both in symmetric and asymmetric directions, for example between family members of similar status (spouses, cousins, etc.) and of lower genealogical rank (parents to adult children, etc.). *Tú* was mainly used in certain intimacy relations (e.g., among lovers) towards unreal entities (deities, mythological figures, etc.), family members of lower genealogical rank (particularly children), and to people of lower rank (e.g., servants).

The pronominal system gradually moved on a scale oriented from more distance to less distance, marked by four degrees (Table 12.1).

Vos and *tú* came to be equated during the 16th century, which caused the slow but certain disappearance of *vos* in Spain in the late 17th century, while *tú* gained the former functions of *vos* and became the pronoun *par excellence* in

TABLE 12.1 Scale of address pronouns (Spain, 16th century)

+ distance	+ – distance	– + distance	– distance
vuestra señoría ~ excelencia ~ alteza ~ majestad	vuestra merced	vos	tú

the field of confidence (Moreno, 2003).[3] On the other hand, *vuestra merced* – > *usted* became the distance-marking pronoun, which evolved to the pronominal system of most of European Spanish:[4] *tú/vosotros* for intimacy situations, and *usted/ustedes* to mark distance (Fontanella, 1999, p. 1402, Cabal-Jiménez, this volume).

Although the aforementioned pronominal system in Table 12.1 was present in Tierra Firme by the time of the Spanish settlements there, the analysis of the historical documentation at hand shows that the situation in Panama changed over time and differed from that in Spain, as will be seen in the following sections.

4 The Destiny of Vuestra Señoría and Vuestra Excelencia

The courtesy formulas, such as *Vuestra Señoría* and *Vuestra Excelencia*, were used throughout the Panamanian Colonial times in order to mark distance and formality and were addressed to people in the government (governors, royalty), as the following examples illustrate:

> Darién, 1518: Nobles señores, Hernando de Argüello, en nombre del adelantado Vasco Nuñez de Balboa, beso las manos de *vv ss.*, é *mercedes*; bien saben el tiempo que por *sus* instrucciones *dieron* al dicho Adelantado para lo que habrá de hazer despues que desta cibdad partió para poblar á Acla y para hazer este viaje. (Pacheco et al., 1864, pp. 556–557).

> Panama City, 1539: Por la vía de Guatem*a*la *le* escreví a *v*uestra *señoría* biendo relaçión / de lo q*u*e al presente p*a*sava. Las q*u*ales c*a*rtas vie*n* creo / que *vuestra señoría* las *avrá resçibido* (Panama, 1539, private letters, cordiam.org)

> Yaviza, 1797: V*uestra* E*xcelencia se ha Seruido* determinar [...] como *podrá* Vuestra Excelencia Reconocerlo (Panama, 1797, administrative documents, letter to the Viceroy of Lima, cordiam.org)

---

3 In fact, testimonies of *tuteo* are found in letters from Spanish immigrants in Panama to their wives in Spain, from the end of the 17th century (Stangl, 2012, pp. 525–527; Bravo, 2002–2004, pp. 261–262).
4 West Andalucia and some areas around Salamanca show a hybrid pronoun system that differs from the rest of the country, with a combination of *ustedes* + second / third plural verb forms in West Andalucian, or a combination of *usted* / *ustedes* + second verb forms in Salamanca (Fernández Martín, 2012, pp. 169–194).

In the documentation analyzed, these formulas were in the process of extinction from the 19th century onwards and were replaced by *V.M.* ~ *usted* in written discourse.

5   The Emergence of *Usted*

The pronoun *usted* derived from a fusion of the nominal phrase *vuestra merced*, and together with *vuestra majestad ~ señoría ~ excelencia*, were used in late Medieval times to fill the empty field of distance that *vos* had left as it passed over to the level of confidence and posterior extinction (Rey, 2005, p. 3; Sáez, 2006, p. 1204; Rószavári, 2015, p. 267).[5] Besides, *usted* adopted a conjugation with the third-person (singular or plural, depending on the number of recipients) verb forms, with its corresponding pronouns (*le/lo/la, su*, etc.):

> Nombre de Dios, 1584: en ella no pude escribir, mas de que habia recibido *sus* cartas de *v.m.* [...] En la cual lo primero sera decir que tengo salud, y que deseo que lo mismo sea en *v.m.* [...] por ahora no conviene que vengan ambos, sino solo *su* hijo de *v.m.* [...] Y *adviertale v.m.* que ha de tratar en Sevilla con gente muy puntosa. (a man to his brother; Otte, 1988, letter 311)

Practically throughout the colonial period and in the 19th century, the abbreviations *V.M. ~ Vmd ~ U.*[6] are found in official and formal correspondence,

---

[5] Sáez (2006, p. 1204), following the theory of grammaticalization, explains how the nominal phrase *vuestra merced* [possessive + noun] evolved to a pronoun *usted*, passing through a process of attrition, desemantization and condensation: "De este modo, *vuestra merced* pasó de pertenecer a un inventario abierto (léxico) a formar parte de un inventario cerrado (gramatical)."

[6] Actually, any addressing indicating distance was abbreviated in writing; for instance, *v.s.* for *Vuestra Señoría, V. E. ~ Vex^a* for *Vuestra Excelencia*:

"abian desembarcado en Manta seis buzos mas que remitió *v.s.* a este destino" (Panamá, 1801; AGI, Lima, 1440, N. 3; fo. 91, http://pares.mcu.es/ParesBusquedas20/catalogo/show/7253686 [Consulted: 30.12.2020]).

"Dios guarde a *V. E.* muchos años." (Panamá, 1793; AGS: SGU. LEG. 7061. 23; folio 1. [Consulted: 29.12.2020]); "Seré muy honrrado si *V.E.* se dignase ofrecerme ..." (Panamá, 1798: AGI, ESTADO, 51, N.9.

http://pares.mcu.es/ParesBusquedas20/catalogo/show/65333. [Consulted: 29.12.2020]).

"Y también por la prosperidad de *V. Exª*" (Panamá, 1797; AGI, https://www.archivesportaleurope.net/es/ead-display/-/ead/pl/aicode/ES-41091-AGI10/type/fa/id/ES-41091-AGI-UD-1928215/unitid/ES-41091-AGI-UD-1928215+-+ES-41091-AGI-UD-65328/search/o/panamá [Consulted: 30.12.2020]).

which makes it almost impossible to know which of them, if *vuestra merced*[7] or *usted*, were orally expressed in daily speech:[8] "Para que esta sea conseguida en toda su corrección, es necesario que *Ud.* como se lo encargo, cuide mucho que en esa plaza no se invierta el buen orden." (José de Fábrega, Panamá 1821; in Soler, 1988, p. 27). Thus, the first and certain documentation of *usted* in Panama comes from an anonymous poem around 1700: "No puede tener *Usted / do menear este caso*" (Miró, 1999a, p. 56).[9]

In opposition to its use solely as a distance marker in most of Spain, *vuestra merced* > *usted* developed another sphere of use, very widespread in Spanish America, denoting closeness, affection and trust, brotherhood or friendship, known as *ustedeo* (Quesada, 2010, pp. 107–111).[10] This use is recorded in Panama since the beginning of the colonial period:

> Panama City, 1524 (to a cousin): en merced tengo a *vuestra merced* lo que *hizo* de enviar esa patena a mi hermano, ella va muy bien que de mano de *vuestra merced* no se esperaba menos. (Mena, 2013, letter 5)

> Panama City, 1737 (to a brother): digo que *vuestra merced administre y cuide*, hasta nueba orden mía. *Vuestra merced perdonará* las herratas de esta [...] por anticipar a *vuestra merced* esta noticia, y *vuestra merced* me *participará* quantas se ofrecieren por esos países. (Panama, 1737, letters and other documents, cordiam.org)

"*v.s.* tomó la voz y me dijo: Bernal, por mí lo dice *U.?*" (Panamá, 1800; AGI: Estado 51; No. 13; fo. 134).

7   See AGI, *Cartas y expedientes del presidente, oidores y fiscal de la Audiencia de Panamá*. AGI: ES.41091.AGI/24//PANAMA,19 http://pares.mcu.es/ParesBusquedas20/catalogo/descripcion/381020 [Consulted: 21.12.2020]. "encargo a *vmd* que immediatamente proceda a recoger dha perla." (Panamá, 1800; AGI, Estado 55, N. 13, Bloque 5 1r) http://pares.mcu.es/ParesBusquedas20/catalogo/show/65337 [Consulted: 02.01.2021].

8   There are testimonies in Spanish grammars written by foreigners, which indicate that people wrote *v. m.* but said *usted*: "Dans la conversation, on pronounce *usted* et *ustedes*, mais on écrit *Vm.* et *Vms.*" (Josse, 1824 [1799], p. 54). An earlier testimony comes from 1697: "Les Espagnols se servent du mot *vsted*, qui est le pronom de la personne à qui on parle, & *vstedes*, quand on parle à plusieurs. Mais en ecrivant ils mettent *v.m.* pour le singulier, qui veut dire *vuestra merced*; & au plurier *vs. ms.*, qui vaut autant que *vuéstras mercedes*; mais en parlant ils disent toujours *Vsted*, & *Vstedes*." (cited by Sáez, 2006, p. 2904). Though both citations concern Peninsular Spanish, it is plausible to think that the same happened in the New World.

9   Miró does not give an exact date for this poem.

10 Kany (1969: 124–129), who does not apply the term *ustedeo*, explains the use of the affective *usted*, as characteristic of many Hispanic regions, including Spain. However, neither he nor Stanziola & Quilis (1983, 1989) record it as a feature of Panamanian Spanish.

Panama City, 1800 (friend to friend). Tocayo mi mui estimado [...] por esta razón no *le* remito a *Vmd* los encargos que me *hace* del maní y del arroz. (AGI: Estado 51, No. 13; fo. 129)

Ustedeo is also observed in the *costumbrista* literature from the 19th to the 20th century and comes from authors from the mid-western part of the country (e.g., Veraguas and David) which could be interpreted as a regionalization of its use; in fact, in the ALEP (Tinoco 2010) no form of *ustedeo* appears in the middle of the country, but rather towards the west and east. According to Quesada and Tinoco (2013, p. 352):

> Dialectalmente visto el panorama, cuando el tratamiento se da dentro del campo de la solidaridad, y es simétrico (tratamiento entre esposos, entre hermanos, entre amigos y entre novios), se observa una tendencia a incrementarse el uso de *usted* cuanto más se aleja uno del centro del país, tomando la capital como centro irradiador tuteante, y cuanto más se acerca uno a las fronteras nacionales: al occidente con Costa Rica, y al oriente con Colombia.

Teixeira and Leal (2019, p. 433) affirm that *ustedeo* exists in Panama City today, contrary to what is stated by Quesada and Tinoco (2013). However, after analyzing their data, it is clearly observed that *tuteo* dominates in symmetric relationships (siblings, friends and couples), while an increase in the use of *usted* is observed only in asymmetric formal relationships, i.e., children addressing their parents, and in situations of distance (to a stranger). Thus, the aforementioned authors fail to show that *ustedeo*, understood as *usted*-addressing in symmetrical situations of confidence, is not registered in their survey. The problem lies in Teixeira and Leal's confusion of *usted* as a distance marker, with *ustedeo* as a confidence marker.

6 Evolution of Panamanian *voseo*

The pronoun *vos*, with its corresponding second person plural verbal system comes from the etymological use from the Middle Ages (see Table 12.2).

In the corpus, two types of *vos* are found: etymological or reverential *vos*, and familiar *vos*, both following the morphological pattern in Table 12.2. The use of the first type is recorded from the first half of the 16th century until the 19th century, and its use is restricted to formal situations on the level of formality, particularly from a high-ranking to a lower-ranking person:

TABLE 12.2 Etymological *vos*

Subject	D.O.	I.O.	Prepositional	Possessive	Verb form
vos	os (vos)	os (vos)	vos	vuestro	2nd. pl. (cantáis, coméis, vivís)

> Nombre de Dios, 1524 (Pedrarias Dávila to his lieutenant): Con Juanillo, mi negro, recibí *vuestras* cartas y las tres arrobas de vino que *enviasteis* con los indios, y en mucha merced *os* tengo el cuidado que *tuvisteis* de hacerme saber de la venida de ese navío. (Mena 2013: letter 7)

In the 19th century, the etymological *vos* appears in poetic and political discourses:[11]

> *Vos* que *amáis* la virtud como ninguna,
> *fundad* en *vuestra* fe *vuestra* esperanza;
> que el Cielo hará que para siempre *os* sobre
> con que ofrecerle caridad al pobre. (1856, in Miró, 1999a, p. 104)

> *Os* lo repito, Sr. Obaldía, no tuvo el tinte que *habéis querido* darle [...] *vos* que *datáis* desde entonces *vuestros* servicios. (1851; in Soler, 1988, p. 156)

The second type of *vos* is seen from the second half of the 16th century, its use being observed in informal discourses within the level of confidence, among family members of the same rank, as well as in generational situations from top to bottom:

> Nombre de Dios, 1560 (a husband to his wife): *Traed* con *vos* a Juana y a Leonor, si quisiere[12] traer todas *vuestras* cajas de ropa y cama, lo demas *vended*. [...] aunque *vos vengais*, no estaré aquí cuatro años [...]. Y esto *haced*, porque conviene. (Otte 1988, letter 302)

---

11 Some poems have been recorded, both from the Colonial period and later—at least those found in Miró's compendium (1999a)—where the determinative *vuestro* appears, together with the verbal endings of the second person plural (*-áis, éis*, etc.), but without their corresponding pronominal form, so they have not been taken into account for the present analysis, since it is not known whether they referred to *vos* or *vosotros*.

12 This verb in the third singular refers to Eleanor, not to the writer's wife.

TABLE 12.3 Panamanian *voseo*

Subject	D.O.	I.O.	Prepositional	Possesive	Verb form
Vos (*tú*)	te	te	*vos*	*tu*	2nd. pl., diphthongized (*-áis, -éis*)

Panamá, 1573 (a father to his son): En la segunda flota, y aun en la tercera, de que vino por general Diego Flores de Vaides, *os* escribí largo, *dandoos* cuenta de mi vida y suceso, y de como a *vuestra* hermana le va bien. (Otte, 1988, carta 275)

From this type of use, the mixed paradigm of the Spanish-American *voseo* must have been gestated and developed, where tonic forms of the medieval *vos* were mixed with unstressed forms of *tú*, and in Panama their verb forms were diphthongized (Table 12.3).

No instances of this type of *voseo* have been found in the Colonial period, so far. The first manifestations of it come from the beginning of the 20th century, featured in the *costumbrista* literature, appearing exclusively in rural, peasant, informal discourse, on the level of confidence:

—¡Jesú, anda! *parecéi qu'estái* movía [...]
—*Vos* aquí, acá *vos*, que se vea la capitana. (Garay, 1999 [1930], pp. 63–64)

—¿*Te habei* juntado con Anselmo? (Miró, 1999b, p. 158)

—Urelia ... *Venite* ya ... Los muchachos tan llorando —llama Pascual (Miró 1999b: 170)
—¿Y qué vamos a hacer, pues? ... *Tú sabei* que esa es la suerte [...] *Mirá* pa' al cielo. (Miró, 1999b, pp. 183–184)

A conversation between an elderly couple:

—¿Jumo? ... El jumo no ej na. Jumo a ejtáo bebiendo dej' que me junté con *voj*. (Miró 1999b: 223)

And in a curse of a widow to her late husband:

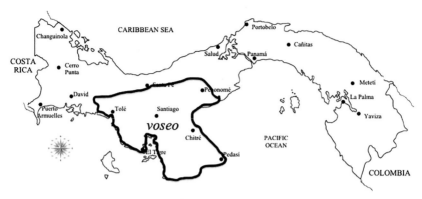

MAP 12.1   *Voseo* regions in Panamá (approximate situation today)

La curpa, sí, ay Vale mío, la curpa la *tenéi Voj* ... [...] *Voj* sólo *tenéi* la curpa. (Miró 1999b, p. 230)[13]

The fact that Panamanian *voseo* comes to light in the *costumbrista* literature indicates that its use was popular, rural and informal (cf. Robe, 1950, p. 146). In addition, it only appears among people from the mid-western part of the country. This indicates that by the beginning of the 20th century its use was not national but had already been reduced geographically.

There remains a gap of almost four centuries where the way in which the process of change from the medieval paradigm to Panamanian *voseo* is not documented; thus, little is known about the geographical reduction that it suffered throughout these centuries.[14] It is clear, however, that *voseo* had to be displaced by the slow, but sure interference and propagation of *tuteo*, structurally affecting it and reducing its use to rural areas of the provinces of Veraguas, Coclé, Herrera, and Los Santos (Robe, 1950, pp. 146–148; Quilis and Graell, 1989, p. 177), as well as to the indigenous groups of the Comarca Ngäbe-Buglé (Quesada, 2019, p. 242) (see Map 12.1).

Referring to the two types of *voseo* in Spanish America, De Granda (1978) states that, during the Colonial period, there was a kind of competition between the diphthongized *voseo* (*-áis*, *-éis*), of a cultured, courtly character by people of the upper social class, and the monophthongized forms (*-ás*, *-és*),

---

13   A particular case of Panamanian *voseo* used in the plural is observed in a traditional song of the *Diablicos*, by a native of La Chorrera (middle of the country): "Ola, habitantes del infierno,/ Qué *hacéis* que no *te lleváis*/A esta Alma/A los profundos infiernos?" (Garay 1999 [1930]: 219). This could be due to the decline in the use of *vos* in La Chorrera, or taken from a tradition coming from the Colonial times.

14   M. Jamieson (1996) does not mention it, nor does he refer to the *ustedeo* during the Panamanian Colonial period.

predominantly used by the lower social classes (p. 468). However, a careful review of the existing documentation shows no samples of monophthongized *voseo*, neither during the Colonial period, nor in later centuries.

7   Coexistence of *Vos* and *Usted*

The fluctuation in the use of the pronouns *vos* (medieval type) and *usted* (formerly *Vuestra Merced*) is observed in the corpus since the beginning of the colonial era:

> Nombre de Dios, 1569 (a brother to a brother): Muy gran merced recibire *procure* de *se* aviar y venir, y *traiga* consigo a nuestro sobrino, que no *venga* sin el, si ser pudiere, porque ya estoy viejo, y deseo mucho *verlos* aca en esta tierra, porque yo no puedo ir por ahora a España. Y esto sea que *se venga* en los primeros navios que salieren para el Nombre de Dios, o para Cartagena o para esta Tierra Firme. [...] Y *mirad*, si le *debeis* alguna cosa, *pagadselo*, porque el señor Zuazo *os* dara todo lo que *hubieredes* menester, que asi quedo conmigo, y lo hara. El señor dean me dijo como *os* dio diez ducados, de que lo ha hecho muy mal conmigo en no *os* aviar y traer con el a estas partes. [...] *Decirle ha* que en los navios que aca quedaron le enviare el dinero de ella, y que le suplico yo sea parte para aviar a *v.m.* y a nuestro sobrino, que yo lo servire. Y *confiesense* como buenos cristianos antes que *entren* en la mar, y *acomodense* lo mejor que *pudieren* con el maestre del navio. (Otte, 1988, letter 305)

Around the same period, there are alternations in the three pronouns *vos*, *tú*, and *vuestra merced*, such as in a letter sent by a man to his nephew, written in Panama City in 1592:

> Y si *os* venis hasta aca con *vuestra* mujer e hijos, que *os* estoy aguardando por horas, que si ya pudiera *enviaros* lo poco que tengo, lo hiciera, pero soy *vuestro* tio, y no *os* puedo negar que *sois* mi sobrino, y tengo de acudir a *vuestras* necesidades. [...] Y no quiero que *entiendas* de mi otra cosa mas de esto. *Hazme* merced de dar mis besamanos a don Luis [...] *Su* tia *le* besa las manos, y *su* prima ni mas ni menos. *Adviertote* que estoy viudo, y que mi hija se ha muerto, y estoy solo. Por eso *mira* que no sea la tardanza mucho tiempo. (Otte, 1988, letter 294)

So far, no alternations of *vos*—*usted* have been found in the 17th century, but at the end of the 18th century we find a poem written by Antonio Castrellón

(1796), in which the second person plural verb form alternates[15] with those corresponding to the third plural (*ustedes*). The poem is addressed to the inhabitants of Santiago de Veraguas, in the mid-western part of the country:

> Santiagueños ya *habéis visto*
> erradas las profecías.
> ¿*Esperábais* al Mesías? [...]
> *Ustedes* en un escollo
> *han dado* con su paisano [...]
> pero en un continuo embrollo
> *los* trae todos los días, [...]
> pero *ustedes*, a porfías,
> nunca *estuvieron* contentos,
> antes bien, siempre violentos,
> *esperaban* al Mesías [...]
> *Tenedle*, pues, voluntad
> Y en su servicio *andad* listos [...]
> ¿No *queríais* redentor?
> in MIRÓ, 1985, pp. 14–15

The same alternation is observed in the *costumbrista* literature of the early 20th century; for example, in a conversation between an older woman and her husband:

> – ¿Jumo? ... El jumo no ej na. Jumo a ejtáo bebiendo dej' que me junté con *voj*. No ej er jumo, no. Ej er ardor. A mo' que juera leña e balo.
> – ¿Balo?—refunfuña el Abuelo—. Ni que juera yo tan pendejo. Matillo mejmo ej y una poquita e nance. Er pereque ej que ya *Ud. ta* muy vieja y *tiene* pereza e sacarla. (in Miró, 1999b, p. 223)

Samples of *ustedeo* are also observed in the *costumbrista* literature of the first half of the 20th century:

> – No *se apelote*, niña ... *Baile* y *escobille* bajito, que esta noche tenemo que estrujasno el alma a tiestos ... Y es que ese marío *suyo* no vale ni un viaje de agua en tulo.
> – *Devore* ese pensamiento, Cirilo.

---

15   The pronominal form is not attested in the poem, so it is not known whether it is *vos* or *vosotros*.

– En *su* bien *encontrará su* mal, niña Panchita. Pero *déle* que me acalambro …
– No *esconda* la boca como puñalá e pícaro, Polita. (in Miró, 1999b, p. 169–170)

Ya mi Abuelo llega con su motete al hombro. Y me dice: —¿Ya *encontró* la vaina? […] —Perros —les grita el Abuelo a los animaluchos delgados que velan el almuerzo—. Luego me dice—: *Sepa Ud.*, que esta Octubrera se va a tirar la cosa. (in Miró, 1999b, p. 223)

These alternations over the centuries show that both *voseo* and *ustedeo* have coexisted in Panamanian informal speech, at least until the middle of last century.[16]

8 Propagation of *tú*

The first manifestations of *tuteo* in Panamanian Spanish date from the beginning of the Conquest and are linked to addressing the following recipients:

a)   deities:

Darién, 1519: ¡Oh, Madre de Dios! *amansa* á la mar, é *háznos* dignos de estar y andar debaxo de *tu* amparo, debaxo del cual *te* plega descubramos estas mares é tierras de la mar del Sur, é convirtamos las gentes dellas á nuestra santa fee católica. (Pacheco et al., 1864, p. 550)

b)   family members of lower genealogical rank:

Panama City, 1573: Esta debe de ser la primera que *has* visto y recibido mia, y asimismo la primera vez que *entiendes* que *te* llamo hijo, pues desde que *naciste* nunca he visto que me *hayas* llamado padre. (Otte, 1988, letter 276)

(12) speakers of Spanish as a second language, such as Indigenous people and Afropanamanians, and vice versa:

---

16   The ALEP registers *ustedeo* zones in the border regions with Costa Rica and Colombia (see Map 12.2).

Quedaua tan corrido el marido de ver, que la yndezuela le negasse, que vuo alguno, que en tal lançe, se boluió a mi, y me dixo; Padre, esta es vna ingrata, *has* lo que ella dize, que *te* doy mi palabra. (an Indian to a priest, in De Ufeldre 1686 [1622], p. 36)

pobre sulia[17] traer mucha hambre coman indio cuando va a *tu* tierra no regalando nada. (an Indian to a mestizo, by Atencio 1891 [1787], p. 326)

Panama City, 1800: Y volviendo al negro le dijo: *Habla*. (AGI, Estado 51, No. 13; fo. 141)

In a poem written by Juan de Miramontes y Zuázola, at the beginning of the 17th century, the African King is addressed by *tú*: "*dime tú* ahora, Rey, si *tus* erarios ..." (Miró, 1999a, p. 42).

d) in the literature of the colonial period and up to the present day:

Canción, aunque cansado de *tu* acento,
te negase Neptuno su elemento,
embárcate en el llanto que *te* baña,
que bien *podrás* por mar llegar a España. (de Ribera, 1985 [1637], p. 77)

Busca, alma, a *tu* esposo amado
sigue a *tu* Jesús divino [...]
síguelo por esta parte
donde *te* llaman sus voces
y por si no los *conoces*
quiero yo sus señas *darte*. (Cayetano de Torres (1719–1780), in Miró, 1985, p. 12)

¡*Quédate* así! Con *tu* cabeza lánguida
apoyada en *tu* mano de jazmín,
no *dejes* nunca esa actitud romántica;
no *te muevas*, mi bien ... ¡*quédate* así!
  Poem from 1857, in MIRÓ 1999a, p. 100

All these uses of *tú* have a common denominator during the Panamanian Colonial period: the interlocutor is *in absentia* (prayers, fiction), or is in the process of learning Spanish (children, Indians, blacks), from which a new paradigm of psycho-ethnolectal kind is shown (Table 12.4).

---

17   *Sulia* 'person of Spanish origin', in Guaymí tongue.

TABLE 12.4 Psycho-ethnolectal level of addressing (Panama, colonial times)

Native speakers of Spanish	People learning Spanish
Vuestra merced (señoría ~ excelencia) *Vos*	*tú*

Alonso Criado de Castilla (1607, p. 61) gives the following linguistic panorama of Panama City: "En la ciudad no hay indios, los españoles hablan la lengua castellana. Los negros entre sí, los de cada tierra la suya; también hablan castellano, pero muy mal, sino son los que dellos son criollos." Thus, if *tú* was used towards those considered inferior, it would be very likely that the Spaniards would address them by *tú*.

Castillo (1982, p. 636), observing the frequency of masters using *tú* when addressing their slaves in Bogotá at the beginning of the 17th century, wonders: "¿Sería *tú* el pronombre más empleado por los esclavos para tratar a sus amos al ver que estos siempre lo usaban para dirigirse a ellos?" Most probably it was so, and the same must have happened in colonial Panama City, as was the case in other regions during the Caribbean colonial period.[18] Besides, the fact that *tú* was spread instead of *vos* among slaves—including *congo* speech—[19] is in my opinion a sign of social and linguistic integration of this group into normative urban colonial Spanish (Sessarego 2018), contrary to the surrounding *voseo* regions, and even to the isolated case in Colombia, where *vos* > *bo* is the regular second person pronoun in Palenquero Creole (Patiño, 1998, 87).

The African presence in Panama dates from the early years of the Conquest, and continued to increase throughout the 16th century (Fortune, 1960, p. 122). By 1575, there were 5,600 blacks but only 800 whites (Mena, 1984, pp. 90–91); that is to say, 12.5% of whites compared to 87.5% of blacks. By 1610, the population is estimated at 4,801 inhabitants, 3,500 of whom (72.9%) were black (Mena, 1984, p. 35). If the black population was addressed with *tú*, the use of *tuteo* in Panama during the Colonial period must have been very frequent (Figure 12.1).

---

18 Gutiérrez (2013, pp. 79, 232–233) observed blacks addressed by *tú* in documents from Santo Domingo and Cartagena (Colombia) in the 17th century. However, he does not go beyond this observation. In his work from 2014 (pp. 463–465), he does not bring anything new to this issue.

19 "Also absent in *congo* speech is the 2nd person singular subject pronoun *vos*, found in other Hispanic and Portuguese creole dialects, despite the fact that most of rural Panama is characterized by a still vigorous *voseo*" (Lipski, 1989, p. 21).

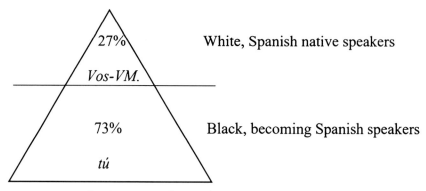

FIGURE 12.1   *Tú* vs. *Vos-VM* according to ethnic groups (Panama, 1610)

The Afro-descendant population was concentrated in the eastern part of the country, from Panama City through Portobelo to Darien; in the rest of the country, it was much smaller (De la Guardia, 1977, p. 7).[20] Robe (1950, p. 146) observed that the use of *voseo* was lower in the black population.[21] On the contrary, the areas with the largest white population are today those where *voseo* and *ustedeo* are best preserved (Arias et al., 2002, pp. 12–15).

Tuteo as a common form of address is widely attested in Panamanian *costumbrista* literature from the 19th century (Miró, 1999b), which suggests that its use had become popular, displacing *voseo* and *ustedeo* (Map 12.2).

The outcomes presented here are in line with Fontanella (1992), for whom the propagation of *tuteo* in Spanish America is a late phenomenon: "Resulta particularmente interesante el hecho de que la imposición del tuteo exclusivo es más reciente de lo que se creía hasta ahora y que en los siglos XVII y XVIII encontramos mezclas de voseo y tuteo en México y Perú." (p. 88). Thus, being a late phenomenon, *tuteo* did not get to spread to the whole country, as De Granda (1978, p. 470) believed.[22]

Summing up, two extra-linguistic factors that favored the spread of *tú* in Panama are (i) the overwhelming presence of the black and mulatto

---

20 According to Sánchez (2013, pp. 21–30), Afro-descendants had different roles in colonial Panamanian society: some worked in the city, others in the fields, others in the Darién mines, and others escaped, who formed their own communities.

21 Amado (1949, p. 376) shows a sample of *voseo* among Afro-descendants: "—Icotea Concha, *vení' a barré!*—No tengo mano', no tengo pie". Icotea Concha, *vení'a comé!*"

22 "Quiere ello decir que el *tuteo* sustituyó al *voseo* en las zonas siguientes: a) islas de las Antillas y Costa atlántica de Venezuela y Colombia junto con la totalidad de Panamá, áreas que experimentaban el influjo lingüístico ejercido por el tráfico marítimo con la Península en forma muy intensa" (de Granda, 1978, p. 470).

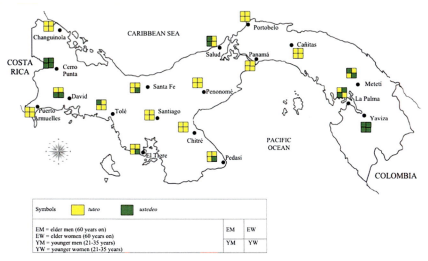

MAP 12.2   *Tuteo* and *ustedeo* in Panama (in present-day Panama)
Symmetrical level of confidence (couples, spouses, brothers, cousins, and friends)
Note: Source: Tinoco (2010; Morfosintaxis, Formas de tratamiento; maps 1, 2, 5, 6, 7, 15).

population, for which this was the unmarked pronoun; and (ii) Panama City's role as a commercial hub between Spain and the New World (cf. Mena, 2001). Initially, *tú* would have spread among the less wealthy classes, slaves and people who were learning Spanish, favored later by their integration and ascent into Panamanian society in the 18th century (Mena, 2000, p. 152–153, 168). Besides, its expansion among *mestizos* and whites would have increased by the influence of linguistic fashions brought from Spain, where *tú* had already begun to be in use by wealthy classes in the 17th century (Moreno, 2003).

9   Final Remarks

Following the premises of the diffusion of linguistic change, previously seen, this study allows us to select three fundamental changes in the use of address forms in Panamanian Spanish throughout its history: changes in its structural, dialectal, and social dimensions.

Firstly, as in the rest of the Spanish-speaking world, *vuestra merced* evolved to *usted*, which in Panama is documented at the end of the 18th century. Furthermore, as in the rest of Spanish America, *voseo* is a hybridized paradigm (*vos* together with forms from *tuteo*), with the particularity that Panama—as eastern Cuba, César (Colombia), Zulia (Venezuela) and Chile—reserved the

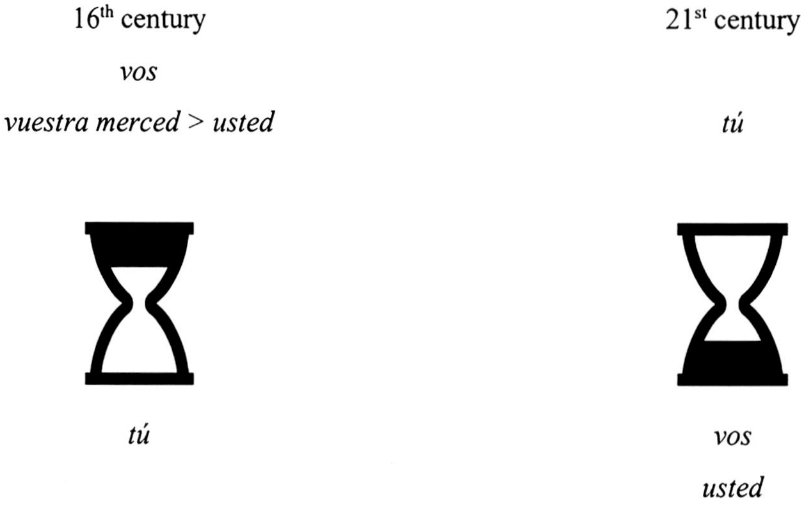

16th century   21st century

vos

vuestra merced > *usted*   *tú*

⧗   ⧗

tú   *vos*

                                       usted

FIGURE 12.2   Pronominal inversion in Panamanian Spanish (confidence level)

diphthongized verb forms (*-áis*, *-éis*) (De Granda, 1978, p. 470). Secondly, *voseo*, which at least during the Colonial period was used throughout Panama, reduced its radius of action to the central-eastern region (Veraguas, Los Santos, Herrera and some parts of Chiriquí), while *ustedeo* was restricted to national border areas.

Regarding the social dimension, *tuteo* began in large urban centers, particularly in Panama City, displacing *voseo* and *ustedeo* to the rural areas.[23] Besides, in the 18th century, the increase and integration of *mestizos* and blacks (Jaén, 1977) might have likely led to an increase in *tuteo* in areas with a high Afro-American population the middle of the country (Panama City, Colón, Portobelo and surroundings).

The evolution in the system of forms of address in Panamanian Spanish at the level of confidence can be compared to an hourglass. As Figure 12.2 illustrates, at the beginning (16th century) the sand represented by *vos* and *vuestra merced* ~ *usted* was in the upper position, but from the 19th century onwards the roles are reversed, and the sand is this time in the lower position. As the use of *tú* spread, *voseo* and *ustedeo* declined.

This goes hand in hand with Croft (2000, p. 178), for whom "The propagation of a linguistic variant is a selection process: one variant is selected over another one." The propagation of *tú* is due to a reorganization in the pronominal system of forms of address on three levels: functional, social, and commercial. Since

---

23   According to Amado (1949, p. 366), "Durante el siglo XVII en el istmo prepondera lingüísticamente la capital."

the beginning of the colonial period *vos* and *usted* were loaded with functions which ranged from formal situations to informal family communication. Thus, *tú* assumed the functions of *vos* and *usted* on the confidence level, leaving only *usted* to indicate distance. On the social plane, *tú* was used by speakers in the lower social class, such as those of indigenous, African or Creole origin, being addressed with *tú*. Thus, the propagation and consolidation of this pronoun (in some parts of the country) was favored by the growth, proliferation, and social rise of these groups. Besides, the strategic position of Panama as a center of commerce in the New World, importing fashions that came from Spain, boosted the spread of *tú* to the areas of major contact with the Peninsula.

The spread of *tú* throughout the country is a process not yet completed, and reduction in the use of *ustedeo* and *voseo* continues. However, there is some hope that it will remain alive because of positive attitudinal change—at least towards *voseo*—in recent decades (Quesada, 2019, pp. 239–240), which could favor its survival to a certain degree.

References

Academia Mexicana de la Lengua; Asociación de Academias de la Lengua Española. *Corpus Diacrónico y Diatópico del Español de América (CORDIAM)*. http://www.cordiam.org.

Aikhenvald, A. & Dixon, R. (2001). *Areal diffusion and genetic inheritance: problems in comparative linguistics*. Oxford University Press.

Amado, M. (1949). El lenguaje en Panamá. *Boletín de la Academia Argentina de Letras 18*, 339–388.

Archivo General de Indias. *Cartas y expedientes del presidente, oidores y fiscal de la Audiencia de Panamá*. ES. 41091. AGI/24//PANAMA, 19. Retrieved April 6, 2023, from http://pares.mcu.es/ParesBusquedas20/catalogo/description/381020.

Archivo General de Indias. *Cartas y expedientes del presidente, oidores y fiscal de la Audiencia de Panamá*. ES. 41091. AGI/24. Retrieved April 6, 2023, from http://pares.mcu.es/ParesBusquedas20/catalogo/description/380233.

Archivo General de Indias. Estado, 51, N. 9. Retrieved April 6, 2023, from http://pares.mcu.es/ParesBusquedas20/catalogo/show/65333.

Archivo General de Indias. Estado, 51, N.6. Retrieved April 6, 2023, from https://www.archivesportaleurope.net/es/ead-display/-/ead/pl/aicode/ES-41091-AGI10/type/fa/id/ES-41091-AGI-UD-1928215/unitid/ES-41091-AGI-UD-1928215+-+ES-41091-AGI-UD-65328/search/o/panamá.

Archivo General de Indias. Estado 55, N. 13. Retrieved April 6, 2023, from http://pares.mcu.es/ParesBusquedas20/catalogo/show/65337.

Archivo General de Indias. Lima, 1440, N. 3. Retrieved April 6, 2023, from http://pares.mcu.es/ParesBusquedas20/catalogo/show/7253686.

Archivo General de Simancas. *Secretaría de Estado y del Despacho de Guerra. Nueva Granada. Tropa e Incidencias.* SGU, LEG, 7061, 23. Retrieved April 6, 2023, from https://www.archivesportaleurope.net/es/ead-display/-/ead/pl/aicode/ES-47161-AGS2/type/fa/id/ES-47161-AGS-UD-117100/unitid/ES-47161-AGS-UD-117100+-+ES-47161-AGS-UD-1299646/search/o/panamá.

Arias, T., Castro, E., Ruiz, E., Barrantes, Ramiro & Jorge-Nebert, L. (2002). La mezcla racial de la población panameña. *Revista Médica de Panamá 27* (1), 5–17.

Atencio, M. (1891 [1787]). Exploración de las playas de la costa norte de la antigua provincia de Veragua. In A. Cuervo (Ed.). *Colección de documentos inéditos sobre la geografía y la historia de Colombia.* Vol. I (pp. 308–327). Zalamea Hermanos.

Bertolotti, Virginia (2015). *'A mí de vos no me trata ni usted ni nadie'. Sistemas e historia de las formas de tratamiento en la lengua española en América.* México D.F.: Universidad Nacional Autónoma de México / Montevideo: Universidad de la República.

Bravo, E. (1990). Fórmulas de tratamiento americanas y andaluzas en el S. XVI. *Philologia Hispalensis V* (I), 173–193.

Bravo, E. (2002–2004). Tratamientos y cortesía en la correspondencia familiar Indiana del siglo XVIII,. In R. M.ª Castañer & J. M.ª Enguita (Eds.). *In memoriam Manuel Alvar* (pp. 249–264). Institución Fernando el Católico.

Castillo Mathiew, N. (1982). Testimonios del uso de "vuestra merced", "vos" y "tú" en América (1500–1650), *Thesaurus XXXVII* (3), 602–644.

Codita, V. (2020a). La documentación de archivo y la historia del español panameño. *Scriptum digital 9,* 237–251.

Codita, V. (2020b). Aproximación al español de Panamá en el siglo XVIII. In M. Fernández Alcaide, and E. Bravo-García (Eds.). *El español de América: morfosintaxis histórica y variación* (pp. 411–434). Tirant lo Blanch.

Criado de Castilla, A. (1607). Descripción de Panamá. In P. de Valencia (Ed.). *Descripción de las Indias.* Vol I (pp. 53–82). Retrieved April 6, 2023, from http://bdh.bne.es/bnesearch/detalle/bdh0000023116.

Croft, W. (2000). *Explaining language change: an evolutionary approach.* Longman.

De Granda, G. (1978). Las formas verbales diptongadas en el voseo hispanoamericano. Una interpretación sociohistórica de datos dialectales. *Nueva Revista de Filología Hispánica 27,* 80–92.

De la Guardia, R. (1977). *Los negros del Istmo de Panamá.* INAC.

De Ribera, Mateo (1638/1985). Poema 1. *Revista Lotería 346–347,* 75–77.

De Ufeldre, A. (1682). Conquista de la provincia del Guaymí, por el venerable Padre Maestro Fr. Adrián de Ufeldre, en el Reino de Tierra Firme. In J. Meléndez (Ed.).

Tesoros verdaderos de las Yndias en la historia de la gran provincia de San Juan Bautista del Perú. Vol. III. (pp. 1–56). Nicolas Angel Tinassio Press. (Original work published 1622).

Fernández Alcaide, M. (2009). *Cartas de particulares en Indias del siglo XVI. Edición y estudio discursivo*. Iberoamericana.

Fernández Martín, E. (2012). *La oposición vosotros/ustedes en la historia del español peninsular (1700–1931)*. [Doctoral dissertation, University of Granada].

Fontanella de Weinberg, M. B. (1970). La evolución de los pronombres de tratamiento en el español bonaerense. *Thesaurus* 25, 12–22.

Fontanella de Weinberg, M. B. (1992). *El español de América*. Editorial MAPFRE.

Fontanella de Weinberg, M. B. (1999). Sistemas pronominales de tratamiento usados en el mundo hispánico. In I. Bosque & V. Demonte (Eds.). *Gramática descriptiva de la lengua española*, vol. 1 (pp. 1399–1425). Espasa-Calpe/RAE.

Fortune, A. (1961). Los orígenes africanos del negro panameño y su composición étnica en el siglo XVII. *Revista Lotería 56*, 113–128.

François, A. (2014). Trees, waves and linkages. Models of language diversification. In B. Claire & E. Bethwyn (Eds.). *The Routledge Handbook of Historical Linguistics* (pp. 161–189). Routledge.

Garay, N. (1999). *Tradiciones y cantares de Panamá. Ensayo folclórico*. Autoridad del Canal. http://bdigital.binal.ac.pa/binal/iframes/cldetalle.php?id=187&from=l. (Original work published 1930).

Gutiérrez, M. (2013). *Pronombres personales sujeto en el español del Caribe. Variación e historia*. [Doctoral dissertation, Universidad de Valladolid].

Gutiérrez, M. (2014). "Pronombres de segunda persona en español del Caribe en torno a 1700". In V. Álvarez et al. (Eds.). *Dándole cuerda al reloj: ampliando perspectivas en lingüística histórica de la lengua española* (pp. 461–482). Tirant.

Hernández Campoy, J. M. (1999). *Geolingüística. Modelos de interpretación geográfica para lingüistas*. Servicio de Publicaciones de la Universidad de Murcia.

Hummel, M. (2010). "Reflexiones metodológicas y teóricas sobre el estudio de las formas de tratamiento en el mundo hispanohablante, a partir de una investigación en Santiago de Chile." In M. Hummel et al. (Eds.). *Formas y fórmulas de tratamiento en el mundo hispánico* (pp. 103–162). El Colegio de México / Karl-Franzens-Universität Graz.

Jaén Suárez, O. (1977). La formación de estructuras económicas y sociales en el Istmo de Panamá: El siglo XVIII colonial (1740–1850). *Revista Tareas 39*, 61–74.

Jamieson, M. (1996). Noticias preliminares sobre el español de la ciudad de Panamá (Siglos XVI a XVIII). *Revista Cultural Lotería 405*, 67–83.

Josse, A. L. (1824 [1799]). *Nouvelle Grammaire Espagnole raisonnée*. Rougeron.

Kany, Ch. (1969). *Sintaxis hispanoamericana*. Gredos.

Lipski, J. (1989). *The speech of the negros congos of Panama*. John Benjamins.

Mena, C. (2000). Religión, etnia y sociedad: cofradías de negros en el Panamá colonial. *Anuario de Estudios Americanos* LVII, 1, 137–169.

Mena, C. (2001). Transportes y comunicaciones en América. Panamá, 'la llave' del Nuevo Mundo. In T. Sánchez-Terán & A. Vaca Lorenzo (Eds.). *La formación del espacio histórico: Transportes y Comunicaciones* (pp. 241–256). Universidad de Salamanca.

Mena, C. (2013). Más allá de la historia oficial. Escritura doméstica y claves secretas en las cartas de los conquistadores del Nuevo Mundo. *Caravelle* [En ligne], 101. https://doi.org/10.4000/caravelle.672.

Miró, R. (1985). Sobre poesía panameña en la Colonia. A propósito del Llanto de Panamá. *Revista Lotería* 346–347, 5–15.

Miró, R. (1999a). *Itinerario de la poesía en Panamá*. Autoridad del Canal.

Miró, R. (1999b). *El cuento en Panamá, estudio, selección, bibliografía*. Autoridad del Canal.

Moreno M. (2010). "Identidad social a través del trataiento a lo largo de la historia del español: propuestas metodológicas." In M. Hummel et al. (Eds.). *Formas y fórmulas de tratamiento en el mundo hispánico* (pp. 80–100). El Colegio de México / Karl-Franzens-Universität Graz.

Moreno, M. (2003). El uso del pronombre *tú* en la España contemporánea: ¿Extensión de un nuevo uso o continuación de una tendencia iniciada en el Siglo de Oro? *Pronombres de segunda persona y formas de tratamiento en las lenguas de Europa. Coloquio de París*. Retrieved April 6, 2023, from https://cvc.cervantes.es/lengua/coloquio_paris/default.htm.

Nocentini, A. (2004). *L'Europa linguistica. Profilo storico e tipologico*. Le Monnier Università.

Otte, E. (1988). *Cartas privadas de emigrantes a Indias, 1540–1616*. Consejería de Cultura.

Pacheco, J.; Cárdenas, F., & Torres, J. (1864). *Colección de documentos inéditos sacados del Archivo de Indias*. Vol. 11. Imprenta Española.

Patiño, C. (1998). Relaciones de contacto del criollo palenquero de Colombia. *Forma y Función* 11, 77–101.

Petyt, K. M. (1980). *The Study of Dialect. An Introduction to Dialectology*. Westview Press.

Quesada Pacheco, M. A. (1988). Uso de las formas de tratamiento en cartas privadas escritas en América en el siglo XVI. *Revista de Filología y Lingüística de la Universidad de Costa Rica* XIV (2), 123–128.

Quesada Pacheco, M. A. (2002). *El español de América*. Editorial del Instituto Tecnológico de Costa Rica.

Quesada Pacheco, M. A. (2019). El voseo panameño: su situación actual y actitudes ante su uso. *Revista de Filología y Lingüística de la Universidad de Costa Rica* 45 (1), 227–245.

Quesada Pacheco, M. A., & Tinoco Rodríguez, T. (2013). Aspectos morfosintácticos del español en Panamá. In M. A. Quesada Pacheco (Ed.). *El español de América Central: nivel* morfosintáctico (341–378). Iberoamericana.

Quilis, A. & Graell Stanziola, M. (1989). El *voseo* en Panamá. *Revista de Filología Española* LXIX (1/2), 173–178.

Rey, M. (2005). *El uso de tú, usted y sumercé como fórmulas de tratamiento en Funza, Cundinamarca.* Instituto Caro y Cuervo.

Robe, S. (1950). The use of *vos* in Panamanian Spanish. *Romance Studies* XII, 145–149.

Robe, S. (1953). Algunos aspectos históricos del habla panameña. *Nueva Revista de Filología Hispánica* VII, 209–220.

Robe, S. (1960). *The Spanish of rural Panama.* University of California Press.

Rószavári, N. (2015). El uso de *vos* y sus formas verbales en obras del Siglo de Oro. *Colindancias* 6, 263–275.

Sáez Rivera, D. (2006). *Vuestra merced > usted: nuevos datos y perspectivas. Actas del* VI *Congreso Internacional de Historia de la Lengua Española* (*Madrid, 29/9/03–4/10/03*), 2899–2912.

Sánchez Fuentes, P. (2013). *Presencia africana en el habla del panameño: estudio sociolinguístico del negro colonial.* INAC.

Sessarego, S. (2018). "On the importance of legal history to Afro-Hispanic linguistics and creole studies." *Lingua* 202, 13–23.

Soler Batista, R. (1988). *El pensamiento político en los siglos* XIX *y* XX. Universidad de Panamá.

Stangl, Werner (2012). *Zwischen Authentizität und Fiktion. Die private Korrespondenz spanischer Emigranten aus Amerika, 1492–1824.* Böhlau Verlag.

Teixeira, F. J. A, & Leal, K. A. (2017). Las formas de tratamiento en el español panameño: la vigencia del "ustedeo". *Travessias Interativas 14* (7), 426–434.

Tejada, P. (2001). El cambio lingüístico. In I. de la Cruz Cabanillas & F. J. Martín Arista (Eds.). *Lingüística Histórica Inglesa* (pp. 1–43). Ariel.

Tinoco Rodríguez, T. (2010). *Atlas lingüístico etnográfico de Panamá. Niveles morfosintáctico y léxico.* Editorial de la Universidad de Panamá.

Wolfram, W. & Schilling-Estes, N. (2003). Dialectology and linguistic diffusion. In J. Brian & R. Janda (Eds.). *The handbook of historical linguistics* (pp. 713–735). Blackwell.

CHAPTER 13

Corner-Store Service Encounters in Nicaraguan Spanish in a Rural Setting

Jeff Michno, Evan Colby Myers and Will Przedpelski

1   Introduction

Nicaragua has been described as the most linguistically understudied region in Central America (Lipski, 2008). While a handful of recent efforts have contributed to descriptions of Nicaraguan Spanish phonetics/phonology (Chappell, 2013, 2014, 2020) and morphosyntax (Christiansen, 2014; Christiansen & Chavarría Úbeda, 2010), studies of pragmatics (i.e., language use in context) and pragmatic variation in the region are still lacking (e.g., Félix-Brasdefer, 2021; Félix-Brasdefer & Placencia, 2020).

Elsewhere in the Spanish-speaking world, studies of pragmatic variation have illuminated similarities and differences across languages (cross-linguistic variation) and among varieties of the same language (intra-linguistic variation). Much of this research has focused on speech acts such as requests, apologies, compliments, compliment responses, greetings, and leave-takings. The body of work has uncovered certain tendencies across Spanish varieties, for example, the use of direct requests, while also revealing important differences, including the varied functions of conversational openings and closings. The value of identifying pragmatic norms and variation, both within and across languages, is amplified in situations of linguistic or cultural contact. When speakers from different linguistic and/or cultural backgrounds come together in a joint interaction, their expectations, and therefore, their perceptions, regarding appropriate behavior (i.e., pragmatic norms) may differ. Such misalignment can result in confusion about participant intentions (e.g., the illocutionary force of their utterances) as well as misunderstandings regarding their orientations to politeness (Mugford & Félix-Brasdefer, 2021; Schneider & Placencia, 2017).

The present study contributes to our knowledge of pragmatic norms and variation in the Spanish-speaking world by analyzing naturally-occurring service encounters in Nicaraguan Spanish. It provides a preliminary description of Nicaraguan Spanish pragmatics while focusing on the speech acts of greetings, requests, and leave-takings; the organization of talk; and the use and functions of relational talk. The study embraces the view of service encounters as "joint actions that are co-constructed and negotiated according to the sociocultural norms dictated by the members of specific communities of practice" (Félix-Brasdefer, 2015, p. 3).

In the following section, we discuss the background literature on pragmatic variation, giving special attention to the Spanish-speaking world and service-encounter contexts. After providing a brief summary of Nicaraguan Spanish, we present the study's four principal research questions. To contextualize the study, we describe the research site, the surrounding community, the participants, and the procedures used to collect and analyze data. We share and discuss our results concurrently to facilitate engagement with the literature at each level of analysis. Finally, we conclude by highlighting the study's main findings, its limitations, and future avenues of research.

2   Background

2.1   *Analyzing Pragmatic Variation*

Pragmatics is broadly understood as the study of language use and meaning in context. Variational pragmatics seeks to identify how language used in interaction varies according to both macro-social and micro-social factors (Schneider & Barron, 2008; Schneider, 2010, 2020). Macro-social factors concern individuals and consist of five social elements: "region, social class, gender, ethnicity, and age," while micro-social factors include "power, distance, and other situational factors" (Barron & Schneider, 2009, pp. 426–427). As Barron and Schneider (2009) point out, these factors not only affect linguistic features traditionally considered in variational linguistics (i.e., those tied to phonetics, phonology, morphology, syntax, and the lexicon) but also pragmatic features. The way sociolinguistic *factors* affect pragmatic *features* of language use is the central object of variational pragmatics. The framework offers five levels of pragmatic analysis: the formal, actional, interactional, topic, and organizational levels. The formal level focuses on linguistic forms, such as discourse markers, hedges, and upgraders, and their discourse functions. The actional level analyzes the strategies speakers use to carry out speech acts, such as requests. The interactional level, on the other hand, considers the sequential patterning of speech acts, for example, the interactional structure of conversational openings and closings. The topic level examines conversational content, considering which conversation topics are selected, and in what types of discourse, and how topic shifts proceed. Finally, the organizational level addresses turn-taking elements, such as overlap, pauses, interruptions, and backchanneling (Schneider & Barron, 2008, pp. 20–21).

Pragmatic variation can be analyzed at both interlingual and intralingual levels. Interlingual analysis examines variation across languages, whereas intralingual analysis explores variation between varieties of the same language. Variational pragmatics orients towards intralingual analysis, promoting the investigation of regional variation in language use, including at the sub-national level.[1] A community-of-practice (Mills, 2003; Wenger, 1998) approach takes this contrastive analysis a step further by recognizing that, even within a regional, sub-national variety of a language, it is possible for distinct communities-of-practice to have different sociocultural expectations regarding what constitutes appropriate, or polite, behavior (e.g., Mugford & Félix-Brasdefer, 2021; Schneider & Placencia, 2017). Consequently, just as studies might compare the varieties of Spanish spoken in the cities of Managua and Matagalpa, Nicaragua, they can also consider how language use might vary at two different corner stores in Managua.

Given the contrastive nature of variational pragmatics research, it is helpful to control for certain elements across studies to increase comparability. For this paper, the service encounter genre serves that purpose. We define service encounters as situations in which participants interact with a specific transactional purpose, with one actor seeking goods or service and the other providing it (Agar, 1985). As a result of their transactional nature, service encounters tend to have a structural consistency across communities of practice. For example, service encounters typically include a request for some type of service or product and an exchange sequence involving payment of some sort. Of course, service encounters do not have entirely preset rules and can vary according to both individual and situational factors. Thus, service encounters are understood to have a semi-institutional character (Kerbrat-Orecchioni & Traverso, 2008). This character strengthens the ability of pragmatic variation scholars to make comparisons between communities and observe differences within communities according to social variables such as gender, age, and familiarity.

To analyze pragmatic variation in service encounters, Félix-Brasdefer (2015) employs a framework with eight levels of analysis. Those relevant to this paper include the actional, interactional, stylistic, and organizational

---

1 Within the variational pragmatics framework, region is considered a social factor alongside age, gender, social class, and ethnicity, mirroring trends in sociolinguistics research that depart from traditional studies of dialectology.

TABLE 13.1 Framework for analyzing pragmatic variation during service encounters adapted from Félix-Brasdefer (2015, pp. 44–46)

Level of analysis	Features of focus
Actional	"Strategies used in speech acts"
Interactional	"Openings, closings, and request-response sequences" through the lens of "speech act sequences"
Stylistic	Notions of "frame and footing" to examine shifts from business talk to phatic (relational) talk and "the choice of forms of address used to open, close, and negotiate a business transaction"
Organizational	"Aspects of turn-taking, overlap, interruption, silence, and preference organization"

levels. The actional, interactional, and organizational levels mirror three of the five identified in Schneider and Barron's (2008) variational pragmatics framework, while the stylistic level, first considered in the context of service encounters by Placencia (2005, 2008), is influenced by the stylistic domain of Spencer-Oatey's (2000) rapport management framework. Table 13.1 provides a summary of the main conversational features analyzed at each level, as described by Félix-Brasdefer (2015).

2.2 *Pragmatic Variation in the Hispanic World*

Research on pragmatic variation during service encounters has shown differences between national varieties of Spanish (Barron & Schneider, 2009; Márquez Reiter & Placencia, 2004), as well as within national varieties (Placencia, 2008; Félix-Brasdefer, 2015). Together, this work has enabled comparative analysis across communities and has enhanced our understanding of how different sociocultural contexts affect discourse.

At the actional level, request types have been analyzed in terms of linguistic form and directness. Table 13.2 displays seven commonly-studied request types. The least direct request type is an indirect request, for example: *puedo tener ...* 'can I have ...'. This is followed by an implicit request, which is typically non-verbal. Next come assertions, such as *me das ...* '[you] give me...', and direct questions, like *¿Cigarillos tenés?* 'Do you have cigarettes?' Want statements include an expression of desire (e.g., *yo quiero ...* 'I want ...'), while ellipticals involve simply stating the desired product (e.g., *un jugo* 'a juice'). Finally, the most direct request form is a command or imperative (e.g., *dame ...* 'give me ...').

TABLE 13.2   Request types with examples

Request type	Example
Indirect	*Puedo tener ...*
Implicit	Non-verbal (lays product down)
Assertion	*Me das ...*
Direct question	*¿Cigarillos tenés?*
Want	*Yo quiero*
Elliptical	*Un jugo*
Command	*Dame ...*

Previous studies have found that Spanish-speakers broadly tend to use more direct request types such as ellipticals and commands across dialects (Félix-Brasdefer, 2015; Félix-Brasdefer & Shively, 2021; Félix-Brasdefer & Yates, 2020; Placencia, 2008; Yates, 2015).[2] As Félix-Brasdefer (2012) points out in the context of Southern Mexico market transactions, it is possible that "direct requests for service do not reflect a lack of politeness" but rather "the appropriate way of expressing a request" (p. 39). However, past research also presents notable differences. Félix-Brasdefer (2015) and Placencia (2008), for example, both find that imperative requests (i.e., commands) predominated in Mexican and Ecuadorian cases respectively. Yates' (2015) study in Buenos Aires, however, found ellipticals to be most common and commands to be relatively rare, representing the request type in only two of 97 interactions (p. 140). Previous studies have also examined the way gender affects request type. For example, Félix-Brasdefer (2015) and Yates (2015) both found that males were more likely to use elliptical requests in Mexican and Argentinian stores respectively. Differences did emerge with respect to assertions, however, with Félix-Brasdefer (2015) finding them to be more common among female customers and Yates (2015) finding similar frequencies across genders.

At the interactional level, similarities across studies have been harder to come by. With respect to openings and closings, for example, studies have shown substantial variation. Placencia (2008) identifies different patterns in openings and closings between varieties of Spanish within Ecuador, noting

---

2   While this pattern in terms of directness may emerge at the level of request type, variation in the use of internal and external modification of requests has also been identified (e.g., Placencia, 2008). Such mitigation may impact the perceived directness and appropriateness of the speech act.

that opening and closing sequences "tend to be rather elaborate for Quiteños ... and swift for Manteños" (p. 18). Yates' (2015) findings in Buenos Aires mirror the swift, transaction-oriented openings and informal closings that Placencia (2008) found in Manta. Félix-Brasdefer (2015), on the other hand, observed that, regardless of gender, 96% of sales transactions at an open-air market in southern Mexico began without a greeting. The same study also found that 65.3% of all "terminal exchanges included a closing expression," though it did not examine this statistic in relation to gender (Félix-Brasdefer, 2015, p. 153). Together, the variation across studies suggests that the significance of openings and closings is not the same in all communities of practice, perhaps due in part to macrosocial, microsocial, and situational factors.

At the stylistic level, researchers principally examine how participants use forms of address and shift between business (transactional) and relational talk during an interaction. The present study focuses primarily on relational talk, understood here to encompass phatic and other social talk (i.e., small talk; Holmes, 2000), including individualized social talk, collectively described as rapport-building talk in the context of service encounters by Placencia and Mancera Rueda (2011). The present study also identifies techniques used by the shopkeeper that serve both stylistic and organizational functions.[3] Previous studies of transactional and relational talk have demonstrated differences between varieties of Spanish. Placencia's (2005) analysis of phatic talk in Quito, Ecuador and Madrid, Spain revealed more "ritualistic behavior" with a "person focus" in Quito and "shorter, less ritualistic" behavior and more "task-orientedness" in Madrid (pp. 584–596). The author offers several potential explanations for this disparity, including the slower "pace of life" in Quito as well as Quiteños' "overall greater attention to the interpersonal dimension" and "preference for personalized service in encounters in which they are involved on a regular basis" (p. 596).

Finally, at the organizational level, Placencia (2008) offers insight into questions of the participatory domain such as overlap and turn-taking. In both Quito and Manta, Placencia (2008) observed that "shopkeepers were not infrequently found to serve more than one customer at the time" (p. 21). Tannen (2006) suggests that "embracing overlap as a show of enthusiasm and interest" reflects a "'high involvement' style" and "the need to be connected" (p. 354). This stands in contrast to "avoiding overlap" which "honors the need not to be imposed on" and is thus associated with a "'high-considerateness' style" (Tannen, 2006, p. 354). The current study examines a corner store where

---

3 See Michno (2020) for a detailed analysis of forms of address used in Nicaraguan service encounters.

simultaneous or overlapping service encounter interactions were common and often contained conversational overlap as well. The analysis contributes to contemporary research by examining techniques that shopkeepers can employ to negotiate dealing with multiple customers at once.

2.3 Nicaraguan Spanish

Nicaragua has been described as the most linguistically understudied Central American nation (Lipski, 2008). Nonetheless, efforts to document the Nicaraguan Spanish lexicon date as far back as Castellón (1939) and include a more recent collection of scholarly essays edited by Arellano (1992). Descriptions of Nicaraguan Spanish phonetics and phonology, on the other hand, begin with Lacayo (1954) and continue through Ycaza Tigerino (1980) and (Lipski 1984, 1994). Lipski (1994, 2008) provides a relatively contemporary overview of the variety across linguistic sub-disciplines. More recent efforts have focused primarily on phonetic features (e.g., Chappell, 2013, 2014) and morphosyntactic features (e.g., Christensen, 2014; Christiansen & Chavarría Úbeda, 2010). Data sources, however, are often limited to the highly-populated central cities of Managua and Granada. Some scholars have begun to examine Nicaraguan Spanish in contact with other varieties and languages (e.g., Chappell, 2020, and Critchfield, this volume, with Miskitu-Spanish bilinguals in Bilwi, Nicaragua; and López-Alonzo, 2016, with Nicaraguan Spanish speakers in Miami, Florida).

Notably absent from the historical trajectory of research on Nicaraguan Spanish is an account of pragmatic norms and variation, although recent work has begun to uncover the pragmatic functions of intonation in absolute questions (Chappell, 2014) and reported speech (Michno, 2021). Additionally, Michno (2020) and Koike and Michno (2020) have examined language use in service encounter contexts to reveal pragmatic variation in forms of address and to document interactive norms in an understudied rural community. This work aligns with new efforts to understand the pragmatic functions of language in other Central American Spanish varieties (e.g., Cabal-Jiménez, this volume, for Costa Rican Spanish). The present study contributes to this emerging body of work by incorporating new levels of analysis of naturally-occurring speech. Crucially, it continues to expand the analysis of Nicaraguan Spanish to understudied linguistic subfields, regions, and populations of speakers.

2.4 Research Questions

The present study contributes new knowledge of pragmatic variation in Nicaraguan Spanish utilizing Félix-Brasdefer's (2015) approach to analyzing service encounters. The following research questions correspond to four of the author's eight analytical levels: the actional, interactional, stylistic, and organizational.

1. What request types are used, and with what frequency, by speakers in this community of practice during service encounters?
2. What is the typical sequence of speech acts during a service encounter? How do openings and closings function within this community of practice?
3. How do speakers integrate phatic (relational) talk and business (transactional) talk during the course of a service encounter? How do they index interpersonal relationships?
4. How does turn-taking function? Is there overlap between interlocutors, and what mechanisms does the shopkeeper use to manage both individual and simultaneous interactions?

3 Methodology

3.1 *Research Site*

This research was carried out in Southwestern Nicaragua in a rural coastal community in the municipality of Tola, Department of Rivas.[4] Historically known as a fertile agricultural zone, the region has nonetheless faced high rates of poverty, with 31.6% of residents living in extreme poverty, and another 41.2%, in moderate poverty,[5] and has had limited access to formal education.[6] Since the late 1990s, however, growth in tourism and coastal property development has increased access to employment and education and led to opportunities for economic and social mobility. The Tola mayor's office highlighted outside

---

[4] According to 2006 Nicaraguan census data, 87% of Tola's estimated 22,012 residents lived in rural communities. This study focuses on a rural area with 2,197 residents, 679 of them in the immediate vicinity of the store where data were collected (Nicaragua, INIDE, 2008). Official estimates list 23,376 residents of Tola in 2015, showing some overall growth (Nicaragua, INIDE, 2014).

[5] Poverty status was assigned according to the *Necesidades Básicas Insatisfechas* 'Unsatisfied Basic Needs' index, calculated using five criteria: dwelling-size-to-occupant ratio, quality of dwelling construction materials, presence of drinking and wastewater utilities, education status of household minors, and a combination of head-of-household education level and occupant employment status (Nicaragua, INIDE, 2008).

[6] Many locals reported achieving a primary school education before leaving to assist their families in agricultural fields, mirroring findings by the Inter-American Development Bank that Nicaragua has the highest percentage among Latin American countries of children who are not enrolled in school, with only 50 percent completing primary school (Näslund-Hadley et al., 2012).

investment interest in the region's coastline in its 2006–2025 strategic development plan, identifying growth in surf and beach tourism as a key element of its strategy (Nicaragua, Alcaldía de Tola, Departamento de Rivas, 2006).

The steady influx of visitors and non-local workers to the region has resulted in regular linguistic and cultural contact between the formerly isolated locals and outsiders representing a variety of languages and dialects. Studies of naturally-occurring social interactions in the community stand to illuminate traditional interactional norms among long-time residents alongside emerging practices in cross-cultural and cross-linguistic interactions.

3.2   *Data Collection*

Data for this study were collected from a center of social interaction in the community: a small corner store at the town's main crossroads where locals frequently gathered throughout the day. Typical of the region and much of Latin America, the one-room convenience store occupied the street-front room of a local family's home and provided household goods such as food, alcohol, cigarettes, and prepaid phone cards. Interactions proceeded solely through a large open storefront window, which required that customers deliver requests for service to the vendor, a 26-year-old local man. The store owner granted permission to record service encounter interactions using a Marantz PMD620 solid-state audio recorder placed just inside the store window. The principal researcher also recorded detailed field notes from nearby to capture demographic attributes of the customers interacting with the vendor and other relevant contextual information.

Three hours of audio recordings yielded 81 analyzable interactions. Audio data were transcribed by the researchers and coded according to the relevant social and linguistic factors: customer age and gender; request type, opening, closing, phatic talk, and pronoun use. Customer age was estimated and placed into buckets: young, medium, and old.

3.3   *Data Analysis*

At the actional level, requests were analyzed according to type: indirect, implicit, assertion, direct question, want statement, elliptical, and command. At the interactional level, openings were coded as customer- or vendor-initiated and classified into one of the following categories: anticipation of customer request, phatic talk, request, or summons (i.e., call to service by the provider). Closings were labeled as customer- or vendor-initiated, as mutual or non-reciprocal, and as containing a thank-you statement or not. At the stylistic level, interactions were evaluated for the presence of relational talk and for the shopkeeper's use of first-person plural *nosotros* ('we') or the command 'wait for me': *espérame* in the *tú* form, *esperame* in the *vos* form. At the organizational level, interactions were coded for both conversational overlap and for overlapping service encounters among multiple customers.

Using the 81 recorded interactions, we performed elementary and complex data analysis to obtain our results. For many conclusions, especially those involving opening and closing frequency, simple calculations and percentages were enough to yield relevant information. For discovering more hidden relationships, such as correlations between illocutionary mechanisms and attributes like gender, we used Weka, an open source data mining tool with machine learning from the University of Waikato in New Zealand (Frank et al., 2016). Techniques employed include association learning (also known as market basket analysis), and various classification algorithms, though association produced the most noteworthy results.

4 Results & Discussion

4.1 Actional Level: Request Type

At the actional level, we examined the types of requests used by customers during 81 service encounter interactions. Because many of the interactions contained multiple requests, there were 126 requests in total. Figure 13.1 shows the overall distribution of the 126 request types.

Based on these data, the preferred request types in this community of practice are elliptical, followed by command, direct question, and assertion. The prevalence of the first two types falls in line with existing research in some other Spanish-speaking communities (e.g., Félix-Brasdefer, 2015: in Mexican markets; Placencia, 2005, 2008: in corner stores in Ecuador and Spain), although

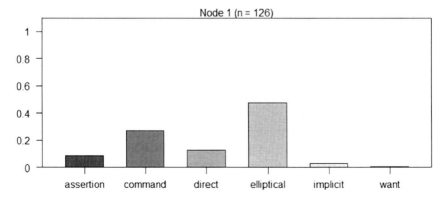

FIGURE 13.1 Distribution of all customer requests by type

the order of the two types is inconsistent across communities. The order differs from similar small shops in Mexico City and Guanajuato (Félix-Brasdefer, 2015), which showed a preference for assertions over ellipticals. These regional comparisons highlight the value of taking a community-of-practice approach to studying pragmatic variation in service encounters.

The relatively high use of direct questions in this data set, on par with assertions, contrasts with most existing accounts. We suggest that this reflects the co-constructed nature of service encounter interactions. This particular shopkeeper regularly interpreted a direct question—in the form of request for information (e.g., price or availability of an item)—as a request, immediately delivering the product to the customer. Consider the following example, in which the customer's direct question in line 1 (*¿Maicena tenés?* 'Do you have cornstarch?') is interpreted as a request by the vendor, as evidenced by his following turn in line 2 (*Sí, o sea, ocho córdobas te cuesta.* 'Yes, or rather, that costs you eight cordobas.') and the initiation of the payment sequence in lines 3 and 4, marked by the use of *entonces*.[7]

Excerpt 1: Shopkeeper (S) and one customer (C)

1   C: *¿Maicena tenés?*
         'Do you have cornstarch?'

2   S: *Sí, o sea, ocho córdobas te cuesta.*
         'Yes, or rather, that costs you eight cordobas.'

3   C: *Ya, ¿entonces?*
         'Ok, so?'

4   S: *Estaríamos hablando de ...* ⟨lists items and calculates total cost⟩
         'We would be talking about ...'

We interpret this behavior as a sales or transaction-oriented strategy, as it was often accompanied by the shopkeeper's description of comparable products, including occasional attempts to 'upsell' or encourage the purchase of a more expensive product. This practice reflects the dynamic nature of service encounter interactions; while the customer might have a particular transactional goal in mind when initiating a request for service (or information), service providers are free to make conversational moves to achieve their own transactional goals (i.e., to encourage the sale, to upsell, or to suggest additional purchases). Such

---

7   See Appendix for transcription conventions.

TABLE 13.3 Request types by customer gender during service encounters

	Customer gender					
Request type	Female		Male		Combined total	
Assertion	6	16%	5	6%	11	9%
Command	13	35%	21	24%	34	27%
Direct question	3	8%	13	15%	16	13%
Elliptical	15	41%	45	51%	60	48%
Implicit	0	0%	4	4%	4	3%
Want	0	0%	1	1%	1	1%
Total	37	100%	89	100%	126	100%

practices are common during service encounters and underscore the value of a turn-by-turn pragmatic-discursive analysis of service encounter data.

Table 13.3 shows a breakdown of the 126 requests according to request type and customer gender.

As shown in Table 13.3, elliptical requests were the most frequently employed request type among both female and male customers (15/37 or 41% and 45/89 or 51%, respectively), suggesting that it is a socioculturally-expected request variant in this context (Félix-Brasdefer, 2015; Shively, 2011). Command was the second-most-common type for both groups: 13/37 or 35% for females and 21/89 or 24% for males. From there the pattern diverges, with females opting for more assertions (6/37 or 16%), followed by direct questions (3/37 or 8%) and males, the opposite trend: 13/89 or 15% direct questions and 5/89 or 6% assertions. There appear to be differences according to customer gender in these data, in terms of percentage of request type used and the order of most-commonly used request types. However, given the relatively low number of female customers and the imbalance in number of requests per customer, we limit ourselves to a descriptive comparison and make no inferences beyond this group of participants. Nonetheless, the observed pattern motivates follow-up research into a potential gender effect for request type use in this community. As detailed in Michno (2020), there was an effect for gender on pronoun and vocative use during service encounters in this community of practice, including an effect on pronoun use in certain types of requests.[8]

---

[8] It is important to note that this analysis focuses on request types and does not consider the internal or external modification of requests. Such mitigation devices have been shown to vary from one Spanish variety to another (e.g., Placencia, 2008, at the sub-national level)

4.2 Interactional Level: Speech Act Sequence

4.2.1 Openings

Turning now to the sequential organization of service encounter interactions, we present the typical structure according to the following segments: opening, request, exchange (of product and money), and closing. Of the 81 interactions, 51 were initiated by some action on the part of the customer, and the remaining 30 by the shopkeeper. Each opening move fell into one of the following categories: anticipation of customer request, phatic talk, request, or summons (see Figure 13.2). Most commonly, the interaction opened with a request sequence initiated by the customer. To a much lesser extent, the customer opened with some type of phatic/relational talk (e.g., a greeting or small talk about the community). When the shopkeeper initiated verbal communication, it was typically in response to the customer's arrival at the shop window (i.e., the summons-response sequence) and overwhelmingly came in the form of *¿Qué quería?* or the truncated *¿Qué querí?* ('What would you like?'). On a few occasions, the shopkeeper opened by anticipating the customer's request, reflecting the regularity of his interactions with his customers. The classification of opening acts by shopkeeper and customer appears in Figure 13.2.

As displayed in Figure 13.2, greetings and other phatic/relational talk were rare in transactional openings with both female and male customers. In line with Félix-Brasdefer's (2015) observations in Mexican market interactions, we suggest that this reflects a speech community norm. Due to the frequent comings and goings of community members in front of the shop window and the

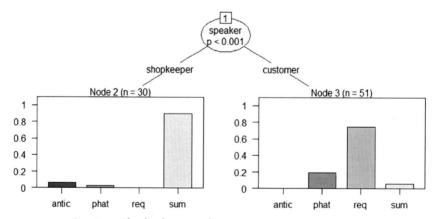

FIGURE 13.2 Opening act by shopkeeper and customer

even when the request types themselves may be similar. The present analysis, therefore, is limited in its ability to fully describe the community's interactional norms in terms of directness and associated perceptions of politeness or appropriate behavior.

high volume of (often simultaneous) service encounter transactions, greetings were not an expected part of the transaction sequence. Instead, vocative and pronoun use played a central role in maintaining and reinforcing social relationships, particularly during openings (see Michno, 2020). During lulls in service, however, passing greetings (see Pinto, 2008) and relational talk were a regular occurrence. The following interaction shows relational talk during an opening sequence that was more typical during slower-paced service encounters. In this case, the customer remained at the window to chat with the vendor while several other customers came and went.

Excerpt 2: Shopkeeper (S) and one customer (C)

1 C: *Buenas.*
       'Good afternoon.'

2 S: *Buenas.*
       'Good afternoon.'

3 C: *¿Cómo estamos?*
       'How are we doing?'

4 S: *Bien, ¿y vos? Aquí esperando el billetito, hermano.*
       'Good, and you? Here waiting to get paid, brother.'

5 C: *Es un gusto tuyo, ¿no?*
       'Lucky you, no?'

6 S: *Camino cansadito a veces.*
       'A tiring road sometimes.'

Such encounters suggest that pace of life in this community would be best analyzed at a micro-/situational level, taking into consideration factors such as time of day (e.g., during the commute to work), or number of simultaneous customers. This approach contrasts with a macro-level view that identifies more general trends, according to region, for example, such as Placencia's (2005) description of relatively slower-paced Quito, Ecuador in comparison to Madrid, Spain.

4.2.2   Closings

Service encounters within this community of practice tended to end without a closing beyond the exchange of product and payment. Closing frequency did

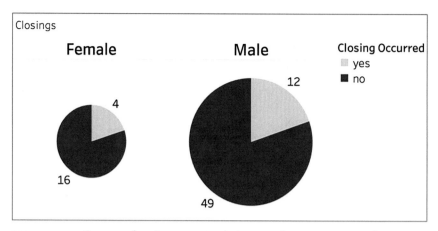

FIGURE 13.3   Presence of service encounter closing according to customer gender

not vary with respect to gender; both female and male customers used closings with a similar level of occurrence (4/20 and 12/61 respectively, or 20% of all interactions), as illustrated by Figure 13.3.

Out of the 16 closing sequences, seven were thank-yous, either customer- or vendor-initiated, and only three were mutual while the remaining were not reciprocated. The general absence of closings—in conjunction with the scarcity of thank-yous—seems to reflect a norm in this community of practice and may be considered appropriate or expected behavior. Similar to openings, the closing sequence patterns mirror findings by Placencia (2008) in the coastal community of Manta, Ecuador, and contrast sharply with the author's findings in Quito, Ecuador. Such sub-national contrasts underscore the importance of taking a local approach to pragmatic variation, which is particularly relevant in this increasingly touristic region. A visitor to this community of practice may not anticipate the lack of greetings or closings, which could lead to a clash in expectations (i.e., perceived politeness norms) between interlocutors and negatively impact in-/out-group relations.

The typically transaction-oriented sequence of acts in these service encounters is similar to those observed by Félix-Brasdefer (2015) in Mexico; Yates (2015) in Buenos Aires, Argentina; and Placencia (2005, 2008) in Madrid, Spain and Manta, Ecuador. Nonetheless, exchanges such as the one in Excerpt 2 illustrate the importance of the interpersonal dimension of service encounters in this close-knit community, as noted by Placencia (2005) among well-acquainted interactants in Quito, Ecuador. It appears that time and attention-related constraints primarily impact the presence of relational talk in this rural Nicaraguan community. This interpretation would account for the often-individualized relational talk woven into interactional sequences during times of low customer volume.

4.3 Stylistic & Organizational Levels: Service Encounter Management Mechanisms

In the following subsections, our analysis will focus on two speech practices employed by the shopkeeper that served primarily stylistic, but also organizational, functions: indexing relationships while simultaneously structuring transactions. This joint analysis facilitates discussion of the data and aligns with Barron and Schneider's (2009) call to interpret data holistically across analytical levels.

4.3.1 Espérame/Esperame Mechanism

The first salient pattern in the shopkeeper's speech directed to customers was the use of the Spanish command for 'wait for me': *espérame* in the *tú* form, *esperame* in the *vos* form.[9] In the present analysis, there is no distinction between the pronominal variants *vos* and *tú*; the "*espérame* mechanism" includes all uses of the command form of *esperar*.

Excerpt 3: Shopkeeper (S) and two customers (C1 & C2)

1	S to C1:	*Cuarenta y siete.*
		'Forty-seven.'
2	S to C1:	*Espérame.* ⟨Begins transaction with C2⟩
		'Wait for me.'
3	S to C2:	*¿Qué quería vos?*
		'What would you like?'
4	C2 to S:	*Dame ( ).*
		'Give me ( ).'

This interaction involves two customers (C1 and C2). While Customer 1 is preparing for the exchange, Customer 2 shows up at the shop window. Thus, as often occurred in this community of practice, the two interactions were overlapping. To manage this situation, the vendor tells Customer 1 to wait (*Espérame* 'Wait for me'), presumably until the transaction with Customer 2 is under way. Once he has time, the vendor returns his attention to Customer 1 to complete the exchange and acknowledge receipt of the money. Such use of command forms to manage service encounter transactions may demonstrate

---

9 Although not of central focus in this study, it is worth noting that pronoun use during service encounters can vary across customers and within a single interaction. See Michno (2020) for a detailed analysis of pronoun variation in this community.

one aspect of stylistic politeness norms (sociocultural expectations) within this community of practice—acknowledging a customer's presence with the understanding that the shopkeeper will eventually return his attention to the customer. As the *"espérame* mechanism" was observed regularly across multiple transactions without adverse response from customers, it may be that direct commands are considered an appropriate way of organizing the complexities of running a busy shop with interactions that regularly overlap. If so, this could also indicate a more general acceptance of commands as a polite (i.e., "appropriate"; Locher & Watts, 2005) way to interact with other members of the community in a "high involvement" culture (see, e.g., Tannen, 2006).

4.3.2 "Ambiguous We" Mechanism

Another recurrent pattern we observed across the service encounters was the shopkeeper's use of first-person plural *nosotros* ('we') when speaking to the customer, which we refer to as the "ambiguous we mechanism" or *nosotros* mechanism. See the following example, which also showcases the common practice of conversational overlap (indexed by brackets).

Excerpt 4: Shopkeeper (S) and two customers (C1 & C2)

| 1 | S: | *¿Qué quería* [( )?] |
| | | 'What would you like[( )?]' |

| 2 | C1: | [*Una*] *libra de pollo.* |
| | | '[A] pound of chicken.' |

| 3 | S: | *Una libra de pollo.* |
| | | 'A pound of chicken.' |

| 4 | S: | *Pound de chicken dice, one pound de chicken.* ⟨While retrieving product⟩ |
| | | 'Pound of chicken she says, one pound of chicken.' |

| 5 | C2: | *¿Coca dos litros, eh?* |
| | | '2-liter coke, eh?' |

| 6 | S to C2: | *Dos litros, sí.* |
| | | '2-liter, yes.' |

| 7 | S to C1: | *¿Y qué están comiendo ustedes?* |
| | | 'And what are you all eating?' |

| 8 | S to C1: | *Entonces tenemos cuarenta ... una libra de pollo, cien ... uno, dos, tres, cuatro. Y te* [*doy—*] |
| | | 'So we have forty ... a pound of chicken, one hundred ... one, two, three, four. And I [give you—]' |

| 9 | C1: | [*¿La*] *maseca? Y* ( ) |
| | | '[The] corn flour? And ( )' |

| 10 | S to C1: | *Esta es la maseca y te doy* [*el vuelto.*] |
| | | 'This is the flour and here is [the change.]' |

| 11 | C1: | [*¿Una bol*]*sa?* |
| | | ['A ba]g?' |

Excerpt 4 shows an example of the vendor's use of "ambiguous we". Again confronted with simultaneous interactions, in line 8, the shopkeeper addresses Customer 1 using a first-person plural form, though its pragmatic clusive function remains somewhat unclear. Generally, first-person plural has four possible levels of clusivity, which are separated into two categories: including or excluding the addressee. Since the comment in line 8 is directed towards Customer 1, this use of *nosotros* naturally includes Customer 1 to the potential exclusion of Customer 2. This suggests that the "ambiguous we" mechanism may serve an organizational purpose of managing simultaneous service encounters.

The levels of clusivity are further divided into two more categories: including or excluding the speaker. On one hand, the service encounter clearly involves both customer and shopkeeper, so we might say it includes the speaker. On the other hand, however, at the point the utterance is made in the service encounter (just before the exchange), the money does not yet belong to the shopkeeper. Thus, we might make the case that *nosotros* does not include the speaker. Regardless, because the clusivity of this mechanism is ambiguous, it functions well as a softening technique for the vendor to maintain face while informing the client of what they owe, serving a relational function (analyzed at the stylistic level).

From an organizational perspective, we might understand the word *entonces* to be a pragmatic technique to structure turn-taking. Given that an interaction can contain multiple requests (e.g., requesting a sandwich, then later asking for a drink), interlocutors may employ certain pragmatic techniques to coordinate movement from the request stage to the exchange sequence. A vendor may use indirect mechanisms to probe whether or not the customer is ready to complete the transaction. The use of *entonces* is likely a strategy to move the transaction along in this very manner; indeed, 'indicating progression' is considered one of the core functions of *entonces* (see, e.g., Travis, 2005). The shopkeeper's regular use of *entonces* in conjunction with *tenemos* (as in Excerpt 4, line 8), on the other hand, could serve a critical dual function: advancing the service encounter into the exchange sequence while also maintaining the relationship between the shopkeeper and customer. We know through ethnographic observations and personal relationships that members of this community of practice generally know each other very well and thus have relationships that require maintenance in one form or another. In certain sociocultural contexts, including many involving English, this may come in the form of a closing or a more elaborate opening involving phatic talk. For example, a comparative study from Vanyan (2017) concluded that English phatic talk that comes at the end of a conversation (i.e., a closing) typically has the purpose of setting the stage for interactions in the future. Analysis of these data, however, showed that neither closings nor phatic talk were particularly common, so we would expect relationship maintenance to appear in alternative forms. The use of *nosotros* could indicate an attempt on the part of the shopkeeper to identify with the customer, thus showing relational closeness during what is often the last significant moment in a transaction (the shift to exchange).

4.3.3 Frequency and Analysis of Mechanism Use

Overall, the shopkeeper used the *nosotros* mechanism in 21% of the interactions (17/81) and *espérame* in 15% of the encounters (12/81). Further analysis showed that, while accounting for the imbalance between male and female customers, the shopkeeper used both mechanisms disproportionately more with males; out of all interactions with female customers, he used *nosotros* only twice (2/17) and *espérame* once (1/12). An initial hypothesis suggested that the vendor might tend to use one or both of these mechanisms when the shop became busy. Coding for these details, "busy" or "overlapping" interactions occurred whenever there were multiple customers at the shop window simultaneously. The shop was considered busy in 51 interactions, and not busy during the remaining 30. When the shop was *not* busy, the shopkeeper only used these mechanisms twice each. Thus, nearly all instances occurred when the shop was busy, which suggests that the shopkeeper employs *nosotros* and *espérame* for reasons mostly relating to time and organizational considerations within the service encounter.

These findings suggest that in high-involvement cultures such as this one, wherein there is a high degree of interpersonal familiarity, relationship maintenance can take different forms depending on the individuals and the interactional and time constraints. While participants may not engage in much relational talk during busy times, they can index interpersonal relationships through other means. The shopkeeper was adept at weaving into the service encounters speech that served both relational and transactional functions. Through certain linguistic practices, such as the use of *espérame* 'wait for me' and ambiguous we (*entonces tenemos …* 'so we have …'), the shopkeeper was able to tend to relationships and minimize face-threat to his customers while also managing turn-taking and negotiating simultaneous interactions. This practice shows the dexterity of participants in successfully co-constructing service encounters and highlights the need for the analyst to consider whether a particular linguistic practice may serve multiple functions across theoretical levels of analysis (e.g., at the stylistic and organizational levels).

5 Conclusions

This study has revealed pragmatic norms during Nicaraguan Spanish service encounters by analyzing naturally-occurring interactions in an understudied rural vernacular. In doing so, it has filled a gap in our understanding of Nicaraguan Spanish while also enabling intra-linguistic and cross-linguistic comparison from a perspective of pragmatic variation. The study has uncovered linguistic and interactional norms in Nicaraguan Spanish that align with some other national and sub-national varieties of Spanish while diverging from others. In the specific context of this community, the findings have potential to raise the awareness of locals and non-locals alike regarding potential mismatches in their expectations during interactions. Future research would complement this study's findings by analyzing interactions with additional vendors and customers, representing a diversity of genders, ages, and other relevant social variables, in this and other Nicaraguan communities. Opportunity also exists to expand the analysis at the organizational level.

Acknowledgements

Author Michno dedicates this chapter to Dale Koike, his model of a thoughtful and caring mentor.

Appendix—Transcription Conventions

- [overlapping talk begins
-] overlapping talk ends
- ( ) unintelligible passage, according to its duration

... pause
- self-interruption; sound or word cut off
⟨ ⟩ transcriber notes, comments

References

Agar, M. (1985). Institutional discourse. *Text, 5*(3), 147–68.
Arellano, J. (1992). *El español de Nicaragua y palabras y modismos de la lengua castellana, según se habla en Nicaragua*. Instituto Nicaragüense de Cultura Hispánica.
Barron, A., & Schneider, K. (2009). Variational pragmatics: Studying the impact of social factors on language use in interaction. *Intercultural Pragmatics, 6*(4), 425–442.
Castellón H. A. (1939). *Diccionario de nicaraguanismos*. Managua: Talleres Nacionales.
Chappell, W. (2013). Intonational contours of Nicaraguan Granadino Spanish in absolute questions and their relationship with pragmatic meaning. In C. Howe, S. Blackwell, & M. Lubbers Quesada (Eds.), *Selected proceedings of the 15th Hispanic Linguistics Symposium* (pp. 119–139). Cascadilla Proceedings Project.
Chappell, W. (2014). Reanalysis and hypercorrection among extreme /s/ reducers. *University of Pennsylvania Working Papers in Linguistics, 20*(2), 5.
Chappell, W. (2020). Social contact and linguistic convergence: The reduction of intervocalic /d/ in Bilwi, Nicaragua. In Rajiv Rao (Ed.), *Spanish phonetics and phonology in contact: Studies from Africa, the Americas, and Spain* (pp. 83–102). John Benjamins. https://doi.org/10.1075/ihll.28.
Christiansen, A. (2014). "El 'vos' es el dialecto que inventamos nosotros, la forma correcta es el 'tú'". *Borealis–An International Journal of Hispanic Linguistics, 3*(2), pp. 259–297.
Christiansen, A., & Chavarría Úbeda, C. (2010). Entre el habla y la escritura: Un análisis de las formas de tratamiento en los anuncios comerciales en Managua, Nicaragua. *Revista Cátedra, 14*(1), pp. 61–74.
Félix-Brasdefer, J. C. (2012). Pragmatic variation by gender in market service encounters in Mexico. In J. C. Félix-Brasdefer & D. Koike (Eds.), *Pragmatic variation in first and second language contexts: Methodological issues* (pp. 17–48). John Benjamins.
Félix-Brasdefer, J. C. (2015). *The language of service encounters: A pragmatic-discursive approach*. Cambridge University Press.
Félix-Brasdefer, J. C. (2021). Pragmatic variation across varieties of Spanish. In D. A. Koike & J. C. Félix-Brasdefer (Eds.), *The Routledge handbook of Spanish pragmatics* (pp. 269–287). Routledge.
Félix-Brasdefer, J. C. & M. E. Placencia (Eds.). (2020). *Pragmatic variation in service encounter interactions across the Spanish-speaking world*. Routledge.
Félix-Brasdefer, J. C. & L Shively, R. L. (2021). *New directions in second language pragmatics*. De Gruyter Mouton.

Félix-Brasdefer, J. C. & Yates, A. (2020). Regional pragmatic variation in small shops in Mexico City, Buenos Aires, & Seville, Spain. In J. C. Félix-Brasdefer & M. E. Placencia (Eds.), *Pragmatic variation in service encounter interactions across the Spanish-speaking world* (pp. 15–34). Routledge.

Frank, E., Hall, M. A., & Witten, I. H. (2016). The WEKA Workbench. *Online appendix for data mining: Practical machine learning tools and techniques (4th edition)*. Morgan Kaufmann.

Holmes, J. (2000). Doing collegiality and keeping control at work: small talk in government departments. In J. Coupland (Ed.), *Small talk* (pp. 32–61). Pearson.

Kerbrat-Orecchioni, C., & Traverso, V. (2008). Presentation. In C. Kerbrat Orecchioni & V. Traverso (Eds.), *Les interactions en site commercial: Invariants et variations* [*Interactions in commercial setting: Invariants and variants*] (pp. 7–42). Ens Éditions.

Koike, D., & Michno, J. (2020). ¿Qué querí?: Shifting frames in Nicaraguan corner shop talk. *International Journal of the Linguistics Association of the Southwest 34*(1–2), 67–81.

Lacayo, H. (1954). Apuntes sobre la pronunciación del español de Nicaragua. *Hispania, 37*, 267–268.

Lipski, J. (1984). /s/ in the Spanish of Nicaragua. *Orbis, 33*, 171–181.

Lipski, J. (1994). *Latin American Spanish*. Longman.

Lipski, J. (2008). *Varieties of Spanish in the United States*. Georgetown University Press.

Locher, M. A., & Watts, R. J. (2005). Politeness theory and relational work. *Journal of Politeness Research, 1*(1), 9–33.

López Alonzo, K. (2016). Use and perception of the pronominal trio *vos, tú, usted* in a Nicaraguan community in Miami, Florida. In M. I. Moyna & S. Rivera-Mills (Eds.), *Forms of address in the Spanish of the Americas* (pp. 197–232). John Benjamins.

Márquez Reiter, R., & Placencia, M. E. (2004). Displaying closeness and respectful distance in Montevidean and Quiteño service encounters. In R. Márquez Reiter & M. E. Placencia (Eds.), *Current trends in the pragmatics of Spanish* (pp. 121–156). John Benjamins. https://doi.org/10.1075/pbns.123.13mar.

Michno, J. (2020). Variation according to gender in Nicaraguan corner store interactions. In J. C. Félix-Brasdefer & M. E. Placencia (Eds.), *Pragmatic variation in service encounter interactions across the Spanish-speaking world* (pp. 77–98). Routledge.

Michno, J. (2021). The functions of prosody in the reported speech of rural Southwestern Nicaraguans. *Semas: Revista de Lingüística Teórica y Aplicada, 2*(3), 45–67.

Mills, S. (2003). *Gender and politeness*. Cambridge University Press.

Mugford, G., & Félix-Brasdefer, J. C. (2021). Politeness research in the Spanish-speaking world. In D. Koike & J. C. Félix-Brasdefer (Eds.), *The Routledge handbook of Spanish pragmatics* (pp. 353–369). Routledge.

Näslund-Hadley, E., Meza, D., Arcia, G., Rápalo, R., & Rondón, C. (2012). *Educación en Nicaragua: Retos y oportunidades*. Inter-American Development Bank.

Nicaragua, Alcaldía de Tola, Departamento de Rivas. (2006). *Plan Estratégico de Desarrollo de Tola 2006–2025*.

Nicaragua Instituto Nacional de Información de Desarrollo (INIDE). (2008). *Tola en Cifras*.

Nicaragua Instituto Nacional de Información de Desarrollo (INIDE). (2014). *Anuario Estadístico 2014*.

Pinto, D. (2008). Passing greetings and interactional style: A cross-cultural study of American English and Peninsular Spanish. *Multilingua, 27*, 371–388.

Placencia, M. (2005). Pragmatic variation in corner store interactions in Quito and Madrid. *Hispania, 88*(3), 583–598.

Placencia, M. E. (2008). Requests in corner shop transactions in Ecuadorian Andean and Coastal Spanish. In K. P. Schneider & A. Barron (Eds.), *Variational pragmatics: A focus on regional varieties in pluricentric languages* (pp. 307–332). John Benjamins. doi:10.2307/20063161.

Placencia, M. E., & Mancera Rueda, A. (2011). *Vaya, ¡qué chungo!* Rapport-building talk in service encounters: the case of bars in Seville at breakfast time. In N. Lorenzo-Dus (Ed.), *Spanish at Work: Analyzing institutional discourse across the Spanish-speaking world* (pp. 192–207). Palgrave/Macmillan.

Schneider, K. (2010). Variational pragmatics. In M. Fried (Ed.), *Variation and change: Pragmatic perspectives* (pp. 239–267). John Benjamins.

Schneider, K. (2020). Rethinking pragmatic variation: The case of service encounters from a modified variational pragmatics perspective. In J. C. Félix-Brasdefer & M. E. Placencia (Eds.), *Pragmatic variation in service encounter interactions across the Spanish-speaking world* (pp. 251–264). Routledge.

Schneider, K., & Barron, A. (Eds.). (2008). *Variational pragmatics: A focus on regional varieties in pluricentric languages*. John Benjamins.

Schneider, K., & Placencia, M. E. (2017). (Im)politeness and regional variation. In J. Culpeper, M. Haugh, & D. Kádár (Eds.), *The Palgrave handbook of linguistic (im)politeness* (pp. 539–570). Palgrave Macmillan.

Shively, R. L. (2011). L2 pragmatic development in study abroad: A longitudinal study of Spanish service encounters. *Journal of Pragmatics, 43*(6), 1818–1835.

Spencer-Oatey, H. (2000). Rapport management: A framework for analysis. In H. Spencer-Oatey (Ed.), *Culturally speaking: Managing rapport through talk across cultures* (pp. 11–46). Continuum.

Tannen, D. (2006). Language and culture. In R. Fasold & J. C. Linton (Eds.), *An introduction to language and linguistics* (pp. 343–372). Cambridge University Press.

Travis, C. (2005). *Discourse markers in Colombian Spanish: A study in polysemy*. Mouton de Gruyter.

Vanyan, A. (2017). Small talk in English and Armenian. *Armenian Folia Anglistika, 13*(1–2 (17)), 59–68. https://doi.org/10.46991/AFA/2017.13.1-2.059.

Wenger, E. (1998). *Communities of practice*. Cambridge University Press.

Yates, A. B. (2015). Pragmatic variation in service encounters in Buenos Aires, Argentina. *IULC Working Papers, 15*(1), 128–158.

Ycaza Tigerino, J. C. (1980). *Situación y tendencias actuales del español en Nicaragua*. Academia Nicaragüense de la Lengua.

CHAPTER 14

Central American Spanish
An Upward Trajectory

John M. Lipski

1   Introduction

The editors of this volume kindly invited me to offer reflections on the finished product, and given that the first chapter begins with an early quote of mine, followed by a reference to Canfield's masterful *Spanish pronunciation in the Americas* (1981), a true confession is in order. When the possibility of conducting field research first came within my reach, shortly after the publication of Canfield's book, I naively consulted the book in search of the least-documented regional variety, and hit upon one country for which the well-traveled and experienced scholar could offer no data: Honduras. Taking advantage of low-cost flights from Houston (my location at the time) to Central America, thus began the forays into one of the linguistically most diverse areas of the Spanish-speaking world, eventually encompassing the entire region. The decision to start in Honduras turned out to be quite fortuitous, revealing a rich tapestry of microdialectal variation in the ruggedly mountainous country, replete with indigenous redoubts, isolated sociolinguistic enclaves, creole languages, and a permeable interface with North American English. Shortly thereafter, I had the opportunity to discuss these findings with Canfield himself, who in turn generously shared his ground-breaking Salvadoran data (Canfield, 1953, 1960) and his broad knowledge of Central American sociolinguistic history. This expertise informed his chronological classification of Latin American Spanish dialects, in which Central American varieties are among the most archaic, a status shared with the traditional Spanish of New Mexico (Canfield, 1981, p. 9).

During the same years I developed a friendship with Tim Hagerty, author of the first major study of Spanish in Belize (Hagerty, 1979). While previously living in Yucatan, I had met Spanish-speaking Belizeans, but the vitality and diversity of Spanish in Belize only came into focus upon listening to Hagerty's recordings. This eye-opening experience highlighted the need to extend the perimeter of Central American Spanish beyond the borders of the former Spanish colonies. The linguistic diversity of Panama, geographically part of Central America although historically part of the Caribbean/NW South American dialect cluster, became apparent to me as I began my research on

© JOHN M. LIPSKI, 2023 | DOI:10.1163/9789004679931_015

the Afro-Panamanian *Congo* language and culture (Lipski, 1985, 1990, 2011b). As successive decades of research—exemplified by the essays in the current volume—have shown, Central America, with Belize now happily included and Panama also added for good measure, is a superb living laboratory for virtually every branch of linguistics, as well as having an equally fascinating sociolinguistic history. Moreover, the massive and ongoing demographic shifts of the past decade, most spurred by failing economies and broken social structures, render any account of a Central American Spanish variety nothing more than a snapshot of a rapidly evolving dialectological landscape that requires constant updating.

2 (Why) Is Central American Spanish "Special"?

The small nations that form Central America exhibit a relatively large dialect diversity as compared to the geographical area, much of it roughly coinciding with national borders, none of which are based on naturally occurring boundaries. Many factors potentially have contributed to this diversification, almost all rooted in colonial and immediately post-colonial history. The nations that now form Central America were never major players in the Spanish colonial enterprise, since the easy mineral resources available in Mexico, Peru, and Bolivia were not to be found, and much of the terrain was mountainous and difficult to access. The Caribbean coast is covered by swamps and dense forests, inhospitable for European settlers, and lacks good natural harbors, and the Pacific coast was equally unpromising, with no rich interior areas to incentivize the founding of ports. Administratively part of the Capitanía General de Guatemala, which originally included the contemporary Mexican state of Chiapas, the capital was moved from Gracias a Dios (Honduras) to what is now Antigua (Guatemala), both remote inland locations that were not conducive to travel to the various outposts. The Capitanía General de Guatemala was in turn subordinate to the Viceroyalty of New Spain (Virreinato de Nueva España) whose capital was Mexico City, but the distance made hands-on administration all but impossible, and the Central American capitaincy general enjoyed de facto autonomy. Overland travel among the Central American colonies was difficult, and only the Pacific coast offered viable possibilities for sea voyages. A voyage from Guatemala to the southernmost colony, Costa Rica, would be most efficient via a maritime route, which may account for some of the phonetic similarities between Guatemalan and Costa Rican Spanish varieties that set them apart from the three central nations: assibilation of final /ɾ/, affrication of the cluster /tɾ/, retention of sibilant [s] in coda position. On the other hand, the uniformly weak posterior fricative /x/, weakening or elision of /j/ in contact with front vowels, and velarization of word-final /n/ are shared among the Central American varieties, and suggest some sociolinguistic continuity since this cluster of featurse was probably not predominant in the speech of colonists arriving from Spain.

A major source of the country-by-country dialect variation was the jealously monopolistic structure of the Spanish colonial enterprise, which forbade commercial transactions among the colonies instead of commerce directly with Spain. Although communication among the Central American colonies was not impeded, the dependence on Spain resulted in de facto city-states with little common cause. In the aftermath of the early 19th century independence movements in Spanish America, the Central American colonies as a block declared their independence from Spain in 1821, and after disputes with the newly independent Mexico, the Federal Republic of Central America was formed in 1823, with the individual ex-colonies known as Provincias Unidas de Centro America. The post colonial legacy of the divide and conquer approach resulted in considerable internal strife, wars, and secession attempts, and the union was formally dissolved in 1840. The remainder of the 19th century and the early 20th century saw several attempts to reestablish the union but none lasted more than a few months, and all created inter-country resentment that made further reunification attempts useless. Perhaps not coincidentally, one of the attempts involved the three nations that share the greatest amount of phonetic and lexical similarities: El Salvador, Honduras, and Nicaragua. These centrifugal political forces contributed to the retention of national dialect enclaves even when dialect homogenization was occurring in other countries.

A final contributor to Central American dialect diversification was the large number of local indigenous languages and the lack of any major precolonial language that could span the region. Unlike the expansion of Guaraní, Quechua, and Nahuatl by Spanish colonizers, who extended the range of these languages as lingua francas for more efficient administrative control, no such language was readily available in the ethnolinguistically rich Central American region. The Mayan empire had already collapsed, and although Guatemala was home to numerous Mayan languages, no single language predominated, and none extended far beyond the Guatemalan borders. Nahuatl words penetrated Pacific coastal regions as far south as Costa Rica as the result of trade with the Aztec empire, but only in El Salvador was a congenor language (Pipil) spoken natively. Other indigenous languages such as Lenca, Paya, Jicaque, were highly regionalized and were not spoken by hegemonic groups, and the Caribbean coast languages such as Miskito, Sumo, Cabécar, and Bribrí had scarce contact with Spanish settlers. Many local words derive from these indigenous languages, but Spanish was the common denominator throughout the colonial period.

3 (Why) Has Scholarship on Central American Spanish Lagged Behind?

Although relatively sparse and slow to take off, the scholarly trek of Central American Spanish research has followed much the same path as other Latin American dialect studies, in terms of both subject matter and the background and preparation of the authors, with many of the first major contributions coming from foreign scholars. Costa Rica has had the largest proportion of within-country linguistic scholarship, although in recent years there has been a heartening trend of linguistic research emerging from the other nations. No single reason accounts for these observations, but many possible contributing factors come to mind. During the first half of the 20th century, when the pioneering dialectological monographs such as those included in the Biblioteca de Dialectología Hispanoamericana (BDH) were being compiled, there were no university-centered linguistic research paradigms in any Central American nation, and the respective Academias de la Lengua Española devoted their attention exclusively to literature. The earliest dialect studies seized upon the low-hanging fruit: lists of vocabulary items rightly or wrongly regarded as regionalisms peculiar to the country in question, and prepared by authors with little or no training in lexicography. The first regional dictionaries tenaciously maintained the academies' insistence on defending the "purity" of the Spanish language by raging against *viciocismos* (e.g. Batres Jáuregui, 1892 and to a certain extent Sandoval, 1941–2 for Guatemala; Gagini, 1893 for Costa Rica; Membreño, 1895 for Honduras; Barreto, 1893 for Nicaragua; Salazar García, 1910 for Central American in general). As a consequence, the general tone of the dictionaries and lexicons produced in Central America from the late 19th century until the middle of the 20th century was one of criticism and implicit apology for harboring so many "improper" items and so many speakers who used them. The quintessentially Central American use of *vos* and the accompanying verbal paradigms were almost universally criticized, despite being present in every other Latin American nation except Puerto Rico and the Dominican Republic, while most of the other *vicios* are archaisms such as *truje, vide*, and *asina* or widely-used analogical creations such as final *-s* in 2nd person singular preterite forms (*hablastes, comistes*, etc.). As with most other regional studies of the time, the authors were largely unaware of variation across the Spanish-speaking world and often implicitly attributed exclusively to their own countries words found throughout Latin America and even Spain. While this nation-centric approach was also found in studies from other Latin American nations, the heavy criticism of demonstrably local usage was largely absent from works produced in larger nations.

The sociolinguistic self-deprecation that permeated Central American scholarship may underlie the fact that the first linguistic (i.e. not simply lexicographic) studies of Central American Spanish were written by scholars from elsewhere. The fourth volume of the BDH, published in 1938, published a translation of Lentzner's (1893) article on Guatemalan Spanish (Lentzner, 1938), and reprinted Cuervo's prologue to the expanded second edition of Gagini's diccionary of Costa Rican lexical items (Gagini, 1919), together with Gagini's introduction (Gagini & Cuervo, 1938). Neither Lentzner (German) nor Cuervo (Colombian) had evidently visited Central America, nor had the Dominican Pedro Henríquez Ureña (1938), who contributed a brief note on the colonial Nicaraguan dramatic sketch *El Güegüense o Macho Ratón*, which exhibits some evidence of contact with Náhuatl (also analyzed by Elliott, 1884).

It was not until the middle of the 20th century that linguistic descriptions produced by Central American authors with personal knowledge of the respective dialects began to appear, largely free from self-criticism and often incorporating atheoretical surveys of phonetics and phonology. Costa Rica, the most prosperous Central American (and having recently disbanded its army and devoted more resources for public benefit) led the group (e.g. Agüero Chaves, 1960, 1962, 1964; Chavarría-Aguilar, 1951; Costales Samaniego, 1962; Villegazs, 1965; Zamora Elizondo, 1945). Salvadoran Spanish was described by Geoffroy Rivas (1975, 1978) and González Rodas (1963), while Lacayo (1954, 1962) offered observations on Nicaraguan Spanish, and Valle (1943) commented on his Nicaraguan regional dictionary (Valle, 1948). Honduras and Guatemala remained under-studied, although research on Guatemalan indigenous languages was on the rise. For Panama, Aguilera Patiño (1947) is the first monograph to appear, followed much later by Alvarado de Ricord (1971). Cedeño Cenci (1960) criticized the Spanish of the creole English-speaking Bocas del Toro region of Panama, in contrast to the non-judgmental monograph by the North American Robe (1960). In view of its status as a nominally English-speaking nation, Belize was not yet included in research on Central American Spanish.

Until the final decades of the 20th century, research on Central American Spanish by scholars from within and outside of the region were largely anecdotal and opportunistic, with few authors having formal training in linguistics and with little empirical evidence to support their observations, however accurate they might be. The advent of empirical studies came with the study of phonetic variability in Central American Spanish dialects. Cedergren's (1973) dissertation on variable consonantal phenomena in Panamanian Spanish was one of the first corpus-based and potentially replicable studies, in this case introducing the scholarly community to logistic regression with the first iteration of the VARBRUL package. Berk-Seligson and Berk-Seligson and Seligson (1978) provide similar variationist data for Costa Rica, while Cowin (1978) describes the regional Costa Rican dialect of Guanacaste, without quantitative data but based on the analysis of a corpus of interviews. A number of other regionally-published studies appeared at the same time (Quesada, 1996 and Quesada Pacheco, 2008 provide many references), increasingly placing emphasis on data sets obtained through interviews and other systematic procedures.

In subsequent years, as exemplified by the studies in the present collection, research on Central American Spanish has rapidly overcome the slow start, and encompasses the full range of empirical investigation, including variationist approaches to segmental and suprasegmental phonetics and phonology, an increased emphasis on pragmatics, and some incursions into psycholinguistics (sentence processing). Recent collections edited by Quesada Pachecho (2010, 2013) are illustrative of the expanding research paradigm, as are the dialect atlases now available for all of Central America: Costa Rica (Quesada Pachecho, 2010); El Salvador (Azcúnaga López, 2018); Guatemela (Richards, 2003); Honduras (Hernández Torres, 2013a, 2013b); Nicaragua (Chavarría Úbeda & Rosales Solís, 2010; Rosales Solís, 2008); Panama (Cardona, 2012).

4 The Newest Frontier: Central Americans in the United States

Although small groups of Central Americans lived in the United States since the early 20th century (e.g. Hondurans in New Orleans), the massive arrival of Central Americans began in the 1980s, largely spurred by the violent political climate and civil wars, including paramilitary death squads, counterrevolutionaries, and national and international military interventions. Salvadorans, mostly from rural areas represented the largest single group, and settled in Houston, Los Angeles, and the Washington, D.C. area. Nicaraguans, many from urban middle-class backgrounds, arrived en masse in Miami and Los Angeles in the aftermath of the 1979 Sandinista revolution. By the end of the 20th century, gangs known as *maras* and formed in U.S. cities, had taken over many urban neighborhoods and rural regions of El Salvador and Honduras, resulting in another mass exodus of Central Americans that continues until the present time. El Salvador, Honduras, and Guatemala account for the majority of Central American arrivals, and the increasingly authoritarian actions by the current (neo-Sandinista) Nicaraguan government are resulting in another large migratory trend, including many working class and rural Nicaraguans. Almost none enter the country with legal immigration status, although quasi-stable Central American neighborhoods can be found in many cities. As a survival mechanism, Central Americans may attempt to "pass" as Mexican, under the assumption that given the large number of Mexicans and Mexican-Americans in the United States, they will attract less attention from immigration and law enforcement authorities. This cultural camouflage can stand in the way of research endeavors specifically focused on Central Americans, and represents a major hurdle to be overcome in field research.

Of the various Central American groups in the United States, Salvadorans have received the most attention from linguists, beginning during the first big wave of refugees in the 1980s (e.g. Lipski, 1986, 1989). Not surprisingly, much research on Central American Spanish in North America has focused on accommodation strategies as well as retention of ethnolinguistic identify markers in dialect contact environments (Lipski, 2000a, 2013, 2016). The quintessential Central America use of the second-person familiar pronoun *vos* and the accompanying verbal paradigms instead of *tú* among Mexican and Caribbean Spanish speakers is a key element that spans speech acts ranging from deliberate dialect masking to tenacious retention of emblematic ethnolinguistic identifiers. A number of studies have examined Central Americans' negotiation of the *vos* ~ *tú* divide (Barahona, 2020; Hernández, 2002; Lipski, 2016; Raymond, 2012a, 2012b, 2019; Rivera-Mills, 2000, 2002, 2011; Schreffler, 1994; Sorensen, 2013; Woods & Rivera-Mills, 2010, 2012; also Cortez, 2021; Villa, Shin, & Nagata, 2014; Villarreal, 2016). Less frequently examined are sociophonetic traits, such as aspiration of /s/ and velarization of final /n/ (Hernández & Maldonado, 2012; Lipski, 1986; Hoffman, 2004 for Toronto, Canada). Guatemalan varieties of Spanish have also made their way into the U.S. Spanish profile, and are examined by Clark (2017), Congosto Martín (2020), Ek (2009, 2010), González (2013), Lavadenz (2008), Montrul (2011), Schreffler (1994), and Villarreal (2016), among others. Bivin (2013), Estrada Andino (2016) and Stover (2016) examine aspects of Honduran Spanish in the United States, while López Alonzo (2016) focuses on Nicaraguan Spanish in the greater Miami area. The linguistic behaior of Belizean immigrants in the United States (e.g. Straughan, 2004) has yet to be examined.

5   To Be Continued …

The studies in the present volume attest to the vitality of Central American Spanish research and the excitement that accompanies the ever-widening scope of inquiry (see Baird et al., this volume). Among topics that deserve additional scrutiny, the syntax and semantics of *hasta* in Central America depart from the Spanish of most other regions, in referring to the inception of an event rather than the end: *La tienda abre hasta las ocho* means 'The store opens at 8:00', not 'The store is open until 8:00' (Bosque & Bravo, 2015; DeMello, 1992; Kany, 1944; Miyoshi, 2004; Rama, 2015; Salazar, 2022; Torres Santos, 2021). The use of non-deictic *vos* (and in Central America sometimes *usted*) in Central American Spanish, as in *Hace mucho calor, vos* 'Hey, it's really hot' has been noted as a discourse marker (Lipski, 2000b) and, in the United States setting, as an identity marker among Central Americans (Rivera Mills, 2002, 2011), but the syntactic structures underlying these combinations have not been fully elucidated. The same holds true for the Salvadoran/Guatemalan combination *un/una* + possessive, as in *Voy a echar una mi siesta* 'I'm going to take a nap' (Lipski, 2000b; Martin, 1985; Pato, 2018, 2020; Quesada, 2000).

Dialect contact is emerging as another relevant research area for Central American Spanish, not only in the United States (as surveyed in the preceding section), but also within Central America and Mexico. Major zones of dialect contact deserving of close examination include Nicaraguans in Costa Rica (Solano-Campos, 2019; Spencer, 2018; Thornton, 2016), Salvadorans in Belize (Collins, 1995; McElroy, 1986; Moberg, 1996; Woods, Perry, & Steagall, 1997), and Central Americans in Mexico, including refugees, immigrants, and migrants attempting to reach the United States (Casillas, 2008; Frank-Vitale, 2020; Gasca Gómez, 2016; Kauffer Michel, 2005; Peña Piña, Francisco Mateo, & López Méndez, 2020).

Taken together, the studies in the present volume as well as those that will inevitably follow point to a very bright future for research on Central American Spanish. Sadly, with the exception of Costa Rica, the triple threat of poverty, authoritarianism, and gang violence imperils the future for Central Americans themselves. In response, we can only hope that Mark Twain's putatively apocryphal "Rumors of my demise have been greatly exaggerated" comes to pass for the long-suffering Central American people.

References

Agüero Chaves, A. (1960). *El español en Costa Rica*. Universidad de Costa Rica.
Agüero Chaves, A. (1962). *El español de América y Costa Rica*. A. Lehmann.
Agüero Chaves, A. (1964). El español de Costa Rica y su atlas lingüístico. In *Presente y futuro de la lengua española* (t. I, pp. 135–152). Cultura Hispánica.
Aguilera Patiño, L. (1947). *El panameño visto a través de su lenguaje*. Ferguson y Ferguson.

Alvarado de Ricord, E. (1971). *El español de Panamá*. Universidad de Panamá.

Azcúnaga López, R. E. (2018). *Atlas lingüístico pluridimensional de El Salvador: nivel fonético*. San Salvador: SEDUCA.

Barahona, S. Y. M. (2020). The Usage of Voseo in Social Media: Hondurans and Salvadorans in the United States. *The Maksey Journal*, *1*(1), article 126.

Barreto, M. (1893). *Vicios de nuestro lenguaje*. Tipografía "J. Hernández."

Batres Jáuregui, A. (1892). *Vicios del lenguaje y provincialismos de Guatemala*. Encuadernación y Tipografía Nacional.

Berk-Seligson, S. (1978). *Phonological variation in a synchronic/diachronic sociolinguistic context: the case of Costa Rican Spanish*. [Doctoral dissertation, University of Arizona].

Berk-Seligson, S. & Seligson, M. (1978). The phonological correlates of social stratification in the Spanish of Costa Rica. *Lingua*, 46, 1–28.

Bivin, A. J. (2013). *"Mi mamá es cuatro pies": a study of the use of calques in Hondurans and Salvadorans in Southern Louisiana*. [Masters' thesis, Louisiana State University].

Bosque, I., & Bravo, A. (2015). Temporal prepositions and intervals in Spanish. Variation in the grammar of "hasta" and "desde". *Isogloss*, *1*, 1–31.

Canfield, D. L. (1951). Guatemalan *rr* and *s*: a recapitulation of Old Spanish sibilant gradation. *Florida State University Studies in Modern Languages and Literatures*, 3, 49–51.

Canfield, D. L. (1953). Andalucismos en la pronunciación salvadoreña. *Hispania*, 36, 32–33.

Canfield, D. L. (1960). Observaciones sobre el español salvadoreño. *Filología*, 6, 29–76.

Canfield, D. L. (1981). *Spanish pronunciation in the Americas*. University of Chicago Press. Cardona, M. (2012). Atlas lingüístico pluridimensional del español de Panamá (ALPEP) Nivel fonético. *Bergen Language and Linguistics Studies*, 2, 48–55.

Casillas, R. (2008). The routes of Central Americans through Mexico: characterization, principal agents y complexities. *Migración y Desarrollo*, *10*, 157–174.

Cedeño Cenci, D. (1960). *El idioma nacional y las causas de su degeneración en la provincia de Bocas del Toro*. Imprenta de la Academia.

Cedergren, H. (1973). *The interplay of social and linguistic factors in Panamanian Spanish*. [Doctoral dissertation, Cornell University].

Chavarría-Aguilar, O. (1951). The phonemes of Costa Rican Spanish. *Language*, 27, 248–253.

Chavarría Úbeda, C. & Rosales Solís, M. A. (2010). *Atlas lingüístico etnográfico de Nicaragua*. Bergen, Norway: Bergen University. Incxludes CD-ROM.

Clark, J. (2017). *Push and Pull: Formation of Guatemalan Expatriate Communities in the Greater Boston Area* [Doctoral dissertation, Harvard University].

Collins, C. O. (1995). Refugee resettlement in Belize. *Geographical Review*, 85, 20–30.

Congosto Martín, Y. (2020). Guatemalan Spanish in contact. Prosody and intonation. *Estudios de Fonética Experimental*, 29, 153–194.

Cortez, D. A. (2021). *Narrando con vos: Central American Transnational Narrative in the United States*. [Doctoral dissertation, Texas A&M University].

Costales Samaniego, A. (1962). *Diccionario de modismos y regionalismos centroamericanos*. Universidad de Costa Rica.

Cowin, S. (1978). *A descriptive phonological study of the Spanish of Liberia, in the province of Guanacaste, Costa Rica*. [Masters' thesis, Florida Atlantic University].

DeMello, G. (1992). 'Hasta' = 'no hasta'—'hasta no' = 'hasta' en el español hablado de once ciudades. *Anuario de Letras*, 30, 5–28.

Ek, L. D. (2009). "Alla en Guatemala": transnationalism, language, and identity of a Pentecostal Guatemalan-American young woman. *The High School Journal*, 92(4), 67–81.

Ek, L. D. (2010). Language and identity of immigrant Central American Pentecostal youth in Southern California. In N. Cantú & M. E. Fránquiz (eds.), *Inside the Latin@ Experience* (pp. 129–147). Palgrave Macmillan.

Elliott, A. M. (1884). The Nahuatl-Spanish dialect of Nicaragua. *The American Journal of Philology*, 5(1), 54–67.

Estrada Andino, M. (2016). *El Tú no es de Nosotros, es de otros Países: Usos del Voseo y Actitudes hacia Él en el Castellano Hondureño*. [Master's thesis, Louisiana State University].

Frank-Vitale, A. (2020). Stuck in motion: Inhabiting the space of transit in Central American migration. *The Journal of Latin American and Caribbean Anthropology*, 25(1), 67–83.

Gagini, C. (1893). *Diccionario de barbarismos y provincialismos de Costa Rica*. San José: Tipografía Nacional.

Gagini, C. (1919). *Diccionario de costarriqueñismos*. Imprenta Nacional.

Gagini, C. & Cuervo, R. J. (1938). El español en Costa Rica. *El español en Méjico, los Estados Unidos y la América Central* (Biblioteca de Dialectología Hispanoamericana IV) (pp. 235–276). Universidad de Buenos Aires.

Gasca Gómez, K. (2016). *Construcción del espacio de tránsito a partir de los trayectos de migrantes guatemaltecos, hondureños y salvadoreños por México en el 2014*. [Master's tesis] El Colegio de México.

Geoffroy Rivas, P. (1975). *El español que hablamos en El Salvador*. Ministerio de Educación.

Geoffroy Rivas, P. (1978). *La lengua salvadoreña*. San Salvador: Ministerio de Educación.

González, D. M. (2013). *Guatemalan-American Heritage Spanish Speakers linguistic identity development*. [Doctoral dissertation, New Mexico State University].

González Rodas, P. (1963). *Jaraguá, una novela salvadoreña: estudio fonológico*. Editorial Universitaria.

Hagerty, T. (1979). *A phonological analysis of the Spanish of Belize*. [Doctoral dissertation, University of California Los Angeles].

Henríquez Ureña, P. (1938). El hispano-náhuatl del *Güegüense*. *El español en Méjico, los Estados Unidos y la América Central* (Biblioteca de Dialectología Hispanoamericana IV, pp. 325–327). Universidad de Buenos Aires.

Hernández, J. E. (2002). Accommodation in a dialect contact situation. *Filología y Lingüística*, 28(2), 93–100.

Hernández, J. E., & Maldonado, R. A. (2012). Reducción de/s/final de sílaba entre transmigrantes salvadoreños en el sur de Texas. *Lengua y migración/Language and Migration*, 4(2), 43–67.

Hernández Torres, R. (2013a). *Atlas lingüístico pluridimensional de Honduras: nivel fonético*. Tegucigalpa: Editorial Universitaria, Ciudad Universitaria.

Hernández Torres, R. (2013b). *Atlas lingüístico pluridimensional de Honduras: nivel morfosintáctico*. Tegucigalpa: Editorial Universitaria, Ciudad Universitaria.

Hoffman, M. F. (2004). *Sounding Salvadorean: Phonological variables in the Spanish of Salvadorean youth in Toronto*. [Doctoral dissertation, University of Toronto].

Kany, C. E. (1944). American Spanish hasta without no. *Hispania*, 27(2), 155–159.

Kauffer Michel, E. F. (2005). De la frontera política a las fronteras étnicas: refugiados guatemaltecos en México. *Frontera norte*, 17(34), 7–36.

Lacayo, H. (1954). Apuntes sobre la pronunciación del español en Nicaragua. *Hispania*, 37, 267–268.

Lacayo, H. (1962). *Cómo pronuncian el español en Nicaragua*. Universidad Iberoamericana.

Lavadenz, M. (2008). Visibly Hidden: Language, Culture and Identity of Central Americans in Los Angeles. *Association of Mexican American Educators Journal*, 2(1), 16–26.

Lentzner, K. (1893). Observations on the Spanish language in Guatemala. *Modern Language Notes*, 8(2), 41–43.

Lentzner, K. (1938). Observaciones sobre el español de Guatemala. *El español en Méjico, los Estados Unidos y la América Central* (Biblioteca de Dialectología Hispanoamericana IV, pp. 227–34). Universidad de Buenos Aires.

Lipski, J. (1985). The speech of the *negros congos* of Panama: creole Spanish vestiges? *Hispanic Linguistics*, 2, 23–47.

Lipski, J. (1986). Central American Spanish in the United States: El Salvador. *Aztlán*, 17, 91–124.

Lipski, J. (1989). Salvadorans in the United States: patterns of sociolinguistic integration. *National Journal of Sociology*, 3(1), 97–119.

Lipski, J. (1990). *The speech of the Negros Congos of Panama*. John Benjamins.

Lipski, J. (2000a). The linguistic situation of Central Americans. In S. McKay, S-l C. Wong (eds.), *Language diversity: problem or resource?* (2nd Edition) (pp. 189–215). Cambridge University Press.

Lipski, J. (2000b). El español que se habla en El Salvador y su importancia para la dialectología hispanoamericana. *Científica* (Universidad Don Bosco, San Salvador), *1*(2), 65–88.

Lipski, J. (2008). *Varieties of Spanish in the United States*. Georgetown University Press.

Lipski, J. (2011a). English and Spanish in the United States: language and immigration. In *Word for word: the social, political and economic impact of English and Spanish in the world/Palabra por palabra: el impacto social, económico y político del español y del inglés* (pp. 245–255). Instituto Cervantes & British Council.

Lipski, J. (2011b). *El habla de los CONGOS de Panamá en el contexto de la lingüística afrohispánica*. Instituto Nacional de Cultura.

Lipski, J. (2013). Hacia una dialectología del español estadounidense. In D. Dumitrescu & G. Piña-Rosales (Eds.), *El español en Estados Unidos: ¿E pluribus unum? un enfoque multidisciplinario* (pp. 107–127). Academia Norteamericana de la Lengua Española.

Lipski, J. (2016). Dialectos del español de América: los Estados Unidos. In J. Gutiérrez-Rexach (ed.), *Enciclopedia de lingüística hispánica* (vol. 2, pp. 363–374). Routledge.

López Alonzo, K. (2016). Use and perception of the pronominal trio vos, tú, usted in a Nicaraguan community in Miami, Florida. In M. I. Moyna & S. Rivera-Mills (Eds.), *Forms of address in the Spanish of the Americas* (pp. 197–232). John Benjamins.

Martin, L. (1985). Una mi tacita de café: the indefinite article in Guatemalan Spanish. *Hispania, 68*, 383–387.

McElroy, C. S. (1986). *The El Salvadoran refugee move to Belize: A geographic study of refugee migration*. [Master's thesis, Texas A&M University].

Membreño, A. (1895). *Hondureñismos*. Tipografía Nacional.

Miyoshi, J. (2004). Sobre el uso peculiar americano de HASTA. *Anuario de Letras. Lingüística y Filología, 42*, 161–179.

Moberg, M. (1996). Transnational labor and refugee enclaves in a Central American banana industry. *Human Organization, 55*(4), 425–435.

Montrul, S. A. (2011). First language retention and attrition in an adult Guatemalan adoptee. *Language, Interaction and Acquisition, 2*(2), 276–311.

Pato, E. (2018). Indefinite article + possessive + noun in Spanish: A case of refunctionalization?. *Languages, 3*(4), 44.

Pato, E. (2020). Posesivos pleonásticos, redundancia y énfasis: de nuevo sobre la construcción una mi amiga en las variedades mexicano-centroamericanas. *Moderna Språk, 114*(3), 141–160.

Peña Piña, J., Francisco Mateo, J. L., & López Méndez, Y. C. (2020). Migración forzada y refugiados guatemaltecos en México: Relaciones transfronterizas e interculturalidad. *Punto Cunorte* (11 Julio–Diciembre), 104–128.

Predmore, R. (1945). Pronunciación de varias consonantes en el español de Guatemala. *Revista de Filología Hispánica, 7*, 277–80.

Quesada, D. J. (2000). On Language Contact: Another Look at Spanish-speaking (Central) America. *Hispanic Research Journal, 1*(3), 229–242.

Quesada, J. D. (1996). A Glance at Studies on Central American Colloquial Spanish. *Hispanic Journal, 17*, 235–257.

Quesada Pacheco, M. Á. (2008). El español de América Central ayer, hoy y mañana. *Boletín de Filología, 43*(1), 145–174.

Quesada Pacheco, M. A. (2010). *Atlas lingüístico-etnográfico de Costa Rica*. San José, Costa RIca: Editorial UCR. Includes CD-ROM.Quesada Pacheco, M. A. (Ed.). (2010). *El español hablado en América Central: nivel fonético*. Frankfurt & Madrid: Vervuert.

Quesada Pacheco, M. A. (Ed.). (2013). *El español hablado en América Central: nivel morfosintáctico*. Frankfurt & Madrid: Vervuert.

Rama, P. R. (2015). Intensividad y preposiciones de trayectoria: la sintaxis dialectal de hasta y desde. *Revista Española de Lingüística, 45*(2), 95–114.

Raymond, C. W. (2012a). Reallocation of pronouns through contact: In-the-moment identity construction amongst Southern California Salvadorans. *Journal of Sociolinguistics, 16*(5), 669–690.

Raymond, C. W. (2012b). Generational divisions: Dialect divergence in a Los Angeles-Salvadoran household. *Hispanic Research Journal, 13*(4), 297–316.

Raymond, C. W. (2019). Negotiating language on the radio in Los Angeles. In *The Routledge handbook of Spanish in the global city* (pp. 406–425). Routledge.

Richards, M. (2003). *Atlas lingüístico de Guatemala*. Guatemala: Editorial Serviprensa. Includes CD-ROM.

Rivera-Mills, S. (2000). *New perspectives on current sociolinguistic knowledge with regard to language use, proficiency, and attitudes among Hispanics in the U.S.: the case of a rural Northern California community*. E. Mellen Press.

Rivera-Mills, S. V. (2002, April 19). *The use of voseo as an identity marker among second and third generations Salvadorans* [Conference Presentation]. XIX Congreso internacional del español en los Estados Unidos, San Juan, Puerto Rico.

Rivera-Mills, S. V. (2011). Use of voseo and Latino identity: an intergenerational study of Hondurans and Salvadorans in the western Region of the US. In L. Ortiz López (ed.), *Selected proceedings of the 13th Hispanic linguistics symposium* (pp. 94–106). Cascadilla Proceedings Project.

Robe, S. (1960). *The Spanish of rural Panama*. University of California Press.

Rosales Solís, M. A. (2008). *Atlas lingüístico de Nicaragua: nivel fonético (análisis geolingüístico pluridimensional)*. Managua: Academia Nicaragüense de la Lengua.

Salazar, L. D. C. C. (2022). Aspecto en dos preposiciones: El caso de hacia y hasta. *Normas, 12*(1), 152–168.

Salazar García, S. (1910). *Diccionario de provincialismos y barbarismos centro-americanos, y ejercicios de ortología clásica* (2nd edition). Tipografía "La Unión".

Schreffler, S. B. (1994). Second-Person Singular Pronoun Options in the Speech of Salvadorans in Houston, TX. *Southwest Journal of Linguistics, 13*, 101–19.

Sandoval, L. (1941–2). *Semántica guatemalense*. Tipografía Nacional.

Solano-Campos, A. (2019). The Nicaraguan Diaspora in Costa Rica: Schools and the Disruption of Transnational Social Fields. *Anthropology & Education Quarterly*, 50(1), 48–65.

Sorenson, T. (2013). Voseo to tuteo accommodation among Salvadorans in the United States. *Hispania*, 96, 763–781.

Spencer, A. T. (2018). Nicaraguan Immigration to Costa Rica: Understanding power and race through language. In S. Croucher, J. Caetano, & E. Campbell (eds.), *The Routledge Companion to Migration, Communication, and Politics* (pp. 266–281). Routledge.

Stover, L. M. (2016). *Consecutive Connectors: A Study on Discourse Markers in Honduran Speech* [Master's thesis, Louisiana State University].

Straughan, J. F. (2004). *Belizean Immigrants in Los Angeles* [Doctoral dissertation, University of Southern California].

Thornton, M. (2016). Negotiating Nicaraguan Identity in Costa Rica: The Performance of Affect in Desde el barro al sur. *Hispanic Journal*, 37(1), 11–28.

Tinoco Rodríguez, T. S. (2010). *Atlas lingüístico-etnográfico de Panamá: nivel morfosintáctico nivel léxico*. Panamá: Imprenta Universitaria. Includes CD-ROM.

Torres Santos, M. D. L. L. (2021). *The scalar focus operator hasta: an experimental study on processing costs in Spanish* [Doctoral dissertation, Universität Heidelberg].

Valle, A. (1943). *Filología nicaragüense: puntos y puntas, cogidos en el Diccionario de nicaraguanismos*. Editorial Nuevos Horizontes.

Valle, A. (1948). *Diccionario del habla nicaragüense*. Editorial "La Nueva Prensa."

Villa, D. J., Shin, N. L., & Nagata, E. R. (2014). La nueva frontera: Spanish-speaking populations in Central Washington. *Studies in Hispanic and Lusophone Linguistics*, 7(1), 149–172.

Villarreal, B. (2016). El habla y las actitudes de los hispanohablantes de Los Ángeles: síntesis y ampliación del trabajo de Claudia Parodi. *Cuadernos AISPI*, (8), 217–233.

Villegas, F. (1965). The voseo in Costa Rican Spanish. *Hispania*, 46, 612–15.

Woods, M. R., & Rivera-Mills, S. V. (2010). Transnacionalismo del voseante: salvadoreños y hondureños en los Estados Unidos. *Lengua y migración/Language and Migration*, 2(1), 97–111.

Woods, L. A., Perry, J. M., & Steagall, J. W. (1997). The composition and distribution of ethnic groups in Belize: immigration and emigration patterns, 1980–1991. *Latin American research review*, 32(3), 63–88.

Woods, M. R., & Rivera-Mills, S. V. (2012). El tú como un "mask": Voseo and Salvadoran and Honduran Identity in the United States. *Studies in Hispanic and Lusophone Linguistics*, 5(1), 191–216.

Zamora Elizondo, H. (1945). Los diminutivos en Costa Rica. *Thesaurus*, 1, 541–546.

Index

address, forms of   1–3, 8, 215–18, 220–34, 260–64, 267, 274–79, 286, 287–90, 301
adjectives. *See* grammatical categories
adverbs. *See* grammatical categories
Africa and Africans   10, 23, 88, 274–75, 279. *See also* Spanish, Afro-Bolivian, *and* enslaved people
age. *See* sociolinguistic variables
allophonic variation   6, 17–22, 33, 34, 36, 62, 73, 76– 78, 81–91, 94, 97, 105–10, 112, 114–16
Andalucía   123. *See also* Spanish
anterior aspect   8, 238–42, 244–46, 251, 253–54, 256
Antigua   18, 41, 44, 47, 309
approximants   17–20, 22, 44–46, 48–49, 50–55, 56, 60–61, 63–65
Areal Norms Theory   260
Argentina   122, 131, 137, 154–55, 161, 175, 182, 184, 186, 248, 298. *See also* Spanish, Argentinian
aspiration   74–76, 78, 81, 87–90, 314
Assamese   17
Asturian   99–100
attitudes   2, 26–27, 47, 148, 232

Basque   41, 239
Belize   1–4, 10, 17–18, 21–27, 34, 308–9, 312, 314–15. *See also* Spanish, Belizean
bilinguals and bilingualism   2–4, 6, 10, 41–48, 57, 60–67, 99, 145–51, 153–55, 157–60, 162–64, 198, 211, 290
biological sex. *See* sociolinguistic variables
Bolivia   123, 309. *See also* Spanish, Afro-Bolivian
Brazilian Portuguese   197, 199, 209
British settlers   23

Caribbean   1, 3, 10–11, 17, 194, 210, 218, 275, 308–10. *See also* Spanish, Caribbean
Chile   122, 131, 182, 184, 186, 277. *See also* Spanish, Chilean
chronological classification   308
code-switching   3

colonial period   8–9, 215–18, 220, 262, 264–66, 268–71, 274–76, 278–79, 309–10, 312
contact between languages   1–3, 6–7, 9–10, 17–18, 21, 25, 33–34, 36, 41–45, 63, 65, 67, 72, 74, 99–100, 104, 111, 145–150, 153–56, 159–63, 189, 194–95, 198, 210–12, 260, 279, 284, 290, 292, 310, 312, 314–15
corpus linguistics   4, 7, 23, 41, 47, 126, 131, 148–49, 150–51, 153, 156, 160, 163, 168, 170, 174, 179, 180–82, 187–89, 240–43, 253, 262, 267, 271, 313
Costa Rica   1–10, 95, 112, 121–23, 129, 169–70, 182–88, 215–17, 224, 235, 238, 242, 245, 248, 251, 253–56, 267, 273, 309, 311, 313, 315. *See also* Spanish, Costa Rican
Creoles   1, 3, 10–11, 23, 34, 279, 308, 312
  Afro-Panamanian Congo language   309
  Belizean Kriol   2–3, 10, 23, 27, 45
  English-based   1, 3, 10, 23, 34
  Miskito Coast Creole   10
  Palenquero Creole   275
  Panamanian Creole   10
  Rama Cay Creole   10
Cuba   18

debuccalization. *See* sound change
deferentiality   215–17, 224, 231, 234
deixis   8, 154, 234, 315
deletion. *See* sound change
determiners. *See* grammatical categories
dialects and dialectology   1–4, 9, 17–25, 30, 34–36, 44, 61–62, 72–77, 94–96, 98–99, 110–11, 121, 123–24, 142, 162, 168–69, 170–71, 177, 179, 180–83, 187–89, 239, 240, 243–44, 249, 256, 261–62, 267–77, 292, 308–15
Dominican Republic   131–32, 170, 193. *See also* Spanish, Dominican

Ecuador   18–19, 95, 98–99, 112, 248, 288–89, 293, 297–98. *See also* Spanish, Ecuadorian
education. *See* sociolinguistic variables

El Salvador   1–4, 72, 74–75, 91, 94–95, 100, 104, 110–14, 169–70, 172–73, 177–78, 182–84, 186, 188, 241, 248, 256, 310, 313. *See also* Spanish, Salvadoran
elision. *See* sound change
English   1–3, 10–11, 21, 23–24, 27, 34, 36, 45–46, 61, 96–97, 99, 114, 171, 196, 245, 302, 308, 312
enslaved people   23, 72, 275, 277
ergativity   160, 171, 175
ethnicity as sociolinguistic variable   63, 145, 149, 274–76, 285–86, 302, 310, 314

face   7, 9, 218–34, 301
    threatening   7, 9, 219–20, 227–28, 303
flaps   21, 33
Florida   3, 240
fricatives   20, 45–46, 62, 73–74, 76, 310

Galician   57
gay speech. *See* sociolinguistic variables
gender. *See* sociolinguistic variables *and* grammatical gender
gestural undershoot   94–96
globalization   111
glottal abduction. *See* sound change
grammatical categories
    adjectives   169, 175, 182–83
    adverbs   8, 240, 243, 245–46, 249–50, 253, 255
    determiners   183
    nouns   183, 194–95, 197, 199, 200, 202, 205, 209, 215–217, 222, 224
    prepositions   6, 146, 159–64, 169, 171, 173–74, 176–79, 182–83, 185, 186–89, 268, 269
    pronouns   6–8, 146, 149–52, 154–61, 195, 199–200, 202, 205, 210, 215–18, 221–28, 230–34, 249, 276, 262–67, 271, 275, 277, 279, 292, 295, 297, 299, 314
    verbs   3, 6, 7, 10, 74, 100, 146–47, 154, 156, 159, 160–63, 169–71, 174–77, 179, 181–83, 187–89, 193–99, 204–5, 209–11, 216, 219, 222, 225–26, 229–30, 234, 239, 240, 243–44, 247, 254, 264, 265, 267–68, 269, 272
grammatical gender   147, 150–54, 156, 160–61

grammaticalization   7–8, 146–47, 163, 169–70, 176, 179, 186, 224, 232, 235, 239, 240–41, 242–43, 247, 250, 254, 256, 265
grammatical number
    object   243–44, 249, 250, 253, 255, 265
    subject   7, 147, 150–56, 160, 161, 193–99, 202–12
Guatemala   1–4, 9–10, 18, 41, 43–44, 47, 60, 63, 66–67, 72, 74–75, 145, 149, 159, 164, 171, 182–84, 186, 264, 309–13. *See also* Spanish, Guatemalan

habituality   183
heteronormativity. *See* sociolinguistic variables, sexuality
historical linguistics   4
Honduras   1, 3, 4, 9, 72–73, 75–76, 86, 169–170, 172–173, 176, 182–86, 188, 308–13. *See also* Spanish, Honduran
hypoarticulation   97

indigenous languages
    Achi   145
    Akateko   145
    Awakateko   145
    Bribrí   310
    Cabécar   310
    Ch'orti'   145
    Chalchiteko   145
    Chuj   145
    Garifuna   145
    Guaraní   147, 310
    Itza'   145
    Ixil   145
    Jakalteko/Popti'   145
    Jicaque   310
    K'iche'   18, 145
    Kaqchikel   2–5, 41–42, 44–45, 47, 57, 60–66, 145
    Lenca   310
    Mam   145
    Miskitu   3, 194–95, 198, 200, 203, 226, 212, 290
    Mopan   145
    Náhuatl   310
    Ocotepeque   75, 77
    Otomi   147
    Paya   310
    Pipil   310

INDEX

indigenous languages (*cont.*)
    Poqomam   145
    Poqomchi'   145
    Q'anjob'al   145
    Q'eqchi'   145
    Quechua   41, 147, 241, 310
    Sakapulteko   145
    Sipakapense   145
    Shipibo-Konibo   44, 46, 61
    Sumo   210
    Tektiteko   145
    Tepehuano   147
    Tz'utujil   3, 6, 145–50, 154, 159, 160–64
    Ulwa   3
    Uspanteko   145
    Xinka   145
indigenous substrates   72
intentionality   220–21
Internal Linguistic Diffusion   261
intervocalic position   4, 17, 19, 20, 22–23, 25–26, 28–29, 32–33, 35, 36, 44–46, 48, 94, 98–99, 112
intonation   6, 121–25, 142, 146, 290

lenition. *See* sound change
lexical change   174, 177, 180–81, 186, 188–89

Mestizos   23, 145, 290
Mexico   9, 10, 17, 22–24, 122, 137, 146, 169, 182, 184, 186, 240, 241, 248, 255–56, 288–89, 294, 298, 308–10, 315
migration   10, 23, 73, 111, 148, 264, 314–15
minimal pairs   5, 17, 22, 42, 44, 53, 54, 56, 64, 66
monolinguals   1–2, 6, 11, 27, 44, 46–47, 60–63, 146, 148–51, 153, 155, 157–58, 160, 163, 194
morphology   23, 179, 193–99, 209, 285
multinomial logistic regression model   81
Munda   17

nasals   35, 198–99
nasalization   197
New Mexico   10, 308
Nicaragua   1–4, 7–8, 10, 72, 74, 168–70, 176, 182–86, 188, 194, 198, 201, 210, 286, 290–91, 310, 311. *See also* Spanish, Nicaraguan
nouns. *See* grammatical categories
number. *See* grammatical number

Panama   1–4, 8–9, 18, 62, 182–84, 186, 262–64, 266–67, 269, 271, 274–79, 308, 312
pan-Hispanic linguistic norms   63
perceptions   5, 33, 41, 64–66, 97–99, 114, 117, 124–25, 161
perfective aspect   8, 241, 253–54, 256
phatic utterances   287–89, 291–92, 296, 302
phonemic tap   45–49, 53–54, 56–61, 63–66
phonemic trill   44–46, 53–57, 62, 64–66
phonetic inventories   62, 66
phonic salience   7, 196–97, 199, 202–9, 211
pirates   72
pitch accents   122, 125, 127, 129, 130–135, 138–42
polarity   183, 185, 188
politeness   9, 97, 208, 218, 221, 284, 286, 288, 296, 298, 300
Praat   48, 101, 126
pragmatic exploitation   226–27, 234
pragmatic strengthening   224, 247
Pragmaticalization   8, 222, 228, 232, 234
pragmatics   4, 232, 284–87, 313
prepositions. *See* grammatical categories
pronouns. *See* grammatical categories
prosody   121, 164

refugees   314–15
retroflex consonants   4, 18, 20–23, 26–34, 36, 46
rhoticism   4–5, 17–23, 25–29, 30–36, 41–42, 44–49, 52–56, 60–67
Rimland   11
ruralness. *See* sociolinguistic variables

semantic change   178, 221–32
semantics   2, 314
social class. *See* sociolinguistic variables
sociolinguistics   88, 112, 114, 208, 211, 286
sociolinguistic variables
    age   4, 6, 7, 21, 25–28, 30–34, 42, 62, 64, 53–54, 57–58, 60, 63, 65–66, 73, 77–80, 82–84, 86–88, 90–91, 101–9, 111, 113, 123, 130, 131, 135, 139, 142, 182, 198–99, 201–3, 207–9, 211, 242, 285–86, 292
    biological sex   6–7, 27–28, 30–31, 33, 48, 53, 57–60, 73, 77–79, 80, 82–84, 87–88, 91, 106, 114, 125, 129, 130, 133–34, 138–39, 142

sociolinguistic variables (*cont.*)
    education   63, 73, 77–80, 82, 85–91, 98,
        104, 106, 111, 113, 123, 141, 145, 148–49,
        162, 194, 197, 199, 201–3, 208–11, 291
    ethnicity   63, 145, 149, 274–76, 285–86,
        302, 310, 314
    gender   96, 98–99, 101, 105–9, 112–13,
        133, 151–56, 160–61, 163, 197, 199,
        201–3, 207–9, 211, 242, 285–86, 288–89,
        292–93, 295, 298, 303
    ruralness as a sociolinguistic variable   8,
        9, 95, 99–102, 105, 114, 197, 269–70, 275,
        278, 290–91, 298, 303, 313
    sexuality   96, 98, 102, 114
    social class   73, 76, 78, 80, 82, 84–85,
        87–89, 91, 104, 271, 279, 285–86
    urbanicity as a social variable   99,
        100–101, 113
sociophonetics   4, 5, 97, 99, 114, 133
sound change
    debuccalization   94, 98
    deletion   5, 74–76, 78, 81, 84, 87–90, 94,
        98, 110, 195–96, 212
    elision   19, 310
    glottal abduction   63, 95, 110, 112
    lenition   21, 53, 94, 112
Spain   17, 41, 74, 122, 169, 171, 178, 182, 184, 186,
    222, 240, 248, 254, 255, 263, 264, 266,
    277, 279, 289, 293, 297, 298, 309. *See
    also* Spanish, Peninsular
Spanish
    Afro-Bolivian   193, 196
    Andean   142, 218, 241
    Argentinian River Plate   240
    Belizean   4, 18, 21, 22–25, 27, 32–34,
        36, 46
    Caribbean   44, 132, 142, 195, 196, 314
    Colombian   6, 95, 121, 122, 131, 142
    Costa Rican   1–3, 6–9, 34, 36, 96, 98–99,
        104, 112, 121–26, 132, 135, 139, 140–42,
        215–18, 222, 231, 239, 241–49, 250–51,
        253–56, 290, 309, 313
    Costa Rican Central Valley   18, 20, 32
    Costa Rican colonial   215, 217, 220
    Extremadura   123

Guatemalan   5, 6, 9, 10, 47, 62, 67, 74, 76,
    309, 312, 315
Honduran   2, 5, 7, 72–76, 78–79, 88, 91,
    313, 314
Mexican   3, 7, 8, 10, 19, 27, 33, 62, 98, 240,
    253–56, 288, 293, 296, 314
Mosquito Coast   7, 193
Nicaraguan   2, 3, 7, 72, 74, 87, 194, 210–12,
    284–85, 290, 303, 312, 314
Panamanian   2, 3, 8, 62, 276, 262, 267,
    269, 270, 273, 277–78, 313
Peninsular   7, 62, 147, 161, 241–42, 247,
    251–55, 266
Peruvian   241
Puerto Rican   98
Taos New Mexican   21, 34
United States   196
Venezuelan   132, 142
Veracruz Mexican   45
Yucatan   18, 22, 34, 37, 63, 308
spectrographic analysis   19
speech acts   7, 9, 222–23, 226–27, 284–85,
    287, 291, 314
Stammbaumtheorie   260
standardization   111
stress   53–54, 123, 125–27, 129, 137, 140,
    146–47, 150, 160–61, 163, 220, 269
subjectification   222, 234

tense   8, 183, 229, 243, 245, 247, 250–51, 255
Temne   33
transitivity   160, 183–85, 188

United States   10, 46, 75, 104, 154, 170, 184,
    186, 196, 313–15
urbanicity. *See* sociolinguistic variables
urbanization   111

variational pragmatics   285, 286–87
variationist method   25, 242
Venezuela   18, 122, 137, 154–55, 161, 218
verbs. *See* grammatical categories
Viceroyalty of New Spain   309
voseo americano   216, 231

Yucatec Caste War   24

Printed in the United States
by Baker & Taylor Publisher Services